HERMAN MELVILLE

Other titles in the Greenhaven Press Literary Companion Series:

AMERICAN AUTHORS

Nathaniel Hawthorne
Ernest Hemingway
Arthur Miller
John Steinbeck
Mark Twain

BRITISH AUTHORS

Jane Austen

WORLD AUTHORS

Sophocles

BRITISH LITERATURE

The Canterbury Tales
Shakespeare: The Comedies
Shakespeare: The Sonnets
Shakespeare: The Tragedies

THE GREENHAVEN PRESS
Literary Companion
TO AMERICAN AUTHORS

HERMAN MELVILLE

David Bender, *Publisher*
Bruno Leone, *Executive Editor*
Scott Barbour, *Managing Editor*
Bonnie Szumski, *Series Editor, Book Editor*

Greenhaven Press, San Diego, CA

Library of Congress Cataloging-in-Publication Data

Readings on Herman Melville / Bonnie Szumski, book editor.
     p.   cm. — (The Greenhaven Press literary com-
panion to American authors)
    Includes bibliographical references and index.
    ISBN 1-56510-584-2 (lib. bdg. : alk. paper). —
ISBN 1-56510-583-4 (pbk. : alk. paper)⁊
    1. Melville, Herman, 1819–1891—Criticism and inter-
pretation. I. Szumski, Bonnie, 1958-   . II. Series.
PS2387.B37   1997
813'.3—dc20   96-20863
                                                 CIP

② American literature — History and Criticism.

Copyright ©1997 by Greenhaven Press, Inc.
PO Box 289009
San Diego, CA 92198-9009
Printed in the U.S.A.

66What I feel most moved to write, that is banned,— it will not pay. Yet, altogether, write the other way I cannot. So the product is a final hash, and all my books are botches.99

Herman Melville, from a letter to Nathaniel Hawthorne, despairing of his lack of success or acceptance

CONTENTS

Chapter 1: Herman Melville: An Introduction to His Works

took that ghastly, bloody, dramatic conflict to inspire some of his greatest poetry. From this point on, Melville's poetry was both more complex and more beautiful.

Chapter 2: A Critical Selection

Chapter 3: *Moby Dick*

Hinduism that clearly influenced the work, especially in the sections that compare the Judeo-Christian and pagan traditions.

FOREWORD

> *"'Tis the good reader that*
> *makes the good book."*
> Ralph Waldo Emerson

The story's bare facts are simple: The captain, an old and scarred seafarer, walks with a peg leg made of whale ivory. He relentlessly drives his crew to hunt the world's oceans for the great white whale that crippled him. After a long search, the ship encounters the whale and a fierce battle ensues. Finally the captain drives his harpoon into the whale, but the harpoon line catches the captain about the neck and drags him to his death.

A simple story, a straightforward plot—yet, since the 1851 publication of Herman Melville's *Moby Dick*, readers and critics have found many meanings in the struggle between Captain Ahab and the whale. To some, the novel is a cautionary tale that depicts how Ahab's obsession with revenge leads to his insanity and death. Others believe that the whale represents the unknowable secrets of the universe and that Ahab is a tragic hero who dares to challenge fate by attempting to discover this knowledge. Perhaps Melville intended Ahab as a criticism of Americans' tendency to become involved in well-intentioned but irrational causes. Or did Melville model Ahab after himself, letting his fictional character express his anger at what he perceived as a cruel and distant god?

Although literary critics disagree over the meaning of *Moby Dick*, readers do not need to choose one particular interpretation in order to gain an understanding of Melville's novel. Instead, by examining various analyses, they can gain numerous insights into the issues that lie under the surface of the basic plot. Studying the writings of literary critics can also aid readers in making their own assessments of *Moby Dick* and other literary works and in developing analytical thinking skills.

The Greenhaven Literary Companion Series was created with these goals in mind. Designed for young adults, this unique anthology series provides an engaging and comprehensive introduction to literary analysis and criticism. The essays included in the Literary Companion Series are chosen for their accessibility to a young adult audience and are expertly edited in consideration of both the reading and comprehension levels of this audience. In addition, each essay is introduced by a concise summation that presents the contributing writer's main themes and insights. Every anthology in the Literary Companion Series contains a varied selection of critical essays that cover a wide time span and express diverse views. Wherever possible, primary sources are represented through excerpts from authors' notebooks, letters, and journals and through contemporary criticism.

Each title in the Literary Companion Series pays careful consideration to the historical context of the particular author or literary work. In-depth biographies and detailed chronologies reveal important aspects of authors' lives and emphasize the historical events and social milieu that influenced their writings. To facilitate further research, every anthology includes primary and secondary source bibliographies of articles and/or books selected for their suitability for young adults. These engaging features make the Greenhaven Literary Companion series ideal for introducing students to literary analysis in the classroom or as a library resource for young adults researching the world's great authors and literature.

Exceptional in its focus on young adults, the Greenhaven Literary Companion Series strives to present literary criticism in a compelling and accessible format. Every title in the series is intended to spark readers' interest in leading American and world authors, to help them broaden their understanding of literature, and to encourage them to formulate their own analyses of the literary works that they read. It is the editors' hope that young adult readers will find these anthologies to be true companions in their study of literature.

INTRODUCTION

This volume in the Greenhaven Press *Literary Companion Series* illuminates the work of novelist and poet Herman Melville. Although Melville's works may seem overly wordy and philosophically heavy to many readers today (as indeed they did to readers in his own time), there are few more satisfying endeavors than discovering Melville's peculiar blend of humor and depth. Although best known for his novel *Moby Dick*, to which volumes of analysis have been devoted, Melville's other works are just as deeply satisfying, as is his poetry.

A reader approaching Melville today perhaps will need more patience than ever to delve deeply into his work. A lover of words and the timeless themes that have intrigued all truly great writers, Melville demands much of his readers. He expects a tolerable understanding of Western and Eastern religious philosophy, a knowledge of the great Western philosophers, and a desire to explore uniquely human qualities: the capacities to think, question, and ponder our place in the world. This pursuit may seem less intriguing, perhaps, in an age when many writers spoonfeed us, rarely referring to the immense religious and philosophical tradition that Herman Melville demands we acknowledge. Yet those who decide to pursue Melville will be participating in the thoughts of one of our greatest religious thinkers, as profound a theologian as any called by such a name.

Readings on Herman Melville helps the reader gather information and gain insight into what Melville cared about and why. Essays cover and clarify the themes that intrigued Melville and the way in which these themes were vital to his work. Chosen for their readability, essays both point out to readers the breadth of Melville's talents and place him in a historical context.

Each volume in the *Literary Companion Series* includes helpful features for those new to literary criticism. Each essay's introduction summarizes the article's main ideas and gives a bit of background on the author. Notes explain difficult or unfamiliar words and concepts throughout the book. A chronology lists important dates in the life of the author and presents him in a broader historical context. A bibliography includes works for further research as well as historical works of interest. Finally, a detailed table of contents and thorough index make each volume in the *Literary Companion Series* a complete research tool in itself as well as a launching point for further exploration.

While examining the work of Herman Melville, or any author who demands the best of us as readers, it may be useful to remember what the author himself, in his usual half-mocking, half-serious way, said of pursuing the depths of the intellect and the soul:

> It is a frightful poetical creed that the cultivation of the brain eats out the heart. But it's my *prose* opinion that in most cases, in those men who have fine brains and work them well, the heart extends down to hams. And though you smoke them with the fire of tribulation, yet, like veritable hams, the head only gives the richer and the better flavour. I stand for the heart.

HERMAN MELVILLE:
A BIOGRAPHY

During his lifetime, Herman Melville was acknowledged as a great writer only for his early adventure novels, *Typee* and *Omoo*. Like fans who typecast an actor, the public would not accept the later work that Melville believed to be his true destiny. As Melville's work became more obscure, more deep, and more demanding, the few readers who had retained any loyalty abandoned him. He found little support in family members who were similarly puzzled by his work. Even *Moby Dick*, Melville's best-known novel, received accolades in some publications as a realistic sea adventure but was panned for its more philosophical insights. Melville, of course, was more interested in the philosophical insights, and refused to write what he termed "the other way." He wanted to join the "corps of thought-divers, that have been diving and coming up again with bloodshot eyes since the world began." The struggle to maintain a belief in his work in the face of strong public resistance often left him alternately depressed and raging. Melville's almost contemptuous lack of respect for his reading public and simultaneous desire for public appreciation dogged his career.

Herman Melvill was born on August 1, 1819, in New York City. (The family would add the final *e* much later.) He was the third child of Allan Melvill and Maria Gansevoort Melvill. The Melville family would eventually consist of eight children, four boys and four girls, of whom Melville was the second son. Both Herman's father and mother came from distinguished American families. Major Thomas Melvill, Herman's paternal grandfather, had been a Mohawk at the Boston Tea Party and was appointed Collector of Port of Boston by President Washington in 1789. Herman's maternal grandfather, General Peter Gansevoort, had prevented the British from reinforcing General Burgoyne before the

Battle of Saratoga during the American Revolution.

With his father a world traveler and both his grandfathers Revolutionary War heroes, Melville grew up hearing tales of adventure. As a boy, Herman was especially intrigued by the mementos and souvenirs from distant lands that filled his home. His family owned several pieces of furniture from Europe that became objects of his contemplation. He later wrote: "These [pieces] I examined again and again, wondering where the wood grew: whether the workmen who made them still survived, and what they could be doing with themselves now." He seemed, from a young age, preoccupied with travel.

Melville's father, an importer of French goods, was a wealthy businessman whose success in Herman's early childhood enabled him to move his growing family to more and more expensive homes in New York. But Allan Melvill's business was always unpredictable, and when in 1830 the American economy took an unfortunate downturn, Melvill's business suffered greatly. The family was forced to move nearer to Maria's parents in Albany. There, unable to rescue his business from debt, Allan Melvill died two years later, when Herman was twelve years old.

GROWING BITTER BEFORE HIS TIME

Allan Melvill's death left his family in poverty. Since women of Maria Gansevoort's social stature did not do paid work, she and her family were supported by her brothers. The Melville boys were taken out of school and put to work. Herman was placed as a bank clerk and his seventeen-year-old brother Gansevoort was hired into the family's fur business. Melville would never again attend school regularly, though he would fit in several semesters of schooling over the next five years whenever he was able to take time away from the need to make money for his family. Melville recalled the crushing weight of responsibility placed upon him for the family's well-being years later in a letter chastising a friend:

> Talk not of the bitterness of middle age and afterlife . . . a boy can feel all that, and much more, when upon his young soul the mildew has fallen. . . . Before the death of my father I never thought of working for my living, and never knew there were hard hearts in the world. . . . I had learned to think much, and bitterly, before my time.

Herman alternated between jobs at the bank and the fur

business while his mother and other siblings spent winters in Albany and summers in Pittsfield, Massachusetts, on the farm of Thomas Melville, Herman's uncle. In 1837 a financial panic put Gansevoort out of business. Seeking to reduce expenses, Maria Melville moved to Lansingburgh, New York, in November 1838. Herman tried to help the family financially by teaching at various schools, but found the work unrewarding, boring, and poorly paid. In May 1839, Melville published his first known fiction, "Fragments from a Writing Desk," in a Lansingburgh newspaper.

FIRST VOYAGE

Soon after, unable to find consistent work in what was then a serious economic depression, Herman decided to attempt his first voyage to Liverpool and back. Herman's cousin Leonard Gansevoort had just come back from a four-year whaling cruise, and his tales were so exciting that Herman decided to try his hand at working on a ship. So on Monday morning, June 5, Melville signed on as "boy," or low-ranking hand, on a merchant ship, the *St. Lawrence*. On his return later that year, Herman found his mother in even more desperate straits than on his departure. Mortgages on her property were being foreclosed and she was auctioning off her furniture. Herman responded to her plight by taking several teaching jobs, which paid little to nothing and which convinced him that teaching was a hopeless career. He then visited his uncle Thomas Melvill in Galena, Illinois, hoping to find work out west. When no work materialized, he returned to New York in the fall of 1840.

LATER VOYAGES

Frustrated by his lack of employment, Melville decided to try his hand at whaling, leaving for Nantucket near Christmas of 1840. There he joined the crew of the *Acushnet*, a new two-masted whaling vessel. The *Acushnet* sailed on January 3, 1841. Hunting whales in the South Atlantic, it then rounded Cape Horn, cruised the Galapagos Islands region and sailed to the Marquesas Islands—where Melville deserted.

Melville had grown to hate the *Acushnet*'s tyrannical captain, who neglected and starved his crew. He and companion Toby Greene jumped ship with some sea biscuits, tobacco, and a roll of cloth to barter with the native Typee tribe. Most scholars believe that Melville lived with the

Typees, rumored to be cannibals, for about a month. During this time, Melville suffered some type of leg injury, and when the wound refused to heal, Toby left to find help. Melville did not see Toby again or learn what happened to him until years later. It is his experiences among the Typee tribe that are immortalized in Melville's first novel, *Typee*. In scenes reminiscent of Paul Gauguin's paintings, Melville lived a day-to-day peaceful existence among the Typees. He soon grew tired of this unchallenging environment, however, and allowed himself to be "rescued" and brought aboard the *Lucy Ann*, an Australian whaler.

The captain of the *Lucy Ann* was ill, and the crew did no whaling. When they landed in Papeete, Tahiti, to get medical treatment, the captain transferred authority to his first mate, James German. Most of the crew hated German, and many, including Melville, refused to serve under him. In Tahiti, Melville and several shipmates mounted a failed mutiny and were imprisoned under the stewardship of "Captain Bob," a native who ran the local jail. After the *Lucy Ann* left port, without her rebels, Captain Bob allowed his prisoners to roam the islands at will. Melville met an eccentric doctor (on whom most scholars believe Dr. Long Ghost in *Omoo* is based) and the two decided to live among the natives as beachcombers. It was during these ventures that Melville became thoroughly disgusted by the Christian missionaries who attempted to convert the natives. "No race upon earth is less opposed by nature to the munitions of Christianity than the people of the South Seas. . . . They can hardly even be said to reflect," Melville wrote during this period. After traveling among the tribes of Tahiti, Melville decided to join another whaler, the *Charles & Henry*, on November 4, 1842, arranging to be discharged on the Hawaiian island of Maui. Moving on to Honolulu, Melville worked as a pin boy in a bowling alley, then as a bookkeeper, but left suddenly to avoid being arrested for desertion when the *Acushnet* pulled into port.

Melville enlisted in the U.S. Navy for a homeward voyage aboard the USS *United States*. Once again home in Boston on October 3, 1844, Melville regaled his family with his adventures, which they encouraged him to try to write down and sell.

The result was *Typee*, published in 1846. *Typee* was extremely popular; in it Melville played up the more exciting aspects of his travels, including having his main character wonder whether the Typees were cannibals. A reader from a publishing house that did not publish *Typee* wrote, "This work if not as good as *Robinson Crusoe* seems to be not far behind it."

Melville quickly followed up on the success of *Typee* by writing *Omoo*, published in 1847. And he coupled his writing career with successes in love, as well. He married Elizabeth Shaw the same year, moving to New York, where he and his new wife lived with Melville's younger brother and his wife. In New York, Melville met and befriended Evert Duyckinck, an editor for several book publishers who ran his own writing circle. Duyckinck invited Melville to borrow from his extensive library, and this is where Melville undertook his extensive literary education. He read Shakespeare, Dante, Montaigne, Coleridge, Browne, and Rabelais.

Perhaps influenced by his newly acquired intellectual friends and pursuits, Melville's next book was quite a departure from his adventure novels. *Mardi* explores the themes of passion and innocence through its hero's attraction to a dark temptress while he pursues a light-haired heroine. *Mardi* also experiments with what would later become a Melville trademark, expressing religious, philosophical, and political attitudes. Unfortunately, *Mardi*, published in 1849, failed to sell.

A GROWING FAMILY

Melville's first child, Malcolm, was born in February 1849. Perhaps the need to support a child drove Melville to abandon the flight into philosophical allegory he began in *Mardi* and return to the more adventurous style found in the first two novels. Melville wrote a straightforward novel loosely based on his trip to Liverpool in 1839. Called *Redburn*, it focuses on a young sailor's introduction to a heartless and indifferent world. In quick succession, Melville wrote *White Jacket*, which capitalized on his experiences aboard the *United States*. Although his publishers were grateful that Melville had returned to a more realistic narrative, Melville believed himself compromised by *White Jacket*'s publication. He wrote to his father-in-law that "no reputation that is gratifying to me, can possibly be achieved by either of these books. They are two *jobs*, which I have done for money— being forced to it, as other men are to sawing wood. . . . So far as I am individually concerned, and independent of my pocket, it is my earnest desire to write those sort of books which are said to 'fail.'"

Melville traveled to England to negotiate a contract for *White Jacket* with an English publisher in 1849. There he may also have gathered material on Revolutionary War figure Israel R. Potter. When Melville returned to the United States in February 1850, he brought his family to Pittsfield, Massachusetts, the family's country retreat, for a vacation and began working on the novel that would become *Moby Dick.*

MEETING HAWTHORNE

During this time Melville met fellow writer Nathaniel Hawthorne, and the two became friends. Hawthorne describes Melville as a "tolerably well-educated bear; although, in his gentler moods, there was a tenderness in his voice, eyes, mouth, in his gesture, and every indescribable manifestation, which few men could resist, and no women." Although he had probably not read much of Hawthorne's work when they met, Melville quickly read *Mosses from an Old Manse,* which he would review for Duyckinck's *Literary Messenger* as "Hawthorne and His Mosses." Melville believed he had found a soul mate in Hawthorne, seeing Hawthorne's attraction to dark themes as a reflection of his own interests. In his review, Melville writes, "Now it is that blackness in Hawthorne . . . that so fixes and fascinates me. . . . This blackness it is that furnishes the infinite obscure of his background— that background, against which Shakespeare plays his grandest conceits, the things that have made for Shakespeare his loftiest but most circumscribed renown, as the profoundest of thinkers."

Melville and Hawthorne's friendship was like a lifeline to Melville. He had been feeling increasingly isolated and unappreciated in the country, and Hawthorne seemed to not only support his work but *understand* it. Hawthorne, however, fifteen years older, seems a bit more reserved toward Melville, although scholars have a difficult time reconstructing the friendship, as Melville did not save Hawthorne's correspondence. Hawthorne's wife left a vivid description of Melville in a letter:

> I am not quite sure that I do not think him a very great man.
> . . . A man with a true, warm heart, and a soul and an intellect—with life to his finger-tips; earnest, sincere and reverent; very tender and modest. He has very keen perceptive power; but what astonishes me is, that his eyes are not large

and deep. He seems to me to see everything accurately; and how he can do so with his small eyes, I cannot tell. They are not keen eyes either, but quite undistinguished in any way. His nose is straight and rather handsome, his mouth expressive of sensibility and emotion. He is tall and erect, with an air free, brave and manly. When conversing, he is full of gesture and force, and loses himself in his subject. There is no grace or polish. Once in a while his animation gives place to a singularly quiet expression, out of these eyes to which I have objected; an indrawn, dim look, but which at the same time makes you feel that he is at that moment taking deepest note of what is before him. . . . It does not seem to penetrate through you, but to take you into itself.

Melville bought a 160-acre farm called Broadhall in Pittsfield from his Aunt Mary. With a loan from his father-in-law he moved his family, his mother, and his sisters to the new home in September 1850. Melville began to work hard on the farm, spending his time cultivating plants and repairing farm buildings, while setting up a routine of writing in the winter months. As he wrote to Hawthorne in 1851: "I have been busy . . . building and patching and tinkering away in all directions. Besides, I had my crops to get in. . . . I work myself; and at night my bodily sensations are akin to those I have so often felt before, when a hired man, doing my day's work from sun to sun."

During the winter of 1850–1851, Melville continued a friendship and correspondence with Hawthorne, who lived in nearby Salem. After rereading *The House of the Seven Gables*, Melville wrote to Hawthorne that he had admired his ability to portray "the visible truth . . . the apprehension of the absolute condition of present things as they strike the eye of the man who fears them not, though they do their worst to him."

BETWEEN THE WHALE'S FLUKES

For a year Melville labored away at his most famous novel, *Moby Dick*, which he dedicated to Hawthorne. Published in 1851, the year his second son, Stanwix, was born, the book was generally praised but condemned as blasphemous. While newspaperman Horace Greeley reviewed the book with the utmost praise, "We think it the best production which has yet come from that seething brain," another contemporary review by George Washington Peck claimed, "The rarely-imagined character has been grievously spoiled, nay altogether ruined, by a vile overdaubing with a coat of book-learning and mysticism; there is no method in his madness; and we must needs pronounce the chief feature of the volume a perfect failure, and the work itself inartistic." Apparently, Hawthorne praised the work, although his letter to Melville no longer exists. In his reply to Hawthorne's praise, Melville wrote, "Your appreciation is my glorious gratuity.... A sense of unspeakable security is in me at this moment, on account of your having understood the book. I have written a wicked book, and feel spotless as the lamb."

DAMN DOLLARS

The following year, 1852, Melville seems to have plunged into a state of deep moodiness, if not depression, over the failure of *Moby Dick* to provide any sort of economic security for his family. "Dollars damn me," Melville wrote to Hawthorne. He began work on *Pierre, or the Ambiguities*, reassuring his wife that he was writing a "rural bowl of milk." Unfortunately, hints of incest and a disintegrating family provoked outrage among reviewers when the book was published in 1852. *Pierre* permanently destroyed Melville's reputation in the United States, and because Melville did not allow the novel to be published in England where it may have achieved more success, the book succumbed to poor sales. Melville grew increasingly despondent and withdrawn, prompting his wife to have him examined for insanity. She tried to find Melville a steady job to ease the financial burden writing had imposed on the family, to no avail. During this period, Melville's third child, Elizabeth, was born, bringing the Melville family yet another member to support.

Melville began to contribute magazine stories to *Putnam's Monthly Magazine* and *Harper's Magazine* to make ends meet after *Moby Dick* and *Pierre* failed to generate income. The short pieces *Bartleby the Scrivener, The Encantadas,* and *Benito Cereno* were first published in this way. *Israel Potter* was also published serially in *Putnam's*. During the winter of 1855–1856, Melville wrote *The Confidence-Man,* perhaps his most modern and bleakest novel. His fourth child, Frances, was born in 1855. At this point, Melville suffered from deep depression and financial desperation. Forced to sell half the farm, his father-in-law saved the family from debt. When his wife despaired of living with him in this state, Melville's father-in-law proposed a four-month trip to Europe and the Middle East, hoping travel might revive Melville's spirit. On October 11, 1857, Melville sailed for Scotland. He went first to Glasgow, then to Liverpool to visit Hawthorne, then serving as U.S. consul. Hawthorne describes Melville's mood:

> We took a pretty long walk together, and sat down in a hollow among the sand hills (sheltering ourselves from the high, cool wind) and smoked a cigar. Melville, as he always does, began to reason of Providence and futurity, and of everything that lies beyond human ken, and informed me that he had "pretty much made up his mind to be annihilated" but still he does not seem to rest in that anticipation; and, I think, will never rest until he gets hold of a definite belief. It is strange how he persists—and has persisted ever since I knew him, and probably long before—in wandering to and fro over these deserts, as dismal and monotonous as the sand hills amid which we were sitting. He can neither believe, nor be comfortable in his unbelief; and he is too honest and courageous not to try to do one or the other. If he were a religious man, he would be one of the most truly religious and reverential; he has a very high and noble nature, and better worth immortality than most of us.

AN ECCENTRIC BEACHCOMBER

Melville traveled on to Egypt and Constantinople; many of his journal entries betray a resigned disappointment toward the marvels of the Holy Land. The journal includes descriptions of ruined mosques and blind men with flies crawling on their eyes, "nature feeding on men." He was grimly fascinated by Jerusalem, writing that "the diabolical landscape of Judea must have suggested to the Jewish prophets their ghastly theology. . . . Is the desolation of the land the result of the fatal embrace of the Deity?" Melville would later put these morbid reminiscences to work in his profound and lengthy poem *Clarel*, but the trip to the Middle East did nothing to lift his spirits. He then toured Europe, returned to England, and went home.

Again driven by the need to make money, Melville tried the lecture circuit between 1858 and 1860. He prepared two lectures, "Statues in Rome" and "The South Seas." Some reviewers were enthusiastic, but on the whole Melville failed to support himself with the lectures, which some reviewers claimed to be overly metaphysical and philosophical. In response to continued calls for his return to writing romances, Melville became especially cynical toward his first books, sarcastically calling them "Peedee, Hullabaloo, and Pog-

Dog." He despaired of being remembered for more than these books, once writing to Hawthorne:

> Think of it! To go down to posterity is bad enough, any way; but to go down as a "man who has lived among the cannibals"! When I speak of posterity, in reference to myself, I only mean the babies who will probably be born in the moment immediately ensuing upon my giving up the ghost. I shall go down to some of them, in all likelihood. *Typee* will be given to them, perhaps, with their gingerbread.

In 1859, a fan of the earlier books, college student Titus Coan, found him in this mood, and wrote to his mother that

> he would not repeat the experiences of which I had been reading with rapture in his books. In vain I sought to hear of Typee and those Paradise islands, but he preferred to pour forth his philosophy and his theories of life. The shade of Aristotle arose like a cold mist between myself and Fayaway. ... With his liberal views he is apparently considered by the good people of Pittsfield as little better than a cannibal or a "beach comber."

In 1860 Melville decided to sail around the world, but the outbreak of the Civil War brought him home again. Still attempting to locate a permanent job, Melville traveled to Washington in 1861, only to return when his father-in-law died. In 1863 Melville sold the farm in Pittsfield and moved his family back to New York City. After the fall of Richmond in 1865, Melville wrote a series of poems entitled *Battle-Pieces and Aspects of the War*, published by Harpers in 1866. Sales of this work, too, proved disappointing, although today his war poetry is rated second only to Whitman's *Drum-Taps*.

Finally, in 1866, Melville found permanent work as deputy inspector in the New York Custom House. The job did not eliminate his moodiness and depression, however, and Lizzie, his wife, was so miserable that even her minister suggested she leave her husband. In the midst of this family struggle, Melville's son Malcolm killed himself by gunshot, evidently committing suicide, although publicly it was called an accident. Second son Stanwix had gone to sea and begun a lifetime of wandering that ended with his death, alone in San Francisco, in 1886.

While at the customhouse job, Melville continued to write poetry, completing his eighteen-thousand-line poem *Clarel*, which depicts a group of international travelers in the Holy Land. He filled the poem with the religious dilemmas he himself faced, including an almost hopeless attempt to believe in God in a secular world. Melville self-published *Clarel* in book form in June 1876. A failure initially, the book remains obscure to today's readers.

In 1885, with a moderate inheritance from Elizabeth's family, Melville retired from the customhouse to write, primarily poetry; his collections include *John Marr and Other Sailors*, self-published in 1888, and *Timoleon*, in 1891. His final collection, *Weeds and Wildings*, was published posthumously.

A QUIET CONTENTMENT

Melville spent the last few years of his life in obscurity, although toward the end he seems to have achieved a quiet contentment he was unable to find throughout much of his life. Highly regarded in Britain, Melville's last years were punctuated by letters from several admirers that anticipated in a very minor way that his work would one day be appreciated by millions. In 1889 Melville received one such letter from Archibald MacMeehan, Ph.D.: "For a number of years I have read and reread *Moby Dick* with increasing pleasure in every perusal: and with this study, the conviction has grown up that the unique merits of that book have never received due recognition. . . . I beg the honor of corresponding with you." Melville declined the opportunity to correspond with MacMeehan, who was planning a work of literary criticism based on *Moby Dick*, claiming that "I have lately come into possession of unobstructed leisure, but only just as, in the course of nature, my vigour sensibly declines. What little of it is left I husband for certain matters as yet incomplete, and which indeed may never be completed."

Melville was referring to his last short novel, *Billy Budd*, one of his most admired and well known works. It brings forth, with the maturity and command of Melville at the height of his writing powers, the religious and philosophical themes that obsessed him throughout his life: faith versus envy of faith, innocence versus evil, and the blindness of mankind to appreciate any of this cosmic struggle. Compelled to rework the piece again and again, Melville died in 1891 with *Billy Budd* not quite completed. The *New York Times* published this obituary: "There has died and been buried in this city, during the current week, at an advanced age, a man who is so little known, even by name, to the generation now in the vigor of life that only one newspaper contained an obituary account of him, and that of only three or four lines."

THE OTHER SIDE OF MELVILLE

A more revealing and touching commemoration of his life
was written by his granddaughter Elizabeth:

> I was not yet ten years old when my grandfather died. To put
> aside all later impressions . . . results in a series of childish
> recollections, vivid homely scenes wherein he formed a pal-
> pable background for my own interested activities.
>
> Setting forth on a bright spring afternoon for a trip to Central
> Park, the Mecca of most of our pilgrimages, he made a brave
> and striking figure as he walked erect, head thrown back,
> cane in hand, inconspicuously dressed in a dark blue suit
> and a soft black felt hat. For myself, I skipped gaily beside
> him, anticipating the long jogging ride in the horse cars, the
> goats and shanty-topped granite of the upper reaches of our
> journey, the broad walks of the park, where the joy of all ex-
> istence was best expressed by running down the hills, head
> back, skirts flying in the wind. He would follow more slowly
> and call "Look out, or the 'cop' may catch you!" I always
> thought he used funny words: "cop" was surely a jollier word
> than "policeman."
>
> We never came in from a trip of this kind, nor indeed from
> any walk, but we stopped in the front hall under a coloured
> engraving of the Bay of Naples, its still blue dotted with tiny
> white sails. He would point to them with his cane and say,
> "See the little boats sailing hither and thither." "Hither and
> thither"—more funny words, thought I, at the same time a lit-
> tle awed by something far away in the tone of his voice. . . .
>
> His own room was a place of mystery and awe to me; there I
> never ventured unless invited by him. The great mahogany
> desk, heavily bearing up four shelves of dull gilt and leather
> books; the high dim book-case, topped by strange plaster
> heads that peered along the ceiling level, or bent down,
> searching blindly with sightless balls; the small black iron
> bed, covered with dark cretonne; the narrow iron grate. . . .
>
> Sad it is that he felt his grandchildren would turn against him
> as they grew older. He used to forebode as much. As it is, I have
> nothing but a remembrance of glorious fun, mixed with a
> childish awe, as of some one who knew far and strange things.

Only decades later would the world appreciate Melville's
knowledge of "far and strange things." Today, he is remembered, read, and pondered by scholars and studied and re-
discovered on a daily basis. Indeed, it seems distinctly
"Melvillian" that Herman Melville could only achieve the
fame and recognition he craved in life after his death.

CHAPTER 1

Herman Melville: An Introduction to His Works

Melville as a Great Tragedian

Lewis Mumford

Lewis Mumford was an American social philosopher and educator who criticized society, especially modern technology and urban planning. His many works include a critical study entitled *Herman Melville*, from which the following article is excerpted. In it, he argues that like Shakespeare, Dostoyevsky, Dante, and other great writers, Melville chose among his themes humanity's tragic struggle against life's circumstances and elevated that struggle through his work.

Why does Herman Melville mean so much more to us than he did to his own contemporaries? What has his thought done for us, and what has his vision given?

The change that has come about is not merely a change of style.... The things that concerned Melville are, like the cubist quilts and coverlets of the 1850's, distinctly modern. ... Moby-Dick, the more closely we consider it, mounts to that lonely wind-swept plateau in whose rarefied air only the finest imaginations can breathe. Distinctly, Moby-Dick belongs with The Divine Comedy and Hamlet and The Brothers Karamazov and War and Peace; and if it does not establish its right to this company, it must occupy a lower place than the successful novels of its period, a David Copperfield or a Pendennis, books written with a complete acceptance of the current limitations and provincialities.

Melville's work, taken as a whole, expresses that tragic sense of life which has always attended the highest triumphs of the race, at the moments of completest mastery and fulfilment. Where that sense is lacking, life shrivels into small prudences and weak pleasures and petty gains, and those great feats of thought and imagination which transform the

From *Herman Melville* by Lewis Mumford. Copyright ©1929, renewed 1957 by Lewis Mumford (New York: Harcourt, Brace, 1929). Reprinted by permission of Gina Maccoby Literary Agency.

very character of the universe and relieve human purpose from the scant sufficiency of toiling and eating and sleeping, in a meaningless, reiterative round, shrivel away, too. John Ruskin saw the truth of this when, in spite of his pacifist convictions, he praised the art of war, for its effect upon the human spirit: life is intensified and purposive when the battle with the inimical forces that surround us, like Ahab's battle, is a deliberate pursuit and challenge, and not merely an apathetic waiting for a purely physiological end.

The tragedy of life, its evanescence, its frustrations, its limitations within physical boundaries almost as narrow as a straitjacket, its final extinction, becomes, in a day that consciously embraces its fate, the condition of an heroic effort. Death, which biologically is merely the terminus of a natural process, acquires significance for man because he anticipates it and modifies his activities so as to circumvent it: by memory and foresight, by choosing his ends, dreaming of immortality, erecting monuments and statues and museums, and above all, by transmitting the written word, man creates a destiny beyond his life's physical span. It is just because the worms lie in wait that man defies the gods, cherishes the images he has created and the relations he has solidified in custom and thought, and centres his efforts on those things which are least given to meaningless change. Though the sensible world is not derived, as Plato thought, from the heaven of ideas, the opposite of this is what every culture must strive for: to derive from the sensible world that which may be translated to a more durable world of forms.

THE TRAGIC STRUGGLE

Within the world of these forms there is Life, a thing of value, and not merely living, a matter of fact and habit and animal necessity. Whether one develops this tragic sense of values on a battlefield, like Sophocles, or in a whaleboat, like Melville, it is a precious experience: for living, merely living, as every profane writer from Petronius Arbiter to Theodore Dreiser has shown, brings boredom, satiety, despair: whereas Life is eternal, and he who has faith in it and participates in it is saved from the emptiness of the universe and the pointlessness of his own presence therein. Living, for man, in all but the most brutish communities, like those of the savages of the Straits of Magellan or the outcasts of a Liverpool or New York slum, includes and implies this Life;

and when Melville summons into his whaler the several races of the world, he is expressing the universal nature of that effort which caps nature with culture, existence with meaning, and facts with forms. Ahab's tragic struggle is the condition of every high endeavour of the mind, even though Death be its tragic reward; while adjustment, acquiescence, accepting outward conditions as inward necessities, though they may prolong living in the physical sense, effectually curtail Life: this attitude, the attitude of Melville's contemporaries, the attitude of the routineers and Philistines of all times—and they have never perhaps been so numerous as today—disrupts life more completely than illness and death do; for it brings about a deliquescence of forms, such as the nineteenth century showed in all its common arts, and a disintegration of human purposes. When that happens, the White Whale of brute energy reigns supreme: Life itself is denied: living produces no values, and men hide their emptiness by embracing dull counterfeits of purpose.

Melville's younger contemporaries, who fought in the Civil War, knew Life and Death; but those who prospered in the years that followed knew something more dreadful than simple death: they knew chaos and purposelessness and disintegration, such chaos and purposelessness, mixed with a wan, reminiscent hope, as Henry Adams pictured in his Education. Herman Melville portrayed a human purpose, concentrated to almost maniacal intensity, in Moby-Dick; and in Pierre and The Confidence Man, he showed the black aftermath, when the purpose was not sustained and carried out in art, and when he himself was deserted in his extremity, by contemporaries who neither understood nor heeded nor shared his vision. No single mind can hold its own against all that is foreign to it in the universe: Shakespeare's solitary heroes issue their brief defiance only to be blotted out: such unity of spirit as one may possess, as philosopher or poet, must be sustained in the community itself. Now, a new culture, the product of two hundred and fifty years of settled life in America, had produced Walden, Leaves of Grass, Emerson's Notebooks, and Moby-Dick; but that culture, instead of supporting and carrying forward the integration of man and nature and society shadowed forth in those books, was completely uprooted by the Civil War, and a material civilization, inimical in many aspects to the forms and symbols of a humane culture, was swept in by the very act of destruction.

Two generations of that material civilization have shown us its lopsidedness, its aimlessness, its grand attempt to conceal its emptiness by extending concrete roads and asphalted streets and vacuum cleaners to more and more remote terrains. Our most humane writers, like Mr. Sherwood Anderson, have proved how mercilessly the whole human being is crippled by this one-sided triumph; and even our most bewildered writers, who have exulted in all these maimed energies, have shown in their very act of deification how brutal and aimless they are. We realize that the effort of culture, the effort to make Life significant and durable, to conquer in ourselves that formidable confusion which threatens from without to overwhelm us—this effort must begin again. And in thus making a beginning we are nearer to Whitman with his cosmic faith and Melville in his cosmic defiance than we are to a good part of the work of our own contemporaries. It is not that we go back to these writers: it is, rather, that we have come abreast of them; for in creating that new synthesis, in lieu of the formless empiricisms and the rootless trancendentalisms of the last three centuries, the writers of our own classic past were nearer to the contemporary problem than almost any of the Europeans have been—since the physical remains of another culture in Europe give the mind a false sense of stability and security.

Herman Melville's world is our world, magnificently bodied and dimensioned: our synthesis must include and sublimate that very quest of power which Melville portrayed with such unique skill, as a combination of science and adventure and spiritual hardihood, in Typee, Mardi, and Moby-Dick. Melville's life warns us not to stop here: men must test their strength in surrender as well as in lonely conquest: he who knows neither social union nor sexual passion nor love is indeed an Ishmael, who finds himself an outcast because he has cast out that which was most precious to his own nature: there is love in the universe as well as power: the sun warms and the rain slakes the thirst: the whales dally and the first song of creation is the song of sex.

A SEARCH FOR SOLUTIONS TO LIFE'S PROBLEMS

The synthesis that Melville foreshadowed in his ideas is not simply a logical structure: Melville's synthesis was embodied in acts and deeds. During the years of his early manhood, as he wandered about the world and contemplated existence under the stars and bore a hand in working the ship, his environment, his experience, and his vital relationships were an integer. He did not lack what libraries and cities and the social heritage of man gives: indeed, he enjoyed fully the resources of a sound literary and philosophic scholarship; but he mixed this with activities that gave back to books the subtle properties that cannot be transmitted to the printed page, but must be derived directly from living. The reviewers in London might well have been shocked by the spectacle of a common sailor writing Typee or White-Jacket. Melville had bridged in his life that great gap between the respectable, learned professions and the common trades that had hitherto been crossed, with rare exceptions, only by those who definitely had lost caste, or who, like Burns, had risen with a sense of uneasy, sullen pride to acceptance among people of high rank.

Melville was an American—and that implied the dissolution of spiritual frontiers. America had taken all the established castes and classifications of Europe and left them to sort themselves out according to nature and ability: this was the true and beneficial result of eighteenth-century thinking and its political accompaniments. By a singular dissociation of ideas, which involved the destruction of an old social tissue, it had permitted a free and disinterested creature, a man, to emerge from a conglomeration of classes and practical interests. Melville was not primarily a sailor; he was not an adventurer; he was a man sailing, a man adventuring, a man thinking, proving in his early manhood that a whole and healthy life may involve many functions, without sacrificing its wholeness and health to any one of them. Whitman with his carpentering and his nursing, Thoreau with his pencil-making and gardening, were Herman Melville's brothers in the way and the life. They did not disdain practical life: they faced it manfully: but instead of neglecting every other activity for "business" they saw that what was called business was only a small part of the totality of living: they behaved toward it *as if it were real*, as Whitman said, with the knowledge that merely getting a living was not a sufficient contribution to Life. Brutal though Melville found whaling to be, it communicated, nevertheless, a sense of Life: there was astronomy and natural history and art and religion within the bulky hold of a whaler, as well as technics and business and the daily logbook.

The vision that grew out of this experience was a whole one, not, like the science of its time, subordinated to practical interests or even narrower metaphysical schemata. Through its dissociation from inherited values all things began at scratch: no one element in life, except sex, carried a handicap. Melville's settling down was inevitable, inevitable and difficult: but the difficulty was not due to the inability of a restless adventurer to accept a tamer and more even existence: it was due to the fact that, having known a rounded and cultured life, however savage and exacting, he could not submit to the desiccated routine of Western civilization, with its contempt for art, its gross disregard for the higher manifestations of science, its dislike for meditation, its subservient religion, its frank subordination of all other values to that of Comfort. Melville's contemporaries, with chance exceptions, neither lived as full a life as he had lived in the South Seas, nor were able to understand it, even as a theory. For these contemporaries, Melville's vision was an example of Bedlam literature: they did not realize that Bedlam was precisely the world they lived in, and that Melville's vision, like Emerson's, like Whitman's, like Thoreau's, was a part, and a great part, of a new cultural synthesis.

The stripping down of Herman Melville's ego, which he began in Mardi and finished in Pierre, was a sloughing away of labels, nicknames, party war-cries, habits, conventions, and acceptances; it was, necessarily, a prelude to that building up of a new ego, a surer and more central, a social and participating self, which is the task of our own time for both men and communities. Melville was crippled in the work of reconstruction by a hiatus in his own career, which was followed and made final by the social hiatus of the Civil War: though he sought to carry the work further in Clarel, one cannot pretend that he did anything but give a hint of this mended psyche, this more richly integrated self: one of his last poems, The Lake of Pontoosuce, perhaps approaches nearer to the goal than any other work of his. Had he built up that ego, his vision might have fully complemented Whitman's—land and sea, day and night, sunlight and shadow, triumph and tragedy. That union was latent: it is for us to effect it. It is useless, however, to speculate upon what might have been. The accidents that befell Melville, as he rounded his own Cape Horn, were part of that malign doom he himself pictured in Moby-Dick, and they do not affect the essence of his work. Whatever Melville's life was, his art in Moby-Dick exhibits that integration and synthesis which we seek. Through his art, he escaped the barren destiny of his living: he embraced Life; and we who now follow where his lonely courage led him embrace it, too. This embrace was a fertile one; and in each generation it will bring forth its own progeny. The day of Herman Melville's vision is now in the beginning. It hangs like a cloud over the horizon at dawn; and as the sun rises, it will become more radiant, and more a part of the living day.

Melville's Obsessive Hatred of God Limited His Greatness

Lawrance Thompson

In the following article, Lawrance Thompson argues that Melville's "quarrel with God" limited him as a writer. Melville, he writes, was obsessed with one theme: God is to blame for creating an unjust world. Thompson argues that this one-dimensional obsession made his works hopelessly flawed. Thompson was a professor at Princeton University and the author of works on Robert Frost, William Faulkner, and Henry W. Longfellow, and a controversial book on Melville entitled *Melville's Quarrel with God*, from which this viewpoint is excerpted.

In my analysis and interpretation of Herman Melville's art and thought, I have consciously and arbitrarily restricted my approach: I have tried to present and resolve what I see as the basic or fundamental problems posed by Melville's artistic and non-artistic attitudes toward his materials, and toward his readers; also, the related problems as to the readers' aesthetic responsibility to Melville's art. . . .

Because Melville's responses to life were what they were, he needed a scapegoat: someone to blame. Having started with hating Christians because they were not sufficiently Christian, he proceeded to hate Christians because they were Christians. When that scapegoat failed to satisfy him, he went on to hate the Calvinistic concept of God, and then proceeded to hate God. It never seemed to occur to him that he had merely declared his independence from the ideal of Calvinism in order to pledge his allegiance to an inverted form of that same ideal.

Let me say again that I am not urging that Melville should not have been inconsistent, or that he would have been a bet-

ter artist if he had been more consistent. He might never
have been an artist, in any sense, if he had gotten his own
inner conflicts straightened out. For our aesthetic satisfaction, then, it is fortunate that Melville was exactly what he
was. Nevertheless, if our ultimate concern is to understand
Melville's art, there is value in recognizing how it happened
that his non-artistic spiritual idiom made his artistic idiom
the complex thing it certainly is.

As I see it, the major problem which confronts the reader,
as he comes to Melville for the first time, is the problem of
recognizing, and learning to cope with, those different forms
of artistic deception and hoodwinking which he developed
and employed, because of his embarrassment over the
heretical and blasphemous nature of his views. . . . His own
disillusionment forced him into such a private preoccupa-
tion with, and employment of, ambiguities and equivoca-
tions that he did not need to contrive any principles or prac-
tices of artistic subterfuge. It is apparent, however, that the
persistent and concealed sadness of his long experience as a
human being was alleviated for him by the happiness of his
long experience as a literary artist: the retaliatory triumph
which he achieved came to him through the act of pushing
words around, to make those words do what he wanted
them to do. And a very high degree of that pleasure, certainly, was derived from his skill in pushing words around
in such a way that some of his readers would not understand
what he wanted those words to do and say. Like his early literary idol, John Milton, he was haughty enough to be content with fit audience, though few.

LITERARY DECEPTION

Part of that major problem which confronts the first-reader
of Melville is the problem of recognizing, and learning to
cope with, his adaptation of moral allegory to his own peculiar uses, in such a way as to create ambiguous allegorical
meanings. Once again, this adaptation of moral allegory
should be recognized as a significant element in his principle and practice of literary deception. Melville knew that the
allegorical mode of storytelling had so largely gone out of
fashion, in his day, that many of his readers would be completely oblivious to his use of allegory in any form. That disposed of "the superficial skimmer of pages." He also knew
that those readers well versed in the principles of moral al-

legory would naturally be the devout and unconsciously bias-bound Christian readers, who would quickly recognize his use of allegory and would instinctively prefer to make a conventional interpretation of his allegorical meanings. That disposed of a second category of readers. He also knew that his sustained irony, created by endowing allegory with sinister or inverted meanings, belonged in a "high hushed" literary tradition.... Considering this threefold appeal, I think it justifiable to call Melville's literary formula a kind of artistic triple talk. Artistically, he fulfilled his responsibilities to us, on this score; but we as readers have generally failed to pay enough attention, and in this sense we have not fulfilled our responsibilities to him. Yet, because he encouraged most of his readers to misunderstand him, perhaps things have worked out for Herman Melville, very much as he desired.

AN ODD BOOK

Melville was not appreciated by his contemporaries, who concurred that he went downhill after he wrote the adventure novels Typee *and* Omoo. *In an excerpt from a review published in London's* Literary Gazette *on December 6, 1851, a frustrated critic grapples with understanding the later novel* Moby Dick.

This is an odd book, professing to be a novel; wantonly eccentric; outrageously bombastic; in places charmingly and vividly descriptive. The author has read up laboriously to make a show of cetalogical learning. He has turned over the articles Whale, Porpoise, Cachalot, Spermaceti, Baleen, and their relatives, in every Encyclopædia within his reach.... Herman Melville is wise in this sort of wisdom. He uses it as stuffing to fill out his skeleton story. Bad stuffing it makes, serving only to try the patience of his readers, and to tempt them to wish both him and his whales at the bottom of an unfathomable sea.

Finally, we may quite easily summarize the essential element in the general range of Melville's vision, because that element remained so constant throughout so much of his later life. As I have been obliged to reiterate, the general range of Melville's vision is somewhat disappointing (not nearly so exciting and fascinating as the infinite variety of his devices for representing it) because that vision narrows down to the sharp focus of a misanthropic notion that the world was put together wrong, and that God was to blame. The gist of it is that simple. He spent his life not merely in sneering at the gullibility of human beings who disagreed with him but also in sneering at God, accusing God, upbraiding God, blaming God, and (as he thought) quarreling with God. The turn which his life had taken translated him from a transcendentalist and a mystic into an inverted transcendentalist, an inverted mystic. To this extent, then, he was consistent, in spite of all his concomitant inconsistencies, to the very end of his life. Like his own Captain Ahab, he remained a defiant rebel, even in the face of death.

Emblems delighted Melville so much (particularly when he could invert them) that his grave-stone emblem should be the Melville coat of arms, on which the motto indicates the ultimate irony of his triumphant departure from the Hell of this life:

"Denique Caelum." (Heaven, at last.)

The Adventure Novels Prove Melville Is a Humorist

Edward H. Rosenberry

Literary critic Edward H. Rosenberry argues that while most people dwell on Melville's sophistication and literary density, few notice that Melville was quite a humorist. In the following selection, Rosenberry focuses on the adventure novels, *Typee, Omoo, Redburn,* and *White-Jacket,* to show how Melville uses humor to poke fun at institutions, people, and ideas. Rosenberry is professor emeritus at the University of Delaware, where he served as the chairman of the English department and acting dean of the College of Arts and Sciences. Rosenberry was also president of the Melville Society in 1981. He is the author of *Melville,* numerous articles on Melville and other American authors, and *Melville and the Comic Spirit,* from which this selection is excerpted.

The story of Melville's literary comedy begins in the racy and circumstantial pages of his first four adventure stories—*Typee, Omoo, Redburn,* and *White-Jacket.* The old delusion that these books are faithful self-portraits of the artist as a young man has been dispelled, but they remain collectively the most reliable portrait of the man as a young artist that we are likely to get. Whatever their departures from literal autobiography, they have a broad common foundation in the actual experiences of their roving author. In his reactions to certain preposterously altered orders of life across the world from Lansingburgh, New York, we can see his sense of humor most instinctively reflecting the values that color the elemental chiaroscuro of fact and fancy. . . .

Melville's adventures before the mast in the 1840's were so fraught with crudity, privation, and danger that one's hair

Reprinted by permission of the publisher from *Melville and the Comic Spirit* by Edward H. Rosenberry (Cambridge, MA: Harvard University Press, 1955). Copyright ©1955 by the President and Fellows of Harvard College.

rises at the thought of the reality behind many of his casual and ludicrous descriptions. Yet, like scores of budding Western humorists around their prairie campfires, Melville learned on midnight watches before the flaring try-works [brick furnaces holding metal pots for rendering whale oil from blubber] how whalemen "narrated to each other their unholy adventures, their tales of terror told in words of mirth." After three years of practice in sharing horrors with his shipmates and matching their mountainous comic lies about them, he was marvelously equipped to shock the mere "state-room sailors" he turned to entertain in his books. With relish he recalled the great tobacco famine on the *Highlander*, which the crew combatted by renovating their "chaws" in the ship's oven, then combing dark corners for discarded plugs, and finally settling for the "cheese-like" yarn of old ship's cable, a delicacy marred only by the tar "with which the flavour of all ropes is more or less vitiated." There is no dread, only a wry exhilaration, in his description of the nauseous *Julia*, whose forecastle was "like the hollow of an old tree going to decay" and was so overrun with cockroaches and rats that "the business of eating and drinking was better done in the dark than in the light of day." "Lucky for us Melville makes it fantastic," D.H. Lawrence has remarked. "It must have been pretty sordid." Like the fantasy-makers of the West of whom Constance Rourke tells us, Melville had swung "from an impinging terror to a gross and often brutal comedy."

The variety of terrors and hardships which Melville turned to comic account in his early books extends over a considerable range. One thinks of the "midnight misgivings" of Tommo and Toby at their first cannibal campfire, of the battle with the "small swordfish" that were the Polynesian mosquitoes, of the incredible obstacles to sleep in both the Navy and the merchant marine, of the perils of shaving, either with a dull blade in a rocking storm or with a shark's tooth in a cannibal hut. But the unmistakable keynote in Melville's comedy of hardship is a gastronomic one. The bias is evident in both the rope-yarn episode and the account of the *Julia*'s vermin. The cannibal scare of Tommo and Toby adds to this element the terror of death; but at bottom, and quite overtly as the scene progresses, the central point of attack is the digestive sensibility. When it becomes clear that the Typees are planning to feed rather than eat their guests, a new and even more plausible horror replaces the old:

> "I say, Tommo, you are not going to eat any of that mess there, in the dark, are you? Why, how can you tell what it is?"
>
> "By tasting it, to be sure," said I, masticating a morsel that Kory-Kory had just put in my mouth; "and excellently good it is too, very much like veal."
>
> "A baked baby, by the soul of Captain Cook!" burst forth Toby, with amazing vehemence; "veal! why there never was a calf on the island till you landed."

"Emetics and luke-warm water!" Melville remarks in our stead. "What a sensation in the abdominal regions!"

No qualms disturb the playfulness with which he damns the miserable fare he had managed to thrive on as a sailor. Evert Duyckinck, after reading about the grim larder of the *Dolly*, wrote to Hawthorne that Melville had actually preferred "the society of cannibals to the interminable casks of corned beef and impracticable bread which so afflicted his imagination in the hold of that vessel." It might easily have seemed so from the description in the fourth chapter of *Typee*, but, as another writer of sea stories observed with British understatement, "Melville romances somewhat when he approaches the galley; and you are scarcely sure that he means all he says." The mess of the *Julia*, on which the fictional Melville escaped from Nukuheva, was evidently worse than that of the ship that had brought him there, but its only literary effect is a heightened humor. The pork "looked as if preserved in iron rust"; the beef gave rise to a "story of a horse's hoof with the shoe on having been fished up out of the pickle"; the biscuits were "hard little gunflints, honey-combed through and through, as if the worms usually infesting this article on long tropical voyages, had, in boring after nutriment, come out at the antipodes without finding anything." The Liverpool packet on which young Redburn sailed may have had less appalling food, but the coffee it served is described with compensatory eloquence. Generally cold, and inexhaustible in its variety of bad flavors, it was prepared by an unhygienic Negro cook who was never seen to wash but once, "and that was at one of his own soup pots." Standard fare on all ships was a concoction called *duff*, "made of flour and water, and of about the consistence of an underdone brick."

The zenith—or nadir—of Melville's gastronomic humor, the episode that comes closest to turning "impinging terror" into "gross and brutal comedy," is the story of the practical

A TYPICAL DAY

In this excerpt from a letter to prominent New York editor and critic Evert Duyckinck, quoted in Willard Thorp's Herman Melville, *Melville writes about a typical day. Here he reveals the rather scathing humor that Rosenberry notes in his article.*

I have a sort of sea-feeling here in the country, now that the ground is all covered with snow. I look out of my window in the morning when I rise as I would out of a porthole of a ship in the Atlantic. My room seems a ship's cabin; & at nights when I wake up & hear the wind shrieking, I almost fancy there is too much sail on the house, & I had better go on the roof & rig in the chimney.

Do you want to know how I pass my time?—I rise at eight—thereabouts—& go to my barn—say good-morning to the horse, & give him his breakfast. (It goes to my heart to give him a cold one, but it can't be helped) Then, pay a visit to my cow—cut up a pumpkin or two for her, & stand by to see her eat it—for its a pleasant sight to see a cow move her jaws—she does it so mildly & with such a sanctity.—My own breakfast over, I go to my work-room & light my fire—then spread my M.S.S. on the table—take one business squint at it, & fall to with a will. At 2½ P.M. I hear a preconcerted knock at my door, which (by request) continues till I rise & go to the door, which serves to wean me effectively from my writing, however interested I may be. My friends the horse & cow now demand their dinner—& I go & give it them. My own dinner over, I rig my sleigh & with my mother or sisters start off for the village—& if it be a Literary World day, great is the satisfaction thereof.—My evenings I spend in a sort of mesmeric state in my room—not being able to read— only now & then skimming over some large-printed book.— Can you send me about fifty fast-writing youths, with an easy style & not averse to polishing their labors? If you can, I wish you would, because since I have been here I have planned about that number of future works & cant find enough time to think about them separately.

But I dont know but a book in a man's brain is better off than a book bound in calf—at any rate it is safer from criticism. And taking a book off the brain, is akin to the ticklish & dangerous business of taking an old painting off a panel —you have to scrape off the whole brain in order to get at it with due safety—& even then, the painting may not be worth the trouble.

joke played on Surgeon Cuticle by the wardroom officers in
White-Jacket.

> Once [it begins] when they had some sago pudding for din-
> ner, and Cuticle chanced to be ashore, they made up a neat
> parcel of this bluish-white, firm, jelly-like preparation, and
> placing it in a tin box, carefully sealed with wax, they de-
> posited it on the gun-room table, with a note, purporting to
> come from an eminent physician in Rio, . . . begging leave to
> present the scientific Senhor Cuticle—with the donor's com-
> pliments—an uncommonly fine specimen of a cancer.

SELF-RIDICULE

. . . Self-ridicule, in the halcyon atmosphere of *Typee, Omoo,
Redburn,* and *White-Jacket,* is for the most part purely jocu-
lar. The richest vein occurs in *Redburn,* not unnaturally,
since the theme of the book is the practical education of a
greenhorn. But the attitude is maintained as consistently, if
with less concentration, in the other narratives. One strongly
anti-romantic episode in *Omoo* is characteristic of Melville's
gleeful exposures of his own punctured pride. Languishing
in the stocks of a makeshift Tahitian prison, Melville and his
fellow mutineers from the *Julia* are mortified by a stream of
native sight-seers and particularly by one light-minded
beauty, who laughs and points at each successive absurdity
sprawled before her. Melville determines to stifle her
ridicule with a show of manly dignity.

> Ere her glance fell upon me, I had, unconsciously, thrown
> myself into the most graceful attitude I could assume, leaned
> my head upon my hand, and summoned up as abstracted an
> expression as possible. Though my face was averted, I soon
> felt it flush, and knew that the glance was on me: deeper and
> deeper grew the flush, and not a sound of laughter.

> Delicious thought! she was moved at the sight of me. I could
> stand it no longer, but started up. Lo! there she was; her great
> hazel eyes rounding and rounding in her head, like two stars,
> her whole frame in a merry quiver, and an expression about
> the mouth that was sudden and violent death to anything like
> sentiment.

In some such light-hearted vein Melville treats every instance in which he appears in these books as the traditional
"goat"—every instance, that is, but one. The occasion is
young Redburn's departure from home on a river boat, a
ragged, hungry pauper, armed with a fowling piece to be
pawned for sea-togs, and a single dollar to pay his boat fare.
He becomes a "goat" when he discovers that the fare has

gone up to two dollars and that he is reduced to still more abject disgrace before his fashionable fellow-travelers, who have already been eyeing his patches askance.

> I stood their gazing some time, but at last could stand it no more. I pushed my seat right up before the most insolent gazer, a short fat man, with a plethora of cravat around his neck, and fixing my gaze on his, gave him more gazes than he sent. This somewhat embarrassed him, and he looked around for someone to take hold of me; but no one coming, he pretended to be very busy counting the gilded wooden beams overhead. I then turned to the next gazer, and clicking my gun-lock, deliberately presented the piece at him.

> Upon this, he oversat his seat in his eagerness to get beyond my range, for I had him point-blank, full in the left eye; and several persons starting to their feet, exclaimed that I must be crazy. So I was at that time; for otherwise I know not how to account for my demoniac feelings.

It is the first dramatic instance we have of the peculiar perversity of humor which Melville so suggestively labels for us as "demoniac." The episode is striking here because of its singularity in the midst of a sunnier humor, but it was destined to cast a long shadow after it.

Around the central self-portrait Melville's memory drew, with comic distortion, the myriad figures that had peopled his transposed frontier world. Fortunately, Melville's forte, like every true humorist's, was the human comedy, and it is to the enduring humor of his portraiture, more than anything else, that the survival of his "popular" novels is due. The raw material was perfect, and the artist evidently knew what it was good for. "At sea a fellow comes out," he wrote to Duyckinck years later. "Salt water is like wine, in that respect." The young Melville simply capitalized on a matchless opportunity to study all kinds of men under the influence of both salt water and wine, frequently both at once. The resulting gallery is heavy in rogues, most of them at sea and most of them drunk, but some merely at sea or merely drunk, and a few even on land and sober. . . .

Redburn, despite Melville's apparent contempt for it, is anything but "beggarly" in the caliber of its salt-fed comic portraiture. One searches very nearly in vain, before *Moby-Dick,* for anything surpassing the sure, full-bodied artistry displayed in the sketches of the cook, the steward, and Jack Blunt. The *Highlander*'s cook takes on a more memorable charm than his coffee and his grooming would suggest. Be-

hind an imposing façade of doormat, knocker, and name-
plate, the devout "Mr. Thompson" presides with sovereign
dignity over his stove-filled cubicle, earnestly poring over a
greasy Bible as he stirs his pots, but occasionally forgetting
his piety with a high sea running in his firebox. His boon
companion is the mulatto steward, an ex-Broadway barber
named Lavender, who perfumes his hair, affects a glass "di-
amond" and a turban, reads sentimental novels, and wears
cast-off clothing "in the height of exploded fashions." It is the
incontestable hand of an artist that brings these two together
to finish their own portraits by the mutual illumination of
their humors:

> And sometimes Mr. Thompson would take down his Bible,
> and read a chapter for the edification of Lavender, whom he
> knew to be a sad profligate and gay deceiver ashore; addicted
> to every youthful indiscretion. He would read over to him the
> story of Joseph and Potiphar's wife; and hold Joseph up to
> him as a young man of excellent principles, whom he ought
> to imitate, and not be guilty of his indiscretion any more. And
> Lavender would look serious, and say that he knew it was all
> true—he was a wicked youth, he knew it—he had broken a
> good many hearts, and many eyes were weeping for him even
> then, both in New York, and Liverpool, and London, and
> Havre. But how could he help it? He hadn't made his hand-
> some face, and fine head of hair, and graceful figure. It was
> not *he*, but the others, that were to blame; for his bewitching
> person turned all heads and subdued all hearts, wherever he
> went. And then he would look very serious and penitent, and
> go up to the little glass, and pass his hands through his hair,
> and see how his whiskers were coming on.

Jack Blunt, who comes in for a somewhat fuller treatment in
the next chapter, is that rare gift to the humorist, the happy
sucker. A devotee of fortune-telling, "Balm of Paradise" hair
oil, miscellaneous quack pills, and mathematical horo-
scopes, Blunt is also God's gift to the confidence man; but
the gentle whimsicality with which Melville here handles
both the fleecer and the fleeced stands in striking contrast to
the acerbity of the book he was one day to write on that special theme. . . .

DEDICATED DRINKERS

The majority of Melville's sailors are dedicated drinkers.
Some are the heroic type who, like Mad Jack of the *Nev-
ersink*, seem to have been "suckled at a puncheon [cask]."
Some are the narcotic type, maintaining, like the pilot at

Nukuheva, "that interesting state of intoxication when a man is amiable and helpless." All are men of little discretion and no shame at all; according to Redburn's prim characterization, they "only blush after the third bottle." The degree of their dedication may have been a matter of sober regret to Melville. He suggests as much in his assertion that the Navy was an "asylum for drunkards ... driven back to the spirit-tub and the gun-deck by [their] old hereditary foe, the ever-devilish god of grog." As an artist, however, he wrung a good deal of excellent comedy from it. Writing of those very man-of-war's men he pitied for their addiction, he made a good thing of the occasion when the grog gave out on the *Neversink*. Deprived of their daily tot, the crew suffered an alarming slump in morale until ten curiously stiff and sweet-smelling fellows were laid out in the brig to sleep off a mysterious drunkenness, and it became known below decks that the ship's store was amply supplied with Eau de Cologne.

> The news spread far and wide among the men, being only kept secret from the officers and underlings, and that night the long, crane-necked Cologne bottles jingled in out-of-the-way corners and by-places, and, being emptied, were sent flying out of the ports. With brown sugar, taken from the mess-chests, and hot water begged from the galley-cooks, the men made all manner of punches, toddies, and cocktails, letting fall therein a small drop of tar, like a bit of brown toast, by way of imparting a flavour.... Next day, fore and aft, the whole frigate smelled like a lady's toilet.

Even Melville's own disapproval of intemperance is turned to comic account in *Redburn*, where he portrays himself as a member of the "Juvenile Total Abstinence Association," driven to apostasy by being seasick among a crew well stocked with the standard cure, "which they had brought along to sea with them, *to taper off with*, as they called it.". . .

MELVILLE POKES FUN AT SEX

Sex, the universal joke, is a recurrent theme in the writing of Melville's jocular-hedonic period. It appears most unreservedly in *Omoo*, under the combined influence of Long Ghost and the free-and-easy mores of the islands, where "the best dress in courting is motley" and the courtesies of hospitality may be extended by a native hostess "to a degree altogether superfluous." Even in the absence of these priming influences its persistence reflects the normality of

Melville's masculine bias and adds to the comic zest of his early books. In *Pierre* he was to take on a new gravity in dealing with intersexual relations, but until then his literary women were no more than a piquant diversion. Melville on his canoeing excursions in *Typee* sounds a good deal like Long Ghost on his botanical ones: "But I was ever partial to what is termed in the *Young Men's Own Book*—'the society of virtuous and intelligent young ladies;' and in the absence of the mermaids, the amusement became dull and insipid." Thus we are introduced to the famous *affaire* Fayaway, which, notwithstanding its theatrical romanticism and careful narrative propriety, is essentially a gambol on the part of a Male Animal frankly stimulated by a young lady's smoking, standing naked in a canoe, and otherwise wearing a dress which "began at the waist, and terminated sufficiently far above the ground to reveal the most bewitching ankle in the universe."

Elsewhere the rovings of the healthy masculine eye are chronicled in an even more clearly picaresque mood. When, in *Omoo*, the author caught sight of a beautiful girl on horseback, he promptly enlisted Long Ghost, identified the young lady as the wife of an English planter ("happy dog"), and undaunted by that intelligence, put in an appearance at the plantation with a view to making her acquaintance. There they were graciously entertained by the lady's husband, who appealed to their secondary weaknesses by offering them fresh melons filled with sherry. "Now this was extremely polite in Mr. Bell," says Melville, keeping his eye on the ball; "still, we came to see *Mrs.* Bell." A similar incident in *Redburn*, allowing for a more appropriate naïveté in the telling, achieves its comic effect by the same subordination of lesser appetites. Attracted to an English cottage by three beautiful girls, young Redburn rises to the challenge of a suspicious mother and talks himself into an invitation to tea, where even the presence of fresh milk and "such buttered muffins [as] never were spread on the other side of the Atlantic" fails to deflect his interest. "There they sat—the charmers, I mean—eating those buttered muffins in plain sight. I wished I was a buttered muffin myself.". . .

The common stratum of material that underlay the autobiographical romances lent itself by and large to the jocular-hedonic air to which Melville was both inclined and committed in works of popular entertainment.

Melville's Short Stories Prove His Greatness as a Writer

Q.D. Leavis

Q.D. Leavis argues that Melville's short stories "are some of the finest . . . short stories in the language." He contends that the shorter works show Melville as a great humorist, social commentator, and novel thinker. Leavis is a literary critic and author of *Fiction and the Reading Public*, as well as a contributor to the anthology *New Perspectives on Melville*, from which this viewpoint is excerpted.

Julian Hawthorne wrote in an otherwise percipient reminiscence of Melville's character and disposition that 'His later writings are incomprehensible'. This from [Nathaniel] Hawthorne's son, who had presumably been initiated into the meaning and method of his father's work and so should have had some insight at least into that art which derived from Hawthorne's, suggests how inevitable it was that Melville could find no public for his fiction after his early phase as a writer of adventure books about voyages by sea. Even the incomparable *Benito Cereno* made no real impact in America in Melville's long lifetime.

But to the modern English and American reader, well trained in practical criticism and knowing with regard to myth, symbol, allegory and imagery, the writings of the great 1853–6 phase are of more interest than the earlier novels, evidently more accomplished as art, more varied—written in the short space of three years and with desperate need of money, they show an astonishing range of subject-matter, attitude, tone and style—and are noticeably more condensed, controlled and mature than either *Moby-Dick* or *Pierre*, the two previous major works; and this in spite of the discouraging fact that even *Moby-Dick* had not been a finan-

From "Melville: The 1853–56 Phase" by Q.D. Leavis, in *New Perspectives on Melville*, edited by Faith Pullin (Kent, OH: Kent State University Press, 1978). Copyright ©1978 by Edinburgh University Press. Reprinted by permission of the Kent State University Press.

cial success while *Pierre* had been and remained a dead loss. Yet Melville rallied from the disappointment, though it seriously affected his health, and triumphantly wound up this last phase of prose creativeness with an ironic masterpiece, *The Confidence-Man.* But in order to understand this difficult and still highly controversial work one must, it seems to me, have grasped the nature of the tales written while he was gestating the novel. Published mostly in magazines, they were reprinted as *The Piazza Tales* and reveal his interests and preoccupations in these fertile years as well as the kinds of technique he was inventing for these new purposes.

THE ENCANTADAS

The Encantadas is simply a series of ten sketches which have as unifying theme the horrors of a tropical waterless Nature which sustains only equally infernal forms of animal and human existence. They show how Melville's imagination at this period was haunted by the memory of the histories of the wretched castaways with their inhuman treatment by fellow-men who exceed them in cruelty. This culminates in the history of the poor half-breed woman Hunilla, treacherously deserted with her family by the captain committed to returning for them and, as sole survivor, raped by whaleboatmen to whom she looked for rescue. A pious Catholic, Hunilla had the fortitude to preserve her sanity and faith. Melville concludes her history with Hunilla riding away Christ-like on an ass, eyeing 'the beast's armorial cross', and 'Humanity, thou strong thing, I worship thee, not in the laureled victor, but in this vanquished one'—an affirmation of faith, in humanity at least and in spite of its worst manifestations, which must not be overlooked in any discussion of Melville's attitude to God and man at this period.

The others really are integral tales. They fall into groups, for instance three double tales each consisting of a contrasted pair. . . . These all spring from experiences in England and America that aroused Melville's generous indignation at social conditions—treatment of the poor, class snobbery extending even to religious worship, and surprisingly, in view of the exclusion of women from his previous novels except as ideas in *Pierre* and *Mardi*, to the treatment of women, who are seen as victims of Nature as well as of man and society. Thus in these years Melville was manifesting a considerable degree of emotional and moral involvement in social life on land, both in England and America. In *The Piazza Tales* we are not living in 'The World in a Man-of-War' as in *White-Jacket* or in the world in a whaling-ship as in *Moby-Dick*, but are taken into the full living world of the Anglo-American mid-nineteenth century, a very great step forward for Melville as an artist into the complexities of living, even, into the difficulties of family life for the man and the artist. We remember that Melville was married in 1847 and by now had children, a family to support, and was living in a household that contained also his mother and three of his sisters, a concentration of women with claims on him that inevitably forced on his attention the woman's point of view, and which also obliged him to reconsider the man's role as individual (as in *I and My Chimney*), and as artist tormented by the rival claims of his work and the support of his family.

BARTLEBY

The tale of *Bartleby the Scrivener* (1853) has received plenty of critical attention and there is no disagreement as to its meaning and the nature of its techniques, which present no difficulty. But recognition has not been given to the fact that it is one of Melville's try-outs and not an adopted position, much less a personal admission of neurosis. This is the only tale of the batch that ends in limbo. Bartleby is posited as the man who adopts a consistently negative response to the demands of unsatisfactory living in the Wall Street society (copying while facing a blank wall). His unshakable 'I would prefer not to' which he persists in until it inevitably leaves him dead of starvation in prison, with 'peering out upon him the eyes of murderers and thieves', is yet felt, like Hunilla's tragedy, to be a triumph of the indomitable spirit: Bartleby, even the lawyer his employer feels, is at rest 'with kings and counselors'. Melville himself concludes with 'Ah, Bartleby! Ah, humanity!' which is unfathomably ambiguous, perhaps a sad recognition of the human condition. Bartleby's suicidal choice is not so much the centre of Melville's attention as the complex reaction to it of his employer, whose mixture of exasperation and pity in his efforts first to save Bartleby and failing this, to wash his hands of him—all too human—are examined not without sympathy. For what could be done for a Bartleby? Can one envisage a society composed of Bartlebies? ... Bartleby's having been a clerk in the Dead

Letter Office, and then a mere copyist of other people's compositions, are not very obscure references to the kind of literary non-life Melville saw he himself would be relegated to in all likelihood after the failure of *Pierre* and the destruction by fire in 1853 of the plates of all his novels, and with the increasing weakness of his eyesight (like Bartleby's). Not surprisingly, several tales of this period are discussions of the problem of the artist who has to earn a living in mid-nineteenth-century America—*Cock-a-Doodle-Doo!, The Fiddler, I and My Chimney.* Only two years before (1851) Melville had praised Hawthorne for as an artist always 'saying No! in thunder'—'the Devil himself cannot make him say *yes'*—and had since been inclined to castigate all those who do say *yes*, an indication of the line Melville was to explore systematically in *The Confidence-Man.* Characteristically, Melville had proceeded from his ardent endorsement of Hawthorne's apparent attitude to testing its validity by actualizing it in the case of a consistent practitioner, Bartleby, when he recognizes that however heroic it is impracticable; Bartleby's employer, the average citizen, had always been convinced, he says, that 'the easiest way of life is the best', which though ignoble is a means of survival, we see. And a year after *Bartleby* Melville tried out such an alternative to Bartleby's in an odd short sketch *The Fiddler.*

This opens with the despair of the narrator, a poet named Helmstone: 'So my poem is damned, and immortal fame is not for me! Intolerable fate!' But he is 'instantly soothed' by being introduced to the amiable and winning genius Hautboy (presumably meaning 'a high-flier') whose fame has passed and his fortune with it. But he is quite content to drudge for a living by teaching the fiddle: '*With* genius and *without* fame, he is happier than a king', his friend Standard (the average man) assures Helmstone, who feels 'I wish I were Hautboy'. So he tears up his manuscripts and follows this model's example. The tale is merely an annotation of an idea and has none of the convincing detail, the sensitive complexity and the involved technical devices Melville found necessary for the more substantial tales, showing he did not entertain this alternative very seriously. I simply cite it as another proof that his mind worked from theory to posited embodiments in alternative forms of life (like Dickens). For these he drew equally on incidents in his own experience, on documents and historical facts, and on the lives of real people, thus doing his best to keep his theorizing in touch with actuality and to direct his abstract thinking on to the life of the individual and the welfare of society.

COCK-A-DOODLE-DOO!

Nearly a year before, Melville had published the very remarkable tale *Cock-a-Doodle-Doo!* In this case Melville took off from Wordsworth's poem *Resolution and Independence* which must have exasperated him since, starting from reflections of a kind relevant to Melville's own position, on the disastrous fate of poets who from beginning in gladness pass through despondency to madness owing to poverty, Wordsworth apparently found arguments in the fortitude of the Leech-gatherer for reassurance and trust in Providence. To Melville, in debt, and in fear of blindness and possibly also of the madness from which his father died, such optimism was superficial. Accordingly, his tone in this tale is harsh and jeering. He exhibits in refutation of Wordsworth the painful history of Merrymusk (that is, 'Merry Music', creative genius) and his family, the tale being for the most part a rude parody of the poem. The narrator, in financial trouble himself and not finding comfort in Nature like Wordsworth, is cheered by the 'prodigious exulting strains' of a cock which ring through the whole countryside and throw him into a rapturous, buoyant state. It turns out to be owned by a desperately poor but dignified wood-sawyer who proudly declares: 'I raised it'. He calls it Trumpet and it crows only at his command—evidently the voice of his art which, while it can't bring him an income, makes up to him and his sick wife and children for their deprivations in material things. The narrator watches them all die happy in hearing to the last the 'glorious and rejoicing crow' of their unique Trumpet. This part is not satiric: the uncomplaining wife is heroic in her 'long-loving sympathy' with her husband, and as for the four children—listening to the cock 'Their faces shone celestially through grime and dirt. They seemed children of emperors and kings, disguised'. Merrymusk himself insists as he dies that he and all of them are well, 'in a kind of wild ecstacy of triumph over ill'. Last of all Trumpet dies, and the narrator buries them all in one grave with on the gravestone 'a lusty cock in act of crowing' and the possibly unironic inscription 'O death, where is thy sting? O grave, where is thy victory?' and—reverting now to the original tone—ends: 'and never since then have I felt the doleful dumps'.

A SMOKED HUMAN HEAD

This excerpt is taken from a review of Typee *written by author Nathaniel Hawthorne and published in the Salem, Massachusetts,* Advertiser *on March 25, 1846. Hawthorne praises the book, pointing out the wide range of experiences Melville writes about.*

The book is lightly but vigorously written; and we are acquainted with no work that gives a freer and more effective picture of barbarian life, in that unadulterated state of which there are now so few specimens remaining.... On one page, we read of manners and modes of life that indicate a whole system of innocence and peace; and on the next, we catch a glimpse of a smoked human head, and the half-picked skeleton of what had been (in a culinary sense) a *well-dressed* man. The author's descriptions of the native girls are voluptuously colored, yet not more so than the exigencies of the subject appear to require. He has that freedom of view—it would be too harsh to call it laxity of principle—which renders him tolerant of codes of morals that may be little in accordance with our own; a spirit proper enough to a young and adventurous sailor.

I have never encountered an explanation of why Merrymusk should have named his cock 'Trumpet'. My own conjecture is that Melville had several poems of Wordsworth's, besides *Resolution and Independence*, in his mind when composing this tale, all of them having in common the theme of the poet's creative powers. So Wordsworth's sonnet on The Sonnet was brought in by naming Merrymusk's art after what Wordsworth tells us was the favourite poetic form of great poets, as of Wordsworth himself; and the account culminates in Milton's use of the sonnet, when

> In his hand
> The Thing became a trumpet; whence he blew
> Soul-animating strains—alas, too few!

So in this complex and subtly Wordsworthian tale, which is surprisingly like D.H. Lawrence in tone and content, Melville registers belief in the sustaining and revivifying power of art, and in support of my interpretation we note that the rustic humour and scoffing tone are abandoned whenever the narrator confronts the Merrymusk household. And he is genuinely disturbed by the mighty power of Trumpet: 'the cock frightened me, like some overpowering angel in the Apocalypse'—as well as sincerely humbled by the character of Merrymusk who denies he deserves pity, declaring with superb conviction:

> Why call *me* poor? Don't the cock *I* own glorify this otherwise inglorious, lean, lantern-jawed land? Didn't *my* cock encourage *you*? And *I* give you all this glorification away gratis. I am a great philanthropist. I am a rich man—a very rich man, and a very happy one. Crow, Trumpet.

The narrator admits he 'was not wholly at rest concerning the soundness of Merrymusk's views of things, though full of admiration for him. I was thinking on the matter before my door, when I heard the cock crow again. Enough. Merrymusk is right. Oh, noble cock! oh, noble man!'

Note that New England is envisaged here as a Puritan; that is to say, the land of Puritan settlers was ignorant of art though desperately in need of it. Also, it is unable to appreciate art—no one in the countryside but the narrator and the Merrymusk family is able to hear the cock, a sly touch. An 'inglorious land' indeed! An interpretation that, because the rest can't hear the cock, the voice is imaginary and Melville trying to come to terms with a neurosis; or alternatively, that 'cock' being a sex-term the tale must be understood as a sexual *double-entendre*—are equally instances of perverse critical sophistry. The identification of cocks with poets is made beyond doubt by Melville's parody of Wordsworth's lines (at the end of the seventh stanza of *Resolution and Independence*) on the sad history of poets:

> Of fine mornings,
> We fine lusty cocks begin our crows in gladness;
> But when eve does come we don't crow quite so much,
> For then cometh despondency and madness.

And in his description of the cock's crow we see the characteristics of his own literary voice: 'full of pluck, full of fire, full of fun, full of glee. It plainly says—"*Never say die!*"'

Merrymusk then is Melville's idea of a more convincing model for Wordsworth's Leech-gatherer and he is also, with his inspiring voice Trumpet, Melville the artist (who thought of himself as poet-novelist)—we are told Merrymusk had been first a sailor, then a small farmer, and was now a hired drudge, Melville's own history. The story of the family dying prematurely as they do from harrowing poverty is surely an ironic comment on Wordsworthian trust, carrying on the ridicule with which the tale started. There is also satire in the reiterated fact that the baseless self-confidence the cock's crowing gives the narrator inspires him to reckless financial behaviour and evidently future ruin. Yet there is no doubt that Trumpet is 'the cheerer', and when he perches on the sick children's bed 'All their wasted eyes gazed at him with a wild and spiritual delight. They seemed to sun themselves in the radiant plumage of the cock'. This is sincere and moving. Melville seems to be trying to explain that though the dolours of the poet's life of poverty that Wordsworth brushes aside are inescapable and bear hardest on his family, *yet* they all, and everyone else in the world too, have thereby the consolations of art which can make life blissful and suffering negligible. The artist's support therefore can only be looked for in his sense of achievement, Melville argues.

Wordsworth's 1815 sonnet to the unfortunate painter Haydon is another that Melville seems to me to have drawn on as a help to expressing his theme in *Cock-a-Doodle-Doo!* It is next but one to the 'Trumpet' sonnet in the 1849–50 edition of Wordsworth's poems and is of such importance in elucidating Melville's argument and the conclusion we should extract that I will cite it in full:

> High is our calling, Friend!—Creative Art
> (Whether the instrument of words she use,
> Or pencil pregnant with ethereal hues,)
> Demands the service of a mind and heart,
> Though sensitive, yet, in their weakest part,
> Heroically fashioned—to infuse
> Faith in the whispers of the lonely Muse,
> While the whole world seems adverse to desert.
> And, oh! when Nature sinks, as oft she may,
> Through long-lived pressure of obscure distress,
> Still to be strenuous for the bright reward
> And in the soul admit of no decay,
> Brook no continuance of weak-mindedness—
> Great is the glory, for the strife is hard!

It is important to note that in these tales Melville shows he is as much concerned as Henry James or Hawthorne with the problems of the life of the artist and the necessity of art for the life of the spirit, because we must also note that these considerations are completely absent from the picture of life in the America of the 1850s drawn for *The Confidence-Man* shortly after. Something he knew to be central and vital has there been deliberately omitted. And these tales, particularly the complex *Cock-a-Doodle-Doo!*, show the kind of difficulty we are faced with in reading these later Melville works. The complexity does not disguise the meaning but it shows that several meanings are intended which, united, provide the means of arriving at a just conclusion. He is in his creative activity exploring all the possibilities in a given human problem, facing and considering them in turn and playing one off against the other, the changes of tone and direction giving us guide-lines. Thus in these tales he developed the method he was to need for *The Confidence-Man*, and one may well feel that tales like *Bartleby*, *Benito Cereno*, *Cock-a-Doodle-Doo!* and *The Tartarus of Maids* are almost inexhaustible. . . .

In none of the tales of this period can I find any justification for Hawthorne's opinion (*English Notebooks*, 20 November 1856) that Melville's 'writings, for a long while past, have indicated a morbid state of mind'. In *I and My Chimney* (published 1855) there is reassuring good-humour in the narrator's recognition that the women of his family suspect the soundness of his home's exceptionally tall and finely-wrought chimney, resent its bulk and mysterious foundations, which they fancy must contain a secret chamber with hidden treasure, and believe that the house would be safer and more comfortable without such a chimney. They torment the old man by getting in 'a master-mason' to test it and arrange if unsound for its removal, but the narrator circumvents them all. He has explained that the chimney 'is my backbone', 'the one grand permanence of this abode' and that 'when all the house shall have crumbled from it, this chimney will still survive'. The tale ends: 'I and my chimney will never surrender'. Thus the chimney is a composite symbol standing, apparently, for his morale, his immortal soul (which he is determined to call his own), the source of his creative power (the chimney's foundations are buried in darkness, deep down), his intellect, his personality, and his inherited traditions (a kinsman named Dacres—that is, 'Sacred'—built the house); the chimney also seems to stand, like the personal tree in European folk-tales, for his life-force, for it is sinking into the ground and crumbling as he himself grows old. This is one of Melville's most intimate and most suggestive tales. It is surely also good proof of its author's mental health. There is much wry amusement at the narrator's situation and some sympathy for the wife, misguided though she is, who has to put up with the disadvantages of living with an obstinately conservative and privacy-loving intellectual, one resigned to old age and death but not to interference with his essential self.

In short, it must be generally recognized that the tales of Melville are some of the finest *contes* and short stories in the language, as well as some of the most original, and that, like D.H. Lawrence and Hawthorne, his claim to stature as an artist is to be based on his tales at least as much as on his novels.

The Bible in Melville's Work

Nathalia Wright

In the following selection, Nathalia Wright argues that Melville not only makes extensive use of biblical quotations and anecdotes in his books, but also patterns many of his characters after personages in the Bible. Wright gives several examples of Melville's use of the Bible and concludes that Melville intended to correlate his characters' struggles with those of biblical heroes. A professor of English, Wright has written *Horatio Greenough: The First American Sculptor*, *American Novels in Italy*, and *Melville's Use of the Bible*, from which this article is excerpted.

In all that Melville wrote he was no nearer saying what he had to say at the end than he was at the beginning. His effect, like Shakespeare's, is one of extension rather than of volume. One receives the impression of spaces and distances, of approaches and retreats, of vistas opened but not entered upon. One is always traveling but never arrives....

Above all, one is made to feel that what has been left unsaid is unspeakably vaster than what has been said. The superabundance of material appalls him, and he is driven at last to think of all truth as voiceless and of the question as more final than any answer. "God keep me from ever completing anything," cries Ishmael. "This whole book is a draught—nay, but the draught of a draught.."...

To this desire to extend the scope of his work, to this fear of appearing final, all Melville's rhetorical devices and all his voluminous sources are subservient. So indiscriminately are they introduced and associated that they tend at last to lose their separate identities. They are but fragments of a boundless creation, undistinguished otherwise in the hands of its creator. Of them all, however, no single one so far ex-

From Nathalia Wright, *Melville's Use of the Bible.* Copyright 1947, Duke University Press, Durham, N.C. Reprinted with permission.

tends the bounds of what Melville wrote as the Bible. However he alluded to it he was assured of a contrast with his immediate material: between the common and the great, the present and the past, the natural and the supernatural. And though each is a contrast achieved by many other means as well, only this one enabled him to make them all simultaneously, at once magnifying his characters and their affairs, establishing for the briefest moment a background of antiquity, and suggesting the presence of yet another, unseen world beyond the vast scene which meets the eye.

Originally and essentially, of course, all Melville's material is simple and commonplace, becoming transformed through a marvelous imagination. Viewed strictly in the light of fact his characters are of limited powers and lowly station. Yet as their lives unfold in passion and in problem, they seem to be supermen, inhabiting a world one degree larger than life. The effect is deliberate, and it is deliberately more than the general exaggeration of his pen. Thus did he justify it [in *Moby-Dick*]:

> If, then, to meanest mariners, and renegades and castaways, I shall hereafter ascribe high qualities, though dark; weave round them tragic graces; if even the most mournful, perchance the most abased, among them all, shall at times lift himself to the exalted mounts; if I shall touch that workman's arm with some ethereal light; if I shall spread a rainbow over his disastrous set of sun; then against all mortal critics bear me out in it, thou just Spirit of Equality, which hast spread one royal mantle of humanity over all my kind! Bear me out in it, thou great democratic God! who didst not refuse to the swart convict, Bunyan, the pale, poetic pearl; Thou who didst clothe with doubly hammered leaves of finest gold, the stumped and paupered arm of old Cervantes; Thou who didst pick up Andrew Jackson from the pebbles; who didst hurl him upon a war-horse; who didst thunder him higher than a throne! Thou who, in all Thy mighty, earthly marchings, ever cullest Thy selectest champions from the kingly commons; bear me out in it, O God!

This effect of magnitude in Melville's characters is achieved largely by figurative language, since his imagery contains references to so many great personages of history and literature. Side by side with the nameless crews of his ships walk Henry VIII, Charlemagne, Xerxes, Apis, Ammon, Jove, Perseus, Prometheus, Mohammed, Faust, Hamlet, Beelzebub, Abraham. With many of them Melville briefly compared his own characters: Daggoo and Hivohitee to

Ahasuerus, Jarl at his supper to Belshazzar at his feast, the helmsman of the *Highlander* to Ixion, General McPherson to Sarpedon, the carpenter at his forge to Prometheus, Ahab to Adam: "'I feel deadly faint, bowed, and humped, as though I were Adam, staggering beneath the piled centuries since Paradise.'" The Bible, in fact, provides genealogies to ennoble the meanest of men, for all, it asserts in various accounts, are descendants of the Jehovah-created Adam, of the sons of God who intermarried with the daughters of men, of the patriarch Noah, and spiritually of the New Testament Father. Melville cited them all.

More important . . . is the deeper relationship which is made to exist between some of these personages and Melville's characters, whereby the patterns of their lives are both clarified and given significance. Some of them are named for the great, and thus the parallel moves with them: a whaling captain for a king of Israel, a Revolutionary soldier for Jehovah's chosen people, a sailor for the son of a patriarch, another sailor for a Norse jarl [nobleman], two lunatics for a prophet and an archangel, a religious fanatic for the rebuilder of Jerusalem, a ship owner for an advisor of Job. Even ships are so titled: the *Jeroboam*, the *Rachel*. The historical *Serapis* might have sprung from the same fancy, for to Melville the white-sailed naval vessels, like the albatross, the whale, the skyhawk, were nothing less than archangelic beings. . . .

[Melville's] characters . . . wrestle with problems which have preoccupied heroes, sages, prophets, and gods. They seek the truth in exile and loneliness, in the wilderness of Ishmael and Hagar, of Moses, of John and Jesus. They pursue the demonic phantom despite testimonies of Faust and Prometheus and Jeremiah that they cannot survive the experience. Some announce with Solomon and with Seneca that the wisdom of this world is equivocal, while others, like Enceladus, Hamlet, Jesus, seek to reconcile it with the wisdom of another, absolute realm. At least one meets disaster through the simple opposition of his nature to evil. . . .

LANGUAGE

The speech of these people, too, is appropriate, containing some of the most magnificent of stylistic echoes from the seventeenth century, the Elizabethans, the Anglo-Saxons, the authors of the Bible. The quotations Ishmael makes from

JONAH AS A PREVIEW FOR AHAB

In Moby Dick, *Father Mapple gives a sermon based on the biblical tale of Jonah and the Whale that remarkably echoes what Ishmael will encounter when he meets Ahab and learns of his reasons for hunting the white whale. In this excerpt from the sermon, Father Mapple chides those who, like Jonah, try to shirk their duty to God's requests.*

How being an anointed pilot-prophet, or speaker of true things, and bidden by the Lord to sound those unwelcome truths in the ears of a wicked Nineveh, Jonah, appalled at the hostility he should raise, fled from his mission and sought to escape his duty and his God by taking ship at Joppa. But God is everywhere; Tarshish he never reached. As we have seen, God came upon him in the whale, and swallowed him down to living gulfs of doom, and with swift slantings tore him along 'into the midst of the seas,' where the eddying depths sucked him ten thousand fathoms down, and 'the weeds were wrapped about his head,' and all the watery world of woe bowled over him. Yet even then beyond the reach of any plummet—'out of the belly of hell'—when the whale grounded upon the ocean's utmost bones, even then, God heard the engulphed, repenting prophet when he cried. Then God spake unto the fish; and from the shuddering cold and blackness of the sea, the whale came breeching up towards the warm and pleasant sun, and all the delights of air and earth; and 'vomited out Jonah upon the dry land;' when the word of the Lord came a second thee; and Jonah, bruised and beaten—his ears, like two sea-shells; still multitudinously murmuring of the ocean—Jonah did the Almighty's bidding. And what was that, shipmates? To preach the Truth to the face of Falsehood! That was it!

"This, shipmates, this is that other lesson; and woe to that pilot of the living God who sights it. Woe to him whom this world charms from Gospel duty! Woe to him who seeks to pour oil upon the waters when God has brewed them into a gale! Woe to him who seeks to please rather than to appal! Woe to him whose good name is more to him than goodness! Woe to him who, in this world, courts not dishonor! Woe to him who would not be true, even though to be false were salvation! Yea, woe to him who, as the great Pilot Paul has it, while preaching to others is himself a castaway!"

Job, Father Mapple's sermon on Jonah, the Confidence-Man's reading from Ecclesiasticus, Pierre's relation of the adulteress's story, Nehemiah's recapitulation of obscure biblical events, countless echoes of the Hebrew prophets, poets, and sages—all add eloquence to pretentiousness. Like the Teutonic war song of Yoomy and the Shakespearean ranting of Pierre, these words, whether spoken by or about Melville's characters, make each of them seem less and less like a single individual, more and more like Everyman.

It is in just this conception of character, in fact, that the intricate connections between Melville's religious thought, his use of the Bible, and the entire Romantic school to which he belonged are most clearly revealed. Quite likely its belief in the dignity and the possibility of the individual more than all else commended Christianity to him. For this he held to be the great value, the field on which all conflicts were fought, the divinity shaping every end. Man, by the very fact of his being, could be neither common nor insignificant, and often the darkest of skin and the most primitive of mind held closest communion with the heart of the universe. . . .

All Melville's characters have something in common with the Renaissance and with the Byronic hero. And hence all those in the Bible on whom he depended most to magnify his own were carefully chosen: the ambitious Ahab rather than the repentant David, the rebellious Jonah and the lonely Jeremiah rather than the priestly Isaiah, the aspiring but not the obedient Jesus. For all this is more than magnitude; this is the assault upon the bastions of heaven.

Nor do these characters come alone to Melville's pages. The ancient past to which most of them belong, and which inevitably accompanies them, towers up everywhere, a presence of which he was constantly aware. And again, since none of the scenes of his narratives is older than the eighteenth century, it is largely a figurative method he adopted. The whalemen live together like some old Mesopotamian family. No dying Chaldee had higher or holier thoughts than Queequeg approaching death. Nantucket is the Tyre of New Bedford's Carthage. [In *Pierre*,] the pines on the hill are as "lofty archers, and vast, out-looking watchers of the glorious Babylonian City of the Day." Of the civilizations of Egypt and Assyria, whose secrets were just being excavated, he was particularly fond. . . .

BIBLICAL EPISODES

With such intimations . . . the Bible, of course, abounds; and Melville exploited certain episodes thoroughly: the Creation, the Garden of Eden, the Flood. Sometimes the extent of time is suggested, as when Ishmael is brooding over the dead in the Whaleman's Chapel: "... in what eternal, unstirring paralysis, and deadly, hopeless trance, yet lies antique Adam who died sixty round centuries ago. ..." Again the emphasis is upon the youthfulness of the world at the time of creation. Exclaimed the champion of contemporary authors, in "Hawthorne and His Mosses": "The world is young to-day as when it was created; and this Vermont morning dew is as wet to my feet as Eden's dew to Adam's."

These allusions are the major part of Melville's effort at "oldageifying youth in books," re-creating as they do an ancient background for his narratives. But he also selected certain strategic points in those narratives to "oldageify" and thereby made them discourses upon themes as old as history. ...

So in his first novels, wherein Melville compared the life of the Pacific islanders with the life in Eden before the fall, and in his last, which broaches the doctrine of original sin to explain Claggart's character, the entire sequence of events is thrown backward to the beginning of time. The men of the *Pequod* are engaged in no new business: their vessel bears the name of an Indian tribe as extinct as the Medes and the Persians, and the whales they secure contain the stone spearheads of ancient Indian seamen. As Ishmael puts it: "Who can show a pedigree like Leviathan: Ahab's harpoon had shed blood older than the Pharoah's. Methuselah seems a schoolboy. I look round to shake hands with Shem." Nor does the youthful Pierre confront a new problem: it is older than the Glendinning genealogy, older even than Memnon, Solomon, or the Titans, as old as the inscrutable stones of nature. *Clarel*, too, is an old story. Wherever the pilgrims go they are met by memorials of the first century and of the dateless ages preceding it. ...

For the past he saw was not a separate segment of time but an inextricable part of the present, of which the ruins strewn upon the earth are but the most obvious evidence. From them each succeeding age is built, for time, as he consistently personified it, is the mason, not the destroyer. It sets one generation's life upon its predecessor's, as it did for both Hebrews and Greeks: Ahab's upon Jeroboam's, Orestes' upon Clytemnestra's, Pierre's upon Mr. Glendinning's. ...

MELVILLE'S USE OF BIBLICAL HEROES

Dreams and portents, hypersensitive natures, and miraculous events—these outline Melville's invisible world. Most of them are described with some reference to supernatural phenomena recorded by history and many in terms of Biblical parallels. The visions of Babbalanja and of Pierre have Hebrew, Miltonic, and Greek echoes; clairvoyants such as Tistig, Elijah, Gabriel, the Manxman, the Dansker resemble and even bear the names of Jewish angels and prophets; spectacles of nature, like the whale's peaking its flukes, are in a class with the activities of Dante's devils and Isaiah's angelic beings; occurrences like Macey's death and the *Pequod's* disaster seem to be the fulfillment of prophecies as divinely inspired as Zoroaster's or as John's. Seeing the dead Claggart lying before him Captain Vere exclaims: "'It is the divine judgment of Ananias! Look!... Struck dead by an angel of God. Yet the angel must hang!'"

Like the past and the present in Melville's pages, moreover, these two spheres of existence are not mutually exclusive, but constantly impinge on each other. They are synchronized. And as natural circumstances are deliberately compared with supernatural ones, a whole undercurrent of affairs is set in motion. Watching Starbuck visit the sleeping Ahab in his cabin and move to slay him with the musket at hand, one suddenly perceives another sequence of events happening at the same moment in quite another world when the mate is said to be wrestling with an angel. These are no theatrical figures of speech; these are glimpses of a realm more dynamic than any other.

Now in his belief in the existence of this world beyond the world of sense Melville has often been called, and even called himself, Platonic. Like the Platonists, he did believe truth resided in the unseen world of ideas and conceptions rather than in the world of material manifestations. But in his essentially romantic conception of this invisible sphere he was closer to the Hebrews than to the Greeks. Order, rhetoric, and logic did not represent the primal truth to him as did elemental and undisciplined energy....

As the sea and the land thus alternate as symbols in his scenes, so the calm and the storm alternate on Melville's sea. For though calmness is sweet and agreeable, the motionless ship is destined to decay. In the rack of the storm it leaps forward, drawing fire from heaven, approaching its goal according as it courts disaster. At the heart of the storm, in the midst of the Great Mutiny, Melville's seekers of truth find and worship it.

This is all in the great tragic tradition of the Hebrews, who regarded the creation, for all its mystery and terror, as the garment of Jehovah....

GOD'S DARK SIDE

It was with something of the primitive spirit of the Hebrews that Melville, too, was more inspired by this manifestation of greatness than of simple goodness. Many were the passages he marked in his Bible illustrating the unequaled and often curiously demonstrated power of Jehovah: his use of Necho the Egyptian to slay Josiah and of Assyria to destroy Samaria. Many were the verses he checked describing Jehovah's darker designs: "... for who can make that straight, which he hath made crooked ?" [Eccles. 7:13] "... for it must needs be that offences come; but woe to that man by whom the offence cometh!" [Matt. 18:7] "He made darkness his secret place; his pavilion round about him were dark waters and thick clouds of the skies." [Ps. 18:11]

The picture which emerges from all these suggestions, while hardly that which Melville was made acquainted with in the orthodox circles of his youth, is nevertheless one which must have been closer to his heart. Nothing less than a spirit touching good and evil was adequate to preside over the universe he envisaged. Even in his earliest voyages he found that the green valley of the Typee was, like the Garden of Eden, but a small plot of the earth. And to the end, side by side in the Maldive sea, swam the pilot fish and the white shark, as long before the white whale swam ahead of Ahab while the beckoning breezes blew softly from the green shore. The law which could hang a criminal could also hang the purest of the pure, and that without shattering the universe, but only dyeing its vast sky a deeper rose....

It is significant that Melville's persistent image for truth, too, is of something hidden. Ultimate reality exists at the core of this complex universe, at the very heart of its vast reaches, indeed well-nigh impossible to attain for the superficies which surround it. Like Donjalolo [in *Mardi*] "universe-rounded, zodiac-belted, horizon-zoned, sea-girt, reef-sashed, mountain-locked, arbour-nested, royalty-girdled, arm-clasped, self-hugged, indivisible," it dwells at the center of many circumferences. It is a face behind a mask. It is a mummy wrapped in cerements. It is a kernel within a husk. It is deep within a subterranean tunnel. It is at the bottom of a spiral stair. . . .

So all Melville's art and all the vast scene it reared are not ends in themselves but means to an end. All his borrowings and all his conjurings are but approximations. They are circumferences of the center, cerements around the mummy, antechambers to the throne room, husks about the kernel. Not truth itself is his culminating vision, but "cunning glimpses," "occasional flashings-forth," "short, quick probings at the very axis of reality"; symbolic and fragmentary manifestations of the one absolute, which is in the last analysis inviolable.

The Civil War Made Melville a Poet

Robert Penn Warren

Named America's poet laureate in 1986, Robert Penn
Warren was a three-time recipient of the Pulitzer
Prize, both as a poet and as a novelist. His best-
known novel, *All the King's Men*, won the Pulitzer for
fiction in 1946. In the following article, Warren comments on the poetry of Herman Melville. Warren
maintains that it took the Civil War to turn Melville
into a great poet, one who dealt with complex
themes in moving verse.

If we are completely to understand Melville's poetry, we
must see it against the backdrop of his defeat as a writer,
from which he suffered not only the pangs of disappointment and rejection, but the associated distress of ill health,
disturbance of vision, and undoubtedly, since his father,
after failure, had died mad, the fear of madness. He had
reached the hour which he had described in *Pierre*, the time
when a man "learns that in his obscurity and indigence humanity holds him a dog and no man," and even the harder
hour "when he learns that in his infinite comparative
minuteness and abjectness, the gods do likewise despise
him." We must see Melville's poetry, too, against the backdrop of grim fortitude and sporadic gaiety, perhaps even
grimmer, with which he met the failure; for he clung to the
thought, again expressed in *Pierre*, that only after man has
passed the hour of total rejection may his soul be "born from
the world-husk" and learn to "stand independent.". . .

Part of the effort Melville made to master his fate, and
himself, was a trip, in 1856, on the charity of his father-in-
law, to Europe and the Holy Land. The family presumably
saw travel merely as a distraction from overwork and self-
absorbed brooding, and the trip most likely did benefit Mel-

65

ville in such obvious commonsensical ways. In his ill-starred venture on the lecture platform two of his offerings were to be "Roman Statuary" and "Traveling, Its Pleasures, Pains, and Profits." But Melville sought more than subjects for lectures; in the journey to the Holy Land Melville saw, or came to see, a symbolic import. He was a seeker of ultimates, a hater of illusion. On his way to the Holy Land, Melville had his last encounter with the admired Hawthorne, who, according to Melville, had had the courage to repudiate all easy solutions to the tragic problem of life. Now on the dunes of Southport, a watering place near Liverpool, where Hawthorne was consul, they talked of the great questions. In his journal Hawthorne reports the occasion:

> Melville, as he always does, began to reason of Providence and futurity, and of everything that lies beyond human ken, and informed me that he had "pretty much made up his mind to be annihilated"; but still he does not seem to rest in the anticipation; and I think, will never rest until he gets hold of a definite belief.

Melville had touched bottom, and he was now seeking a belief by which life could be considered and his own life rebuilt; and his poetry, in one dimension, may be read as a record of that search. . . .

BATTLE-PIECES

The first volume of poems which Melville published was *Battle-Pieces and Aspects of the War*, which appeared in 1866. It is, in many ways, a very remarkable document in the history of American poetry, and a remarkable commentary on the moment in American history. It is also to be remarked in the personal history of the author. War, despite suffering and horror, fulfills certain deep-seated needs in men, affords certain releases, offers certain compensations. Men yearn for significance in life, for the thrill of meaning in action, for communion in a common cause, for the test of their fiber, paradoxically for both the affirmation of, and the death of, the self. Even Hawthorne, despite a premature sense of age, a bleak awareness of the loss of his life-sense and of his creative force, and a peculiarly detached and ironical view of the conflict, could say that the Civil War had a "beneficial effect upon my spirits," and that "it was delightful to share in the heroic sentiment of the time, and to feel that I had a country—a consciousness which seemed to make me young again.". . .

A POET'S SUBJECT

In a very profound way it can be said that the Civil War made Melville a poet. It gave him the right "subject"; and for him the right subject, in prose or poetry, was absolutely essential. For all Melville's metaphysical passion and thirst for ultimates, his creative mind could work only from the stimulation of the concrete, the specific. I do not mean this merely in the sense that all poets, to be poets at all, must be concerned with the physicality of the world. Melville had, in a very special way, a mind that could be truly stirred, be fully engaged, only by what was urgently human, and such a subject had to be come upon in life, had to be torn from actual life, with the raw validation of life.

The Civil War gave Melville the kind of big, athletic, overmastering subject which he always needed for his best work, and it was bloodily certified by actuality. But there was a paradox in Melville's appetite for the violent subject; such a subject would serve his need only if the centrifugal whirl toward violent action was perfectly balanced by the centripetal pull toward an inwardness of apparently unresolvable mystery, or tormenting ambiguity. Of such inward issues, this outwardly and violently overmastering subject of the Civil War offered God's—and the devil's—plenty.

This complexity in the subject itself—or, rather, the complexity that Melville saw in the subject—had a deep psychological consistency with the kind of style toward which he had been groping in the recent poems. Now, in *Battle-Pieces*, he achieves his best things not by directly imitating the English Metaphysical poets, but by aiming, however uncertainly, at what we may think of as a metaphysical style of his own, which, though vastly different in effect from that of the English poets of the seventeenth century, shared with their style certain assumptions, and even certain methods. He was aiming at a style rich and yet shot through with realism and prosaism, sometimes casual and open and sometimes dense and intellectually weighted, fluid and various because following the contours of his subject, or rather the contours of his complex feelings about his subject. . . .

"THE MARCH INTO VIRGINIA"

Few of Melville's poems are as good, as deeply coherent, as "The March into Virginia," but some of the principles of its

THE MALDIVE SHARK

Perhaps Melville's best-known poem, "The Maldive Shark" encompasses the themes to which the author continually returned. Melville comments on both the natural phenomenon of the habit of pilot fish to swim unharmed around a shark, and the terrible shark itself.

About the Shark, phlegmatical one,
Pale sot of the Maldive sea,
The sleek little pilot-fish, azure and slim,
How alert in attendance be.
From his saw-pit of mouth, from his charnel of maw
They have nothing of harm to dread,
But liquidly glide on his ghastly flank
Or before his Gorgonian head;
Or lurk in the port of serrated teeth
In white triple tiers of glittering gates,
And there find a haven when peril's abroad,
An asylum in jaws of the Fates!
They are friends; and friendly they guide him to prey,
Yet never partake of the treat—
Eyes and brains to the dotard lethargic and dull,
Pale ravener of horrible meat.

style do appear rather generally. For example, the use of precise, realistic detail, which was outside the prevailing practice. But not merely the fact of such detail deserves comment; what merits more emphasis is the way in which such prosaic materials are played against the more conventional poetic elements. This contrast occurs at the level of mere vocabulary, for Melville, as Newton Arvin has pointed out in his biography, was given to poeticisms like *fain, deem,* and *wight*; technical terms like *caloric, integral, fraction, escheat, foreclosure*; and coined words like *rugged* (covered as with a rug), *vowelled, sliddery* (as in the sliddery ledges of ice in "The Berg").

Vocabulary is, however, only a starting point for such contrasts. For instance, take the first stanza of "Malvern Hill":

Ye elms that wave on Malvern Hill
    In prime of morn and May,
Recall ye how McClellan's men
    Here stood at bay?
While deep within yon forest dim
    Our rigid comrades lay—
Some with the cartridge in their mouth,

> Others with fixed arms lifted South—
>   Invoking so
> The cypress glades? Ah wilds of woe!

The cartridge clenched in the teeth of a dead man, held there as he prepared for loading, suddenly vivifies the stanza. And we may note, too, how the flattened rhythm of the line strikes across the lyricism of the rest.

The whole of "The Armies of the Wilderness" is based on a system of counterpointing; and one of the elements counterpointed is the sort of realism indicated above. The Federal soldiers look across with a telescope to see a "baseball bounding sent," and would like to join the game. Or:

> By the bubbling spring lies the rusted canteen,
> And the drum which the drummer-boy dying let go.

Or:

> The wagon mired and cannon dragged
>   Have trenched their scar. . . .

Long sections of realistic dialogue mark the poem; for instance, these lines spoken by a Confederate prisoner being interrogated by his captors as they overlook the Confederate camp:

> ". . . on the crest,
> The Carolinians; lower, past the glen,
> Virginians—Alabamians—Mississippians—Kentuckians
> (Follow my finger)—Tennesseans; and the ten
> Camps *there*—ask your grave-pits; they'll tell.
>   Halloa! I see the picket-hut, the den
> Where I last night lay."

Over against such passages we find a lyricism like:

> *Where are the birds and boys?*
> *Who shall go chestnutting when*
> *October returns? The nuts——*
>   *O, long ere they grow again.*

Such stylistic contrasts are most obvious, of course, when occurring within a single poem, but the principle sometimes appears in the juxtaposition of separate pieces. There are poems like the elaborately lyrical "Shiloh" and poems as scrupulously prosaic, except for rhyme, as "Running the Batteries." The most clearly marked instance of stylistic contrast among poems themselves is in the pairing of two poems suggested by the fight between the *Monitor* and the *Merrimac*—the requiem for the "fighting Temeraire," supposed to be spoken by "an Englishman of the old order," and "A Utilitarian View of the Monitor's Fight." The first poem ends:

> But Fame has nailed your battle-flags—
>   Your ghost it sails before:
> O, the navies old and oaken,
>   O, the Temeraire no morel

The second poem begins, "Plain be the phrase," and the plain-ness of phrase is part, as it were, of the subject matter of the poem—of "The clangor of that blacksmiths' fray," in which

> . . . all went on by crank,
>   Pivot, and screw,
> And calculations of caloric.

The poem ends with a brilliant metaphor which snatches the poem from the jaws of prose:

> War shall yet be, and to the end;
>   But war-paint shows the streaks of weather;
> War yet shall be, but warriors
>   Are now operatives; War's made
>   Less grand than Peace,
> And a singe runs through lace and feather.

The poem itself states, as well as illustrates, the assumptions behind Melville's style: a world in which a singe runs through lace and feather demands an appropriate style.

THE END OF ILLUSION

Melville saw, however, another kind of singe running through the lace and feather of life. Every man must con-front it, sooner or later, the painful end of illusion, the dire destiny of the passage round the Horn, just as America was confronting it in the Civil War. But not only in the moment of great crisis is there the "singe": in the ordinary course of life, there is a doubleness in things. If Nature seems benefi-cent and beautiful, that is only one aspect, for, as it is put in "Misgivings," there is "Nature's darker side," and as, in "The Stone Fleet," the sailor says, "Nature is nobody's ally."

Such doubleness lies in history, too. Man is doomed to exert will to control events, but even when he seems to act effectively, the process in which his will operates may be only a mask for a secret process of which he has suspected nothing. So we find it said in "Misgivings," in which, as of 1860, the poet broods on the impending conflict:

> And storms are formed behind the storm we feel:
>   The hemlock shakes in the rafter, the oak in the driving
>   keel.

And in "The Conflict of Convictions," the wind of History "spins *against* the way it drives." For example, by the victory of "Right" in the Civil War, certain undreamed-of forces may be released so that

> Power unanointed may come—
> Dominion (unsought by the free)
> And the Iron Dome,
> Stronger for stress and strain,
> Fling her huge shadow athwart the main;
> But the Founders' dream shall flee.

But there are other polarities and ambiguities in life. A decision presumably made on idealistic grounds may simply be the reflex of a historical situation. "On the Slain Collegians" shows young men of both North and South "swept by the wind of their place and time." Even if an ethical distinction is to be made at the level of the cause for which war is being waged, at another level such a distinction is irrelevant:

> Warred one for Right, and one for Wrong?
> So be it; but they both were young—
> Each grape to his cluster clung,
> All their elegies are sung.

Each was doomed to cling to his cluster, and in this fact is implicit the polarity of "ideology" ("Law," "Right," or even "Destiny") against human values, human suffering, human aspiration, qualities of personality and spirit.

The human bond may be as important as the bond of ideology. As "On the Photograph of a Corps Commander" puts it:

> Nothing can lift the heart of man
> Like manhood in a fellow-man.

And the fellow-man may be a fellow, not by ideology but only in his manhood. Stonewall Jackson and Lee are noble enemies, are nobly wrong. In "Donelson," we find that the "Rebel," though he is in the wrong, defends "a perverted Bunker Hill." A recognition of the human community is an essential virtue, and the human community is, in one perspective, a community of guilt, as we find in "The Swamp Angel," the poem on the bombardment of Charleston, South Carolina:

> Who weeps for the woeful City
> Let him weep for our guilty kind;
> Who joys at her wild despairing—
> Christ, the Forgiver, convert his mind.

A recognition of the human as distinguished from the ideological makes magnanimity possible, and Melville ends the volume with a poem called "A Meditation," and the lines:

> When Vicksburg fell, and the moody files marched out,
> Silent the victors stood, scorning to raise a shout.

"Man honors man" beyond "cause," as Melville says in "Magnanimity Baffled," knowing, if he is wise, that even the best cause does violence to some values, and that, as William James remarks in "Pragmatism and Religion," after victory "something apparently drastic and bitter always remains in the bottom of the cup."

THE FACT OF DEATH

The most painful polarity of all is that between all values and the blank fact of annihilation. As in "Sheridan at Cedar Creek,"

> There is glory for the brave
> Who lead, and nobly save,
> But no knowledge in the grave
> Where the nameless followers sleep.

But the same fact of annihilation—the subject on which Melville had brooded so much—which appears in this poem as mere blankness may elsewhere be regarded as a peace, with the problem of values in the flux of history resolved, however perilously and equivocally, in the context of natural process. For instance, in "Malvern Hill," the elms remember the horror and heroism of the battle,

> *But sap the twig will fill:*
> *Wag the world how it will,*
> *Leaves must be green in Spring.*

But if death is blankness—or even blankness regarded as elegiac peace—how can values be found in action desperately foredoomed to blankness? The answer is by a stoicism at once self-assertive and self-denying. It is self-assertive in the courage to endure, and by endurance to define its own value, outside of time, as in the poem on the prisoners who died at Andersonville, in Georgia, "On a Natural Monument":

> Their fame is this: they did endure—
> Endure, when fortitude was vain
> To kindle any approving strain
> Which they might hear. To these who rest
> This healing sleep alone was sure.

But stoicism may be self-denying in the will to sink the personal pain in a compassionate and ennobling awareness of the general human lot, as in another poem on a forgotten monument, "An Uninscribed Monument":

> Thou who beholdest, if thy thought,
> Not narrowed down to personal cheer,
> Take in the import of the quiet here—
>   The after-quiet—the calm full fraught;
> Thou too wilt silent stand—
> Silent as I, and lonesome as the land.

There is, however, another way of regarding action, another polarity involving it. The act is in time. It is at the knife-edge moment of the present, between the past and the future, and at this moment it both projects and fulfills life. But as the life projected into the future is fulfilled, the act with all its urgencies disappears into the past. Action becomes legend.

This theme is continually implicit in *Battle-Pieces*, but its fullest poetic embodiment is in "Battle of Stone River, Tennessee," which is described in the subtitle as "A View from Oxford Cloisters." Here, half a world away from the battle, a learned don might ironically convert his distance in space into a distance in time, and muse that the present conflict, with all its issues and urgencies, will soon be no more for America than the War of the Roses is for England: "In legend all shall end."

In the very moment of action, action enters into legend:

> But Rosecrans in the cedarn glade,
>   And, deep in denser cypress gloom,
> Dark Breckinridge, shall fade away
>   Or thinly loom.
> The pale throngs who in forest cowed
>   Before the spell of battle's pause,
> Forefelt the stillness that shall dwell
>   On them and on their wars.
>   North and South shall join the train
>   Of Yorkist and Lancastrian.

TRAGIC INSIGHT

... The underlying tragic insight of *Battle-Pieces* is ... the necessity for action in the face of the difficulty of knowing truth. In this situation man becomes fully man only if he submits himself to the complications of the inwardness of life in order to be returned, chastened and enlightened, to the objective world of action. In this case—the case of the Civil War—Melville, speaking for and to the victors, holds that the chastening would lie in the discovery of the victorious *self* as blood kin, in the human plight of virtue-in-guilt and guilt-in-virtue, to the defeated *other*, and that this enlightenment would, in the end, be Melville's way of trying to follow the prescription of William James for doing "justice to the ideals in which the vanquished interests lay."...

A FAILURE

When *Battle-Pieces* appeared, Melville had been desperately in need of money as well as appreciation; and with a book on such a topic, and in a period when a volume of poetry not infrequently sold like a popular novel today, Melville's hope, a hope that today would mark a poet as a certifiable lunatic, had some grounding in reality. With this hope blasted, Melville faced the brute fact that he could make neither a living nor a name, by his pen. He had failed, too, in his hope to convert his guttering fame into a competence by means of a consular appointment. He was now ready to descend into his Tartarus, the Customs House of the Port of New York, where he became an inspector—an occupation which, years before, in *Redburn*, he had described as more inglorious than "driving geese to water." So now, at the age of forty-seven, at the wage of four dollars a day, Melville made his terms with the world, and with fate.

CHAPTER 2

A Critical Selection

READINGS ON
HERMAN MELVILLE

Typee and *Omoo*: Melville's Contemplation of Paradise

D.H. Lawrence

In this unique essay excerpted from D.H. Lawrence's collected literary criticism, *Studies in Classic American Literature*, novelist Lawrence critiques Melville's successful early novels *Typee* and *Omoo*. Lawrence claims that Melville proves a bitter truth: No matter how much humanity yearns to return to the time of Eden, it cannot. Modern humans cannot coexist in a paradisical environment, argues Lawrence, that ultimately produces childlike and irresponsible adults. English novelist D.H. Lawrence's most famous works include *Lady Chatterley's Lover*, *Women in Love*, and *The Plumed Serpent*.

The greatest seer and poet of the sea for me is Melville. His vision is more real than Swinburne's, because he doesn't personify the sea, and far sounder than Joseph Conrad's, because Melville doesn't sentimentalize the ocean and the sea's unfortunates. Snivel in a wet hanky like Lord Jim.

Melville has the strange, uncanny magic of sea-creatures, and some of their repulsiveness. He isn't quite a land animal. There is something slithery about him. Something always half-seas-over. In his life they said he was mad—or crazy. He was neither mad nor crazy. But he was over the border. He was half a water animal, like those terrible yellow-bearded Vikings who broke out of the waves in beaked ships. . . .

Melville was a northerner, sea-born. So the sea claimed him. We are most of us, who use the English language, water-people, sea-derived.

Melville went back to the oldest of all the oceans, to the Pacific. . . .

Without doubt the Pacific Ocean is aeons older than the Atlantic or the Indian Oceans. When we say older, we mean it has not come to any modern consciousness. Strange convulsions have convulsed the Atlantic and Mediterranean peoples into phase after phase of consciousness, while the Pacific and the Pacific peoples have slept. To sleep is to dream: you can't stay unconscious. And, oh heaven, for how many thousands of years has the true Pacific been dreaming, turning over in its sleep and dreaming again: idylls: nightmares.

The Maoris, the Tongans, the Marquesans, the Fijians, the Polynesians: holy God, how long have they been turning over in the same sleep, with varying dreams? Perhaps, to a sensitive imagination, those islands in the middle of the Pacific are the most unbearable places on earth. It simply stops the heart, to be translated there, unknown ages back, back into that life, that pulse, that rhythm. The scientists say the South Sea Islanders belong to the Stone Age. It seems absurd to class people according to their implements. And yet there is something in it. The heart of the Pacific is still the Stone Age; in spite of steamers. The heart of the Pacific seems like a vast vacuum, in which, mirage-like, continues the life of myriads of ages back. It is a phantom-persistence of human beings who should have died, by our chronology, in the Stone Age. It is a phantom, illusion-like trick of reality: the glamorous South Seas. . . .

To this phantom, Melville returned. Back, back, away from life. Never man instinctively hated human life, our human life, as we have it, more than Melville did. And never was a man so passionately filled with the sense of vastness and mystery of life which is non-human. He was mad to look over our horizons. Anywhere, anywhere out of *our* world. To get away. To get away, out!

To Another Life

To get away, out of our life. To cross a horizon into another life. No matter what life, so long as it is another life.

Away, away from humanity. To the sea. The naked salt, elemental sea. To go to sea, to escape humanity.

The human heart gets into a frenzy at last, in its desire to dehumanize itself.

So he finds himself in the middle of the Pacific. Truly over a horizon. In another world. In another epoch. Back, far back, in the days of palm trees and lizards and stone implements. The sunny Stone Age.

Samoa, Tahiti, Raratonga, Nukuheva: the very names are a sleep and a forgetting. The sleep-forgotten past magnificence of human history. "Trailing clouds of glory."

Melville hated the world: was born hating it. But he was looking for heaven. That is, choosingly. Choosingly, he was looking for paradise. Unchoosingly, he was mad with hatred of the world.

Well, the world is hateful. It is as hateful as Melville found it. He was not wrong in hating the world. . . . He hated it to a pitch of madness, and not without reason.

But it's no good *persisting* in looking for paradise "regained."

Melville at his best invariably wrote from a sort of dreamself, so that events which he relates as actual fact have indeed a far deeper reference to his own soul, his own inner life.

So in *Typee* when he tells of his entry into the valley of the dread cannibals of Nukuheva. Down this narrow, steep, horrible dark gorge he slides and struggles as we struggle in a dream, or in the act of birth, to emerge in the green Eden of the Golden Age, the valley of the cannibal savages. This is a bit of birth-myth, or re-birth myth, on Melville's part—unconscious, no doubt, because his running underconsciousness was always mystical and symbolical. He wasn't aware that he was being mystical.

There he is then, in Typee, among the dreaded cannibal savages. And they are gentle and generous with him, and he is truly in a sort of Eden.

Here at last is Rousseau's Child of Nature and Chateaubriand's Noble Savage called upon and found at home. Yes, Melville loves his savage hosts. He finds them gentle, laughing lambs compared to the ravening wolves of his white brothers, left behind in America and on an American whaleship.

The ugliest beast on earth is the white man, says Melville.

In short, Herman found in Typee the paradise he was looking for. It is true, the Marquesans were "immoral," but he rather liked that. Morality was too white a trick to take him in. Then again, they were cannibals. And it filled him with horror even to think of this. But the savages were very private and even fiercely reserved in their cannibalism, and he might have spared himself his shudder. No doubt he had partaken of the Christian Sacraments many a time. "This is my body, take and eat. This is my blood. Drink it in remembrance of me." And if the savages liked to partake of their sacrament without raising the transubstantiation quibble, and if they liked to say, directly: "This is thy body, which I take from thee and eat. This is thy blood, which I sip in annihilation of thee," why surely their sacred ceremony was as awe-inspiring as the one Jesus substituted. But Herman chose to be horrified. I confess, I am not horrified; though, of course, I am not on the spot. But the savage sacrament seems to me more valid than the Christian: less side-tracking about it. Thirdly, he was shocked by their wild methods of warfare. He died before the great European war, so his shock was comfortable.

Three little quibbles: morality, cannibal sacrament, and stone axes. You must have a fly even in Paradisal ointment. And the first was a ladybird.

UNHAPPY IN PARADISE

But Paradise. He insists on it. Paradise. He could even go stark naked, as before the Apple episode. And his Fayaway, a laughing little Eve, naked with him, and hankering after no apple of knowledge, so long as he would just love her when he felt like it. Plenty to eat, needing no clothes to wear, sunny, happy people, sweet water to swim in: everything a man can want. Then why wasn't he happy along with the savages?

Because he wasn't.

He grizzled in secret, and wanted to escape.

He even pined for Home and Mother, the two things he had run away from as far as ships would carry him. HOME and MOTHER. The two things that were his damnation.

There on the island, where the golden-green great palmtrees chinked in the sun, and the elegant reed houses let the sea-breeze through, and people went naked and laughed a great deal, and Fayaway put flowers in his hair for him—great red hibiscus flowers, and frangipani—O God, why wasn't he happy? Why wasn't he?

Because he wasn't.

Well, it's hard to make a man happy.

But I should not have been happy either. One's soul seems under a vacuum, in the South Seas.

The truth of the matter is, one cannot go back. Some men can: renegade. But Melville couldn't go back: and Gauguin couldn't really go back: and I know now that I could never go back. Back towards the past, savage life. One cannot go back. It is one's destiny inside one.

There are these peoples, these "savages." One does not despise them. One does not feel superior. But there is a gulf. There is a gulf in time and being. I cannot commingle my being with theirs.

There they are, these South Sea Islanders, beautiful big men with their golden limbs and their laughing, graceful laziness. And they will call you brother, choose you as a brother. But why cannot one truly be brother?

There is an invisible hand grasps my heart and prevents it opening too much to these strangers. They are beautiful, they are like children, they are generous: but they are more than this. They are far off, and in their eyes is an easy darkness of the soft, uncreate past. In a way, they are uncreate. Far be it from me to assume any "white" superiority. But they are savages. They are gentle and laughing and physically very handsome. But it seems to me, that in living so far, through all our bitter centuries of civilization, we have still been living onwards, forwards. God knows it looks like a *cul de sac* now. But turn to the first negro, and then listen to your own soul. And your own soul will tell you that however false and foul our forms and systems are now, still, through the many centuries since Egypt, we have been living and struggling forwards along some road that is no road, and yet is a great life-development. We have struggled on, and on we must still go. We may have to smash things. Then let us smash. And our road may have to take a great swerve, that seems a retrogression.

But we can't go back. Whatever else the South Sea Islander is, he is centuries and centuries behind us in the life-struggle, the consciousness-struggle, the struggle of the soul into fulness. There is his woman, with her knotted hair and her dark, inchoate, slightly sardonic eyes. I like her, she is nice. But I would never want to touch her. I could not go back on myself so far. Back to their uncreate condition.

She has soft warm flesh, like warm mud. Nearer the reptile, the Saurian age. . . .

WE CAN'T GO BACK TO PARADISE

We can't go back. We can't go back to the savages: not a stride. We can be in sympathy with them. We can take a great curve in their direction, onwards. But we cannot turn the current of our life backwards, back towards their soft warm twilight and uncreate mud. Not for a moment. If we do it for a moment, it makes us sick.

We can only do it when we are renegade. The renegade hates life itself. He wants the death of life. So these many "reformers" and "idealists" who glorify the savages in America. They are death-birds, life-haters. Renegades.

We can't go back, and Melville couldn't. Much as he hated the civilized humanity he knew. He couldn't go back to the savages; he wanted to, he tried to, and he couldn't.

Because, in the first place, it made him sick; it made him physically ill. He had something wrong with his leg, and this would not heal. It got worse and worse, during his four months on the island. When he escaped, he was in a deplorable condition—sick and miserable, ill, very ill.

Paradise!

But there you are. Try to go back to the savages, and you feel as if your very soul was decomposing inside you. That is what you feel in the South Seas, anyhow: as if your soul was decomposing inside you. And with any savages the same, if you try to go their way, take their current of sympathy.

Yet, as I say, we must make a great swerve in our onward-going life-course now, to gather up again the savage mysteries. But this does not mean going back on ourselves.

Going back to the savages made Melville sicker than anything. It made him feel as if he were decomposing. Worse even than Home and Mother.

And that is what really happens. If you prostitute your psyche by returning to the savages, you gradually go to pieces. Before you can go back, you *have* to decompose. And a white man decomposing is a ghastly sight. Even Melville in Typee.

We have to go on, on, on, even if we must smash a way ahead.

So Melville escaped, and threw a boat-hook full in the throat of one of his dearest savage friends, and sank him, because that savage was swimming in pursuit. That's how he felt about the savages when they wanted to detain him. He'd have murdered them one and all, vividly, rather than be kept from escaping. Away from them—he must get away from them—at any price.

And once he has escaped, immediately he begins to sigh

and pine for the "Paradise"—Home and Mother being at the other end even of a whaling voyage.

When he really was Home with Mother, he found it Purgatory. But Typee must have been even worse than Purgatory, a soft hell, judging from the murderous frenzy which possessed him to escape.

But once aboard the whaler that carried him off from Nukuheva, he looked back and sighed for the Paradise he had just escaped from in such a fever.

Poor Melville! He was determined Paradise existed. So he was always in Purgatory.

He was born for Purgatory. Some souls are purgatorial by destiny.

The very freedom of his Typee was a torture to him. Its ease was slowly horrible to him. This time *he* was the fly in the odorous tropical ointment.

He needed to fight. It was no good to him, the relaxation of the nonmoral tropics. He didn't really want Eden. He wanted to fight. Like every American. To fight. But with weapons of the spirit, not the flesh.

That was the top and bottom of it. His soul was in revolt, writhing for ever in revolt. When he had something definite to rebel against—like the bad conditions on a whaling ship—then he was much happier in his miseries. The mills of God were grinding inside him, and they needed something to grind on.

When they could grind on the injustice and folly of missionaries, or of brutal sea-captains, or of governments, he was easier. The mills of God were grinding inside him.

They are grinding inside every American. And they grind exceeding small.

Why? Heaven knows. But we've got to grind down our old forms, our old selves, grind them very very small, to nothingness. Whether a new somethingness will ever start, who knows? Meanwhile the mills of God grind on, in American Melville, and it was himself he ground small: himself and his wife, when he was married. For the present, the South Seas.

He escapes on to the craziest, most impossible of whaling ships. Lucky for us Melville makes it fantastic. It must have been pretty sordid.

And anyhow, on the crazy *Julia*, his leg, that would never heal in the paradise of Typee, began quickly to get well. His life was falling into its normal pulse. The drain back into past centuries was over.

Yet, oh, as he sails away from Nukuheva, on the voyage that will ultimately take him to America, oh, the acute and intolerable nostalgia he feels for the island he has left.

The past, the Golden Age of the past—what a nostalgia we all feel for it. Yet we don't want it when we get it. Try the South Seas.

SEARCHING FOR THE IDEAL

Melville had to fight, fight against the existing world, against his own very self. Only he would never quite put the knife in the heart of his paradisal ideal. Somehow, somewhere, somewhen, love should be a fulfilment, and life should be a thing of bliss. That was his fixed ideal. . . .

That was the pin he tortured himself on, like a pinned-down butterfly.

Love is never a fulfilment. Life is never a thing of continuous bliss. There is no paradise. Fight and laugh and feel bitter and feel bliss: and fight again. Fight, fight. That is life.

Why pin ourselves down on a paradisal ideal? It is only ourselves we torture.

Melville did have one great experience, getting away from humanity: the experience of the sea.

The South Sea Islands were not his great experience. They were a glamorous world outside New England. Outside. But it was the sea that was both outside and inside: the universal experience.

The book that follows on from *Typee* is *Omoo*.

Omoo is a fascinating book; picaresque, rascally, roving. Melville, as a bit of a beachcomber. The crazy ship *Julia* sails to Tahiti, and the mutinous crew are put ashore. Put in the Tahitian prison. It is good reading.

Perhaps Melville is at his best, his happiest, in *Omoo*. For once he is really reckless. For once he takes life as it comes. For once he is the gallant rascally epicurean, eating the world like a snipe, dirt and all baked into one *bonne bouche*.

For once he is really careless, roving with that scamp, Doctor Long Ghost. For once he is careless of his actions, careless of his morals, careless of his ideals: ironic, as the epicurean must be. The deep irony of your real scamp: your real epicurean of the moment.

But it was under the influence of the Long Doctor. This long and bony Scotsman was not a mere ne'er-do-well. He

haps his half-sentimental love for Jack Chase, in *White-Jacket.*

Yet to the end he pined for this: a perfect relationship; perfect mating; perfect mutual understanding. A perfect friend.

Right to the end he could never accept the fact that *perfect* relationships cannot be. Each soul is alone, and the aloneness of each soul is a double barrier to perfect relationship between two beings.

Each soul *should* be alone. And in the end the desire for a "perfect relationship" is just a vicious, unmanly craving. . . .

Melville, however, refused to draw his conclusion. *Life* was wrong, he said. He refused Life. But he stuck to his ideal of perfect relationship, possible perfect love. The world *ought* to be a harmonious loving place. And it *can't* be. So life itself is wrong.

It is silly arguing. Because, after all, only temporary man sets up the "oughts."

The world ought *not* to be a harmonious loving place. It ought to be a place of fierce discord and intermittent harmonies: which it is.

Love ought *not* to be perfect. It ought to have perfect moments, and wildernesses of thorn bushes—which it has.

A "perfect" relationship ought *not* to be possible. Every relationship should have its absolute limits, its absolute reserves, essential to the singleness of the soul in each person. A truly perfect relationship is one in which each party leaves great tracts unknown in the other party.

No two persons can meet at more than a few points, consciously. If two people can just be together fairly often, so that the presence of each is a sort of balance to the other, that is the basis of perfect relationship. There must be true separatenesses as well.

Melville was, at the core, a mystic and an idealist.

Perhaps, so am I.

And he stuck to his ideal guns.

I abandon mine.

He was a mystic who raved because the old ideal guns shot havoc. The guns of the "noble spirit." Of "ideal love."

I say, let the old guns rot.

Get new ones, and shoot straight.

Benito Cereno Reveals Melville's Belief in Racial Equality

Edward S. Grejda

Literary critic Edward S. Grejda is the author of *The Common Continent of Men: Racial Equality in the Writings of Herman Melville*. Many critics have puzzled over Melville's dark tale *Benito Cereno*, contending that it stereotypes blacks as savage and uncivilized. In the following article, Grejda argues the opposite. He contends that the tale is about mutual distrust between the races, which, he argues, is inspired by whites' condescending stereotypes of and attitudes toward blacks.

Benito Cereno, Melville's tale of mutiny aboard the Spanish ship *San Dominick* captained by Don Benito Cereno, is a drama in which nonwhites occupy center stage. The story unfolds through the consciousness of a native of Duxbury, Massachusetts, Captain Amasa Delano, who, seeing the *San Dominick* in a shocking state of decay floundering toward a reef, comes to its aid. Once aboard, Delano cannot know what Benito does—that the principal cargo of the vessel, 160 Negro slaves, have mutinied and killed most of the crew. Their leader is the Senegalese Negro Babo, who, disguised as the solicitous body servant of Cereno, has organized every person aboard in an ingenious masquerade to deceive the American captain. Alternating between mistrust and reassurance over the ambiguous actions of Cereno, crew and slaves, but failing to penetrate the true nature of the mystery, Delano's mind makes *Benito Cereno* a masterpiece of suspense, many particulars of which are not known until after the narrative climax. At this point, the specifics of the revolt are revealed through lengthy extracts from the testimony of Benito, who gives his deposition during the trial of the mu-

From *The Common Continent of Men: Racial Equality in the Writings of Herman Melville* by Edward S. Grejda (Port Washington, NY: National University Publications, 1974). Copyright ©1974 by Kennikat Press Corp.

tineers. Suspense, however, is of secondary importance. The fascinating enigma of *Benito Cereno* revolves around the question of what Melville intended his blacks to be. . . .

EVIL AND GOOD ARE BLURRED

Melville's characters in *Benito Cereno* cannot be placed within a strict good-evil framework. White sailors and black slaves, rather than being "whitened" and "blackened," merge into gray, a color which blurs any distinction between them. Interestingly, Melville sets the tone of his tale with an early emphasis on gray:

> Everything was mute and calm; everything gray. The sea, though undulated into long roods of swells, seemed fixed, and was sleeked at the surface like waved lead that has cooled and set in the smelter's mould. The sky seemed a gray surtout. Flights of troubled gray foul, kith and kin with flights of troubled gray vapours among which they were mixed, skimmed low and fitfully over the waters, as swallows over meadows before storms. Shadows present, foreshadowing deeper shadows to come.

In the world of gray shadows, this "smelter's pot," humans cannot be readily dichotomized. Man, as evidenced by the duality (i.e., man-devil, lion-lamb) of many of Melville's earlier characters, may evoke both admiration and revulsion. In this connection, Melville offers a revealing observation in his "Sketch Second" of "The Encantadas":

> Even the tortoise, dark and melancholy as it is upon the back, still possesses a bright side; its calipee or breast-plate being sometimes of a faint yellowish or golden tinge. Moreover, everyone knows that tortoises as well as turtles are of such a make, that if you but put them on their backs you thereby expose their bright sides without the possibility of their recovering themselves, and turning into view the other. But after you have done this, and because you have done this, you should not swear that the tortoise has no dark side. Enjoy the bright, keep it turned up perpetually if you can, but be honest, and don't deny the black. Neither should he, who cannot turn the tortoise from its natural position so as to hide the darker and expose its livelier aspect, like a great October pumpkin in the sun, for that cause declare the creature to be one total inky blot. The tortoise is both black and bright.

Like the tortoise, Babo and the Negroes aboard the *San Dominick* are neither black (pure evil) nor bright (angels avenging a moral wrong). By showing both sides of whites and blacks, by illustrating the universality of the savage impulse, Melville again dramatizes the sameness of man. But, as Melville says in "The Encantadas," "Let us to particulars."

Trusting and benevolent as Captain Delano is, one cannot ignore the possibility of his being an object of satire, what [critic] Charles I. Glicksberg calls "a composite reflection of the righteous stereotyped attitudes prevalent at the time." To the good American captain, "a man of such native simplicity as to be incapable of satire or irony," the Negro is simply not an individual; he takes "humane satisfaction" in seeing the blacks dutifully performing their designated roles in life. He notes the "peculiar love in negroes of uniting industry with pastime," and he is amused by "the African love of bright colours and fine shows." He admires in the Negro servant "that affectionate zeal which transmutes into something filial or fraternal acts in themselves but menial; and which has gained for the negro the repute of making the most pleasing body-servant in the world; one, too, whom a master need be on no stiffly superior terms with, but may treat with familiar trust; less a servant than a devoted companion." To the "blunt thinking" American, the "menial familiarity" of the black servant is marked by the "charm of simple-hearted attachment." That "charm" is also evident in Delano's pastoral view of the female slaves: Negresses are "unsophisticated as leopardesses; loving as doves"; another is "like a doe" and her infant a "wide-awake fawn." In Delano's consciousness no detail of the Negro stereotype is overlooked:

> There is something in the negro which, in a peculiar way, fits him for avocations about one's person. Most negroes are natural valets and hair dressers; taking to the comb and brush congenially as to the castanets, and flourishing them apparently with almost equal satisfaction. There is, too, a smooth tact about them in this employment, with a marvellous, noiseless, gliding briskness, not ungraceful in its way, singularly pleasing to behold, and still more so to be the manipulated subject of. And above all is the great gift of good humour. Not the mere grin or laugh is here meant. Those were unsuitable. But a certain easy cheerfulness, harmonious in every glance and gesture; as though God had set the whole negro to some pleasant tune.

FATAL STEREOTYPES

... Even when a Spanish lad is knifed by a Negro boy and a sailor is trampled by two Negroes, Delano's veil of bias enables him to rationalize. His comfortable assumptions about the Negro character do not allow for the possibility of their being savage; his superficial appraisal does not admit that

Negroes might seek their freedom. After all, "Newfoundland dogs" are domesticated and loyal. . . .

DELANO'S RACISM

Throughout Benito Cereno, *the character of Captain Delano sees many strange and blatant actions by the crew that should tip him off that a mutiny has occurred. Yet, because of his stereotypes of blacks, who are the mutineers, Delano cannot interpret the events correctly. In this excerpt, Delano puzzles over Don Benito's (Benito Cereno's) criticisms of his crew, and again misses the point when he stereotypes the blacks onboard.*

Was it from foreseeing some possible interference . . . that Don Benito had, beforehand, given such a bad character of his sailors, while praising the negroes; though, indeed, the former seemed as docile as the latter the contrary? The whites, too, by nature, were the shrewder race. A man with some evil design, would he not be likely to speak well of that stupidity which was blind to his depravity, and malign that intelligence from which it might not be hidden? Not unlikely, perhaps. If the whites had dark secrets concerning Don Benito, could then Don Benito be any way in complicity with the blacks? But they were too stupid. Besides, who ever heard of a white so far a renegade as to apostatize from his very species almost, by leaguing in against it with negroes?

If Delano's "weakness for Negroes" causes their image to be distorted, what, then, is the reality of the blacks? From the . . . extracts from Cereno's deposition during the trial, we discover that the man whom Delano sees as a solicitous and charming menial is capable of animal savagery. The Negroes murdered "eighteen men of those who were sleeping upon deck, some with handspikes and hatchets, and others by throwing them alive overboard, after tying them." The owner of the slaves, Don Alexandro Aranda, was dragged mangled and half alive to the deck where his murder was completed before the eyes of Babo. His body, stripped of flesh "in a way which [Benito Cereno], so long as reason is left him, can never divulge," was then mounted below the ship's figurehead to remind the other whites of what could be their fate. The Negresses, had they not been restrained, "would have tortured to death, instead of simply killing, the Spaniards slain by command of the negro Babo." From the deposition we also learn "that the negroes broke an arm of one of the cabin-boys and gave him strokes with hatchets." Another Spaniard had hot tar poured over his hands. Still others, their arms bound, were thrown alive into the sea. Of the thirty-six crewmen, only six remained alive. In this document of horror, Delano's Newfoundland dogs become wolves. . . .

It is not surprising, then, that many readers, repelled by the Negro atrocities and by the animal images, view the blacks as a malignant, destructive force and, accordingly, empathize with the helpless, victimized whites. In a sense, such readers have greater perception than Delano; whereas he acknowledges neither the man nor the beast, they see at least the beast. The man, however, is also there.

The Negroes in *Benito Cereno* are neither Delano's docile subservients nor ravenous animals. Both assessments represent an extreme, an indictment of an entire race by a man whose concern lies with the "common continent of men." As with the Galapagos tortoise, Melville has not denied the dark side of the Negroes. But neither are they "one total inky blot.". . .

WHITE ATROCITIES

How do the whites act when they recapture the *San Dominick*? Do their civilized natures emerge? Are their acts marked by Christian, civilized justice? The deposition provides some answers. In it we find evidence of white barbarity balancing that of the slaves. Several Negroes were killed at night while shackled to the ring bolts on deck. Martinez Gola was caught aiming a razor at the throat of a chained slave. Bartholomew Barlo was stopped from stabbing a shackled black. Perhaps the most damning illustration of white barbarity is the account of Babo's punishment: "dragged to the gibbet at the tail of a mule, the black met his voiceless end. The body was burned to ashes; but for many days the head, that hive of subtlety, fixed on a pole in the Plaza, met, unabashed, the gaze of the whites.". . . The description of Babo's execution [is] an indictment of a society which, even within the framework of law, is as capable of barbarity as is the "unenlightened" savage. . . . By reserving Babo's death for the final paragraph and thereby emphasizing it, Melville reinforces what, throughout his fiction, he repeatedly stated—that no great disparity exists between the nonwhite savage and the white civilized man. The severed black head facing St. Bartholomew's church—an ironic and tragic juxtaposition of two worlds, two cultures, two races—renders incredible the argument that Melville has "whitened the whites." Following the above passage from *Typee*, Melville indicted "the white as the most ferocious animal on the face of the earth." In *Benito Cereno*, he shows both white and black as equally capable of ferocity, equally capable of reducing men to the level of brutes. Babo, it should be noted, was a slave in both black and white societies. In merging the "civilized" brutality of the whites with the animal ferocity of the blacks, Melville has dramatized the universality of the savage impulse. . . .

Babo deserves considerable credit for being the awesomely clever mastermind of a plot so well implemented that it almost succeeds. . . .

The mind that devised such a scheme may be a "hive of subtlety," but it is a mind which commands respect. Central to that scheme is Babo's masquerade as a menial. Like the mask of the confidence man, it is based on a shrewd understanding of the white man's attitudes toward the black. Babo is also to be respected for his determination and spirit. Never panicking, never faltering, even during the fury of the revolt, he steadfastly keeps in mind the main objective. Neither does he bow; captured, "he uttered no sound, and could not be forced to." And like the unquailing, kingly Atufal before the sickly Cereno, Babo even in death remains defiant, his head meeting "unabashed, the gaze of the whites." Depending on the degree to which one can sympathize with Babo's motives, the black's performance could be called heroic. One thing is certain: Babo is no inferior. His dominant traits are intelligence, determination, firmness of will and command, and defiant pride. Except in the beclouded mind of Delano, the stereotype darky complete with castanets and good-natured grin is not aboard the *San Dominick*; an individual is. We may admire or despise Babo, but our response is not dictated by his color; Melville has created a memorable human being. . . .

HUMAN SAVAGENESS

Benito Cereno is neither an abolitionist tract nor a condemnation of the Negro race. Evil and ferocity are not confined to the blacks; heroism and virtue are not the exclusive traits of the whites. Both blacks and whites are part of the humanity whose dark side Melville will not deny. Like the satyr on the stern-piece, Babo is part man, part beast. Like

Bembo of *Omoo,* he is man (in that his response to humiliation is courageously human) and devil (in that his vengeance takes a particularly vicious turn). But the white man,
who ironically espouses a religion of charity, forgiveness,
and brotherhood, is also a beast. Who can say where the
blame rests for the carnage unleashed aboard the floating
coffin? The untamed and demoniac forces rampant on the
San Dominick characterize not a particular race, but all of
mankind. *Benito Cereno* poses the problem with which Herman Melville grappled from *Typee* to *Billy Budd*: the
"primeval savageness which ever slumbers in human kind,
civilized or uncivilized.". . .

BARRIERS TO EQUALITY

In Melville's fiction the several races of mankind are insep-
arably intertwined, united by his acknowledgment of the individual's special worth. Through the interaction of characters of all colors, Melville dramatizes how in the ideal
society the nonwhite should be regarded. The foolish, the
cruel, the ignorant, and the sheltered categorize the nonwhite in accord with the role the "bland hypocrisies" of society assign him, that of inferior buffoon or of scowling savage; the humane and the wise see him as an individual to be
liked or disliked for his human traits. . . . In [Melville's] fictional world, men have a fundamental claim to humanity.
Such democratic faith is echoed and reechoed from the first
book to the last. We see that faith in Tommo's warm admiration of the physical perfection and the harmonious social
order of the "savage" Polynesians; in his indictment of the
white race, which, in imposing its values on the Polynesians,
is responsible for corroding the racial identity of these people; in the anger and pity evoked by the plight of Negro
slaves in *Mardi*; in Redburn's recognition of the black man's
humanity; in White-Jacket's acknowledgment of man, white
or dark, as the image of God; in the "champions from the
kingly commons," dark as well as white, embraced by Ishmael's "just spirit of equality"; in the striking resemblances
between General Glendinning, John Paul Jones and Ethan
Allen, and the Typee warriors and Queequeg; in the universe
of *The Confidence-Man* and *Benito Cereno,* where black is
indistinguishable from white; and, finally, in the simple
recognition that the "handsome sailor"—a cynosure of
"strength and beauty"—can be either a Billy Budd or a

Negro on a Liverpool dock.

The barrier to equality, Melville suggests, is the absence of mutual respect which, in turn, becomes mutual distrust. Significantly, the white man is usually the architect of the wall which separates the races. If Melville's nonwhites are scowling barbarians or grinning stereotypes, they are made so by the whites who refuse to acknowledge their humanity. The denial takes many forms: "wanton acts of cruelty" for "mere amusement" by white seamen who "hardly consider [Polynesians] human"; the humiliation and endless rounds of practical jokes inflicted on black seacooks; the brute level to which Negro slaves are degraded by the lash; the stares and grimaces of local greenhorns at the Queequegs, Samoas, and Lavenders; a Spaniard's racial insult flung at Daggoo; Stubb's abandoning "insignificant" Pip and ridiculing Fleece; river-boat passengers tossing pennies at the mouth of a crippled Negro; an American captain's fondness for Negroes as though they were Newfoundland dogs.

Such treatment is best explained by White-Jacket: ". . . There is something in us, somehow, that in the most degraded condition, we snatch at a chance to deceive ourselves into a fancied superiority to others, whom we suppose lower in the scale than ourselves." Melville's fictional world refutes this self-deception, this "fancied superiority" which degrades others. There can be no preeminent race, no mastery of one people over another in a world where white American heroes are remarkably similar to dusky Polynesians; where "the New Zealander's tattooing is not a prodigy nor the Chinaman's way an enigma"; where "we may have civilized bodies and yet barbarous souls"; where "primeval savageness ever slumbers in human kind, civilized or uncivilized"; where "a man can be honest in any sort of skin"; where Indians, Orientals, Polynesians, Negroes, and Caucasians are "sprung from one head, and made in one image." Such a world, dark as well as bright, is Herman Melville's "common continent of men."

Melville's *Battle-Pieces* Is Moving Civil War Poetry

Stanton Garner

In the following article, Stanton Garner analyzes several of Melville's poems from his Civil War collection, *Battle-Pieces*. Garner takes issue with critics who argue that Melville was trying to "cash in on" the Civil War, contending that the poems prove Melville's talent as a poet. In addition, Garner maintains that Melville, like a modern-day prophet, was trying to guide the nation away from making the same mistakes again. Stanton Garner's book, *The Civil War World of Herman Melville*, from which this viewpoint is taken, is both a biography and a work of literary criticism.

As the fighting died away, Herman began sustained work on *Battle-Pieces*. . . . Like the violent upheavals of the [Civil War] themselves, the immediate reactions of an artist to events were subject to excesses of grief, anxiety, anger, and exultation; it was necessary to wait until the flux of the conflict had subsided into a coherent memory. The end of the war, then, was the point at which Herman began to make his book. . . .

It deals with a war so lavish in emotion and so profligate in event that to the present day it affords historians an inexhaustible field for inquiry. . . .

"THE APPARITION"

"The Apparition (A Retrospect)" was inspired by Frank Bartlett's experience in the great mine explosion at Petersburg. Herman could imagine the horror of the Confederate soldiers as they felt the solidity of the earth swell and burst beneath their feet, which suggested an important qualification of the meliorative tone of the latter part of *Battle-Pieces*. The poem is central to the meaning of the book in that it fo-

From *The Civil War World of Herman Melville* by Stanton Garner. Copyright ©1993 by the University Press of Kansas. All rights reserved. Reprinted with permission.

cuses and completes the initiation into war's horrors of earlier poems. It is final proof that the worldview of the "bachelor," who sees only the cheerful, comfortable side of the human condition, is incomplete and therefore false. That had been the error of those who had trusted in Raphael and Michael. This poem invokes a pastoral, Shenandoah-like America, a green and growing world signified here in Herman's poetic shorthand as "Solidity." Even after John Brown's shadow had fallen across the "pastoral green," the nation remained confident in its promise and its belief in an orgiastic future. But Solidity is not the way of the world, in the past or in the future. It is only an appearance concealing behind it a central fact of man's existence, Satan's "eruptions of a darkness always lurkingly present in human affairs." When the union is severed and the consequences are felt, America is blasted by an eruption of violence and malignity. In a convulsion, a "goblin-mountain" pushes up from beneath the verdure and fertility is replaced by marl, slag, and clinkers: "The unreserve of Ill was there," Satanic ill. Yet before the senses can fully absorb and the mind comprehend, the eruption disappears as though it had never existed, leaving behind it the great philosophical lesson of the war: "Solidity's a crust— / The core of fire below." The appearance of wholeness returns, but the existence of Satan has been established for all time; he retreats back to his abyss to await another moment when man's imperfection will renew his opportunity to seize the reins of events. Preserving the memory of the goblin-mountain is a major purpose of *Battle-Pieces*: if future fields for fight are congealing beneath the sea, awareness must protect the nation from again becoming the battleground. An entire people must be educated to distrust the illusion that Solidity is dependable and to prevent the apparition from appearing again. . . .

"AMERICA"

"America" is more notable for its vision than it is for its originality. Embodying America in a conventional feminine figure, it is an allegory that the general public would have understood, and as such it has been criticized as tepid and derivative and as a "ritual of a sleazy sort." But when it is understood as a culminating point of *Battle-Pieces*, a counterpoint to "The Apparition," and the final appearance of the mother figure introduced in "Apathy and Enthusiasm," it gains purpose and dignity. To quote Milder, the poem "shapes the confusion of events [of the preceding poems] into an over-arching national myth and clarifies the process of moral growth the poems have occasioned in the reader all along."

SHILOH: A REQUIEM

In a poem from Battle-Pieces *entitled "Shiloh," Melville speaks of the aftermath of that battle.*

Skimming lightly, wheeling still,
   The swallows fly low
Over the field in clouded days,
   The forest-field of Shiloh—
Over the field where April rain
Solaced the parched ones stretched in pain
Through the pause of night
That followed the Sunday fight
   Around the church of Shiloh—
The church so lone, the log-built one,
That echoed to many a parting groan
    And natural prayer
  Of dying foemen mingled there—
Foemen at morn, but friends at eve—
  Fame or country least their care:
(What like a bullet can undeceive!)
  But now they lie low,
While over them the swallows skim,
  And all is hushed at Shiloh.

If "The Apparition" invokes the dark side of the war experience, this poem is a reminder that there is also hope. It begins with a vision of an American flag "where the wings of a sunny Dome expand"—suggesting the Capitol dome as well as the firmamental dome—with the antebellum land reposing "in peace below." In this green world, the children (the states and the citizens alike) of the young mother were "folded to the exulting heart / Of young Maternity." Then in the earlier days of the war the flag streamed not in peace but "in fight / When tempest mingled with the fray," and over the flagstaff there was "ambiguous lightning." As her children strove "Valor with Valor" in their fierce Pride and Despair, "the lorn Mother speechless stood, / Pale at the fury of her brood." The children descend into Satan's primal world while the mother lapses into unconsciousness, seemingly dead and wrapped as on a bier in the flag that had once flown so grandly above. It is the dark night of the soul for America, as in sleep she sees the dark truths that *Battle-Pieces* has revealed. Her face is contorted by the vision "revealing earth's foundation bare, / And Gorgon in her hidden place." It is fearful to see "so foul a dream upon so fair a face." In short, she has glimpsed the "unreserve of Ill" of "The Apparition," the "core of fire" beneath Solidity. The "foul" dream serves the additional purpose of affirming that "the world's fairest hope linked with man's foulest crime" in "Misgivings" refers not to slavery but to the fratricidal battle which threatened "the Founders' dream."

The nightmare is necessary as a prelude to spiritual renewal. Thus America awakens with slavery crushed ("At her feet a shivered yoke") and with "no trace of passion or of strife" in her "clear calm look." The hope for the future lies in the belief that the nation may not only survive the primitive passions of war but may also transcend them into greatness. America is no longer innocent; pain has purified her and knowledge has repressed her triumph; her power is dedicated and her hope informed. "Law on her brow and empire in her eyes. / So she, with graver air and lifted flag" stands on her promontory, the shadow that had fallen over her gone. The innocent and ineffective Raphael has been replaced on the pinnacle by the newly wise and mature America who, ideally, will never again fall victim to Satan. Thus the outcome of the war would justify its terrible suffering.

It is disquieting to read of an America with "empire in her eyes," since that suggests a nation vying with the crowns of Europe for colonial dominion in Africa, Asia, and the Pacific isles. Indeed, it would hardly be surprising, considering his late brother Gansevoort's oratory on behalf of the annexation of Texas, to learn that Herman's vision of America included Manifest Destiny in the sense of southwestern territorial expansion that would stretch the nation's borders from Atlantic to Pacific; *that* empire was already all but achieved, its borders essentially established. But he would not have approved of interference with primitive cultures, as on the island paradises of the Pacific, the spoliation of which by "Paul Pry" with his "Pelf and Trade" he lamented in his late poem, "To Ned." Empire in this poem may be understood in terms of Frederick Merk's "Mission," as distinguished from territorial aggrandizement: the capture of men's minds rather than their lands. The Mission of America is "to redeem the Old World by high example": the example of liberty, democracy, human rights, public spiritedness, compassion, and all of the other ideals that the nation, however imperfectly, stood for.... The American empire would come to pass when, from one margin of the globe to the other, feudalism had given way to democratic equality....

SLAVERY

For the most part, Herman avoided the issue of slavery. He might not have written any poem at all on the subject had he not attended the National Academy of Design Exhibition. ... Hundreds of paintings were hung in the North, South, East, and West Rooms and in a central corridor. It was in the corridor that Herman saw Sanford Gifford's "The Coming Storm," which inspired his poem about Edwin Booth. War illustrators, such as Thomas Nast and Winslow Homer, were represented by camp scenes, while other artists exhibited a large cross section of the most memorable works of a notable era in American art: Albert Bierstadt, Frederick Church, Eastman Johnson, William Sidney Mount, Asher B. Durand, William Bradford, George Innes, William M. Hunt, Jasper Cropsey, Thomas Hicks, and Elihu Vedder, among others.

The paintings by Vedder, which included "The Arab Slave," "Jane Jackson, Formerly a Slave," "Lonely Spring," and "A Lost Mind," hung in the West Room. The *New York Times* critic was both impressed and perplexed by them. He admired their "absolute power," but he was put off by their darkness and by their enigmatic character. About the portrait of Jane Jackson, he decided that "the subject is not a very attractive one, but it is handled with great fidelity and strength." For Herman, the subject *was* attractive, and Vedder's dark vision was preferable to the conventionality of much of the show.

The inspiration for Herman's "'Formerly a Slave': An idealized Portrait, by E. Vedder, in the Spring Exhibition of the National Academy, 1865," then, was a rendering by a painter to whom he was particularly attracted of an old black peanut-seller encountered by Vedder on the streets of New York. Although "the sufferance of her race" is plain in her face, for her "too late deliverance dawns." Like the old crippled slave of "The Scout toward Aldie," she has no youth to squander on dreams, on education, and on personal fulfillment. For many like her, and even much younger, a past of servitude has bred a present of ignorance, dependence, and long-ingrained servility that makes them unemancipated slaves of fate. Even her son (a Union soldier, she told Vedder) may never gain full freedom. But "her children's children they shall know / The good withheld from her" as they break free of the yoke of the American black's special inheritance, and then emancipation will have come to an entire people. Thus from "down the depth of thousand years" she sees the good that is to come—not to her but to hers—and "her dusky face is lit with sober light."...

THE FINAL POEM

The final poem of *Battle-Pieces*, "A Meditation: Attributed to a Northerner after attending the last of two funerals from the same homestead—those of a National and a Confederate Officer (brothers), his kinsmen, who had died from the effects of wounds received in the closing battles," is set in a separate section following "Lee in the Capitol," thereby suggesting, along with its content and tone, that it is another late addition. Its heavily contrived dramatic situation refers back to the brothers who had parted in hatred in "Apathy and Enthusiasm," but where another poet might have focused his attention on the sentimental cliché of the fraternal deaths, Herman chose instead to dwell on the brotherly bonds that the war never sundered.

It is largely a compendium of recorded incidents of the war, and there were many, in which the bond of common humanity reasserted itself. An emissary from one army finds old friends in the other with whom to spend a warm social hour. Soldiers fronting each other at close range exchange compliments and food instead of bullets. In an event that occurred before Marye's Heights at Fredericksburg, a Confederate soldier risks his life to bring water to a Union soldier lying gravely wounded between the battling armies. Generals who had been schoolmates at West Point battle one another, and when armies pause during a truce, friends and relatives glimpse each other across the chasm of divided loyalties: "And something of a strange remorse / Rebelled against the sanctioned sin of blood, / And Christian wars of natural brotherhood." At such moments they feel "the god within the breast" and doubt "each plea and subterfuge of earth," asking rebelliously, "Can Africa pay back this blood / Spilt on Potomac's shore?"

In 1866, while the nation was searching for the means of reunification, this godly pull of brotherhood had special significance. If the two sides were to become one again, it would be necessary to abandon the vindictiveness of Emerson and Stevens: "*'The South's the sinner!'* Well, so let it be; / But shall the North sin worse, and stand the Pharisee?" To feel the old bonds now is as manly—and at least as easy—as it was to feel them during the bloodiest moments of the war. Southerners inspired admiration for their bravery in battle; so much the more should they be treated with dignity now: "When Vicksburg fell, and the moody files marched out, / Silent the victors stood, scorning to raise a shout." If Herman had refused to celebrate the starvation of the Vicksburg defenders in his battle poems, now he could find in their surrender a trenchant example of respect for the defeated to guide the North. . . .

THE BRADY OF CIVIL WAR VERSE

Like *Moby-Dick, Clarel,* and *Billy Budd, Battle-Pieces* is the only book of its type ever written or ever likely to be written in America. Calling him "the Brady [Matthew, Civil War photographer] of Civil War verse," [critic Newton] Arvin claims that "Melville is the first poet in English to realize the meaning of modern technological warfare." But the book is more. In the realm of imaginative literature, it is the only important attempt ever made to grapple intellectually with a distinctly *American* war, which is not to deny that there are other notable war books with different aims. There have been only two *American* wars, wars in which Americans battled to create and define their political identity, the Revolutionary War and the Civil War. All others have been foreign expeditions. But these two were truly national, the first the crucible from which the new country was poured and the second the agony that seems to have been necessary to resolve unanswered questions about the national identity. Of the Revolutionary War, it is safe to say that it inspired no literary work of distinction other than prose advocacy. Those who experienced it left that task to future writers. . . . But these later works have never attained the first rank of literary merit. . . .

A POLITICAL BOOK

Battle-Pieces is entire unto itself. It is a political book. . . . Fogle has described Melville's "public role" as "an unofficial poet laureate of the American nation, who tries to register in poetry the impact and the scope of the Civil War in all representative aspects." Melville asked what nation this was, why Fate had dashed it against the rocks of war, and what sort of future might await it. That future could be bright if the author were permitted to enter the "historical breach" caused by the war "to help refound America upon a worthier ideal of character." The resulting poetry is the product of restless wisdom, sharp sight and insight, high patriotism, unfailing compassion, religious fatalism, both tragic and epic intentions, and the poetic will to weave these elements into a single, unified expression. It is a revolt against the genteel and ideal sentiment that told readers what they wished to hear about the nobility and sanctity of their cause and their warriors, substituting grittiness that told readers who they were, what they had done and why, in what direction they might be headed, and what hope remained that the American experiment might yet ennoble mankind. It is a literary achievement that could have come only from Herman Melville. . . .

THE WAR AND MELVILLE'S BELIEFS

It is doubtful that the war revolutionized Melville's religious beliefs, but it affected them by subjecting them to the severest of tests. If one believed in a god at all, one was forced to reconcile the ravages and sufferings of war, and even the outbreak of the war itself, to that belief. What kind of god would decree such suffering? . . .

In *Battle-Pieces*, the analogues to Ormuzd, the son, and Ahriman, his evil twin, the subordinate gods of constructive good and anarch evil in Zoroastrianism, are, to further confuse matters, named Christ and Satan. In a book of war poems, there is little room for Christ except as "the Forgiver" of "The Swamp Angel," whose wish it is to convert those who would celebrate the sufferings of the innocent. He appears most frequently in the "Supplement," where both charity and benevolence are Christian principles. The war is the province of Satan, its instigator. He is the god of dissonance, malignancy, disruption, derangement, and suffering. He is the author of original sin, of which war is the ultimate celebration. In "Misgivings," he is the spirit of Nature's "dark side." Yet he cannot prevent even war from having a favorable outcome—because in the end God's plan governs.

It is difficult to determine precisely what Melville meant

Christ and Satan to be. It is possible that they are intended to be genuine deities—or angels—but it is equally possible that they represent elements, good and evil, of man's moral or psychological nature. In the latter case, Christ would represent man's higher values, his compassion, forgiveness, conscience, while Satan would represent his innate malevolence, belligerence, hatreds, bigotries, callousness. Nevertheless, in *Billy Budd* Melville implicitly deplored the decline of "that lexicon which is based on Holy Writ" and protested against the idea that a theological explanation of evil would be "subject to the charge of being tinctured with the biblical element." Other members of Melville's celestial host are canards. Raphael and Michael are human fabrications, and the holy angels who stand behind the Union sailors at Mobile Bay are no more than baroque figurines introduced for ornament. Thus the population of Melville's unseen world numbers three, at most.

It is safe to say that, other than Father Mapple, Melville never created a clergyman that he liked, and at the time of *Battle-Pieces* this anticlericism was in full flower. If the battle-poems offered him little opportunity to introduce clerics as dramatic characters, in "The Battle of Stone River" he did so by allusion, recalling that during the Wars of the Roses "monks blessed the fratricidal lance, / And sisters scarfs could twine." He would take up that theme again in *Billy Budd*, in which the chaplain, a man of Christ who should oppose war, permits himself to be enlisted in the ranks of Satan's warriors. He is the "church" in "church and state," an instrument of feudal tyranny. In "The Scout toward Aldie," the chaplain, far from sustaining others spiritually, is intent on curing his own spiritual ailments. Melville's complaint was not that these clergymen were evil or ill-intentioned men, only that they were inadequate to the daunting task they undertook. . . .

AN END TO HOPE

There was only one antidote to the pain and suffering, the prospect that fear and pity would guide the nation toward a better future in which it would abandon the follies and vanities of the past to embrace faith, humility, Christian charity, and its destiny of leading the world toward a future of moral progress. At some midwar point, Melville dedicated his artistry to that future, and when the government divided and faltered over the proper postwar path, he was ready with his pen to lead the way toward justice and tolerance. He was wrong in believing that he would be heard, but that miscalculation does not invalidate the achievement of *Battle-Pieces.*

Thus for five intense years Melville was a man dedicated to a cause, not the man of uncertainty and clouded aims he had been before the war. His subsequent fall was as precipitous as his ascent had been steep. A new America was emerging, but it was not his chastened mother. His hopes for national rededication were shattered and his poetic aspirations were crushed. Never again would he delude himself into thinking that he might be recognized in his own time, nor would he ever again see himself as the bard of national destiny.

Israel Potter as a Historical Novel

Alfred Kazin

Alfred Kazin is a well-known literary critic and
writer praised for his works *On Native Grounds* and
the autobiographical *New York Jew*. In the following
article, Kazin argues that although Israel Potter is a
rather inept and uninteresting hero, Melville prevents
the novel from being mundane by using it as a foil to
characterize several well-known historical figures.

Israel Potter: His Fifty Years of Exile has probably been the
least read of Melville's novels up to now; it has rarely been
available outside of Melville's collected works. The book has
a curious history, and it is certainly a curious book. Though
Melville's heroes are mostly himself under various disguises
(he was complicated enough to be both Ishmael and Ahab),
nowhere did he describe his psychic monomania of exile,
drift, homelessness, so pointedly as he did in emphasizing
Israel Potter's continual misfortunes and final beggary for
almost fifty years. Yet never did he have a character less re-
flective, less like himself, than Israel Potter. What Israel
shares with Herman Melville is "exile" seemingly perpetual,
exile as a lifetime experience, exile as a feeling about life un-
explained by the circumstances of exile. Fortunately, it is not
Israel who dominates the book but Israel's often cliffhanger
adventures. And the book has some historical actors—Benjamin Franklin, John Paul Jones, Ethan Allen—who are as
powerful in their way as Melville was in his secret soul,
powerful as only a great writer can be.

In 1854 Melville picked up a ragged, slatternly paperback
book called *Life and Remarkable Adventures of Israel R. Potter, A Native of Cranston, R.I.* This was the hack "life and adventures" of a Revolutionary War veteran, an agile but by no
means unusual man who had been captured by the British

at Bunker Hill, was taken to England as a prisoner in January, 1776, escaped, was recaptured, but served under John Paul Jones in the famous battle of the *Bon Homme Richard* with the *Serapis.* Israel Potter was an unlucky fellow; even after the victory of the American cause, he was unable to get home to Rhode Island until 1823. He lived out much of his English "exile" among the poorest of the poor in London, weaving cane chairs and crying his wares.

The *Life and Remarkable Adventures of Israel R. Potter* is a conventionally written, stilted autobiography of a bizarre life that became so by accident. Israel was, you might say, one of history's sad sacks, and his book is not stimulating. Melville, back in 1849, visiting London, wrote in his diary that he "looked over a lot of ancient maps of London. Bought one (A.D. 1776) for 3 & 6 pence. I want to use it in case I serve up the Revolutionary narrative of the beggar." In short, when Melville was still the well-known and "successful" author of such best sellers as *Typee* and *Omoo,* and before he had injured his reputation (!) by baffling his audience with the "metaphysical nonsense" of *Moby Dick,* Melville was thinking of exploiting, for his own novelistic purposes the undistinguished, pathetic figure of Israel R. Potter. Melville had some vague plans in the back of his head—it was possible that he might yet "serve up the Revolutionary narrative of the beggar."

MELVILLE'S FASCINATION WITH ISRAEL POTTER

Something about the extraordinary adventures but miserably rootless life of Israel R. Potter fascinated Melville. The "Revolutionary" period was one of heroic individuals, like Melville's own grandfathers. But even more, the idea of using another man's actual and reported life appealed to Melville's habitual strategy as an author. This strategy was always to convert some piece of actual experience, so long as it was bizarre, exotic, unduplicated by the middle-class respectable life Melville was leading as an author, husband and father into a loose, episodic, nicely spiced novel of adventure for the general public. But this genial popular adventure story also had to dramatize Melville's favorite idea of himself as a literary warrior at odds with his time. A book had to dramatize the epic struggle with the universe of Melville's own rebellious idiosyncrasy. This explains the ups and downs of his literary fortunes.

Melville, born into the best society of New York (Dutch and British), a descendant on both sides of famous (and dashing) Revolutionary War generals, had been driven, like his alter ego, Ishmael, into the "wilderness." His father, a hard-driven New York merchant, had gone bankrupt, then gone to pieces and died when his son was thirteen. Melville went to sea as a cabin boy; at twenty-two he embarked in a whaler from New Bedford on the three-and-a-half-year voyage that was to lead him to the South Seas, and into every possible scrape and adventure as a sailor. This was his making as an author. Melville began his literary career with best-selling nonfiction novels, *Typee* and *Omoo*, based on his adventures in the South Seas. Then, with *Mardi*, Melville showed that he could write a bad "visionary" novel to please himself—then turn back to more acceptable books, like *Redburn* and *White-Jacket*, just to keep the pot boiling. He could also, as all the world knows now but didn't during his lifetime, write a book of headlong genius, *Moby Dick*, that would for all practical purposes sink him as a professional author.

By 1855, when Melville finally did "serve up the Revolutionary narrative of the beggar," Melville was thirty-six, had published seven books, had a wife and children, but was no longer considered a reliable literary property by publishers in New York and London. He wrote as fast as any Irving Wallace or Harold Robbins who nowadays serves up a "quick read" for the hurried man dashing to a plane. But though Melville's works usually dealt with out-of-the-way adventures in remote parts of the world, this strange philosophical streak in him, this determination to be perpetually in mutiny against a genteel American upper-crust that claimed to have the final answers to all human questions and difficulties, had made Herman Melville a most difficult and unassimilable literary property.

ISRAEL POTTER AS AUTOBIOGRAPHY

Here is the personal drama behind *Israel Potter*—this peculiar, fascinating, uneven, often richly comic book. We cannot overlook the (still?) surprising fact that a leading American author (admittedly of somewhat dubious reputation) took a hack book and turned it into an allegory of his own life. Melville wrote it just to make some money. But with his unstoppable creative force he turned *Israel Potter* into a satiric picaresque novel that is much more about the real Herman Melville than it is about the real Israel Potter.

Yet there *was* a real Israel Potter. And in this book he remains an historic personage even though Melville moves his birthplace from Rhode Island to the Berkshires, then puts him through adventures that are not in the original text or are jauntily expanded out of all resemblance to the humdrum original.

Most strikingly, Melville puts into his "Revolutionary narrative" one of the great satires on Benjamin Franklin, plus a brilliantly overcolored view of Ethan "Ticonderoga" Allen as an American Samson among the (British) Philistines who have captured him. There is a view of the American Navy's John Paul Jones as a restless masculine desperado who feels cooped up to the point of madness when he is not fighting. In two successive chapters, Melville gives us a marvelously old-fashioned naval battle—John Paul Jones's almost suicidal victory in the *Bon Homme Richard* over the *Serapis*—a gory killing fight to the finish that went on into the night under the light of the moon over the Cliffs of Dover, from which a crowd of spectators gaped.

Melville's *Israel Potter* is at its best as a book about American men in the old, slashing, heroic style of romantic war, escapade, incessant movement. It is a book about warriors who have the character of brigands and pirates, ferocious toughies who fight for the pleasure of fighting, and who are never so happy as when they are knocking down the enemy with everything in sight. At Bunker Hill, writes Melville, "Not one American musket in twenty had a bayonet to it. So, wielding the stock right and left, the terrible farmers, with hats and coats off, fought their way among the furred grenadiers, knocking them right and left, as seal-hunters on the beach knock down with their clubs the Shetland seal."

BENJAMIN FRANKLIN

Israel Potter is about men who are ruled less by loyalty to a specific place or country than by their own irresistible feeling for adventure, risk, deception. The portrait of Benjamin Franklin is a masterpiece of irreverence. Franklin was without doubt a genius, as he was certainly one of the most useful men who ever trod the American earth. But also an intriguer, entrepreneur, publicist, speculator, and above all a wily old hypocrite, Franklin is beautifully portrayed by Melville as a man of infinite cunning, as classical in his wiles and stratagems as Ulysses or the Biblical Jacob.

The scenes between Israel and Benjamin Franklin are straight comedy—with poor, innocent, always besought and unlucky Israel as the straight man. Franklin is shown as the gay deceiver and unctuous man of affairs in all things—above all, the canniest man with a penny in American history before Calvin Coolidge. "Every time he comes in," poor Israel soliloquizes dolefully, "he robs me; with an air all the time, too, as if he were making me presents."

John Paul Jones, who cries out when he is not on duty—"My God, why was I not born a Czar!"—is deliciously a savage. "He was a rather small, elastic, swarthy man, with an aspect of a disinherited Indian Chief in European clothes. An unvanquishable enthusiasm intensified to perfect sobriety, couched in his savage, self-possessed eye." He runs his warships right into one English harbor after another. And spiking the cannon in Whitehaven, talks to them like a Shakespearean brigand—"I'll tongue-tie the thunderers."

This emphasis on heroic, military, hell-for-leather grappling with the enemy is the really decisive element in Melville's narrative. It reflects Melville's own passionate admiration for masculine power, headlong independence at any price, a damn-the-torpedoes resistance to the hindrances that life may raise. John Paul Jones is also plainly mad; the American "Samson" in English captivity, Ethan Allen, is willfully mad, histrionically defiant, a ham acting it up. Franklin is wily to the point of being inhuman. But these are men, as we say now, in the "classic" mold—they are meant to portray the American Revolution as perhaps the last time when men could be heroes (and cutthroats) on an unlimited scale. Melville is amused by his characters, but he loves them and he loves a time when the heroic individual like Franklin, Jones, Allen, seemed to incarnate fierce strength and unquestioning self-trust. In a revolutionary period such men incarnated the energy, the new hope, of revolution.

Melville felt that to be a man of power, a true hero and rebel in behalf of "nature," you had to be somewhat touched. Like Herman Melville. Nature, the "world," are not "sane," only society tries to be. The heroic individual, striking out for a vision that exists nowhere but in his own head, does so at the expense of his "balance."

About John Paul Jones, Melville says, typically,

The career of this stubborn adventurer signally illustrates the idea that since all human affairs are subject to organic disorder, since they are created in and sustained by a sort of half-disciplined chaos, hence he who in great things seeks success must never want for smooth water, which never was and never will be, but with what straggling method he can, dash with all his derangements at his object, leaving the rest to Fortune.

Israel Potter is thus a very personal and positive novel about masculine force. The vitality is mock-heroic, lovingly satiric about American demigods like Franklin. But what of Israel Potter himself? Israel, as his Biblical name testified in Melville's time, is the perpetual victim and wanderer. He is the man things happen to—he is the dummy on whom Melville, pent up as usual in this strange, uneven book, put all the pain of his own wandering, his orphanage, his bereftness from God and society.

Poor Israel! He never really makes it. He is always out of luck. Although his creator, Herman Melville, does give him a yellow mane and once calls him a "lion," Israel is really the average man, caught up in a series of adventures and escapes. Melville was not at his best writing about the average man. But fortunately, it is not Israel himself who holds our attention in this book. It is Israel as the occasion for Melville to write about Bunker Hill, Israel as an occasion for Melville to write about Franklin, John Paul Jones, George III, various English radical sympathizers with the American Revolution, Paris during the American Revolution. Melville's versatile, comic, beautifully extreme talent came through in this book despite every possible handicap from Israel Potter himself.

Themes in *The Confidence-Man*

H. Bruce Franklin

H. Bruce Franklin was a professor of English and American literature at Rutgers University in New Jersey. A well-known critic, Franklin's several books include *Prison Literature in America, Robert A. Heinlein: America as Science Fiction*, and a work on Melville, *The Wake of the Gods*. In the following article, Franklin lays out what he believes are the primary themes in *The Confidence-Man*. Franklin contends that the book is both an adept social commentary and a complex mythological work.

America in the 1850's was a jungle in which all kinds of hunters pursued their quarry: slaves, factory workers, buffalo, Indians, Mexicans, Mormons, Catholics, Protestants, gold, land, and suckers. American troops had just seized almost half of Mexico, were now busy exterminating Indians from Florida to Oregon, and were preparing to attack the Mormons in Utah. Slavery had already caused much blood to flow, and the nation was on the brink of civil war. Bands of killers roamed almost at will on both sides of the Mississippi and far to the west, undaunted by meeting the heads of other killers stuck on poles. Violence came from the Gold Rush, land claims, competing settlements, economic catastrophes, obscure feuds, racism, and plain blood lusts. This is the immediate world of *The Confidence-Man*, which refers again and again to the violent events of this world and presents many kinds of men who had their being in these events.

But, though the scene is the central Mississippi, the symbolic center of America, the story contains the violence of many human places and times, from primitive tribes to the ancient Greek and Roman conquerors, from Phalaris and Nero to Torquemada, Cesare Borgia, and Pizarro, from the

From *The Confidence Man* by Herman Melville, edited, with an introduction and annotation, by H. Bruce Franklin. Copyright ©1967 by The Bobbs-Merrill Company, Inc. Reprinted by permission of the author and Prentice Hall, Upper Saddle River, New Jersey.

French Revolution to the revolutions of 1848–1849 and the Crimean War, which had just ended. Only one physical blow is struck on board the riverboat *Fidèle*, but its decks are slippery with the blood of history.

All the varieties of fraud and swindling are also here. On board the *Fidèle* are American representatives of herbdoctors, land agents, counterfeiters, impostors, charity agents, card sharps, divines, transcendental philosophers, con men of all kinds. They and their victims discuss, quote, and reenact the roles of the other con men of history, such as Plato, Pontius Pilate, Seneca, Augustine, Machiavelli, Bacon, Rochefoucauld, Chesterfield, and P.T. Barnum.

Many American types and American figures are passengers on the *Fidèle*. While we are on this ornate riverboat we are floating down the Mississippi River in the middle of nineteenth-century America, surrounded by local forms, local customs, local language, local characters. But just as black turns out to be an appearance of white, this West is also the East, and this time conjoins past with future.

FICTION, READERS, CHARACTERS, AUTHOR

The Confidence-Man makes many extraordinary demands on the reader. By reference, allusion, parody, and quotation, it appropriates and incorporates whole works into itself: many of Shakespeare's plays, many books of the Bible, Ovid's *Metamorphoses*, the *Aeneid*, *Paradise Lost*, and numerous other works are as integral to *The Confidence-Man* as the little stories told by its own characters. Furthermore, some of these characters are caricatures of historical personages (such as Diogenes, Cooper, Socrates, Emerson, Timon, Thoreau, Poe) and others represent mythic figures (such as Manco Capac, Christ, Orpheus, Satan, Vishnu, Buddha)....

Nothing in *The Confidence-Man* is wasted, misplaced, or merely decorative. The difficulties of syntax are not mere rhetorical flourishes or meaningless obscurities but constant invitations to the reader both to see all the multiple possibilities they create and to feel the sinuous rhythms and sinister weavings that are entrapping him in a dialectical web. Only a few of the ever present syntactical snares are annotated. Many, many of the words of *The Confidence-Man*, including its title, are significant puns.... Nothing in the book, from the most physical of objects to the most metaphysical of arguments, can, in the last analysis, be separated from every other thing in the book; so the cross-references in the foot-notes only hint of the intricacy of the book's design.

Perhaps the most perplexing thing about the book is its diabolical suggestiveness. Elaborate solutions for all problems and mysteries are suggested; but they turn out to be incomplete or ambiguous. Hints are dropped about financial chicanery, religious imposture, physical disease, and sexual perversion; but they usually remain only hints. Darkness obscures all lights. The book ends by asserting that "something further *may* follow of this Masquerade." Behind and through all appearances peeps an author who suggests that he knows all. He asks the reader for his confidence while making it impossible to hear that word again without a most suggestively knowing smile.

FAITH IN MAN?

The Confidence-Man at first may seem to be a debate about the question, Should one have confidence in Man? One should resist the temptation to read the book as an argument for or against this position. One must also resist the temptation to read it as an unresolved debate; the debate serves to establish a dialectic, and the dialectic serves not to analyze the world that is but to create a new cosmos out of the materials of an old chaos. The principal materials of that old chaos exist within each reader, and it is he who is asked to re-form Man by entering a world in which an author and he define each other in terms of objects and characters they join in creating.

A reader begins, innocently perhaps, trying to read this book as though it were a novel. If he is a good novel-reader, he pays careful attention to the words and the physical objects and actions created out of these words. In the very first words of the book the reader discovers that the actions about to be described take place on April Fools' Day. At this point, he may suspect that the title character is going to be playing tricks on other characters; he may even suspect that the author is going to be playing tricks on him. But will he suspect the possibility that each physical object and action may be an All-Fools' joke because he will either see that it is not physical or else become its victim? Everything he is to see will be like a left-handed monkey wrench, a skyhook, or a can of striped paint, that is, a verbal thing, a tricky fiction created by the interaction of at least two minds. The first action of the book consists of a mysterious stranger coming upon a placard that presents "what purported to be a careful description" of "a mysterious impostor"; the stranger may read this description, but the reader may not. All he can read is the author's description of the stranger, who is a "lamb-like" mute on a riverboat named the *Fidèle.*

Soon, however, the reader finds himself, together with the passengers on the *Fidèle,* receiving descriptions of all the subsequent avatars of the Confidence Man in the form of a list of "ge'mmen" reeled off by Black Guinea, a crippled Negro beggar, himself apparently a principal avatar. One by one these avatars appear in person, that is to say, in the author's words rather than in the words of Black Guinea, who is one of his characters. In this world a character creates his author by creating other characters who speak words formed by both of them.

CHARACTERS CREATE CHARACTERS

This only begins the involutions of fictive realities. Many subsequent characters at times become authors who create characters, some of whom then create other characters. Melville interpolates three chapters (14, 33, 44) addressed by the author to his readers about the relations among fiction, authors, characters, readers, and the rest of reality. Two characters try to get each other dizzy and confused with bad wine, cheap cigars, and a discussion of what authors mean by the words they put in the mouths of characters (Chapter 30). One of these characters later victimizes the other by telling him a story which he claims to have "told with the purpose of every storyteller—to amuse"; "Hence, if it seem strange to you, that strangeness is the romance; it is what contrasts it with real life; it is the invention, in brief, the fiction as opposed to the fact" (Chapter 35). One character hears a "true" story from two other characters who are evidently the same character in two different forms, and then repeats it, in a somewhat different version, to someone evidently a third form of the same character; we are not permitted to hear any of these versions because, as the authorial "we" tells us: "But as the good merchant could, perhaps, do better justice to the man than the story, we shall venture to tell it in other words than his, though not to any other effect" (Chapter 11). Now what in the world does it mean to do better justice to a man than to a story told about that man? And what then can "not to any other effect" possibly mean?

And what is all this hazy shadow play about? Part of the answer lies in the relations between man's imaginative reality, what he thinks, and man's identity, what he is.

Most of us wander through life identifying people in terms of such things as external characteristics (tall, fat, brown, bowlegged, eagle-beaked) or easily labeled groups (Negro, Methodist, Communist, worker, Indian) or more-or-less temporary states (rich, well-dressed, gloomy, angry, young, on a battlefield, in the cabin of the boat) and so forth. When we read most fictions, we are asked to behave in this usual way—only more so. If we are presented with a character described as a crippled Negro beggar on a Mississippi riverboat, we expect that character to remain the same except as he is changed by circumstances we are told about or may infer. He may get off the boat, stop begging, become healed, or, even more miraculously, lose his identity as a Negro; but he changes only as we accept the author's manipulations. If, in the next chapter, there appears a character who does not *appear* to be the same character, he *is* not the same character unless and until we are convinced that he is. Black Guinea's list exposes some of the consequences of these ordinary assumptions about fiction and other forms of existence.

BLACK GUINEA'S LIST

Black Guinea's list of the avatars of the Confidence Man is a list of only the most external characteristics:

> Oh yes, oh yes, dar is aboard here a werry nice, good ge'm-man wid a weed, and a ge'mman in a gray coat and white tie, what knows all about me; and a ge'mman wid a big book, too; and a yarb-doctor; and a ge'mman in a yaller west; and a ge'mman wid a brass plate; and a ge'mman in a wiolet robe; and a ge'mman as is a sodjer; and ever so many good, kind, honest ge'mmen more aboard what knows me and will speak for me, God bress 'em; yes, and what knows me as well as dis poor old darkie knows hisself, God bress him! Oh, find 'em, find 'em. . . .

We share the plight of the bystander who immediately wants to know, "But how are we to find all these people in this great crowd?" Apparently we are supposed to find out who people *are*—and who the Confidence Man *is*—by examining the colors each man wears, the objects he carries, and the role he plays. This is precisely what we see the people on the *Fidèle* doing and what we customarily do in our daily lives.

"AM I AN ACTOR?"

The Confidence-Man is a book full of characters who are all, ostensibly, the same man—the confidence man. Throughout the book, this man, in his various guises, casts aspersions on the other characters' lack of faith, or "confidence" in their fellow man. In this excerpt, "the man in gray," a guise for the confidence man, accompanied by a reverend, accosts a one-legged man about his conviction that a black crippled beggar, Guinea, was really a white man masquerading as a black.

"This reverend gentleman tells me, sir, that a certain cripple, a poor negro, is by you considered an ingenious impostor. Now, I am not unaware that there are some persons in this world, who, unable to give better proof of being wise, take a strange delight in showing what they think they have sagaciously read in mankind by uncharitable suspicions of them. I hope you are not one of these. In short, would you tell me now, whether you were not merely joking in the notion you threw out about the negro. . . .

"Well, he's just what I said he was."

"A white masquerading as a black?"

"Exactly."

The man in gray glanced at the young clergyman a moment, then quietly whispered to him, "I thought you represented your friend here as a very distrustful sort of person, but he appears endued with a singular credulity.— Tell me, sir, do you really think that a white could look the negro so? For one, I should call it pretty good acting."

"Not much better than any other man acts."

"How? Does all the world act? Am *I*, for instance, an actor? Is my reverend friend here, too, a performer?"

This is precisely what Black Guinea—almost certainly an avatar of the Confidence Man—wants us to do, and what we have to do in order to read the book with any coherence.

At the same time, Guinea's list, like everything else in *The Confidence-Man*, contains its opposite. We do meet, in order, characters explicitly described as a man with a weed, a man in a gray coat and white tie, a man with a big book, and an herb doctor, all of whom seem to be forms of the Confidence Man. These are precisely half, the first half, of the particularized characters in the list. Of the four who comprise the second half, we meet only one described by the author as described by Guinea (this one is the second of the four). After

"Yes, don't you both perform acts? To do, is to act; so all doers are actors."

"You trifle.—I ask again, if a white, how could he look the negro so?"

"Never saw the negro-minstrels, I suppose?"

"Yes, but they are apt to overdo the ebony; exemplifying the old saying, not more just than charitable, that 'the devil is never so black as he is painted.' But his limbs, if not a cripple, how could he twist his limbs so?"

"How do other hypocritical beggars twist theirs? Easy enough to see how they are hoisted up."

"The sham is evident, then?"

"To the discerning eye," with a horrible screw of his gimlet one.

"Well, where is Guinea?" said the man in gray; "where is he?". . .

"You forget," here said the young clergyman to the man in gray, "that yourself helped poor Guinea ashore."

"So I did, so I did; how unfortunate. But look now," to the other, "I think that without personal proof I can convince you of your mistake. For I put it to you, is it reasonable to suppose that a man with brains, sufficient to act such a part as you say, would take all that trouble, and run all that hazard, for the mere sake of those few paltry coppers, which, I hear, was all he got for his pains, if pains they were?"

"That puts the case irrefutably," said the young clergyman, with a challenging glance towards the one-legged man.

"You two green-horns! Money, you think, is the sole motive to pains and hazard, deception and deviltry, in this world. How much money did the devil make by gulling Eve?"

these eight particular characters, Guinea ends his list with "ever so many good, kind, honest ge'mmen," an indication that there are far more than ten (eight plus Guinea and the lamb-like man) shapes of the Confidence Man in this world and that all shapes may be ambiguous. Furthermore, Guinea speaks in a dialect, making any of his words possibly puns (as he hints by concluding "dis poor ole darkie is werry well *wordy* of all you kind ge'mmen's kind confidence").

Guinea's wordiness, like the muteness of the lamb-like man, expands until it fills the universe of *The Confidence-Man*; his list ultimately includes everybody. To perceive what is involved, one must read his list artfully, always following its movement through precision into ambiguity, through the particular to the universal—or apparently chaotic.

Number 1. "A werry nice, good ge'mman wid a weed." The first listed avatar seems the easiest to find. John Ringman appears with "a long weed on his hat" in Chapter 4 and then is referred to in the title of Chapter 5 as "The man with the weed." But to establish this identity we must assume that the author sticks to Guinea's terms, something later to be made dubious. We might, as one alternative, take Guinea's "weed" to mean tobacco, making each of the two confidence men who force cigars on the other in Chapter 30 a man with a weed; one of them, Frank Goodman, is certainly a "good man wid de weed," to use Guinea's very last words. Or we could take another common meaning of weed, "A covering; that which covers, spreads over vest or vestment, clothing or garment" (Richardson's *Dictionary*, 1844), and see the first of Guinea's listings to be as equivocal and far-reaching as the last. We may create this form of the Confidence Man wherever we see him.

Number 2. "A ge'mman in a gray coat and white tie." In Chapter 6 there appears "a man in a gray coat and white tie." But note that in Chapter 3, when a suspect Methodist minister attacks a cynical cripple, a voice cries out, "The white cravat against the world!"

Number 3. "A ge'mman wid a big book, too." In Chapter 9 there appears a man carrying a ledger-like transfer book; he is the president and transfer agent of the Black Rapids Coal Company. Several characters have small books, so we are asked to distinguish them from the Confidence Man by the size of their books. Then the last character mentioned in *The Confidence-Man* is discovered in possession of the big book of the gentlemen's cabin, the Bible. And both the reader and the author have a book, which may or may not be big.

Number 4. "A yarb-doctor." The relatively unambiguous first half of Guinea's list ends with one of the two unambiguous identifications; the only herb doctor appears just as the sun comes out from behind the clouds in Chapter 16.

Number 6. "A ge'mman wid a brass plate." The relatively unambiguous first half of the book ends with the other unambiguous identification; a man who wears a small brass plate around his neck, having just sold a hypothetical boy, gets ready to disembark as he passes a bluff called the Devil's Joke. As soon as he leaves, Chapter 23, the exact center of the book, describes the ambiguous twilight. After this, not one of Guinea's listings appears as Guinea had described.

Number 5. "A ge'mman in a yaller west" and Number 7. "A ge'mman in a wiolet robe." Neither of these two brightly colored forms is described by the author as described by Guinea. Either or both may be the sun, around which *The Confidence-Man,* like the world it images, revolves. The "man in cream-colors" who appears "at sunrise on a first of April" in the first sentence of the book might be viewed as a *gentle*man in a yellow vest ("vest," from the Latin *vestis,* meant any garment, particularly an outer garment, a robe or coat). Or the last character introduced in the book, a peddler-boy wearing a "fragment of an old linen coat, bedraggled and yellow," may be viewed as a *gamin* in a yellow vest. The herb doctor also wears a yellowish garment; several times he is pointedly identified as the man in the snuff-colored surtout. The sun, which comes out when he does, is then called "a golden huzzar." The Cosmopolitan calls all "moderns" "we golden boys," sees about Shakespeare a "hidden sun . . . at once enlightening and mystifying," and refers to the printing press as the sun, "god Apollo" who "dispenses the day."

As yellow is to the sunrise, violet is to the sunset. The two confidence men who confront each other in Chapters 25 through 35, the extraordinary Cosmopolitan and the ordinary riverboat con man, Charlie Noble, each wear something that resembles a violet robe. The Cosmopolitan "sported a *vest*ure barred with various hues, that of the cochineal predominating"; Charlie wears a "violet vest." A character who flits by in Chapter 6, a "gentleman in a ruby-colored velvet vest," would seem to be merely a red herring. But not to be dismissed is the intensely symbolic "robed man" on the ground-glass shade of the solar lamp in the final chapter; whether or not his robe is violet, the extinction of the solar lamp that illuminates him is much like the setting of the sun. And, after all, what makes colors?

Number 8. "A ge'mman as is a sodjer." Four of the *Fidèle's* passengers play the role of playing the role of soldier. The lamb-like man, though "apparently a non-resistant," moves through the crowd "shield-like bearing his slate before him." Likewise, the Methodist minister, though he says he was thought "a non-combatant," is a "soldier-like," "martial-looking man . . . who in the Mexican War had been volunteer chaplain to a volunteer rifle-regiment." The man with the bandaged nose of Chapter 18, who walks "with a pace that seemed the lingering memento of the lock-step of convicts," is called a "poor wounded huzzar" by the herb doctor. The cripple of the following chapter, entitled "A Soldier of Fortune," claims to the herb doctor to have been crippled in prison but passes himself off to the other passengers as a wounded veteran of the Mexican War. He is both accused of belonging to "the Devil's regiment" (in *White-Jacket* Melville himself had said that any soldier "is but a fiend" who serves the Devil) and acclaimed as a fighter against "Fortune." He illustrates the art of "coming the old soldier," i.e., tricking like "a rogue who pretends to be an old soldier."

Besides these four passengers, there are other gentlemen who appear "as is a sodjer." There is the sun itself, likened to a "golden huzzar." There is a real soldier, Colonel John Moredock, one of the most important metaphysical (though not physical) passengers. The very word soldier—derived from *soldus* and literally meaning one who receives pay—suggests a fundamental ambiguity. And "sodjer" does not even necessarily mean "soldier." "Sodjer" (also spelled "sodger," "sojer," and "soger") in nautical usage meant, as Melville knew, "a red herring." Finally, all these possibilities combine in the possibilities foreshadowed by the final sentence of the book: "Something further may follow of this Masquerade." In apocalyptic visions of both the East and the West, the Savior in his last avatar will return as a destroying soldier.

THE CONFIDENCE-MAN AS MYTH

A reader familiar with no other myths than the Judeo-Christian ones may read through *The Confidence-Man* with a good partial understanding. He may see that the lamb-like man represents either Christ or Satan masquerading as Christ, that Guinea and the later avatars of the Confidence Man represent Satan, that the vision of the final chapter is filled with images from Revelation, and that the sequel hinted in the last sentence may be a fulfillment of that apocalypse. He may describe the Confidence Man's assumption of Christianity in familiar Western terms, such as diabolic, wicked, fiendish; and he may see this role as that of Satan or Anti-Christ.

However, this is not even half the mythic structure. One of

the great achievements of *The Confidence-Man* is its way of relating the principal Western myths to the principal Eastern myths and all myth to all other kinds of fiction. In *The Wake of the Gods: Melville's Mythology*, I discuss these relations in some detail; here I shall just summarize.

The Confidence-Man begins at sunrise on April 1st and ends shortly after midnight. All Fools' Day was generally assumed to be a remnant of the ancient great vernal festival, commemorating the rebirth of the sun, celebrated all around the Northern Hemisphere at the time of the vernal equinox, when the sun returns from "beneath" the equator. (The date of course shifts with the precession of the equinoxes.) Most authorities traced the rituals of All Fools' Day to the most ancient known vernal celebration, a Hindu masquerade called the Huli. These vernal rituals, held on the one day when the duration of light exactly equals and is about to exceed the duration of darkness (a division precisely reflected in the structure of *The Confidence-Man*), greeted the sun as the great savior-god returning from the realms of night, i.e., the Southern Hemisphere (whose best-known incarnation of the sun, Manco Capac, is likened to the lamb-like man in the first sentence of the book).

The Confidence Man is this sun, this god, this savior. But at the same time he is the darkness that obscures this sun (as Black Guinea when he holds up his "old coal-sifter of a tamborine" to indicate the sun, as the President of the Black Rapids Coal Company, as the Cosmopolitan when he extinguishes the last light in the book, a solar lamp); he is the god who struggles against this god; he is the destroyer. This identity of light and darkness, salvation and destruction, inherently alien to Christianity, lies at the heart of both Hinduism and Buddhism.

The avatars of the Confidence Man are quite literally *avatara*, that is, successive incarnations of the great Hindu god of salvation, Vishnu. The first major avatar of Vishnu is as a fish who recovers the lost sacred books; the first avatar of the Confidence Man is, among other things, an "Odd fish!" who brings to the world injunctions from the Bible. The second avatar is as a tortoise who upholds the world; the second avatar of the Confidence Man is as a "grotesque" figure who shuffles around on leather stumps, who lives "all 'long shore," and who holds his symbolic "coal-sifter of a tamborine" "high over his head." After this come eight other major avatars and innumerable minor ones; Black Guinea lists eight other major avatars and innumerable minor ones ("ever so many good, kind, honest ge'mmen"). For Hinduism and for *The Confidence-Man* the two most important are the last avatar which has come, Buddha, and the last avatar, which is to come, Kalki.

The teachings of Buddha ("the enlightened"), who had also the name of Gotamâ (*go*, senses, and *tamá*, darkness: i.e., "he who brings darkness to the senses"), aimed toward the achievement of *nirvana*, which means literally the extinguishing of a flame or lamp. According to Hindus (as opposed to Buddhists), Buddha was Vishnu incarnate as a deceiver, leading his enemies into spiritual darkness. The last avatar of the Confidence Man is the Cosmopolitan, who finally extinguishes the last light, the solar lamp, and leads man into the ensuing darkness.

In Hinduism, Vishnu the Preserver is one face of a three-headed godhood, the Trimurti, whose other two faces are Brahma the Creator and Siva the Destroyer. Brahma has no role in the created world; but Siva, like Vishnu, has periodic avatars. The world of *The Confidence-Man: His Masquerade*, like the world of the Hindus, can be seen as a dialectic masquerade of the two conflicting forms—preservation and destruction, love and hate, confidence and delusion, white and black, Vishnu and Siva. In both Hinduism and *The Confidence-Man* these two forms are shapes of the same being, in fact all forms are shapes of the same being, and all men partake of the unity imaged visually in the god that seems many but is one.

In Vishnu's last avatar, which is to come, he will appear with the attributes of Siva the Destroyer as Kalki, an armed warrior, to end the final age of man, the present age, the Age of Time, by destroying man. This may be both Guinea's "ge'mman as is a sodjer" and what is hinted in the final sentence: "Something further may follow of this Masquerade." And it may also explain why the last character introduced into the book, in the final chapter, is a boy with "leopard-like teeth," with a face that "wore such a polish of seasoned grime, that his sloe-eyes sparkled from out it like lustrous sparks in fresh coal," and clothed in a "red-flannel shirt." For Siva often appears as "a smoke-coloured boy" whose "teeth are as large as an ogre's," who appears "clothed in red raiment," and who "destroys all, or . . . absorbs all essences into himself at last." When the boy winks at the Cosmopolitan and asks, "is the wind East, d'ye think?", one may sense their final apocalyptic union.

Melville makes the Hindu vision of the apocalypse overshadow the Christian vision, in which the armed Word of God vanquishes Satan. Christ in *The Confidence-Man* merges into Satan as the shape-shifting struggles and ultimate identity of Vishnu and Siva generate a world in which all objects and events become fictions, all men become indistinguishable, all gods become the Confidence Man, salvation means destruction, and black is only another appearance of white. This vision, at first appearance so destructive, is in reality most creative. To experience and survive it is to be re-created.

CHAPTER 3

Moby Dick

READINGS ON
HERMAN MELVILLE

Moby Dick: An Introduction

Tyrus Hillway

In a piece meant to be an introduction to *Moby Dick*, Tyrus Hillway outlines the main themes of Melville's greatest novel, including Ahab's rebellion against God. Hillway concludes that Melville implicitly criticizes Ahab for defying destiny. Hillway was one of the founders of the Melville Society in 1945. Author of *Melville and the Whale*, he contributed a large number of articles and reviews to periodicals in American and English literature. His three-act play *Captain Ahab*, based on *Moby Dick*, has been produced in Nantucket, Massachusetts. He has been president of Mitchell College and has been on the faculty of Colorado State College.

"I have written a wicked book, and feel spotless as the lamb," reported Herman Melville to his Berkshire friend and neighbor Nathaniel Hawthorne after the completion of *Moby-Dick* in 1851. Regarding the story as most people do—that is, as the tale of an adventurous whale hunt in the South Seas— one can hardly call *Moby-Dick* a wicked book. What, then, did Melville mean in making such a statement? Attempts to answer this question have resulted in some of the most fanciful and complex writing ever to mar the pages of literary criticism. Yet its meaning is clear, I think, not only in Melville's comments upon his own experiences as an author but in the explanations which he provided within the book itself.

Typee and *Omoo*, his earliest novels of adventure, won Melville an enthusiastic audience. That audience, however, was quickly and rudely turned against him by his third book, *Mardi*, a long and somewhat involved allegory of ideas. The bitterness aroused in Melville by the unfavorable reception of *Mardi* led him to exclaim to Hawthorne, "Truth

Tyrus Hillway, "A Preface to *Moby Dick*," in *"Moby-Dick": Centennial Essays*, edited for the Melville Society (Dallas: Southern Methodist University Press, 1953). Reprinted by permission of the author.

is the silliest thing under the sun. Try to get a living by Truth—and go to the Soup Societies!" Of his literary methods in writing *Moby-Dick* he said, "What I feel most moved to write, that is banned,—it will not pay. Yet, altogether, write the *other* way I cannot. So the product is a final hash, and all my books are botches."

What Melville wanted, of course, was to teach, to deal with moral and philosophical ideas. His readers preferred to be entertained. What evolved, in order to satisfy both reader and writer, was a compromise. For most readers, even today, *Moby-Dick* remains a story of wild adventure. For its author, as creative artist, it was a framework of narrative within which he could raise vital moral, social, religious, and philosophical questions. Those of his novels in which he did not exhaustively ponder such weighty questions he regarded as merely potboilers.

Moby-Dick must be recognized, first of all, for what it is— not only an adventure story, but a profound study of human character and human destiny. The great question which it raises is this: What have the gods to do with man?

AHAB

Captain Ahab, conveyor of the protests of mankind against the injustices of fate, represents one point of view that may be taken toward life. He reveals this, for example, in a conversation with the ship's carpenter on the *Pequod,* when he exclaims, "Thou art as unprincipled as the gods, and as much of a jack-of-all-trades."

"But I do not mean anything, sir," is the reply. "I do as I do."

"The gods again," says Ahab.

Here is the essence of his observations upon divine power. Struck and maimed by the whale, a brute beast of the sea, forced thus to suffer both physical and mental anguish, Ahab refuses to accept the suffering as his just lot. "Why was I singled out," he seems to cry, like so many moderns, "by fate or God for such torment?" His reaction is to roar defiance. If the gods take the liberty of striking him, he will strike back blow for blow. But where shall he strike? What visible form do the gods take? In the most powerful speech of the entire book, Ahab explains matters as follows to Starbuck, his first mate:

All visible objects, man, are but as pasteboard masks. But in each event—in the living act, the undoubted deed—there, some unknown but still reasoning thing puts forth the mouldings of its features from behind the unreasoning mask. If man will strike, strike through the mask! How can the prisoner reach outside except by thrusting through the wall? To me, the white whale is that wall, shoved near to me. Sometimes I think there's naught beyond. But 'tis enough. He tasks me; he heaps me; I see in him outrageous strength, with an inscrutable malice sinewing it. That inscrutable thing is chiefly what I hate; and be the white whale agent or be the white whale principal, I will wreak that hate upon him.

This tokens a kind of heroism, a Prometheanism, in Ahab. He voices the implied protest of all humanity. Yet Ahab is mad. If he utters in his mad raptures a few of the truths with malice in them which trouble saner minds, he is mad none the less. His tremendous power to work his will upon other men seems to be all the more heightened by the form of his insanity; but his futile and unreasonable feud with nature's brute forces, his deliberate courting of destruction, prove the wreck of his essential instruments of mental balance. Melville, of course, knew exactly what he was doing when he made Ahab mad. While he admired, he could not have approved Ahab's theories or his inhuman pride in applying them. Influenced, without any doubt, by his master Shakespeare, Melville created in Ahab a megalomaniac of the modern world.

One result of Ahab's madness is his isolation from the rest of humanity. Like Faust, he has bartered his immortal soul for the right to consider himself a demigod. Fedallah and his mysterious companions appear to be the guides appointed to conduct his soul to hell. In achieving his temporarily exalted status, Ahab, like Hawthorne's Ethan Brand, commits the unpardonable sin of pride and attempts to reject his kinship with other humankind. At more than one point in the story he actually senses the fact that by giving up his defiant quest he can regain his soul and return to sanity. The tragedy of the plot lies in his never quite managing to bring this about, even under the urgings of the kind and sensible Starbuck. His physical and spiritual separation from his wife and child, his disdain for the ordinary comforts of life, his destruction of the helpful quadrant—all these mark his withdrawal from the common level of mankind into an egocentric stratosphere between the world of man and the heaven of God. He remains the defier of fate.

WORSHIPING WITH THE PAGAN QUEEQUEG

In this scene from Moby-Dick, *Ishmael and the pagan Quee-queg spend the night in a rented room before setting sail the next day on the* Pequod. *Melville uses Ishmael, a rather shel-tered "good Christian," as the perfect foil to Queequeg's pagan worship. In a scene filled with irony and humor, Ish-mael ultimately concludes that it is a Christian act to wor-ship Queequeg's idol, an "insignificant bit of black wood."*

Wild he was; a very sight of sights to see; yet I began to feel myself mysteriously drawn towards him. And those same things that would have repelled most others, they were the very magnets that thus drew me. I'll try a pagan friend, thought I, since Christian kindness has proved but hollow courtesy. . . .

He made me a present of his embalmed head; took out his enormous tobacco wallet, and groping under the tobacco, drew out some thirty dollars in silver; then spreading them on the table, and mechanically dividing them into two equal portions, pushed one of them towards me, and said it was mine. I was going to remonstrate; but he silenced me by pouring them into my trowsers' pockets. I let them stay. He then went about his evening prayers, took out his idol, and removed the paper fireboard. By certain signs and symp-toms, I thought he seemed anxious for me to join him; but well knowing what was to follow, I deliberated a moment whether, in case he invited me, I would comply or otherwise.

I was a good Christian; born and bred in the bosom of the infallible Presbyterian Church. How then could I unite with this wild idolator in worshipping his piece of wood? But what is worship? thought I. Do you suppose now, Ishmael, that the magnanimous God of heaven and earth—pagans and all included—can possibly be jealous of an insignificant bit of black wood? Impossible! But what is worship?—to do the will of God—*that* is worship. And what is the will of God?—to do to my fellow man what I would have my fellow man to do to me—*that* is the will of God. Now, Queequeg is my fellow man. And what do I wish that this Queequeg would do to me? Why, unite with me in my particular Pres-byterian form of worship. Consequently, I must then unite with him in his; ergo, I must turn idolator. So I kindled the shavings; helped prop up the innocent little idol; offered him burnt biscuit with Queequeg; salaamed before him twice or thrice; kissed his nose; and that done, we un-dressed and went to bed, at peace with our own consciences and all the world.

PIP

"Oh, ye frozen heavens! look down here," shouts Ahab, observing Pip. "Ye did beget this luckless child and have abandoned him, ye creative libertines." Pip, too, is insane.

Pip, as a matter of fact, constitutes Ahab's foil. A small and cowardly Negro lad, he loses his mind when cast adrift for several hours on the wild and open sea. But the important thing about Pip is that he makes no real protest against his fate. He is at the opposite pole of Ahab's axis. His pathetic figure stirs in Ahab his most disturbing feelings of kinship with humanity. So disturbing to Ahab are these feelings that he consciously resists them, although Pip's influence nearly succeeds in saving him. Pip's reactions to life are almost all passive, and he provides for Ahab a means of salvation by giving him something human to protect and help. Unfortunately, Ahab's pride is never completely mastered by Pip's humility.

STARBUCK

While Pip touches Ahab's heart, Starbuck touches his reason. Starbuck, like a good angel, gradually draws Ahab away from his evil purpose—but too late. Ahab, well aware that Starbuck has common sense in his favor, resists him first by reasoning, then by threats. Even though almost overwhelmed by the force of Ahab's personality, Starbuck holds to his convictions and sets out to save both Ahab and the crew. At one point, convinced of his captain's madness, he is ready to assassinate him in order to preserve the others from being drawn into tragedy with him; yet this contemplated violent act proves too strong for Starbuck's good principles. He cannot force himself to commit murder and returns to the only weapon at his command—reason.

Melville wrote to his friend Hawthorne with some bravado that the secret motto of *Moby-Dick* might be found in Ahab's consecration of the harpoon: *Ego non baptizo te in nomine patris, sed in nomine diaboli* [I baptize thee not in the name of the Father, but in the name of the Devil]. It seems clear, however, that Melville was being more than half humorous in this declaration. A more likely motto can be discovered, I believe, in one of the two important sermons which are preached in the book. One sermon is delivered by the Negro cook on the *Pequod* to the sharks, comparing them in greed and rapacity with men. The other is the beautiful and moving discourse of Father Mapple in the chapel at New

Bedford, on the theme of Jonah. The following words from Father Mapple's great sermon form a motto which is nearer, I think, to Melville's intention in *Moby-Dick* than any other which might be selected:

> All the things that God would have us do are hard for us to do—remember that—and hence, he oftener commands us than endeavors to persuade. And if we obey God, we must disobey ourselves; and it is in this disobeying ourselves, wherein the hardness of obeying God consists.

Here we have Ahab's case exactly. That godless, god-like man has taken the whale's attack upon him as a personal affront, and he consequently blames God for creating a world in which brotherhood is preached while vulturism is practiced.

"Faith? What's that?" cries Ahab derisively, in his bitterness. Yet there rings a hollowness in the cry. Struggle and fume as he will, he cannot escape the suspicion that even his defiance of God is preordained. Perhaps that thought serves to add something to his exasperation. He unhesitatingly accepts Fedallah's prophecies, of course, and so shows himself a fatalist. In the face of nearly certain annihilation he pauses briefly to justify himself by asserting, "I am the Fates' lieutenant; I act under orders."

Perhaps too much has already been written about Melville's powerful symbolism. From the literary point of view, his language is unusually colorful and rich with symbolical import. His use of symbols, however, has led many to look for hidden meanings of all kinds in his works. For the most part, I think, his intentions are plain to see. While it is true that Melville, for fear of losing his readers, may have attempted to clothe his ideas in allegory in order to avoid the shock of the naked thought, I feel sure that his fondness for the symbol came from a natural predilection in which he took a literary delight. He seldom lost an opportunity to turn a physical fact into an artistic device. For this he had to await appreciation until the twentieth century.

The conclusion remains that *Moby-Dick* must be recognized as much less a tale of maritime adventure than a novel of ideas and spiritual conflict. The great White Whale, with all his majesty and frightfulness, becomes inevitably the symbol of a universal power (or its mask) which Ahab feels to be unjust and against which he rebels. The effect of Ahab's mad rebellion upon himself and upon those who surround him, and not the hazards of the chase, however interesting these may be, constitutes the story's theme.

This theme the America of the present century can at last understand. In Melville's own day, engrossed in political and economic expansion, the American public almost angrily rejected any suggestion that it should examine rationally the relation of the individual to his universe, especially when such an examination might weaken some established institutions of considerable popular influence. It was mainly upon the appeal of a direct practical application that an idea could hope to win many followers. We are now willing to listen to Melville because, having exhausted our energies in expansionism and having finally reached a point of disillusionment, we have again become interested in the meaning of man. When the nation was rapt in its great work of colonization and construction, there was little time for such thinking. Truth could be doled out, as it were, by the professionals and accepted substantially without scrutiny.

Even the long struggle between the church and science took place during the nineteenth century on a somewhat superficial plane. Except in the later phases, it resembled less a clash between opposing views of true teaching than a struggle for influence between factions. The underlying contradictions—where faith enters the picture for both religion and science—were only dimly discerned; and the battle raged chiefly over "authorities" and "evidence." As the scientific discoveries placed new emphasis upon the material and rational factors in human life, those who recognized the basic issues were deeply moved. Among these Melville may be numbered; for Melville was habitually one who dived deep. Religious in the sense that he believed instinctively in the need for a firm faith, scientific in the sense that he accepted no dogma without clear evidence, he saw reluctantly the futility of seeking final truth. The knowledge of our common limitation in this respect seems to have aggravated in him the festering of a restless frustration. Emotionally, he hungered for faith, but he could not accept it blindly.

Something of his perplexity pervades the pages of *Moby-Dick*, his masterpiece. Few answers, many questions. Above all, the tragic question: What have the gods to do with man? Whatever the correct answer may be, we know that Ahab's was the wrong one. To rebel against one's destiny, to defy God, leads only, it is clear, to tragedy.

Melville's Use of Greek Myth in *Moby Dick*

Gerard M. Sweeney

Herman Melville uses allegory; literary, mythological, and biblical references; and other devices to reveal layers of meaning in his works. In this article, Gerard M. Sweeney focuses on Melville's use of Greek mythology; specifically, he compares Ahab, the captain of the *Pequod* in *Moby Dick*, to Prometheus, who steals fire from the gods to bring it to humanity. Sweeney claims that Melville patterned Ahab after Prometheus, and that by understanding the parallels we can more deeply understand Ahab's character and, ultimately, *Moby Dick* as a whole. Critic Gerard M. Sweeney is the author of the book *Melville's Use of Classical Mythology.*

No matter how the Romantics interpreted Prometheus, no matter how they transformed and re-created him into a heroic and humanitarian savior, unjustly tortured by a despotic tyrant, an attentive reading of *Prometheus Bound* reveals that Aeschylus conceived of his hero as a flawed sinner. Certainly he deserved admiration because of his fearlessness and massive will, but he was nevertheless a criminal, one who had sinned and who kept on sinning, one who underwent his deserved punishment with continued defiance and unregeneracy. "From Aeschylus to Calderon," according to Lewis Awad, "the role Prometheus played in the cosmos, regardless of our attitude toward that role, implied a high degree of sinfulness for which he was bound and from which he needed to be delivered.". . .

AHAB'S CRIME

[Melville] could not have read Aeschylus' *Prometheus* without recognizing—although perhaps admiring as well—the

From *Melville's Use of Classical Mythology* by Gerard M. Sweeney. Copyright 1975 Editions Rodopi N.V., Amsterdam. Reprinted by permission of the author.

fatal depravity in the heart of its hero. And this is precisely what the reader of *Moby-Dick* must grant Melville: that he had read his Aeschylus perceptively, that he knew who Prometheus was and what he was, and that, when he established the numerous connections between Prometheus and Ahab, he did so in full awareness of the Titan's flawed nature.

Prometheus and Ahab are both criminals. Prometheus stole, as Strength reminds Vulcan in the opening lines of *Prometheus Bound,*

> Thy radiant pride, the fiery flame, that lends
> Its aid to every art . . . and bore
> The gift to mortals; for which bold offence
> The gods assign him this just punishment;
> That he may learn to reverence the power
> Of Jove, and moderate his love to man.

The accusation capsules not only the specific crime of Prometheus, but also the character flaws underlying the crime: immoderation, or a failure to recognize and accept his limitations; and a willful disrespect for the deity. . . . One should note too that Prometheus' crime illustrates not merely his sinful defiance; it suggests as well, as C. Kerenyi claims [in *Prometheus*], a defect in his own being. "The theft of fire—because it is a theft—characterizes the thief as one whose existence is inherently deficient. . . . Neither Hephaistos nor Hermes had any need to steal fire. The darkness of Prometheus signifies precisely the deficiency of one who needs fire in order to achieve a more perfect form of being. In obtaining this higher form of being for man, Prometheus shows himself to be man's double, an eternal image of man's basically imperfect form of being." Ahab's crime consists in his defiant attempt to annihilate Moby Dick, a crime which, even on its surface, is comparable to the mythic theft of fire. For one thing the very business of whaling constitutes a theft of fire. Involving, as a number of readers have noted, the exploitation of nature, its goal is to obtain for men the sperm whale's oil, the fuel for their flames. Then too, the particular pursuit of the White Whale is significantly described by Ishmael as "the fiery hunt"; that it represents a conflict with a deity—such as Zeus or Jupiter—is made clear by the numerous references to Moby Dick as a god.

More importantly, one episode of *Moby-Dick*—the typhoon scene in "The Candles"—seems to be Melville's intentional re-creation of the mythic theft of fire. Prometheus' theft, as he describes it [in *Prometheus Bound*], was accomplished by the stealthy hiding of the divine spark in a fennel stalk.

> For favours shown
> To mortal man I bear this weight of woe;
> Hid in a hollow cane the fount of fire
> I privately conveyed, of every art
> Productive, and the noblest gift to men.

Ahab's "theft," in contrast, is a boldly defiant deed, set amidst elemental nature in furious eruption. (The setting much resembles the stark desolation of Aeschylus' Caucasus, the mountain on which Prometheus is chained, as it explodes with the wrath of Zeus.) The scene depicts corpusants settling on the *Pequod*'s masts, transforming each into a gigantic candle. Hereupon Ahab, his foot resting on the bowed Parsee, grasps the lightning chains. Then, as if dramatically responding to Ahab, the lightning attaches itself to his harpoon, "and from the keen steel barb there now came a levelled flame of pale, forked fire." Immediately Starbuck interprets the omen to signify divine disapproval and frantically begs Ahab to order an end to the voyage.

> Overhearing Starbuck, the panic-stricken crew instantly ran to the braces—though not a sail was left aloft. For the moment all the aghast mate's thoughts seemed theirs; they raised a half-mutinous cry. But dashing the rattling lightning links to the deck, and snatching the burning harpoon, Ahab waved it like a torch among them; swearing to transfix with it the first sailor that but cast loose a rope's end. Petrified by his aspect, and still more shrinking from the fiery dart that he held, the men fell back in dismay, and Ahab again spoke:

> "All your oaths to hunt the White Whale are as binding as mine; and heart, soul, and body, lungs and life, old Ahab is bound. And that ye may know to what tune this heart beats; look ye here; thus I blow out the last fear!" And with one blast of his breath he extinguished the flame.

In Ahab's grabbing the lightning chains and especially in his waving the fiery harpoon—in a way emblematic of all his actions—the reader should see Melville's modified equivalent of Prometheus' smuggling from heaven the fire-laden fennel stalk. It is a striking allusion, one which attests the degree to which Melville was thinking of Prometheus while shaping his conception of Ahab. Perhaps unconsciously, perhaps as a clue to the reader, Melville has Ahab admit he is "bound." (Four chapters later Starbuck will consider, but reject, the idea of binding Ahab in his cabin, and Fedallah will last be seen bound to the White Whale, foreshadowing Ahab's descent to the depths, also tied to Moby Dick.)

Ahab's fire-grabbing re-creates not only the external crime of Prometheus, but the internal crime as well. For although Prometheus' intention is to benefit men, while Ahab's is to coerce them, the essence of both heroes' actions is criminal defiance of the deity. As he addresses the corpusants, Ahab states his case against the god he originally worshipped in the form of fire. "Oh! thou clear spirit of clear fire, whom on these seas I as Persian once did worship, till in the sacramental act so burned by thee, that to this hour I bear the scar; I now know thee, thou clear spirit, and I now know that thy right worship is defiance.". . .

THE HUBRIS OF AHAB AND PROMETHEUS

Not only do Prometheus and Ahab believe they know the mind and workings of the powers above, they also propose to alter or reverse the supernatural design, and herein lies the acme of their tragic hubris. Erroneously convinced that Zeus planned the destruction of man, Prometheus stole fire in order to contravene the will of the god. (And even if Zeus had intended man's annihilation, the crime of Prometheus would still be the same.) His theft exemplified his fatal pride, and his continued refusal to obey the god, to give him the information he desires, is another manifestation of his defiant hubris. . . .

Ahab is infected with colossal pride. He reveals it in thinking that his intellect can penetrate the mystery of evil and even more so in thinking that, by killing Moby Dick, he can expel evil from the cosmos. Starbuck recognizes Ahab's hubris when he calls his goal "blasphemous," a "heaven-insulting purpose." Ishmael notes it too when he surveys Ahab after he has turned the ominously inverted compass needle: "In his fiery eyes of scorn and triumph, you then saw Ahab in all his fatal pride." And Ahab himself admits he is "proud as a Greek god," an admission that makes his pride even greater than Prometheus', since, while Ahab is merely a man, his classical counterpart was in fact a demi-deity. Moreover, Ahab's recognition of his hubris increases his culpability, since, instead of extirpating the sin, he glories in it.

Because of their hubristic activities, both heroes are accused of madness. The Chorus warns Prometheus not to let his love of man "o'erleap the bounds/ Of reason," but he persists in his rebellion, even when Mercury arrives to undertake a final attempt to make him relent.

MER. Thy malady, I find, is no small madness.
PRO. If to detest my enemies be madness,
    It is a malady I wish to have.
MER. Were it well with thee, who could brook thy pride?

Finally the messenger exclaims, totally frustrated with the Titan's continued defiance,

Such ravings, such wild counsels might you hear
From moon-struck madness. What is this but madness?

... Ahab's madness lies in a comparable dissociation from reality—the inscrutable reality of the White Whale—and it is therefore connected with his hubris; it involves his attempting to achieve a goal that is supernatural, that is beyond the limits set in reality for mortal man. So to Starbuck Ahab is "a madman," and his pursuit of Moby Dick is "madness." To Ishmael he is "crazy Ahab." And just as he recognizes his excessive pride, Ahab also realizes he is mad. "I'm demoniac," he soliloquizes, "I'm madness maddened!"...

WARNINGS

Both heroes, moreover, hear a number of direct verbal warnings, Prometheus from the Chorus, and Ahab from Starbuck. Although Prometheus receives explicit reproofs from Oceanus, as well as threats from Mercury and outright abuse from Strength and Force, the choric admonitions are the strongest, from the reader's point of view, since the Chorus sincerely sympathizes with the sufferings of the hero. . . .

ISHMAEL: THE IDEAL SPECTATOR

A number of critics have noted that Ishmael serves a chronic function in *Moby-Dick*. He is akin to the playwright's "ideal spectator," being on the stage throughout the tragedy (like the Greek chorus), observing and commenting on the conflict and the characters. His ever-present voice offers in this sense the narrative equivalent of the dramatic chorus. Ishmael also serves another traditional choric function by providing the audience with relevant factual information: background information on Ahab and discussions of cetology. More importantly, Ishmael is, like the Chorus of *Prometheus Bound*, sympathetic with the hero. In fact for a time he is even an accessory to Ahab's crime, having sworn with the others the blasphemous oath. Nonetheless, he is not completely caught up in Ahab's insanity: Melville wants us to be certain of this. Although Ishmael does take the oath—which he later formally rejects—he takes it in "the abandonment of the time and the place." Moreover, his reasons for battling Moby Dick are not Ahab's reasons. It is not the incarnate evil, but "The Whiteness of the Whale" that most appalls Ishmael. It is a reaction which he feels only "at times"—at other times he lauds the godlike and majestic beauty of the whale—and which, he painstakingly points out, is a common human and animal response. Thus while he sympathizes with and even praises Ahab, Ishmael can, like the Chorus of the *Prometheus*, frequently censure the hero. Furthermore, the narrator's philosophy seems to be most equatable with the author's. Ishmael's acceptance of the White Whale's inscrutability and of the mysteries that are ultimately unsolvable and his consequent acceptance of life's tragic nature appear to be Melville's. This of course is not to deny that Melville accepts these things reluctantly or that Ishmael's sympathy for Ahab—which is so intimately connected with his criticism—is not Melville's as well. . . .

AHAB'S PUNISHMENT

Melville was so influenced by the Aeschylean Prometheus story that he allusively linked Ahab's career not only to the crimes of the Titan, but to the punishments as well. Prometheus' punishment is a triple one, the first part occurring as the play opens when the Titan is chained to the rock. The second and third stages begin at the end of the play and are outlined to the hero by Mercury, threatening the protagonist for the last time.

> But mark me well,
> If not obedient to my words, a storm,
> A fiery and inevitable deluge
> Shall burst in threefold vengeance on thy head.
> First, his fierce thunder winged with lightning flames
> Shall rend this rugged rock, and cover thee
> With hideous ruin: long time shall thou lie
> Astonied in its rifted sides, till dragged
> Again to light; then shall the bird of Jove,
> The rav'ning eagle, lured with scent of blood,
> Mangle thy body, and each day returning,
> An uninvited guest, plunge his fell beak,
> And feast and riot on thy black'ning liver.

Ahab's punishment is clearly structured on Prometheus', but it is chronologically reversed: first he is attacked by Melville's equivalent of the Aeschylean "bird of Jove," and then he is sent to the lower depths, from which, unlike Prometheus, he will never rise.

Central to Melville's implicit comparison of the two punishments is the bird imagery which begins with Ishmael's description of Moby Dick appearing on the first day of the chase accompanied by "hundreds of gay fowl." "Like to some flag-staff rising from the painted hull of an argosy, the tall but shattered pole of a recent lance projected from the white whale's back; and at intervals one of the cloud of soft-toed fowls hovering, and to and from skimming like a canopy over the fish, silently perched and rocked on this pole, the long tail feathers streaming like pennons." Shortly later, "the grand god revealed himself, sounded, and went out of sight," and "the white sea-fowls lovingly lingered over the agitated pool that he left." An hour after this, anticipating Moby Dick's return to the surface, the birds begin "fluttering over the water ... wheeling round and round, with joyous, expectant cries." To enforce the point that these birds constitute a royal entourage of the Whale-as-Zeus, Melville explicitly links Moby Dick to the god by alluding to "the white bull Jupiter swimming away with ravished Europa." Other birds furnish still more specific correspondences. A red-billed sea-hawk—which seems Melville's equivalent of the "rav'ning eagle" of Jove—rips Ahab's hat from his head, and then another (or more likely the same one returning as the classical bird periodically returns) tears away the red flag flying from the ship's main mast. Ahab ironically links himself to the punishment of Prometheus by describing the Parsee's disappearance on the second day of the chase as "a riddle" that pecks his brain "like a hawk's beak." And finally, in light of the previous bird imagery, one should note the sharks that trail Ahab's boat on the last day. They follow "in the same prescient way that vultures hover over the banners of marching regiments in the east." Molesting none of the others, they pursue Ahab's boat alone, snapping at the oars.

Melville's repeated references to attacking birds of prey are doubtless intended to recall the punishment of Prometheus. But they should also remind us that Ahab suffers, like the Greek hero, from a recurring wound. The sufferings of Ahab and Prometheus are unlike those of other tragic heroes, such as Euripides' Pentheus or Sophocles' Ajax, who undergo a single punishment for a single crime. In contrast to these first offenders, Prometheus and Ahab are punished by repeated assaults that are consistent with their careers of unregenerate pride and defiance. The liver of Prometheus is eaten; then it regrows and is eaten again. Since the liver is considered the seat of the very passions which the hero permits to overrule his reason, the cyclical punishment is a fit emblem of his unregeneracy. The symbolic function of Ahab's leg wound is similar. He is dismasted once in his first encounter with Moby Dick; then on shore he breaks the ivory replacement; he later weakens the false leg when recklessly leaving the *Samuel Enderby*, having just received an additional warning from another amputee; and finally he again breaks the ivory replacement in his encounter with Moby Dick on the second day of the chase. Ahab's recurring leg wounds—considered with the fact that he still feels the pain of the absent limb—should be seen as Melville's equivalent of the wounded liver of Prometheus, eaten, regrown, and eaten again. Finally one should note that, while Ahab's on-shore injury clearly has sexual overtones, it also seems Melville's re-creation of an additional wound of Prometheus. Ahab's fall on shore so displaced his ivory leg that "it had *stake-wise smitten*, and all but pierced his groin." The allusive significance of this wound strikes the reader when he recalls that when Prometheus is chained to the rock he is further tormented by having a stake driven through his chest.

While Prometheus' punishment begins with his descent and Ahab's ends with his, the two descents—each being the catastrophe of the respective tragedy—are equatable in light of the context of each work. Prometheus is sent to Tartarus bound to his rock, just as Ahab sinks below the waves tied to the White Whale. In each tragedy, moreover, the hero's associates accompany him in his descent to the depths. The wrath of Zeus being imminent, the Chorus of the *Prometheus* is explicitly warned by Mercury to "remove with speed" from the scene.

> Remember you are warned; if ill o'ertake you
> Accuse not Fortune, lay not the blame on Jove,
> As by his hand sunk in calamities
> Unthought of, unforeseen: no, let the blame
> Light on yourselves; your folly not unwarned,
> Not unawares, but 'gainst your better knowledge,
> Involved you in th' inextricable toils.

The crew of the *Pequod* has received similar warnings, since they have witnessed the same omens and heard the same admonitions that Ahab has. Indeed, knowing the *Town-Ho's* tale of Radney and Steelkilt—a story Ahab is ignorant of—the crew has in fact received an additional warning. So like Aeschylus' Chorus, they sink into calamities that are not unforeseen. This is especially true of Starbuck, who performs so many of the choric functions. More than any of the others Starbuck is acting against his better knowledge. His better knowledge—or his reliable intuition—informs him, as he handles the musket outside Ahab's door, that "come to deadly harm, my soul swears this ship will, if Ahab have his way." But he refuses to act, and therefore the blame is partially his as he sinks, caught in the catastrophe of his Promethean captain.

From both tragedies, however, there exits a single wandering survivor, each of whom suggests a modicum of promise. Io will suffer the torments of the gadfly, but eventually she will settle and conceive a new race, the thirteenth descendent of which will be Hercules, who will free Prometheus from his chains (probably with the permission of Zeus and after some form of reconciliation between the Titan and the god). The promise embodied in Ishmael is that he attains a tragic acceptance, an acceptance which Ahab cannot reach. At the opening of *Moby-Dick*, as Bruce Franklin states, in "Hawthorne and Melville: The Unpardonable Sin," "Ishmael . . . is Ahab in miniature, isolated, defiant, obsessed. But, unlike Ahab, Ishmael changes in the course of the novel; the experience of the sea becomes for him an experience of purgation, purification." Like Noah—and like Deucalion, the son of Prometheus—Ishmael escapes the watery catastrophe which must be viewed as something like a deity's wrathful punishment of an impious man and his cohorts. But before he escapes Ishmael, like Io, suffers. Because of his involvement in Ahab's crime he is sucked into the black abyss, but is released just before the ultimate descent. So for the moments before his release, spinning in the vortex of the sinking *Pequod*, he is "like another Ixion," one of the few Greek sinners who, like Prometheus, was crucified.

Hindu Mythology in *Moby Dick*

H.B. Kulkarni

While Melville's use of Western mythology, especially
Greek and Roman myth and the Bible, has been
noted by many authors, H.B. Kulkarni argues that an
understanding of Hindu mythology is equally impor-
tant in reading *Moby Dick*. In the following article,
Kulkarni argues that Melville was very familiar with
contemporary works on Hinduism, and peppered
Moby Dick with references to the tradition in order to
elevate the novel into a "symbolic quest for God and
Truth." Kulkarni is the author of *Moby Dick: A Hindu
Avatar: A Study of Hindu Myth and Thought in Moby
Dick*, from which this article is excerpted.

Melville's references to Hindu myth and thought, however
peripheral to his works some have thought them to be, are
so numerous that there can be no doubt about his extensive
knowledge of Hinduism. The depth of his understanding,
however, has not been sufficiently explored.

"The only extant account of Melville as an academic student of Oriental mythologies," as James Baird points out, is
to be found in the memoirs of Maunsell Field. Field reports
Melville's conversation with Oliver Wendell Holmes on the
religions and mythologies of India, when he visited Melville
with his friend Darley in the summer of 1855:

> At length, somehow, the conversation drifted to East India re-
> ligions and mythologies, and soon there arose a discussion
> between Holmes and Melville, which was conducted with the
> most amazing skill and brilliancy on both sides. It lasted for
> hours and Darley and I had nothing to do but listen.

Though it is the only account, it is strong testimony for Melville's knowledge of India's religion and mythology.

Howard P. Vincent was, perhaps, the first to raise the
question about Melville's sources of such information,

specifically about Vishnu and his *Matse-Avatar*, mentioned in *Moby-Dick*: "Where did Melville learn about the Matse Avatar, as he called it in chapter 55, or about Vishnu in general?" Although Vincent knows that "a complete answer to this question seems impossible," he suggests and offers some evidence that Melville must have read *Indian Antiquities* (7 volumes) and *History of Hindostan* (3 volumes) by Reverend Thomas Maurice. It is also certain that Melville was familiar with the works of Sir William Jones, who was the first President of the Royal Society of Bengal and Calcutta and was a major promoter of scholarship and research in Asiatic life and letters. Melville mentions him by name in *Moby-Dick* and refers to his knowledge of thirty languages. His acquaintance with the works of these scholars is confirmed by Merton Sealts in his careful compilation of Melville's library.

But going beyond such specifics, it is certain that Melville would not have needed to go out of his way for information on the exotic East. Orientalism was indeed one of the major preoccupations of scholarship in Melville's time, and after the European mastery of Sanskrit and the establishment of correspondence among Indo-European languages, the reading world of America received a generous supply of books, pamphlets, and articles on India and the various aspects of its life and thought. Poole's *Index to Periodical Literature* of the first half of the nineteenth century lists thousands of items on India, Hindu mythology and religion, and allied matter. If this material did not form part of the regular diet of the common American, a sensitive and alert mind like Melville could not have missed encountering it in his normal reading of books and magazines:

> Melville was a voracious reader and he turned to books, magazines, newspapers as an experience, in their relevance to his art, equal to participation and observation; pictures impressed him as deeply as words. He used books for their music as well as for their ideas and information.

Recent critics of Melville seem to be in general agreement on Melville's extensive knowledge of Eastern mythology and religion:

> Melville read widely in the popular sources of mythology—modern periodicals and ancient and modern poetry, fiction, drama, and travel literature. He also read deeply in the central documents of the post-Renaissance mythology—the ponderous polemical tomes of learned heretics and divines. It

has been shown that Melville used as sources, for instance, an English translation of Bayle's *Dictionnaire* and the Reverend Thomas Maurice's *Indian Antiquities.*

Perhaps Melville's reading was neither scholarly nor academic. But it was definitely creative:

> As a man who had barely finished high school, he developed an extraordinary ability to extract the essence of ideas from slight intimations, assimilating his reading with an imaginative intensity not often to be found among "trained minds."

This study, then, assuming Melville's genuine interest in and more than adequate knowledge of Hindu myth and thought, will attempt to demonstrate that the vast amount of information which he picked up in his discursive reading sank into his mind and was transformed into a kind of feeling for things Oriental, which, instead of distorting facts, illuminated them with a native flavor that, perhaps, only a person born into the tradition can sense and understand. James Baird recognises this feeling in Melville, though he identifies it simply in broad terms as a genuine feeling for Primitivism which, he thinks, informs his symbols and makes his works a supreme example of Primitive Art. Baird is convinced that Melville had "an obsession with the primeval East." Melville's interest in Eastern mythology cannot be explained in terms of idle curiosity or desire for exotic novelty, for it is deeply embedded in his intense spiritual questioning and is an integral part of his artistic discipline looking for fresh and appropriate symbols as correlatives of his life's vision. Melville's quest can be understood in the light of Whitman's "Passage to India," for he may be described, in his own words, as a "thought diver" who strives to "*eclaircise* the myths Asiatic, the primitive fables" and in his exploration sounds "below the Sanscrit and the Vedas."

In recent years there have been some significant publications investigating in depth Melville's use of Oriental mythology. Among them, *The Wake of the Gods* by H. Bruce Franklin, *Melville's Orienda* by Dorothee Metlisky Finkelstein, and *Ishmael* by James Baird, referred to earlier, may be mentioned. . . .

In Melville, symbols taken from different mythologies of the world are set side by side with Biblical allusions. Sometimes they merge into one another. One does not eliminate the other, but they all by their juxtaposition, superimposition, and subtle interaction achieve a tremendous extension of metaphysical signification few narratives achieve. Melville presents a supreme example of mythological synthesis accomplished not by elimination but by assimilation of what appears to be its opposite. Did he not celebrate the marriage of a cannibal with a Christian at the very opening of *Moby-Dick* and direct the reader into this channel of synthesis? . . .

KEY PASSAGES ON HINDU MYTH

It is necessary at the very beginning of this study to take cognizance of the objections critics have raised against the relevance of Hindu myth to the structure and significance of *Moby-Dick*. Most critics have noted what may be called the key passages of Hindu myth, but they are either indifferent to them or feel unconcerned about their importance. That Melville should give a fairly detailed description of the story of Vishnu in two places is itself an indication that he did not intend it to be read and forgotten. While trying to present the "true form of this whale," he adverts to those "curious imaginary portraits of him" and describes the Hindu whale as the most ancient portrait available in the world:

> Now, by all odds, the most ancient extant portrait anyways purporting to be the whale's is to be found in the famous cavern pagoda of Elephanta, in India. The Brahmins maintain that in the almost endless sculptures of that immemorial pagoda, all the trades and pursuits, every conceivable avocation of man, were prefigured ages before any of them actually came into being. No wonder then, that in some sort our noble profession of whaling should have been there shadowed forth. The Hindoo whale referred to, occurs in a separate department of the wall, depicting the incarnation of Vishnu in the form of leviathan, learnedly known as the Matse Avatar.

In addition to this reference to the portrait of the Hindu leviathan at Elephanta, Melville mentions the context in which Vishnu incarnates himself as a fish and relates him to the whalemen's fraternity:

> That wondrous oriental story is now to be rehearsed from the Shaster which gives us the dread Vishnoo, one of the three persons in the godhead of the Hindoos; gives us this divine Vishnoo himself for our Lord:—Vishnoo, who, by the first of his ten earthly incarnations, has forever set apart and sanctified the whale. When Brahma, or the God of Gods saith the Shaster, resolved to recreate the world after one of its periodical dissolutions, he gave birth to Vishnoo, to preside over the work; but the Vedas, or mystical books, whose perusal would seem to have been indispensable to Vishnoo before beginning the creation, and which therefore must have contained some-

thing in the shape of practical hints to young architects, these Vedas were lying at the bottom of the waters; so Vishnu became incarnate in a whale, and sounding down in him to the utter-most depths, rescued the sacred volumes. Was not this Vishnoo a whalemen, then? even as a man who rides a horse is called a horseman?

... A close study of these passages shows that Melville was

THE SIGNIFICANCE OF WHITENESS

In the chapter "The Whiteness of the Whale," Ishmael gives a laundry list of the world's mythologies and how they all revere the color white, yet ends with the ways in which white is also terrifying. This excerpt gives just a sampling of Melville's extensive knowledge of world mythologies.

Whiteness has been even made significant of gladness, for among the Romans a white stone marked a joyful day; ... though even in the higher mysteries of the most august religions it has been made the symbol of the divine spotlessness and power; by the Persian fire worshippers, the white forked flame being held the holiest on the altar; and in the Greek mythologies, Great Jove himself being made incarnate in a snow-white bull; and though to the noble Iroquois, the mid-winter sacrifice of the sacred White Dog was by far the holiest festival of their theology, that spotless, faithful creature being held the purest envoy they could send to the Great Spirit with the annual tidings of their own fidelity; and though directly from the Latin word for white, all Christian priests derive the name of one part of their sacred vesture, the alb or tunic, worn beneath the cassock; ... yet for all these accumulated associations, with whatever is sweet, and honorable, and sublime, there yet lurks an elusive something in the innermost idea of this hue, which strikes more of panic to the soul than that redness which affrights in blood.

This elusive quality it is, which causes the thought of whiteness, when divorced from more kindly associations, and coupled with any object terrible in itself, to heighten that terror to the furthest bounds. Witness the white bear of the poles, and the white shark of the tropics; what but their smooth, flaky whiteness makes them the transcendent horrors they are? That ghastly whiteness it is which imparts such an abhorrent mildness, even more loathsome than terrific, to the dumb gloating of their aspect. So that not the fierce-fanged tiger in his heraldic coat can so stagger courage as the white-shrouded bear or shark.

familiar with numerous details regarding the Hindu myth
which he weaves so skillfully into the design of his novel. . . .

MELVILLE'S RIDICULE OF HINDU MYTH

H. Bruce Franklin's major objection to Hindu myth is based
on Melville's ridicule of it in the chapter entitled "Monstrous
Pictures of Whales." He states with unqualified emphasis:

> Melville's obvious ridicule of the Vishnu myth should be suf-
> ficient to discourage identification of Moby Dick with Vishnu.
> Indeed, Melville makes it clear that Vishnu is not to be taken
> as any fish at all.

But obviously Franklin has missed the whole point of Melville's ridicule. It is clear even in casual reading that Melville's ridicule is aimed not at any particular myth, Hindu or
Christian, but at what he calls "this whole blundering business" of picturing the whale. What Melville is clearly suggesting is that all pictorial representations of the whale are
"monstrous," for no one can ever paint the whale accurately.
Many have tried and all have failed, and the Egyptian is no
exception. The Hindus, the Egyptians, the Greeks, the Christians, the professionals, the non-professionals, the artists, and
even those who claim to be scientists have all been victims of
what Melville so aptly describes as "pictorial delusions":

> It may be that the primal source of all those pictorial delu-
> sions will be found among the oldest Hindoo, *Egyptian* [my
> italics], and Grecian sculptures. For ever since those inven-
> tive but unscrupulous times . . . something of the same sort of
> license prevailed, not only in most popular pictures of the
> whale, but in many scientific presentations of him."

Melville elaborates upon the manifold mistakes made in the
depiction of the whale and finally concludes by saying:

> For all these reasons, then, anyway you may look at it, you
> must needs conclude that the great Leviathan is the one crea-
> ture in the world which must remain unpainted to the last.
> True, one portrait may hit the mark much nearer than an-
> other, but none can hit it with any very considerable degree
> of exactness. So there is no earthly way of finding out what
> the whale really looks like.

It is clear that Melville's intention in this chapter on
"Monstrous Pictures of Whales" is not to condemn the
Hindu and Christian myths in order to commend and up-
hold the Egyptian myth, as Mr. Franklin would persuade us
to believe, but to show how all earthly attempts at picturing
the whale, including the Egyptian, are at best "authentic

abortions of the truth."

The impossibility of accurate description of the whale is an idea that persists through the novel. In the chapter on "Cetology," he underscores the idea:

> As yet, however, the sperm whale, scientific or poetic, lives not complete in any literature. Far above other hunted whales, his is an unwritten life.

Franklin makes much of the comic tone with which Melville describes the Vishnu myth and calls it "obvious ridicule." The lighthearted bantering tone of Melville which plays delicately upon most of the serious concerns of the novel deserves better approach than such quick disposal in terms like "ridicule." It is a complex technique aimed not at the thing "ridiculed," but at directing the reader's attention to some underlying significance. Here the comic technique is used to emphasize the metaphysical subtlety and cosmic amplitude of the Leviathan which naturally eludes the grasp of the painter's brush, the sculptor's chisel, or the poet's tongue. Behind the half-serious pose which Melville takes and the comic edge of many of his observations is the suggestive method of poetry, which achieves extension of meaning not by logic or rational argument but by psychological association. Therefore what takes the reader to the Egyptian myth is the very path of nuances and suggestions which can open the door to Vishnu myth and associate both of them to *Moby-Dick*. The solution does not really lie in exclusion but in inclusion which is, perhaps, a better approach to analysing the complex structure of the novel. . . .

VISHNU AND MOBY DICK

Franklin continues his objections to identifying Moby Dick with Vishnu by stating:

> In the Hindu myth, the fish incarnates the preserving power. Moby Dick is the Destroyer, and Melville's precise ridicule of the Matse Avatar forestalls any mythological mitigation of this fact.

As the question of ridicule has been satisfactorily answered, the problem of Vishnu being the preserving power may be considered. It is true that the common notion about Vishnu is that his function is to preserve. But he incarnates himself on earth in order to destroy evil and save the world from degeneration and ruin. The fish-incarnation is the first of Vishnu's ten incarnations, each of which is specifically undertaken to destroy the evil forces of the world. Moreover, in India destruction and creation are not regarded as exclusive terms at all. Wisdom lies in recognising the basic paradox of life, wherein destruction itself is creative. Maurice recognises the true spirit of India's philosophy and religion, when he says: "According to the philosophy of India, 'to *destroy* is only to *generate* and *reproduce* in another way.'"

Melville's vision of life does not admit of neat and simplified categories of destruction and creation, of life and death. If we recognise this, we will discover no incompatibility in identifying Vishnu and Moby Dick; for we cannot really say that one is a preserver, and the other, a destroyer. Melville is aware that Vishnu, the Preserver, does possess attributes of the Destroyer. He describes him as "dread Vishnoo" and in the same sentence calls him "divine Vishnoo." The same fusion of the opposite qualities is to be found in every one of his incarnations: he is tender and terrible and destroys to preserve. Similarly, Moby Dick, the Destroyer, is also not without creative qualities. Moby Dick, we all know, is a sperm whale. His value in commerce depends upon the fact that he is "the only creature from which that valuable substance, spermaceti, is obtained." "Spermaceti" may not actually be the seminal fluid, as the name suggests, but Melville considers it to be so and describes it as "the quickening humor." This fluid was not only used medically for rejuvenation, but also for lighting lamps on ships and in homes. Incidentally, Vishnu, who is supposed to have a thousand names, is called *Vishwaretah,* which means the semen of the universe. It is obvious that Melville intended Moby Dick to represent both the creative and destructive forces of life. . . .

The commingling of diverse mythical material turns whale-hunting into a symbolic quest for God and Truth by elevating the white whale to a cosmic symbol and by bringing into focus the entire history and prehistory of man's religious strivings, recreating imaginatively the mythological splendor and unity of the ancient world. James Baird rightly observes that "Moby Dick in his fullness becomes the whole of man's religious history."

Moby Dick Is an Allegory of Humanity's Struggle with God

William Braswell

In the following selection, William Braswell quotes a
French critic who summarizes the plot of *Moby Dick*
by saying that the "only reason Ahab tries to harpoon Moby Dick is that he cannot harpoon God."
Braswell argues that Ahab's quest to kill the white
whale is an allegory of man's quest for revenge on
God. Braswell is the author of *Melville's Religious
Thought*, a study of Melville's religious background
and its influence on his writing.

In his essay on "Hawthorne and His Mosses," Melville said
that "in this world of lies, Truth is forced to fly like a scared
white doe in the woodlands; and only by cunning glimpses
will she reveal herself, as in Shakespeare and other masters
of the great Art of Telling the Truth,—even though it be
covertly and by snatches." The various interpretations of
Moby-Dick testify to the difficulty of discovering the precise
meaning of the novel from the cunning glimpses of truth it
allows.... The interpretation given here, which agrees with
a number of others in the importance it attributes to certain
passages, confines itself to what seems significant for the
understanding of Melville's religious spirit at the time he
wrote the novel.

To come at once to the central problem, the meaning of
the allegorical conflict between Ahab and Moby Dick, Melville says explicitly what Moby Dick symbolizes for Ahab.
Ever since the combat in which the white whale bit off one
of Ahab's legs,

> Ahab had cherished a wild vindictiveness against the whale,
> all the more fell for that in his frantic morbidness he at last
> came to identify with him not only all his bodily woes, but all

his intellectual and spiritual exasperations. The White Whale swam before him as the monomaniac incarnation of all those malicious agencies which some deep men feel eating in them, till they are left living on with half a heart and half a lung. That intangible malignity which has been from the beginning; to whose dominion even the modern Christians ascribe one-half of the worlds; which the ancient Ophites of the East reverenced in their statue devil;—Ahab did not fall down and worship it like them; but deliriously transferring its idea to the abhorred White Whale, he pitted himself, all mutilated, against it. All that most maddens and torments; all that stirs up the lees of things; all truth with malice in it; all that cracks the sinews and cakes the brain; all the subtle demonisms of life and thought; all evil, to crazy Ahab, were visibly personified, and made practically assailable in Moby-Dick. He piled upon the whale's white hump the sum of all the general rage and hate felt by his whole race from Adam down; and then, as if his chest had been a mortar, he burst his hot heart's shell upon it.

The novel also plainly says that the assault on Moby Dick signifies more than a mere assault on evil. For evil is but an effect, and Ahab is interested in the primary cause. Reasoning by analogy, in the manner of divines arguing for God's beneficence, Ahab concludes that if good is to be attributed to the omnipotent Deity, so must evil. When gazing one day at a calm sea beneath "a smiling sky," he exclaims: "Look! see yon albicore! who put it into him to chase and fang that flying fish? Where do murderers go, man? Who's to doom, when the judge himself is dragged to the bar?" For him the visible world is but the manifestation of the spiritual: "... not the smallest atom stirs or lives on matter, but has its cunning duplicate in mind." When Ahab strikes at Moby Dick, the symbol of all spiritual as well as all physical evil, he does so in a mad desire for revenge on God, whom he holds responsible for its existence. Ahab explains this when he says to Starbuck:

All visible objects, man, are but as pasteboard masks. But in each event—in the living act, the undoubted deed—there, some unknown but still reasoning thing puts forth the mouldings of its features from behind the unreasoning mask. If man will strike, strike through the mask! How can the prisoner reach outside except by thrusting through the wall? To me, the White Whale is that wall, shoved near to me. Sometimes I think there's naught beyond. But 'tis enough. He tasks me; he heaps me; I see in him outrageous strength, with an inscrutable malice sinewing it. That inscrutable thing is chiefly what I hate; and be the White Whale agent, or be the White Whale principal, I will wreak that hate upon him.

HARPOONING GOD

A contemporary French critic got at the heart of the matter when he said that the only reason Ahab tries to harpoon Moby Dick is that he cannot harpoon God.

By various devices Melville makes the white whale an imposing symbol of divine power. The crazy Shaker prophet Gabriel pronounces Moby Dick to be "no less a being than the Shaker God incarnated." Although Moby Dick is represented as an agent for the first cause rather than as the first cause itself, to conceive of a god's being incarnate in a whale

SUPERNATURAL REVENGE

In this excerpt from Moby Dick, *narrator Ishmael ponders Ahab's reasons for pursuing the white whale, coming to the conclusion that it is a monomaniacal hatred too deep to penetrate.*

Ahab had purposely sailed upon the present voyage with the one only and all-engrossing object of hunting the White Whale. Had any of his old acquaintances on shore but half dreamed of what was lurking in him then, how soon would their aghast and righteous souls have wrenched the ship from such a fiendish man! They were bent on profitable cruises, the profit to be counted down in dollars from the mint. He was intent on an audacious, immitigable, and supernatural revenge.

Here, then, was this grey-headed, ungodly old man, chasing with curses a Job's whale round the world, at the head of a crew, too, chiefly made up of mongrel renegades, and castaways, and cannibals—morally enfeebled also, by the incompetence of mere unaided virtue or right-mindedness in Starbuck, the invulnerable jollity of indifference and recklessness in Stubb, and the pervading mediocrity in Flask. Such a crew, so officered, seemed specially picked and packed by some infernal fatality to help him to his monomaniac revenge. How it was that they so aboundingly responded to the old man's ire—by what evil magic their souls were possessed, that at times his hate seemed almost theirs; the White Whale as much their insufferable foe as his; how all this came to be—what the White Whale was to them, or how to their unconscious understandings, also, in some dim, unsuspected way, he might have seemed the gliding great demon of the seas of life,—all this to explain, would be to dive deeper than Ishmael can go.

is not unprecedented, as Melville was aware. Twice in the novel he refers to the oriental myth of "the incarnation of Vishnu in the form of leviathan." And he plays with the idea of a leviathan deity by asserting that "If hereafter any highly cultured, poetical nation shall lure back to their birth-right, the merry May-day gods of old; and livingly enthrone them again in the now egotistical sky; in the now unhaunted hill; then be sure, exalted to Jove's high seat, the great sperm whale shall lord it." He suggestively compares the white whale with Jupiter incarnate in a white bull, and even refers to the whale as "the grand god."

Moby Dick is invested with "terrors unborrowed from anything that visibly appears," and with some attributes unmistakably divine. Haunted by the legends about him, superstitious sailors believe him to be both ubiquitous and immortal. His intelligence is considered far superior to mere animal instinct: "... such seemed the White Whale's infernal aforethought of ferocity, that every dismembering or death he caused, was not wholly regarded as having been inflicted by an unintelligent agent." There is a supernatural awe in his whiteness, which "is at once the most meaning symbol of spiritual things, nay, the very veil of the Christian's Deity; and yet ... the intensifying agent in things the most appalling to mankind." At the end of the novel, just after the whale with "retribution, swift vengeance, eternal malice" in his aspect has rammed the ship, Ahab cries that the hull is "god-bullied.". . .

Since Ahab's attitude toward the Deity is precisely the opposite of Christlike submissiveness, it is ironically appropriate that the *Pequod* sets sail on Christmas Day. Ahab's incantation over the harpoon he tempers in savage blood is also in harmony with his defiance: "*Ego non baptizo te in nomine patris, sed in nomine diaboli.*" The omission of reference to the Son and the Holy Ghost emphasizes the fact that Ahab's feud is with God alone. As Ahab pursues the white whale, he continues venting his blasphemy, though in a veiled way. Since Melville was depending for his livelihood on the sale of his books in a Christian land, and since, moreover, he had no perverted desire to offend good Christian people, he caused Ahab to address his insulting remarks to "the gods," "the heavens," "thou clear spirit," and the like. What Ahab says makes it fitting that he should have been named after King Ahab of old, who, according to the Bible, "did more to provoke the Lord God of Israel to anger than all the kings of Israel that went before him." (He is like the scriptural Ahab also in that a prophetic Elijah foretells his doom.) . . .

FIRE AS SYMBOL

In another scene he calls the gods jacks-of-all-trades, and says that they are unprincipled. In the typhoon he becomes vulgar toward the Deity. "What a hooroosh aloft there!" he cries of the winds. "I would e'en take it for sublime, did I not know that the colic is a noisy malady. Oh, take medicine, take medicine!"

Some of Ahab's more serious charges against the Deity are made in the chapter entitled "The Candles," which tells how during the storm the corposants appeared: "All the yard-arms were tipped with a pallid fire; and touched at each tri-pointed lightning-rod-end with three tapering white flames, each of the three tall masts was silently burning in that sulphurous air, like three gigantic wax tapers before an altar." The symbolism implies what Melville goes on explicitly to say: "God's burning finger has been laid on the ship." Using fire as a symbol for the Deity might have been suggested to him by knowledge of Zoroastrianism, Heraclitus, the Stoics, the Bible, or various other sources.

Instead of being awed by this "Mene, Mene, Tekel Upharsin," Ahab defiantly brings charges against the Deity. One of them is suggestive of Gnostic influence. In primitive Christian times the Gnostics urged rebellion against the Creator of the universe. They taught that He is an emanation from a higher power, that He is ignorant of His genealogy, and that He tyrannically governs the world in the belief that He is the Supreme God. . . .

REASONS TO DEFY GOD

The most important comments that Ahab makes about God are those which give the reason for his defiance. By way of preface to the following quotation, Ahab's being burned in the act of worshiping fire, or God, on the high seas may be clarified by recalling that Melville uses exploring the seas to represent looking for the highest truth and that in *Pierre* he refers to fire as "an eloquent symbol" of the "ultimate Truth itself" (in *Moby-Dick* he says that "clear truth is a thing for salamander giants only to encounter"). Having fire symbolize both the Deity and the ultimate truth is not strange when one recalls the theological notion that God not only is true but is the Truth. As to Ahab's burn, he is described on his first appearance in the novel as bearing a long white scar like that which lightning sometimes makes in the trunk of a lofty tree. . . .

GOD IS WITHOUT LOVE

It is clear that Ahab conceives God to be without love for mankind. When Melville was completing *Moby-Dick*, he wrote to Hawthorne: "The reason the mass of men fear God, and *at bottom dislike* Him, is because they rather distrust His heart, and fancy Him all brain like a watch." Ahab typifies this dislike of God for His heartlessness. Looking upon the misery of the insane black boy Pip, Ahab exclaims: "There can be no hearts above the snow-line. Oh, ye frozen heavens! look down here. Ye did beget this luckless child, and have abandoned him, ye creative libertines." He says that Pip shall henceforth live with him, and Pip, clasping his hand, declares that he will never let go; whereupon Ahab cries: "Lo! ye believers in gods all goodness, and in man all ill, lo you! see the omniscient gods oblivious of suffering man; and man, though idiotic, and knowing not what he does, yet full of the sweet things of love and gratitude." Ahab's severity with his crew should not blind one to the fact that his pity for mankind motivates his hostility toward the Deity.

Ahab maintains that he is predestined to play the role that he plays. "This whole act's immutably decreed," he tells Starbuck. "'Twas rehearsed by thee and me a billion years before this ocean rolled. Fool! I am the Fates' lieutenant; I act under orders.". . .

ADMIRATION FOR AHAB

Though Melville makes it clear that Ahab is responsible for his doom, he also shows great admiration and sympathy for Ahab. Melville considered Hawthorne and himself men of great hearts and keen intellects. He represents Ahab as "a mighty pageant creature"—a man "with a globular brain and a ponderous heart." Some men do not have souls, but Ahab has enough "to make up for all deficiencies of that sort in other chaps"; to use his own bold figure, though his body has but one leg his "soul's a centipede, that moves upon a hundred legs." Possessed of keen perception, Ahab is unable to enjoy the common delights of men. His abnormal consciousness of the grief in the world has made him "impatient of all misery in others that is not mad.". . .

AHAB AS CHRIST

Ahab, one might say, has taken upon himself the suffering of mankind. In a way to remind one of Jesus Christ, he is pictured as standing before his men "with a crucifixion in his face; in all the nameless regal overbearing dignity of some mighty woe." The "Iron Crown of Lombardy" that he wears was made, as Geist observes, "of the nails used in the Crucifixion." Ahab feels as though he "were Adam, staggering beneath the piled centuries since Paradise." His attack on the evil symbolized by Moby Dick, together with this arraignment of God for permitting evil, is madly enacted in behalf of mankind. At the head of thirty-six foreigners, an "embassy of the human race," Anacharsis Clootz in 1790 spoke before the French Assembly for the rights of man. Melville refers to Ahab's crew as an "Anacharsis Clootz deputation from all the isles of the sea, and all the ends of the earth, accompanying Old Ahab in the *Pequod* to lay the world's grievances before that bar from which not many of them ever come back." Most men, like Stubb, laughingly refuse to think about the problem of evil; or, if they do think about it, solve it, like Starbuck, by letting "faith oust fact." If Ahab were not intellectually honest and courageous, if he were less affected by the suffering of mankind, he would not be the tragic figure he is. As it is, too much reflection on the problem of evil brings him to madness. . . .

MOBY-DICK AND MELVILLE'S ATTITUDES

Melville does not try to refute Ahab's criticism of the Deity as hardhearted. He does not say that God is loving and merciful. On the contrary, *Moby-Dick* contains evidence apart from what Ahab says that Melville thought of God as not wholly benevolent. The rhetorical apostrophe to "the great democratic God" is notable of Melville's democracy rather than of his adoration for a benevolent Deity. On the same page he says that "at the undraped spectacle of a valour-ruined man" piety itself cannot "completely stifle her upbraidings against the permitting stars": the thought behind the astrological figure is obvious. . . .

We have Melville's own testimony on the spirit in which he wrote the novel. During the final stages of work on it he declared in a letter to Hawthorne:

> Shall I send you a fin of the *Whale* by way of a specimen mouthful? The tail is not yet cooked, though the hell-fire in which the whole book is broiled might not unreasonably have cooked it ere this. This is the book's motto (the secret one), *Ego non baptiso te in nomine*—but make out the rest yourself.

We know from Ahab's incantation over his harpoon that the secret motto in full is: "*Ego non baptizo te in nomine patris, sed in nomine diaboli.*" In the letter Melville does not say that this is Ahab's motto; he says that it is the book's. And in a letter to Hawthorne just after *Moby-Dick* was published, Melville says: "I have written a wicked book, and feel spotless as the lamb." He does not say a book with a wicked character in it; he says a wicked book. And of course it was a wicked book according to the Christian world in which Melville and Hawthorne lived. Melville's inability to account for evil had made him conclude that the Christian conception of a wholly benevolent Deity is wrong, and he had arrived at the point where he could give full artistic expression to his heretical view without suffering pangs of conscience. Considering how far he had come from his early orthodox position, and how also the everlasting years of Carlyle, Emerson, and a host of others were ringing in his ears, there was reason for him to feel somewhat self-conscious, even though he was writing to a friend whom he believed to be, like himself, a thunderer of no.

Moby Dick Is an Allegory About the Unconscious

D.H. Lawrence

Novelist D.H. Lawrence is best known for his work *Lady Chatterley's Lover*, which caused a scandal when it was published in 1928 because of its sexually explicit content. Lawrence was greatly influenced by psychologists Sigmund Freud and Carl Jung, whose work focused on unconscious motivations for people's conscious acts. In this article, Lawrence argues that *Moby Dick* is an allegory of man's last mythological hunt, which ends with his becoming one with his environment.

Herman Melville's biggest book is *Moby Dick*, or *The White Whale*. It is the story of the last hunt. The last hunt, the last conquest—what is it?

American art symbolises the destruction, decomposition, mechanizing of the fallen degrees of consciousness.... [James Fenimore] Cooper and Melville [show] the deeper worship-through-contumely of the fallen sexual or sacral consciousness; [Edgar Allan] Poe the direct decomposition of this consciousness; and [Richard Henry] Dana and Melville the final hunting of the same consciousness into the very Matter, the very watery material, last home of its existence, and its extinction there. Remains the entry into the last state, and into fulness, freedom.

St. John said, "there shall be no more sea." That was esoteric. Exoterically, Dana and Melville say the same. The Sea, the great Waters, is the material home of the deep sacral-sexual consciousness. To the very depths of this home Melville pursues the native consciousness in himself, and destroys it here. When he has really destroyed this sacral-sexual consciousness, destroyed or over-thrown it, then

From *The Symbolic Meaning: The Uncollected Versions of "Studies in Classic American Literature"* by D.H. Lawrence, edited by Armin Arnold (New York: Viking; Fontwell, U.K.: Centaur Press, 1962). Reprinted by permission of Centaur Press.

John's prophecy will be fulfilled. There will be no more sea.

Moby Dick is the story of this last symbolic hunt. Moby Dick is a great white whale, the Leviathan of the waters. He is old, hoary, monstrous and snow-white; unspeakably terrible in his wrath; having been repeatedly attacked, he swims now alone in the great, pathless seas.

He is the last warm-blooded tenant of the waters, the greatest and last. He is the deep, free sacral consciousness in man. He must be subdued.

In himself he is warm-blooded, even lovable. But he must be conquered. Curious are his counterparts in the world. The whole of the South Pacific seems to worship, in hate, the shark or the crocodile, the great cold-blooded tenants, lords of the water, fiendish and destructive lords. Curious how shark and crocodile patterns, with grinning teeth, dominate aboriginal decoration-designs in those regions. The same crocodile worship is found in Africa, very widespread. In China, however, the dragon, the Leviathan is the dragon of the sun: as the Mantis, surely another dragon of the sun, dominates the Bushmen. Is not this the inordinately ancient relic of the pre-Flood worship, a relic from that era when the upper consciousness was the anathema [thing despised], and the glory and the triumph was all in the sensual understanding, incomprehensible to us now?

Melville writes in the peculiar, lurid, glamorous style which is natural to the great Americans. It gives us at first a sense of spuriousness. To some it merely seems wordy and meaningless, unreal. It comes, I think, from the violence native to the American Continent, where force is more powerful than consciousness, and so is never gracefully expressed. The life-force itself is so strong that it tends to come forth lurid and clumsy, obscure also. It causes also a savage desire to go to extremes, to hasten to extremes, whether of idealism or of violent action.

STRUCTURE

So, in beginning *Moby Dick*, we must be prepared for the curious lurid style, almost spurious, almost journalism, and yet *not* spurious: on the verge of falsity, still real. The book starts off with a semi-metaphysical effusion about water, and about the author's attraction to this element; it goes on with some clumsy humorisms, till it arrives in the sea-town of New Bedford. Then actual experience begins. It is curiously like cold material record, touched-up into journalese: neither veritable nor created. One cannot help feeling that the author is pretentious, and an amateur, wordy and shoddy. Yet something glimmers through all this: a glimmer of genuine reality. Not a reality of real, open-air experience. Yet it is a reality of what takes place in the dark cellars of a man's soul, what the psychoanalysts call the unconscious. There is the old double set of values: the ostensible Melville, a sort of Emersonian transcendentalist, and the underneath Melville, a sort of strange underworld, under-sea Yankee creature looking with curious, lurid vision on the upper world. It is the incongruous mixture of ideal heaven and the uncouth incoherence of a self-conscious adolescent. The reality comes from the adolescent, the uncouth, unformed creature, not from the idealist.

It is no use pretending that Melville writes like a straightforward, whole human being. He is hardly a human being at all. He gives events in the light of their extreme reality: mechanical, material, a semi-incoherent dream-rendering. What the futurists have tried hard to do, Dana and Melville have pretty well succeeded in doing for them. These two are masters of the sheer movement of substance in its own paths, free from all human postulation or control. The result is nearly like artifice, a sort of rank journalism. But we must restrain a too hasty judgment. The author is never quite himself. He is always at the mercy of the rank, self-conscious idealism which still rules white America, he always has to handle artificial values.

Melville tries to square himself with the intellectual world by dragging in deliberate transcendentalism, deliberate symbols and "deeper meanings." All this is insufferably clumsy and in clownish bad taste: self-conscious and amateurish to a degree, the worst side of American behavior. When however he forgets all audience, and renders us his sheer apprehension of the world, he is wonderful, his book commands a stillness in the soul, an awe.

Let us repeat that it is in rendering the sheer naked slidings of the elements, and the curious mechanical cause-and-effect of materials [sic] events, that he is a master. For near as he is to sheer materialism, the central creative spark is still unquenched, the integral soul is present, if alone. His mind lags far, far behind his physical comprehension. His mind is cumbered up with the hopeless aggregation of fixed ideas, which spin on together like little wheels. But his bodily knowledge moves naked, a living quick among the stark elements. In sheer physical, vibrational sensitiveness, like a marvelous wireless-station, he registers the effects of the outer world. And he records also, almost beyond pain or pleasure, the extreme transitions of the isolated, far-driven soul, the soul which is now alone, without human connection.

CHAPTER 4

Billy Budd

READINGS ON
HERMAN MELVILLE

Billy Budd Is a Tale of Acceptance

William Ellery Sedgwick

In the following selection, William Ellery Sedgwick claims that even though Billy Budd is a tragedy, the character of Billy is meant to offset this tragedy. Sedgwick believes that Billy's innocence, goodness, and natural charisma prove that human goodness compensates for all of the tragic, senseless evil in the world. Sedgwick authored the book Herman Melville: The Tragedy of Mind, *from which this article is excerpted.*

It is right and true to call *Billy Budd* Melville's "testament of acceptance"; but we must be careful not to understand either too much or too little by the word acceptance. Melville's "acceptance" was not based on any denial of the tragic facts of life or any ignorance of the inexorable logic of these facts. The world which we are shown in his last book is figuratively—as he had called it long before in *White-Jacket*—and literally, a man-of-war world, and the story of *Billy Budd* is as stark a tragedy as an American writer even to this day has ever penned.

The scene is an English man-of-war, the *Indomitable*, near the close of the eighteenth century, when conservative England and revolutionary France were locked in mortal combat. The hero, a young English sailor, is hanged for an act which his superiors, bound by the articles of war, have to adjudge a crime for which hanging was the only commensurate punishment, but which, in reality, far from being evil, was like the swift retributive stroke of an indignant angel.

Billy is the handsome sailor—guileless, good-natured, loving and beloved. Opposite him, like the bad angel against the good angel in an old morality, is the ship's police officer or master-of-arms, John Claggart. Out of apparently motive-

From *Herman Melville: The Tragedy of Mind* by William Ellery Sedgwick (Cambridge, MA: Harvard University Press, 1944). Copyright 1944 by the President and Fellows of Harvard College. Reprinted by permission of the publisher.

less malice, Claggart is down on Billy and trumps up a charge against him. In the captain's cabin, in the presence of the captain, he accuses Billy of trying to incite the crew to mutiny. Now Billy has one deformity; he stammers. Bewildered and outraged, he cannot find the words to defend himself and repel Claggart's accusation. His whole being rises, and, since words fail him, he takes other means to express himself. Quick as a flash and with the force of a cannon shot, he drives his right fist at Claggart's jaw and floors him. A few moments later the ship's surgeon pronounces the master-at-arms dead. "It is the divine judgment of Ananias," Captain Vere exclaims to the astonished surgeon; but again starting, he vehemently exclaimed, "Struck dead by an angel of God. Yet the angel must hang." From this point on the interest centers in Captain Vere as he faces the dilemma which flashed upon him in these words.

Of the captain's character something more should be told. He is an excellent officer; there are few better than he in His Majesty's service. While always mindful of the welfare of his men, he will not tolerate any infraction of discipline. . . .

VERE

Being the man he is in the position he occupies, Captain Vere acts promptly in the emergency which has taken place before his eyes. He immediately summons his lieutenants to sit in court martial on Billy Budd. Captain Vere's directions to his court martial cannot be overlooked. They bring out a point of special urgency as they also show his character in action. Of Claggart's inexplicable malice, which provoked Billy to strike him, the captain says, "Ay, there is a mystery; but to use a Scriptural phrase, it is 'a mystery of iniquity'; a matter for psychological theologians to discuss. But what has a military court to do with it?" Nor is the question of Billy's intent or non-intent pertinent. "The prisoner's deed, with that alone we have to do." Neither the speculative mind nor the heart has any business here; "the heart is the feminine in man and hard though it be, she must here be ruled out." Captain Vere understands the compunctions that his fellow officers must feel, and he reviews them; "In natural justice is nothing but the prisoner's overt act to be considered? Now can we adjudge to summary and shameful death a fellow-creature innocent before God and whom we feel to be so?— Does that state it aright? You sign sad assent. Well, I too feel

that, the full force of that. It is Nature. But do these buttons
that we wear attest that our allegiance is to Nature? No, to the
King. Though the ocean, which is inviolate Nature primeval,
though this be the element where we move and have our

ENVY

*From the moment he first spies Billy, Claggart tries to undo
him. In this excerpt from* Billy Budd, *the narrator speculates
as to why Claggart is so envious of Billy. Melville's comparison of Claggart to a snake, and therefore a sort of Satan figure, is evident.*

Now envy and antipathy, passions irreconcilable in reason, nevertheless in fact may spring conjoined like Chang
and Eng in one birth. Is Envy then such a monster? Well,
though many an arraigned mortal has in hopes of mitigated
penalty pleaded guilty to horrible actions, did ever anybody
seriously confess to envy? Something there is in it univer-
sally felt to be more shameful than even felonious crime.
And not only does everybody disown it, but the better sort
are inclined to incredulity when it is in earnest imputed to
an intelligent man. But since its lodgment is in the heart not
the brain, no degree of intellect supplies a guarantee against
it. But Claggart's was no vulgar form of the passion. Nor, as
directed toward Billy Budd, did it partake of that streak of
apprehensive jealousy that marred Saul's visage perturbedly
brooding on the comely young David. Claggart's envy struck
deeper. If askance he eyed the good looks, cheery health,
and frank enjoyment of young life in Billy Budd, it was because these went along with a nature that, as Claggart mag-
netically felt, had in its simplicity never willed malice or experienced the reactionary bite of that serpent. To him, the
spirit lodged within Billy, and looking out from his welkin
eyes as from windows, that ineffability it was which made
the dimple in his dyed cheek, suppled his joints, and dancing in his yellow curls made him pre-eminently the Handsome Sailor. One person excepted, the master-at-arms was
perhaps the only man in the ship intellectually capable of
adequately appreciating the moral phenomenon presented
in Billy Budd. And the insight but intensified his passion,
which assuming various secret forms within him, at times
assumed that of cynic disdain, disdain of innocence—to be
nothing more than innocent! Yet in an aesthetic way he saw
the charm of it, the courageous free-and-easy temper of it,
and fain would have shared it, but he despaired of it.

being as sailors, yet as the King's officers lies our duty in a sphere correspondingly natural?" No, for "in receiving our commissions we in the most important regards ceased to be natural free agents. When war is declared, are we the commissioned fighters previously consulted? We fight at command. . . . So now, would it be so much we ourselves that would condemn as it would be martial law operating through us? For that law and the rigor of it, we are not responsible. Our vowed responsibility is in this: that however pitilessly that law may operate, we nevertheless adhere to it and administer it. . . . But while, put to it by those anxieties in you which I cannot but respect, I only repeat myself—while thus strangely we prolong proceedings which should be summary, the enemy may be sighted and an engagement result. We must do; and one of two things must we do—condemn or let go."

Captain Vere reminds the court of the larger situation which they must keep in mind. Their country is at war with another power; conservative England is threatened from without and from within. The sparks from the French Revolution have crossed the Channel. Mutinies have flared up in the English navy—there has been the mutiny at the Nore, the so-called Great Mutiny—and, although quelled, these outbreaks might be repeated at any moment. Hence, more than ever, His Majesty's officers are bound to insist on all points of discipline. A clement sentence in the case of Billy Budd might be construed as timidity and encourage insurrection. Says Captain Vere, turning the case over to his subordinates, "You see then whither, prompted by duty and the law, I steadfastly drive. But I beseech you, my friends, do not take me amiss."

The other officers "hardly had the inclination to gainsay one whom they felt to be an earnest man, one, too, not less their superior in mind than in naval rank." Billy is convicted and sentenced to hanging at the yard arm in the early morning watch, it now being night. The next morning, just at daybreak, the sentence was carried out. . . .

NATURE AND THE WORLD

Of all the ship's company only Captain Vere and Claggart were "intellectually capable of adequately appreciating the moral phenomenon presented in Billy Budd." As for Claggart, as Captain Vere had the insight to discern, in him there was the opposite mystery to Billy's, "the mystery of iniquity." What, Melville asks, "can more partake of the mysterious than the antipathy spontaneous and profound such as is invoked in certain exceptional mortals by the mere aspect of some other mortal, however harmless he be?—if not called forth by that harmlessness itself." Normal human nature affords no explanation of such a one as Claggart, who is at once an object of pity and of the profoundest loathing. He and his kind are free of vulgar vices. He is, says Melville, borrowing a definition attributed to Plato, a case of "Natural Depravity; a depravity according to nature." Melville explains that this is not the same as Calvin's total depravity, because it does not apply to all mankind, but only to certain individuals. This much Melville has to say about the origin of evil. But his interest in his last book is not primarily speculative or metaphysical. It is enough for him that the mysterious facts are confronted—are confronted honestly and honorably.

Melville distinguishes between nature and the world. Primeval nature is good. The world is not under nature's rule. Not nature, not love, but necessity, or fate, rules the world. It is a man-of-war's world and we all fight at command. Idealism which would throw off this yoke of necessity only leads to more misery for man. Of the last decade of the eighteenth century, when the story takes place, Melville wrote, "The opening proposition made by the Spirit of that Age involved the rectification of the Old World's hereditary wrongs. In France, to some extent, this was bloodily effected. But what then? Straightway the Revolution itself became a wrongdoer, one more oppressive than the kings. Under Napoleon it enthroned upstart kings, and initiated that prolonged agony of continual war whose final throe was Waterloo." However unintelligible and arbitrary, there is an organic necessity in the world and it cannot be disregarded. A principle of limitation, it is, nevertheless, also a principle of self-preservation. Even where it allows some latitude for choice, men are wise to conform with it by supplementing it with forms and definitions of their own. Captain Vere only repeats Melville's own, now settled conviction, "With mankind . . . forms, measured forms, are everything; and that is the import couched in the story of Orpheus with his lyre spellbinding the wild denizens of the woods." And "this he once applied to the disruption of forms going on across the Channel and the consequences thereof.". . .

VERE'S SOUL

As an index to Melville's "acceptance," Captain Vere is still more interesting as he faces his own soul. He is obliged by the exigencies of this man-of-war world to disregard all considerations of the absolute good and the ultimate truth. But he does not therefore deny the existence of the absolute good and the ultimate truth. He is the first to recognize Billy's angelic innocence. In the present emergency his innocence cannot excuse the consequences of his act: "We proceed under the law of the Mutiny Act." But he has said, "At the Last Assizes it shall acquit." In his dilemma Captain Vere does not arraign God as a devil-god; nor does he conclude, according to *Pierre*, "that whatever other worlds God may be Lord of, he is not the Lord of this." The words occur in the Plinlimmon pamphlet, and in *Pierre* Melville could not bring himself to accept Plinlimmon's relativistic doctrine of virtue in this world. Like his hero, he would have all or nothing and, like his hero, he got nothing; or, because his imagination could not picture nothing, he got worse than nothing: "Now, 'tis merely hell in both worlds."

As Plinlimmon wrote, "What man who carries a heavenly soul in him, has not groaned to perceive, that unless he committed a sort of suicide as to the practical things of this world, he can never hope to regulate his earthly conduct by the same heavenly soul? And yet by an infallible instinct he knows, that that monitor cannot be wrong in itself." So it was with Captain Vere. As for Melville, it can be said that he has accepted the human predicament,—which follows inevitably from the dualism of human nature.... Now he sees that because a man acts under a worldly necessity he does not therefore debase his humanity: his soul, be it immortal or not, is not soiled thereby. And because a man has accepted the limitations of his nature he is not therefore lacking in human strength and dignity, and is not to be relegated, as we feel that Melville, in the presence of Ahab could not but relegate Starbuck, on the score of "the incompetence of mere unaided virtue or right-mindedness." Further than this he sees that it is possible to be in this world and not of it; that because a man has taken on the burden of human consciousness, with its sad knowledge of good and evil, he is not therefore excommunicated from primal goodness.

Between Billy's instinctive rectitude, that of an upright barbarian, and such as Adam's might have been "ere the urbane Serpent wriggled himself into his company," and Captain Vere's conscious human rectitude there is no estrangement. Far from that, there is a profound reciprocal understanding between the two.

> Fair encounter
> Of two most rare affections! Heavens rain grace
> On that which breeds between them!

It was Captain Vere who, of his own motion, communicated the death sentence to Billy. As to what transpired then, between these two, "each radically sharing in the rarer qualities of one nature," Melville would no more than hint. Captain Vere was old enough to have been Billy's father. "The austere devotee of military duty, letting himself melt back into what remains primeval in our formalized humanity, may in the end have caught Billy to his heart, even as Abraham may have caught young Isaac on the brink of resolutely offering him up in obedience to the exacting behest. But there is no telling the sacrament... wherever under circumstances at all akin to those here attempted to be set forth—two of great Nature's nobler order embrace." The next morning when Billy stood up for execution before the crew, his last words were "God bless Captain Vere." Not long afterward Captain Vere, dying of a wound received in an engagement with the enemy, was heard to murmur words inexplicable to his attendant, "Billy Budd, Billy Budd."

It is possible to see in these intimations the reflection of a heavenly mystery, in which the idea of divine love, as attributed to Christ, is reconciled with the known facts of the rough justice which overrules the world. There is a suggestion of such a reconciliation in terms of Christianity inasmuch as it is just hinted that Billy Budd, a foundling, was in truth, the son of Captain Vere. It should be mentioned, too, since no fact in the story is without some symbolical significance, that the enemy's ship which Captain Vere engaged and overcame, at the cost of his life, formerly named the *St. Louis*, had, by the revolutionary government of France, been re-christened the *Athéiste*. Furthermore, it is impossible not to see in Billy's execution a resemblance to the Crucifixion. Long after his death, his comrades "recalled the fresh young image of the Handsome Sailor, that face never deformed by a sneer or subtler vile freak of the heart within! This impression of him was doubtless deepened by the fact that he was gone, and in a measure mysteriously gone." The spar from which he was hanged was reverently kept track of even long after it had been discarded. To those who had known Billy "a chip of it was as a piece of the Cross." At the moment of his death before the assembled crew, "it chanced that the vapory fleece hanging low in the east, was shot through with a soft glory as of the fleece of the Lamb of God seen in mystical vision, and simultaneously therewith, watched by the wedged mass of upturned faces, Billy ascended; and ascending, took the full rose of the dawn."

MAN'S NATURE IS GOOD

It may be that the visitations of man's best nature signify a more than human reality. It may be that such innocence and goodness as blazed in Billy's heart have a sanction from a higher quarter than the tribunals of this world. Melville does not say. "Doubts of all things earthly,"—that is, doubts of all earthly beliefs and conclusions,—and "intuitions of some things heavenly,"—that was Melville's state of mind in his last book; a state of suspended belief and unbelief, in which, as I quoted Keats as saying, there is no "irritable reaching after facts and reason."

For the rest, in the "testament of acceptance," Melville ascribes a constitutional soundness to humanity. Insofar as it was provoked by wilful idealists, the French Revolution led to worse oppression than before. But taking a long view of it and seeing it as an infection coming to a head in a frame so constitutionally sound as to be able to throw it off, it had a salutary effect which "not the wisest could have foreseen" at the time. In a way "analogous to the operation of the Revolution at large, the Great Mutiny, though by Englishmen naturally deemed monstrous at the time, doubtless gave the first latent prompting to most important reforms in the British navy." Moreover, there is that in the foreground of the story which attests the constitutional soundness of humanity. Between normal human nature and a being like Claggart there is a gap, a "deadly space between." The sailors instinctively distrust him and are repelled by him. Whereas to Billy they respond spontaneously. They are drawn together around him as around a bon fire on a cold day and are stirred to acts of good nature by his cordial influence. . . .

In Billy's life there is more promise of salvation for the world than there is of damnation in his death. And Melville has partaken of its salvation. His intellectual passion spent, and illuminated by his insight of a mind which by accepting its limitations has transcended them and has found within itself, at its own mysterious centre, a calm not to be found elsewhere, Melville has been restored to the radiant visage of life, whose shining secret is, it has its salvation in its own keeping.

Billy Budd Is a Rebel

John Bernstein

John Bernstein graduated from Princeton University and is a professor of English at Macalester College in St. Paul, Minnesota. In the following selection, Bernstein argues that Melville intended *Billy Budd* as a story of rebellion against the constraints of society. Although Bernstein contends that Melville implicitly criticizes both Vere and Billy, Melville finds rebellion a route preferable to following society's arbitrary rules.

"That's rebellion," murmured Alyosha, looking down. "Rebellion? I am sorry you call it that," said Ivan earnestly. "One can hardly live in rebellion, and I want to live. Tell me yourself, I challenge you—answer. Imagine that you are creating a fabric of human destiny with the object of making men happy in the end, giving them peace and rest at last, but that it was essential and inevitable to torture to death only one tiny creature—that baby beating its breast with its fist, for instance—and to found that edifice upon its unavenged tears, would you consent to be the architect on those conditions? Tell me, and tell the truth." "No, I wouldn't consent," said Alyosha softly.

Dostoyevsky, *The Brothers Karamazov*

In *Billy Budd* Melville . . . condemns not only Claggart, but Captain Vere and perhaps even Billy as well, and that though the work is strongly anti-war, the ultimate message, first stated in the Preface, is a call to rebellion, not only philosophical rebellion but violent revolution if necessary.

The seeds for the tragedy of *Billy Budd* are sown when the hero is seized aboard the merchant ship, the *Right-of-Man*, and impressed into service on the British warship, the H.M.S. *Indomitable*. Billy's transfer represents more than a mere change of scenery, for the differences between the two ships are the differences between two worlds with conflicting sets of values, and the young sailor is destroyed because

From *Pacifism and Rebellion in the Writings of Herman Melville* by John Bernstein (The Hague: Mouton, 1964). Reprinted by permission of the author.

he is unable to adjust to the more complex and sinister life on the *Indomitable.*

The *Rights-of-Man,* as the name indicates, is a place in which the rights of every individual are respected. It symbolizes at once an unfallen world in which inherent evil does not exist, and also a primitive world, such as the Valley of the Typees, where man is governed not by a codified set of laws, but by natural law. Billy, who "in the nude might have posed for a statue of young Adam before the Fall" and who is "a sort of upright barbarian, much such perhaps as Adam presumably might have been ere the urbane serpent wriggled himself into his company," is eminently suited for life aboard such a ship as the *Rights-of-Man.* Because of his physical beauty and moral purity, Billy emerges as a natural leader among the crew of this vessel. "Ashore he was the champion; afloat the spokesman; on every suitable occasion always foremost." And, as Captain Graveling remarks to Lieutenant Ratcliffe, the officer who impresses young Budd, Billy is the peacemaker aboard the *Rights-of-Man.*

The world represented by the H.M.S. *Indomitable* is antithetical to Billy's former ship. To begin with, the *Indomitable* is not a vessel of commerce but a ship of war, and as such, is subjected to much the same sort of condemnation as is the *Neversink* in *White-Jacket....* Life on the merchant vessel was governed by the rights of man. Aboard the *Indomitable,* the Articles of War, which have no concern with right or wrong but merely with expediency and which are highly arbitrary, prevail. Under these Articles, the individual has few rights, as Billy's impressment demonstrates, and man is regarded not as a free and thinking being, but merely as a pawn of the King's.

GOOD VERSUS EVIL

Most important of all, however, there exists a type of evil on the warship which was lacking aboard the *Rights-of-Man.* This is embodied in Claggart, the Master-at-Arms, "in whom was the mania of an evil nature, not engendered by vicious training or corrupting books or licentious living, but born with him and innate, in short, 'a depravity according to nature.'" As we have seen, Billy is described as being similar to Adam before the Fall. This Biblical imagery is further developed by Claggart, who assumes the role of the Serpent in the Garden of Eden. (The Master-at-Arms looks at Billy with "serpent fascination," and when Billy and Captain Vere attempt to lift Claggart's corpse, "it was like handling a dead snake."

The Adam-like Billy is an easy victim for the serpent-like Claggart. The young man is so innocent and naive that he is unable to perceive evil, much less to cope with it. Billy's dilemma is instantly recognized by the aged Dansker, who speculates "as to what might eventually befall a nature like that, dropped into a world not without some man-traps and against whose subtleties courage lacking experience and address without any touch of defensive ugliness, is of little avail." When small things start going wrong for Billy— something awry with his hammock or the storage of his gear—he appeals to the oracular Dansker for advice. The old man comments that *"Jemmy Legs"* (a nickname for Claggart), is down on him. Such sinister subtlety completely eludes the young sailor. "'*Jemmy Legs*!' ejaculated Billy his welkin eyes expanding; 'what for? Why he calls me *the sweet and pleasant young fellow*, they tell me.'"

But *Jemmy Legs* is indeed down on Billy, so much so that the Master-at-Arms concocts an elaborate plot and accuses young Budd of planning mutiny. This is a particularly serious charge in the year 1797, the time in which the story is set, for England is not only at war with France, but the British Navy has been rocked with a series of mutinies. When Captain Vere hears this accusation, he summons Billy to his cabin in order for the youth to hear Claggart's charges face to face. Now Billy has one flaw in his otherwise flawless make-up: he stutters. When Claggart repeats his slander, Captain Vere urges Billy to speak in his own defense. But Billy, unable to protect himself in the face of evil, cannot speak. Captain Vere, realizing the problem, tells Billy to take as much time to reply as he needs. But the usually pacifistic Billy still can't utter a word. "The next instant, quick as the flame from a discharged cannon at night, his right arm shot out, and Claggart dropped to the deck." After Captain Vere affirms that the Master-at-Arms has been killed by this blow, he exclaims "'Struck dead by an angel of God. Yet the angel must hang.'"

This rapid evaluation by the *Indomitable*'s captain not only neatly summarizes the basic tension of *Billy Budd*, but sheds a great deal of light on the character of Vere himself. What kind of a man is this who can so quickly size up a situation and so quickly pass judgment? . . .

Captain Vere is a wise man, "mindful of the welfare of his men, but never tolerating an infraction of discipline." Vere's wisdom springs from three sources—from his own personal experience, from his vast reading ("books treating of actual men and events no matter what era—history, biography, and unconventional writers, who, free from cant and convention, like Montaigne, honestly and in the spirit of common sense philosophize upon realities.") . . .

Vere's wisdom is coupled with goodness. Throughout Billy's ordeal, he shows a consummate kindness to the young sailor, so much so, that, during the trial when Billy becomes confused, he turns "an appealing glance towards Captain Vere as deeming him his best friend and helper." After Billy has been sentenced, Vere makes an unprecedented visit to the compartment of the condemned foretopman, and exists from this interview in a greater state of suffering than the prisoner himself. . . . Despite Captain Vere's kindly and paternal feelings towards Billy (Melville likens the older man's attitude toward the condemned youth to Abraham's compassion for Isaac), he nevertheless believes that the young seaman must hang, for since the British Navy is not only involved in a war, but threatened by rebellion from within, to allow the killing of an officer to go unpunished would encourage mutiny among the British sailors and might eventually lead to an overthrow of the entire English system. Moreover, such punishment must be immediate. Thus Vere's sense of duty wins out over his sense of compassion, and he argues to the hastily summoned drumhead court that Billy must be sentenced to death. Chronometrical law must be ignored if the law of man is to survive, as Vere attempts to make clear to the confused and unphilosophical members of the court. . . .

VERE'S DECISION IS EVIL

Though compassionate and kindly as Vere may be, though his plea for Billy's execution is honest, painful, and carefully thought out, the Captain advocates an evil and wrong verdict. Melville is no more able to accept a system founded upon the sacrifice of an innocent babe than is Ivan Karamazov, the intellectual hero of Dostoyevsky's monumental novel *The Brothers Karamazov,* a work which deals with virtually the same theme as does *Billy Budd* and which comes to somewhat the same conclusions. If a system can exist

"FATED BOY"

In this excerpt from Billy Budd, *Captain Vere demands that Billy answer Claggart's accusations against him. Because of his stutter, Billy ends up killing Claggart. Many of the main themes in* Billy Budd *are revealed here, including Melville's likening of Billy to Christ.*

"Speak, man!" said Captain Vere to the transfixed one, struck by his aspect even more than by Claggart's. "Speak! Defend yourself!". . .

Though at the time Captain Vere was quite ignorant of Billy's liability to vocal impediment, he now immediately divined it, since vividly Billy's aspect recalled to him that of a bright young schoolmate of his whom he had once seen struck by much the same startling impotence in the act of eagerly rising in the class to be foremost in response to a testing question put to it by the master. Going close up to the young sailor, and laying a soothing hand on his shoulder, he said, "There is no hurry, my boy. Take your time, take your time." Contrary to the effect intended, these words so fatherly in tone, doubtless touching Billy's heart to the quick, prompted yet more violent efforts at utterance—efforts soon ending for the time in confirming the paralysis, and bringing to his face an expression which was as a crucifixion to behold. The next instant, quick as the flame from a discharged cannon at night, his right arm shot out, and Claggart dropped to the deck. Whether intentionally or but owing to the young athlete's superior height, the blow had taken effect full upon the forehead, so shapely and intellectual-looking a feature in the master-at-arms; so that the body fell over lengthwise, like a heavy plant tilted from erectness. A gasp or two, and he lay motionless.

"Fated boy," breathed Captain Vere in tone so low as to be almost a whisper, "what have you done! But here, help me."

The twain raised the felled one from the loins up into a sitting position. The spare form flexibly acquiesced, but inertly. It was like handling a dead snake.

---

only if its most innocent and just members must be sacrificed, then this system is not worth preserving. Though white civilized man might be appalled at the conclusion that it is better for an innocent man to be spared and society to collapse completely with all the resulting anarchy than it is for society and its institutions to be preserved at the cost of one of its members, this is nonetheless the direction towards which Melville is inexorably pointing in *Billy Budd.*

Though there is no criticism of Vere's integrity, his decision as to the necessity of sacrificing Billy to preserve the law is sharply attacked by Melville. When the Surgeon is summoned into Vere's cabin to ascertain whether Claggart is dead, something in the Captain's attitude makes him wonder if Vere's mind has suddenly become affected. The Surgeon's doubts are echoed and re-echoed in the succeeding pages. "Whether Captain Vere, as the Surgeon professionally and primarily surmised, was really the sudden victim of any degree of aberration, one must determine for himself by such light as the narrative may afford." Even Vere's fellow officers question his wisdom in these proceedings. "Certain it is however that subsequently in the confidential talk of more than one or two gun-rooms and cabins he was not a little criticized by some officers." Nevertheless, it must be emphasized—as the Captain himself stresses—that Vere is acting not through his own volition but as an agent of martial law. The fact that Vere is such a good man makes it even more clear that the responsibility for Billy's death lies with such arbitrary codes as the Articles of War and the Mutiny Act rather than with any specific individual.

I have earlier suggested that Melville takes not only Captain Vere to task, but Billy Budd as well. Moreover, in his criticism of Billy, we find perhaps Melville's most subtle attack on Christ. There is little doubt that by the end of the novel, Billy has acquired Christ-like characteristics. Claggart's accusations bring to Billy's face "an expression which was as a crucifixion to behold." At the moment that Billy is hanged,

> it chanced that the vapory fleece hanging low in the East, was shot through with a soft glory as of the fleece of the Lamb of God seen in mystical vision and simultaneously therewith, watched by the wedged mass of upturned faces, Billy ascended, and ascending, took the full rose of the dawn.

After Billy's execution, the spar from which he was hanged was in great demand among common sailors, for "To them a chip of it was as a piece of the Cross."

BILLY'S WAY IS INEFFECTIVE

As we have seen, Billy was a natural leader aboard the *Rights-of-Man,* a peacemaker and a spokesman among the crew. In an unfallen world, Billy is a tower of nobility and strength, a righter of wrongs. But in a fallen world, a world of innate evil and Claggarts, the philosophy represented by Billy is ineffective. This is indicated immediately when Billy is impressed by Lieutenant Ratcliffe. The Handsome Sailor does not resist this injustice, he seems almost to welcome it. "To the surprise of the ship's company, though much to the Lieutenant's satisfaction, Billy made no demur.... Noting this uncomplaining acquiescence, all but cheerful one might say, the shipmates turned a surprised glance of silent reproach at the sailor." When Billy is questioned by the drumhead court as to whether he would participate in a mutiny, he replies, "'I have eaten the King's bread and I am true to the King.'" This answer indicates that Billy seems completely unaware that not only he, but a large part of the crew which has also been impressed, are unquestionably the victims of injustice, and that the King is ultimately one of the chief sources of this injustice. When shortly before his execution Billy calls out "God bless Captain Vere!" and this shout is echoed by the crew, Billy in one sense is again furthering the system of injustice which has doomed him and others. It is one thing to bless Captain Vere as an individual, and it is another thing to accept so quietly the decisions of the inherently evil authority invested in Captain Vere. In his calm acceptance of what befalls him and others, Billy himself becomes an unconscious tool of injustice, for he is a natural leader, yet he does nothing to help free the mass of mankind from their fetters. Billy's life—as is Billy's death—is meaningless and wasteful, and offers not hope to mankind, but despair. In the character of Billy Budd, whose "smooth face all but feminine in purity" recalls descriptions in the author's earlier writings about the feminine nature of Christ, Melville is making his final and most profound observation on the character of Jesus and the nature of Christianity. To be Christ-like in a Christ-like and unfallen world is well and good. But a Jesus-like meekness in a fallen world does nothing to rectify the evil that exists therein. A more vigorous attitude is necessary if injustice is to be crushed out.

AN APPEAL TO REVOLUTION

The ultimate message of *Billy Budd* is an appeal to revolution, and the work is Melville's most complete statement on rebellion, both political and spiritual. Though critics comment upon the marvelous craftsmanship of *Billy Budd*, most of them ignore the implications of the Preface of the novel, which indicate the course of the action to follow and suggest the moral to be drawn.

> The year 1797, the year of this narrative, belongs to a period which as every thinker now feels, involved a crisis for Christendom not exceeded by its undetermined momentousness at the time by any other era whereof there is record. *The opening proposition made by the Spirit of that Age, involved the rectification of the Old World's hereditary wrongs. In France to some extent this was bloodily effected. But what then? Straightway the Revolution itself became a wrongdoer, one more oppressive than the kings.* Under Napoleon it enthroned upstart kings, and initiated that prolonged agony of continual war whose final throe was Waterloo. *During those years not the wisest could have foreseen that the outcome of all would be what to some thinkers apparently it has turned out to be, a political advance along nearly the whole line for Europeans.*
>
> Now, as elsewhere hinted, it was something caught from the Revolutionary Spirit that at Spithead emboldened the man-of-war's men to rise against real abuses, long-standing ones, and afterwards at the Nore to make inordinate and aggressive demands, successful resistance to which was confirmed only when the ringleaders were hung for an admonitory spectacle to the anchored fleet. *Yet in a way analogous to the operation of the Revolution at large the Great Mutiny, though by Englishmen naturally deemed monstrous at the time, doubtless gave the first latent promptings to most important reforms in the British Navy.* [Italics my own.]

Thus, the Preface implies that though rebellions such as the French Revolution often initially result in confusion and wrongdoing, they eventually may lead to important reforms and political advancement.

The theme of rebellion is further developed throughout *Billy Budd.* There are continual references to such important leaders of the French Revolution as Anacharsis Cloots and General Murat. The owner of the *Rights-of-Man* "was a staunch admirer of Thomas Paine whose book in rejoinder to Burke's arraignment of the French Revolution had then been published for some time and had gone everywhere." Indeed, two entire sections of *Billy Budd* in addition to the Preface—Sections Three and Five—are devoted entirely to an analysis of revolution and mutiny.

Billy Budd, therefore, is a struggle between the forces of rebellion and those who are opposed to rebellion, such as Admiral Nelson, who is continually cited throughout the novel, and Captain Vere, a man who opposes revolutions not because he was a member of the aristocracy but because

"they seemed to him incapable of embodiment in lasting institutions, but at war with the peace of the world and the true
welfare of mankind." But the fate of Billy Budd, who is often
likened to Adam and who on one level is representative of
Everyman, condemns the system and the authority represented by men like Vere and Nelson. Such authority can only
be effectively opposed by active rebellion. Captain Vere is
eventually slain in a combat with the French ship, the
Athéiste, whose name obviously symbolizes the forces of the
French Revolution, which, as may be remembered, Melville
suggests led to "a political advance along nearly the whole
line for Europeans.". . .

Throughout the world, men are suppressed and victimized by systems of authority such as the Articles of War.
Though good men such as Captain Vere often administer
these codes, there can be no justice under a system which is
inherently wrong. Nor can the cause of justice for all be fur-
thered by a Christ-like resignation to the authorities who
represent this system. Freedom and justice can be gained
only by vigorously striking out against the offending system
and its authorities. This rebellion, as evidenced by the
French Revolution, may itself for a time become perverted
and act as a tool of injustice. But in the long run, the force of
rebellion, which is a combination of social and, in a sense,
spiritual protest, is that power which eventually liberates
mankind. . . .

MELVILLE'S PROTEST

In an age and a country which was, for the most part, content to ask orthodox questions and give orthodox answers,
Melville dived deep into the meaning of existence and was
not afraid to face the consequences of his findings. In all of
his major works, we find an unflagging search for truth and
a refusal to accept anything which might be considered unjust or shoddy. Moreover, there is as much idealism and defiance of conventional attitudes in his more mature work as
in his earlier writings. Jay Leyda has noted that "Glued on
the inside of the writing box on which *Billy Budd* and the
last poems were composed was found a tiny clipping—Melville's own motto—'Keep true to the dreams of thy youth.'"
Melville's intellectual wanderings led him to condemn God
and to challenge the basis of Christianity. Though in this
sense Melville might be considered the phenomenologist of

relativism, he was an absolutist in his refusal to compromise his principles. For Melville, the universe was basically hostile to the human race, but like Albert Camus he felt that "there are more things to admire in man than to despise." And, what is perhaps the keynote to Melville as a writer and as a thinker, is his insistence that mankind is never more noble than in this struggle against injustice, both human and universal, that by rebelling against evil, man can wrest meaning from the cosmos and in this struggle find some sort of salvation.

CHRONOLOGY

1819

United States acquires Florida from Spain; Herman Melvill is born in New York City, the third child and second son of Allan Melvill (a merchant and son of a participant in the Boston Tea Party) and Maria Gansevoort (daughter of a revolutionary hero).

1820

National census: population 9,638,453; 7 percent urban, 93 percent rural.

1823–1825

Monroe Doctrine proclaimed; Herman attends New York Male High School but is not fond of books.

1826

Herman contracts scarlet fever.

1827

Herman visits grandparents in Boston.

1828

Herman is named best speaker in his school.

1829

Herman enrolls in the Grammar School of Columbia College.

1830

Father's business fails; Melvill family moves to Albany and Herman attends Albany Academy.

1831

Herman wins first prize in his class for bookkeeping.

1832

After father's death on January 28, Herman and brother Gansevoort are withdrawn from Albany Academy; Gansevoort opens a fur and cap store; Herman is put to work in his Uncle Peter's bank; cholera strikes Albany in summer; mother takes children to uncle Thomas's farm in Pittsfield, Massachusetts; sends Herman back at insistence of Uncle Peter.

1833

Andrew Jackson defeats John Quincy Adams for presidency; Gansevoort adds an *e* to family name.

1834

Herman works in bank; in summer he works in brother's fur and cap store.

1835

Herman enters the Albany Classical School; cousins Thomas W. Melvill and Leonard Gansevoort join crews of whaling ships.

1836

Republic of Texas formed; Herman starts classes at Albany Academy and joins the Ciceronian Debating Society.

1837

Gansevoort Melville's business fails; Herman attends winter term in a rural school near Pittsfield and teaches there until early 1838.

1838

Family moves to Lansingburgh, New York; Herman enrolls in Lansingburgh Academy to study surveying and engineering.

1839

Herman's first known fiction, "Fragments from a Writing Desk," appears in a Lansingburgh paper; signs on a merchant ship to Liverpool as a "boy"; in winter, teaches school near Greenbush, New York.

1840

On December 31 in New Bedford, Massachusetts, Herman signs on the whaling ship *Acushnet* for a voyage to the South Seas.

1842

First message by Morse's telegraph; Herman deserts ship with a companion in the Marquesas Islands and lives with the Typee tribe; Herman is crippled by a leg injury and friend Toby goes for help; Herman rescued by the crew of the whaler *Lucy Ann*; Herman takes part in another rebellion and is imprisoned in Tahiti for several weeks; signs on as a harpooner and boatsteerer to the *Charles & Henry* to go to Japanese whaling grounds.

1843

Melville is discharged in the Hawaiian Islands, works in Honolulu as a pin setter in a bowling alley and as a store clerk; signs on the U.S. Navy frigate *United States*.

1844

Melville discharged from navy in Boston; visits family; writes out his adventures with the Typee tribe.

1845

Gansevoort takes the manuscript of *Typee* with him to London to place with a publisher.

1846–1848

United States engages in Mexican-American War.

1846

Typee published.

1847

Omoo published; Melville marries Elizabeth Shaw in August and moves into a house in New York City with brother Allan and wife and Maria Melville and her four unmarried daughters; Melville joins the literary circle of Evert A. Duyckinck.

1848

Women's Rights Convention at Seneca, New York; Melville begins work on *Mardi*.

1849

The Melvilles' first child, Malcolm, is born; *Mardi* published; Melville writes *Redburn* and *White-Jacket*; *Redburn* published; Melville sails to London to arrange publication of *White-Jacket*.

1850

Melville returns to United States; begins writing *Moby Dick*; meets Nathaniel Hawthorne and buys a farm near Pittsfield; *White-Jacket* published.

1851

Melville manages to work on *Moby Dick* in between planting crops; in October second child, Stanwix, is born; *Moby Dick* published in October under the title *The Whale*.

1852

Melville gets into financial trouble; *Pierre*, published in July, receives terrible reviews and permanently damages his reputation in the United States; since the book is not published in England, his career remains somewhat less tarnished there.

1853

Melville writes *The Isle of the Cross*, but it is not published, forcing him to write a series of short tales to make money; "Bartleby the Scrivener" published; all income from Harper's, American publisher of his books, ends after a fire destroys stock of his books; Elizabeth (Lizzie), third child and first daughter, is born.

1854

Melville begins serializing *Israel Potter*; Putnam's publishes "The Encantadas."

1855

Fourth child, daughter Frances, is born.

1856

The Piazza Tales published; father-in-law funds a vacation for Melville, who sails to Glasgow and visits Hawthorne in Liverpool; continues on to the Mediterranean and Palestine.

1857

Melville goes to Egypt, the Holy Land, Greece, Sicily, Naples, and Rome; *The Confidence-Man* published in London and New York on or around April Fool's Day; Melville continues to tour northern Italy, Switzerland, Germany, and the Netherlands, returning to England and then home in May; begins to lecture on "Statues in Rome."

1860

Abraham Lincoln elected president; Melville sails for Cape Horn and San Francisco on a ship commanded by youngest brother, Thomas; returns in November.

1861–1865

American Civil War.

1861

Father-in-law dies.

1863

Melville sells Pittsfield farm to his brother Allan and moves with family to New York.

1864

Melville visits a cousin serving in the Army of the Potomac.

1865
Lee surrenders at Appomattox Courthouse; Lincoln assassinated.

1866
Battle-Pieces and Aspects of the War published; Melville receives a job as a customs inspector in New York.

1867
Melville's oldest son, Malcolm, shoots himself; Lizzie waits all day for Malcolm to get up, till Melville returns from work, forces open the door, and finds Malcolm dead in his bed.

1870–1875
Melville continues to write poetry, completing the eighteen-thousand-line *Clarel.*

1874
First Impressionist exhibit in Paris.

1876–1877
Clarel published in June; Melville works on several short fictional pieces.

1879
Edison invents workable incandescent lightbulb.

1882
Indian chief Geronimo captured; Plains Indian warfare ends; Melville's first grandchild, Eleanor, is born to Frances.

1885
French chemist Louis Pasteur gives first inoculation against rabies; Melville writes "Billy in the Darbies," receives an inheritance, and resigns from the customhouse.

1886
Melville's second son, Stanwix, dies; Melville works on *Billy Budd.*

1888
John Marr and Other Sailors, with Some Sea-Pieces published in September.

1891
Timoleon and Other Ventures in Minor Verse published in June; Melville suffers a fatal heart attack; *Billy Budd* left incomplete at his death.

Works by Herman Melville

Typee: A Peep at Polynesian Life During a Four Months' Residence in a Valley of the Marquesas (1846)

Omoo: A Narrative of Adventures in the South Seas (1847)

Mardi: And a Voyage Thither (1849)

Redburn: His First Voyage (1849)

White-Jacket; or, The World in a Man of War (1850)

Moby Dick; or, The Whale (1851)

Pierre; or, The Ambiguities (1852)

Israel Potter; His Fifty Years of Exile (1855)

The Piazza Tales (1856) (Contains "Bartleby the Scrivener," "Benito Cereno," "The Lightning-Rod Man," "The Encantadas," "The Bell-Tower," "The Piazza")

The Confidence-Man: His Masquerade (1857)

Battle-Pieces and Aspects of War (1866)

Clarel: A Poem and Pilgrimage in the Holy Land (1876)

John Marr and Other Sailors, with Some Sea-Pieces (1888)

Timoleon and Other Ventures in Minor Verse (1891)

Posthumous Publications

Billy Budd (1924)

Jack Gentian Sketches (1924)

Collections of shorter tales, sketches, first published in magazines

FOR FURTHER RESEARCH

BIOGRAPHIES

Gay Wilson Allen, *Melville and His World.* New York: Viking Press, 1971.

Charles Roberts Anderson, *Melville in the South Seas.* New York: Dover Publications, 1966.

Alice Kenney, *The Gansevoorts of Albany: Dutch Patricians in the Upper Hudson Valley.* Syracuse, NY: Syracuse University Press, 1969.

Herman Melville, *Melville's Journal of a Visit to London and the Continent, 1849–1850.* Eleanor Melville Metcalf, ed. Cambridge, MA: Harvard University Press, 1948.

Eleanor Melville Metcalf, *Herman Melville: Cycle and Epicycle.* Cambridge, MA: Harvard University Press, 1953.

Charles Olson, *Call Me Ishmael.* San Francisco: City Lights Books, 1947.

Raymond M. Weaver, *Herman Melville: Mariner and Mystic.* New York: Pageant Books, 1961.

Robert Wernick, "In Melville's Lifetime, Fame Proved Fickle," *Smithsonian,* July 1995, pp. 100–12.

CRITICISM

James Baird, *Ishmael.* Baltimore: Johns Hopkins University Press, 1956.

William Braswell, "Melville as a Critic of Emerson," *American Literature,* vol. 7 (1950), pp. 283–89.

Ray B. Browne, *Melville's Drive to Humanism.* Lafayette, IN: Purdue University Studies, 1971.

John Bryant, ed., *A Companion to Melville Studies.* Westport, CT: Greenwood Press, 1986.

William B. Dillingham, *An Artist in the Rigging: The Early Work of Herman Melville.* Athens: University of Georgia Press, 1972.

James Duban, *Major Fiction: Politics, Theology, and Imagination.* Dekalb: Northern Illinois University Press, 1983.

H. Bruce Franklin, *The Wake of the Gods.* Stanford, CA: Stanford University Press, 1963.

John Freeman, *Herman Melville.* New York: Haskell House Publishers, 1974.

Brian Higgins and Hershel Parker, eds., *Herman Melville: The Contemporary Reviews.* Cambridge, MA: Cambridge University Press, 1995.

Carolyn Karcher, *Shadow over the Promised Land: Slavery, Race, and Violence in Melville's America.* Baton Rouge: Louisiana State University Press, 1980.

A. Robert Lee, *Reassessments.* London: Vision Press, 1984.

Jane Mushabac, *Melville's Humor.* Hamden, CT: Archon Books, 1981.

Hershel Parker, ed., *The Recognition of Herman Melville: Selected Criticism Since 1846.* Ann Arbor: University of Michigan Press, 1967.

Faith Pullin, *New Perspectives on Melville.* Kent, OH: Kent State University Press, 1978.

John Samson, *White Lies: Melville's Narratives of Facts.* Ithaca, NY: Cornell University Press, 1989.

Merton M. Sealts Jr., *Pursuing Melville, 1940–1980.* Madison: University of Wisconsin Press, 1982.

Neal L. Tolchin, *Mourning, Gender, and Creativity in the Art of Herman Melville.* New Haven, CT: Yale University Press, 1988.

HISTORICAL OR LITERARY BACKGROUND

Ralph H. Gabriel, *The Course of American Democratic Thought.* New York: Ronald Press, 1940.

Daniel Walker Howe, ed., *Victorian America.* Philadelphia: University of Pennsylvania Press, 1976.

John P. McWilliams, *Hawthorne, Melville, and the American Character: A Looking Glass Business.* New York: Cambridge University Press, 1984.

Russel B. Nye, *Society and Culture in America, 1830–1860.* New York: Harper & Row, 1974.

Perry Miller, *The Raven and the Whale: The War of Words and Wits in the Era of Poe and Melville.* New York: Harcourt, Brace, 1956.

Edmundo O'Gorman, *The Invention of America.* Bloomington: Indiana University Press, 1961.

Richardson Wright, *Hawkers and Walkers in Early America.* Philadelphia: Lippincott, 1927.

INDEX

This is Not a
Werewolf
Story

SANDRA EVANS

This is Not a WereWolf Story

ATHENEUM BOOKS FOR YOUNG READERS
New York London Toronto Sydney New Delhi

ATHENEUM BOOKS FOR YOUNG READERS

An imprint of Simon & Schuster Children's Publishing Division
1230 Avenue of the Americas, New York, New York 10020

ATHENEUM BOOKS FOR YOUNG READERS is a registered trademark of Simon & Schuster, Inc.
Atheneum logo is a trademark of Simon & Schuster, Inc.
For information about special discounts for bulk purchases, please contact Simon & Schuster Special Sales at
1-866-506-1949 or business@simonandschuster.com.
The Simon & Schuster Speakers Bureau can bring authors to your live event. For more information or to book an event, contact the Simon & Schuster Speakers Bureau at 1-866-248-3049 or visit our website at www.simonspeakers.com.
Book design by Debra Sfetsios-Conover
The text for this book was set in Garamond 3 LT Std.
Manufactured in the United States of America
0616 FFG
First Edition
10 9 8 7 6 5 4 3 2 1

Library of Congress Cataloging-in-Publication Data
Names: Evans, Sandra, 1970- author.
Title: This is not a werewolf story / Sandra Evans.
Description: First edition. | New York : Atheneum Books for Young Readers, 2016. | Summary: "This is the story of boarding school student Raul, who waits for sunset—and the mysterious, marvelous phenomenon that allows him to go home"—Provided by publisher.
Identifiers: LCCN 2015025074
ISBN 978-1-4814-4480-4 (hardcover)
ISBN 978-1-4814-4482-8 (eBook)
Subjects: | CYAC: Shapeshifting—Fiction. | Wolves—Fiction. | Werewolves—Fiction. | Boarding schools—Fiction. | Schools—Fiction. | Families—Fiction. | BISAC: JUVENILE FICTION / Animals / Wolves & Coyotes. | JUVENILE FICTION / Legends, Myths, Fables / General. | JUVENILE FICTION / Social Issues / Friendship.
Classification: LCC PZ7.1.E93 Th 2016 | DDC [Fic]—dc23
LC record available at http://lccn.loc.gov/2015025074

To Mac and Mike

Nature shows us only the tail of the lion.
—ALBERT EINSTEIN

Chapter 1

THIS IS THE CHAPTER WHERE THE NEW KID RUNS SO FAST, RAUL DECIDES TO TALK

New kid. New kid. The words fly around the showers and sinks. I can almost see them, flying up like chickadees startled from the holly tree in the woods.

All the boys are in the big bathroom on the second floor, washing up before breakfast. The littlest kids stand on tiptoe to peek out the windows that look onto the circle driveway.

I pick Sparrow up and hold him so he can see. He's the littlest of the littles, but the kid is dense—like a ton of bricks.

I can't believe my eyes. No kid has ever come to the school on the back of a Harley. Not in all the years I've been here, and I've been here longer than anyone. The driver spins the back wheel, and a bunch of gravel flies up.

The new kid is holding on to the waist of the driver. He must have a pretty good grip, because the driver looks over his shoulder and tries to peel the kid's fingers away one by one. Then the driver takes off his helmet.

We all gasp, because it turns out the driver is a lady with long straight black hair.

Next to me Mean Jack whistles. "What a doll!"

Mean Jack thinks he's a mobster. A made man, that's what he calls himself. I call him a numbskull, but not out loud.

The pretty lady turns her head again and says something. The new kid folds his arms over his chest. He just sits there with his helmet on, waiting for her to roar them back down the hill to the freeway and freedom. His black leather jacket is way too big for him. Pretty Lady keeps talking. She looks angry the way moms look when they're doing something they don't want to do but think that they have to. The kid's helmet jiggles left to right. *No,* he's saying. *No. No. No. No.*

That's how I felt when my dad brought me here. My chest hurts just thinking about it, and Sparrow starts to weigh as much as a blue whale. I hoist him up onto my shoulders. Sparrow reaches down and pulls on my ears. "Fanks," he says.

Sometimes Sparrow makes an "f" sound when he should make a "th" sound. You can't try to explain it to him because it makes him sad. The last thing I want is for Sparrow to be sad.

I can feel Mean Jack getting ready to say something rude, so I shoot him a warning look that says something even ruder.

Nobody teases Sparrow about the way he talks when I'm around, but Jack's the kind of kid who forgets what's good for him.

While I'm making sure Jack remembers, everyone starts to shout and cheer.

The new boy is making a break for it.

He's jumped off the bike and is racing toward the edge of the cliff. We all run to the windows on the other side of the bathroom to watch. The grown-ups below freeze, but a second later they come running around the corner to watch too.

"Come back here!" The words float out and pop in the grass. It must be Ms. Tern. When she yells, you can tell she knows you're not ever going to do what she wants.

Ms. Tern's bubble-yell is gas in the new kid's tank. His knees and elbows crank and turn. It's like watching a plane just before liftoff.

My heart soars. It really does. I read that saying the other night, and when I see the new boy run I remember it. Now I know what it means—your heart ruffles and beats like a pair of wings. I feel like I'm flying beside him, racing away.

And where he's heading and how fast he's running, man, that kid even has half a chance.

The school sits on a cliff that looks like the letter *M*. See how it has two points at the top, a left one and a right one? Well, the school is at the tip of the left point, about three hundred feet above the beach. Between the left and right points, the cliff drops straight down to sharp rocks and water. Even if you could swim across the ravine to where the other point juts back out of the sea and scale the cliff, you'd get to the top and find yourself at the far end of White Deer Woods. Let me tell you, because I know it for a fact, no new kid would survive in there for more than an hour.

But the new kid is heading to the left of the left tip of the *M. That* side slopes gently down to the water. There's a zigzag path that leads to the beach. You're wondering what happens once he hits the sand, right? Well, there's only one way to go—left, along the water's edge to Fort Casey. And Fort Casey is just what it sounds like—an old military fort. There are tons of barracks and guns and tunnels built into the cliff. It's a big park now. All the new kid will have to do is walk into any one of the fifty tunnels and just sit tight. If he doesn't mind killing time in the dark, chances are good he'll be able to hide from everyone.

Well, at least until the grown-ups find some flashlights and get a search going. Then it's all over for him. He'll meet his fate here like the rest of us. But until then, the race is on.

The girls, whose bathroom is on the other side of the building, must have heard the commotion. They all come out onto the grass to watch.

The kid is running like he's never heard of Consequences.

"Go, kid, go! Go, kid, go!" everyone starts chanting.

I don't say it out loud along with them, but I'm thinking it so hard it's like I'm praying for him.

Then, right before the new kid hits the zigzag path, Mr. Tuffman runs out the side door that leads from the gym.

He's hauling toward that new kid like a Bugatti Veyron (the fastest street-legal car in the world, if you didn't know). Mr. Tuffman was in the Olympics. Three times. He didn't break any records, and it was a long time ago.

But still.

He was in the Olympics. Three times.

We all groan. Jack says a bad word. I set Sparrow down. My back is killing me.

Here they come. Consequences, kid. Nobody wants to find out about them from Tuffman. Mean Jack says Tuffman lost his last coaching job because kids kept disappearing during the 5K runs. I always wonder. When they say "disappear," do they mean the kids got lost but showed up at school later? Or do they mean disappear like never seen again?

I can't look away. It's all over for the new kid.

But then it's not.

"What the—?" Jack says first.

We all look. The kid's legs have started moving so fast that they're a blur. They look like the spokes on a bicycle wheel. He's flying, practically, and he's halfway down the path. Everyone's yelling again.

"Go, kid, go!" the chant starts up again. My skin gets little bumps, and we're all pumping our fists and jumping for him.

But I know Tuffman. And I can tell by the way he's running with his back perfectly straight that he has a lot more juice in him. See, now he's just chugging along. It hurts because of some old spinal injury, but he can go a lot faster. The pain just makes him meaner once he gets you.

And once they're both on the sand, he'll catch the new kid in under a minute.

In fact, just now, I notice Tuffman lean forward from the waist. Oh yeah. He's putting on the speed. I'm gonna hate this part.

Then the back of my neck tingles. The hair on my head stands straight up. Something is about to happen—a magic kind of something that only happens in White Deer Woods. Not hocus-pocus magic with witchy-poo hats and green fizzy drinks, all right? We're not talking werewolves and vampires, either. When it happens it makes you notice things that must have been there all the time. And once it's happened to you, you can never stop noticing.

Tuffman's sprinting. New kid's flying, or just about.

From nowhere a crow darts down and zips right in front of Tuffman.

Right. In. Front.

I see, plain as day, one of its wings slap up and down against Tuffman's face. Slap slap. That was no accident. Crows don't sucker punch Olympic athletes. I move my eyes a little to the left, then a little to the right. Nobody else noticed. A crow just homed in on the gym teacher like a heat-seeking missile and nobody noticed. It wheels around and taps Tuffman's neck with its beak.

Tuffman goes down. Splat, face in the dirt. A huge cheer goes up from the boys in the bathroom. Tuffman's toupee soars through the air and ends up sitting on a round little huckleberry bush. The crow with the attitude swoops down and takes a peck or two at it. Okay, *everyone* notices that.

We all hoot, we're laughing so hard. Some boys are on the floor, bent over, so happy it hurts. Tuffman has made every one of us puke, blush, or run out of gym with a bellyful of sad.

"Who's the punk *now?*" Mean Jack keeps saying.

It's still happening.

From the corner of my eye I see a dark cloud outside the windows across the room. At the far end of the circle driveway a bunch of crows—a "murder" is what you call a group of them—flap up from the old oak tree, clapping their wings.

I watch the crows swarm. I've got what's called "qualms." It means I'm worried about what just happened and what's coming next. Not because Tuffman's eating dirt. I *should* have qualms about that. We're all gonna pay in a big way once he stands up, spits a mud loogie, and starts picking the bird lice out of his toupee.

No, if I've got qualms, it's because those crows and the way they're acting remind me of White Deer Woods magic. Woods magic belongs in the woods. Not in the real world. I don't want my two worlds running into each other, even if it means seeing crusty-shorts Tuffman get some feathers stuck in his teeth.

The new kid jumps from the path onto the driftwood pile. The sky is filled with long low slices of white clouds. A skeleton sky is what I call it.

The crows circle above him, muttering and tumbling on the wind.

Oh, I've got qualms all right.

In the bathroom the boys keep cheering. But I feel very still inside. Scared, but excited, too. For the first time since I found the magic in White Deer Woods, I feel the power of it here at school, in the beat of the black wings against the bone-shaped clouds.

What if everyone found out about the woods magic?

What if everyone found out the truth about me?

I watch the grown-ups below. Not one of them notices the crows.

Then the new kid looks up and raises a fist like he knows we're up here. We all shake our fists back at him and yank the windows up so we're sure he can hear us.

"Go, kid, go!" The chant booms out across the driveway and over the field and down the zigzag path. I'm part of it. This time I'm yelling too.

It's happening.

Maybe the woods magic is everywhere all the time. Maybe it'd be good if everyone knew. Maybe everyone would like me more if they knew.

The grown-ups look up at us now. But we don't stop yelling, even when we see the dean shove his hands in his pockets and start to walk back to the main entrance. He thinks he's gonna come up here and shut us up, but *nothing* will.

Now the new kid stretches both arms above his head and laces his fingers together like a champ taking in the applause from his fans.

And that's when the security guard from Fort Casey rushes at him from behind and tackles him.

We all stop cheering. The new kid is face down in the sand. I know what my dad would say about that. I can hear his voice in my head still. The new kid made the fatal error of celebrating victory before it was his.

The dean must have phoned the Fort Casey Visitors' Center and asked them to send one of their guards in our direction.

Jack swears and points to the path. Tuffman is walking the rest of the way down to the beach, holding his hair in one hand and wiping the blood from his nose with the other. He picks the kid out of the sand and starts marching him up the path back to the school.

Even from here we can see that the kid is crying. Not just a few tears either. He's bawling his eyes out, bent over at the middle. He's sobbing, sniveling, blubbering, driveling. Halfway up, Tuffman stops, squats down, and shakes a finger in his face.

A shiver goes through the room, up and down every spine.

I don't want to go to PE today.

I look up, but the crows have gone back to the woods. The woods magic has left the real world.

It's over.

"Loser," Mean Jack says. Then he remembers his mobster act. *"Mortadella,"* he sneers in his thug voice.

Pretty soon, all the boys who had been cheering the new kid on are calling him a jerk and a poser, a show-off, and, worst of all . . .

"What a crybaby," says Little John.

Little John is one to talk. He cries when a crayon breaks. I've seen every boy in this room cry, and me too, and not just in PE when Tuffman "accidentally" sends the baseball smack into your front teeth.

But I've never seen one of them outrun Tuffman the way that kid just did.

"Shut up," I say.

The room goes totally silent. Not a boy moves. I guess you could say that I'm not a big talker. In fact, I don't think I've said a word to anybody in a month or more.

"Shut up," I repeat. "If I hear even one of you make fun of the new kid for crying, you'll be crying yourself. I guarantee it."

I pat Sparrow on the head and walk out of the bathroom, slamming the door behind me.

In the main hallway on the second floor I cross paths with the dean. He's breathing pretty hard.

"They got him," I say.

The dean stops dead in his tracks and just stares at me. Then he smiles. He wipes a trickle of sweat from the side of his face and leans toward me.

"Thank you, Raul. Thank you for informing me." He talks real quiet, the way you do when you're trying to get a rabbit to come out of the blackberry bush and eat the lettuce in your hand.

I keep walking toward my room. I'm glad me talking makes him so happy, but I'm not gonna do it again just because I like him. Talking is useless. One minute everyone says they love you and the next minute they forget all about you. Nobody listens, and everybody lies.

The only truth is in the woods, and nobody will believe it anyway. Look how they can stand under a sky full of crows on a mission and not even notice.

After a second I hear the dean panting behind me, trying to catch up. *Huff, huff, huff.* The dean needs to take a few laps with Tuffman, if you know what I mean.

"Raul," he says. He sounds like he's had an idea. "I'd like you to take the new boy under your wing. I think you may have a lot in common. Will you help him settle in?" The dean's eyes bug out even when he's not excited about something, but when he is, they look like two big marbles.

I know what he's thinking. He doesn't think I'm gonna help the new kid. He thinks the new kid is gonna help me.

But I nod, mainly so that he'll stop looking at me like that.

"Wonderful!" he says with a huge smile.

He doesn't stop. Now his eyes are the size of alien moons. It's freaking me out. What if they pop?

I'm about to open the fire door to the boys' wing when I hear Dean Swift say something that makes *my* eyes pop. I have pretty good hearing. Once, after she took the headphones off me and stopped fiddling with the dials, the nurse told me she thought I could hear sounds from a mile away. She kind of whispered that like it scared her. But I heard her.

So I can hear the Dean even though he's halfway down the hall. Now, usually when Dean Swift is talking to himself, it's about the refraction of light or bioluminescent fungi or mapping the human genome. So I don't listen too closely because no matter how well I hear it, I don't understand it.

"I wonder. Birds of a feather flock together," Dean Swift is saying to himself.

That gets my attention. Didn't he say I could take the new boy *under my wing*? Why's he talking about birds again?

Did he notice the crows? The thought paralyzes me.

"They will be the best of friends. There is strong evidence that the new one has secrets too." Dean Swift's key turns in the lock.

I push through the fire doors and walk down the hall to my room, chewing on his words like a dog with a bone. I wonder about the new kid's secrets.

Did he say "too"? Does that mean Dean Swift knows what the woods magic does to me?

And if he does, why isn't he afraid of me?

And if he's not afraid of me, could he help me?

Chapter 2

HERE'S WHERE YOU FIND OUT ABOUT THE BONE IN THE BLACKOUT TUNNEL

I remember how it felt when I was the new kid here. I felt like the only one of my kind, and all around me were the other kids in their groups like herds of wildebeests and prides of lions and crashes of rhinos and unkindnesses of ravens and leaps of leopards and wrecks of sea hawks. Remembering makes it hard to breathe, like huge hairy hands have grabbed my heart and lungs and squeezed. (Not *werewolf* hands, if that's what you're thinking, because I'm too old to believe in monsters.)

I sit on my bed and wait until the big hairy paws let me breathe again. On my nightstand is a headband my mom used to wear in her hair. I pick it up and hold it to my face for a second. It doesn't smell like her anymore, but that's okay because I know I'm the one who sniffed the scent away.

The new kid is somewhere in the building. He's probably stopped bawling by now, but I bet he's got a big hard lump in his throat. I bet he feels lost. I'm still the only one of my kind here. But I don't feel lost anymore.

If I *was* gonna show the new kid around, I'd tell him how easy it is to figure out where everything is. *See,* I could say to him, *from the outside the building looks like a castle with turrets and windows and fancy stone carvings. It looks like the kind of place where you'll get lost. But don't let the outside fool you. The outside of anything almost never tells you what's inside. The building's a rectangle with a wing at each end. Ignore the wings on the third floor because that's where the girls are. Ignore the turrets because they're full of stuff nobody uses anymore, and the doors to them are always locked. Classrooms are on the main hallways of each floor, and if you can't find one then you just end up missing twenty minutes of listening to the teacher blab, and is that really so bad?*

Here's all you need to know. First floor, dining hall. Got it? Okay. Second floor, boys' rooms in the north wing and boys' bathroom in the south wing.

Eat, sleep, shower—what else is there to do?

And if you forget to shower a few days or weeks, you're a boy, so it's only expected.

And then, if I liked the look of him, I'd tell him the truth. *The woods are all that matter, kid.* That's what I'd say. I wouldn't mention woods magic. I wouldn't tell him that the woods are alive with secrets. I wouldn't tell him that you'll find everything you've ever lost and everything that has ever lost you in them.

I'd just point him in the right direction.

My stomach informs me that food would be welcome. *Now*. My dad says only a fool argues with his vital organs.

On my way to the dining hall I hear the sound of breaking glass coming from the animal care room. *Sparrow*. If you hear something breaking in this place, nine out of ten times, Sparrow is involved. Then I hear screams. If you hear someone screaming in this place, ten out of ten times, Mean Jack is involved.

I trot over and look through the window set into the top half of the door.

Mean Jack is chasing Sparrow around the room with the business end of a pencil. Barking, squeaking, flapping, hissing—the animals are going wild. As I put my hand on the doorknob to go in and rescue him, Sparrow jumps up on a high table where the aquarium sits, with its fifty tropical fish.

"Do ya feel lucky?" Mean Jack snarls, jabbing the pencil at Sparrow's feet. "Well, do ya, punk?"

Sparrow jumps. Mean Jack misses. Water sloshes out of the top of the tank. A red swordtail goes over the rim, flops on the table, and hits the floor. Gandalf the cat swallows and then stretches. Forty-nine fish.

Sparrow jumps again, and this time he grabs on to the pipe that runs along the ceiling.

Mr. Baggins the hamster is running in his wheel, tossing little looks over his shoulder at me. *Get in here, man,* he's saying. *Get in here and shut this crazy kid down.*

I like to let Sparrow fight his own fights sometimes. I'll go in when he needs me.

Then, as Sparrow's swinging along the ceiling, one of his feet catches the latch on Gollum's cage. Snake loose. His other foot rams Mean Jack in the nose, and the mobster takes the mouse tank to the floor with him. Ten little mice scamper toward freedom . . . and the fangs of Gollum.

I predict a bloodbath.

I'm turning the doorknob, when I smell cinnamon and honey. *Mary Anne.* She pushes me aside and opens the door.

"Put down the pencil, Jack. That's a one-way ticket to juvie," she says.

Mean Jack drops the pencil and puts his hands up. Sparrow lands on the high table with the aquarium. A rainbow fish flops over the rim and into Gandalf's mouth. Forty-eight.

Mary Anne's the same age as me and Mean Jack, but she has amazing power. I've never heard her say, "I'm telling." She doesn't need a teacher.

She pulls me into the room, shuts the door, and drops the blind over the window so that nobody can see in.

"Get to work," she says.

I give her the *What, me?* look, and she says, "You too. Sometimes you must choose to observe and sometimes you must choose to act. *You* made the wrong choice."

My stomach is growling, but I start sweeping sawdust and grabbing mice. I give Mean Jack a little shove every time I come near him. Mean Jack doesn't mess with me. Nobody does.

Then Bobo the German Shepherd growls, low in her throat.

Tuffman opens the door. We all freeze.

He's combed his toupee out pretty good, but there's still one spot in the back that looks a little mangled.

I don't think I'll point that out to him, though.

Mary Anne looks at each of us and shakes her head slightly. *Do not be a rat.* We don't need the warning. At One of Our Kind Boarding School we don't tattle. We don't point fingers. We. Don't. Rat. It's the single most important rule. Dean Swift calls it solidarity. Mean Jack punches his palm with his fist and calls it Stitches for Snitches. I call it keeping my mouth shut, and for me it's pretty much SOP (standard operating procedure).

"Got a problem?" Tuffman asks.

"No problem," Sparrow squeaks. "I'm cleaning the cages since it's my week for pet care, and my friends are helping."

Good cover, I think. It's actually Mean Jack's week for pet care, and he was obviously trying to force Sparrow, at pencil point, to do the work for him. If he'd just turn that graphite tip toward a piece of paper instead of some kid's eyeball, Mean Jack could write a book on it: *A Practical Guide to Extortion for Kids.*

"No problemo, you say? Well, you lost one, pip-squeak." Tuffman pulls a mouse from his pocket and dangles it by the tail.

Sparrow grabs the mouse. He strokes its head and says softly, "You gonna be okay now, little guy."

"You didn't say 'thank you,' short stuff," says Tuffman.

"Fank you, Mr. Tuffman," Sparrow says with big eyes.

"No *fanks* to you, that's what Mr. Mousie says."

Sparrow puts the mouse back in its cage.

"I'm still talking to you, so look at me. Look at me when I'm talking to you," Tuffman says.

Sparrow's lower lip starts to wiggle.

"When you clean these cages, it's your duty to protect these animals. Do you understand the word 'duty'? Do you? Answer me."

Sparrow can't say a word. He's shaking, and I want to grab Tuffman by the throat and make him shake too.

If I met him one weekend in White Deer Woods—when the woods magic was happening to me—I could scare him pretty good. He wouldn't even know it was me.

The idea of me pouncing on him in the woods must have made me smile a little.

"You hear something funny, weirdo?" he asks me.

His eyes paralyze me.

"Nothing about this is funny. I don't like to see

animals in cages. It ain't natural. But you kids want your pets. You make an animal helpless, then you darn well better help it. You turned it into a baby. You're its parents now."

The room is so quiet.

"I can see why a kid like you wouldn't understand." His voice gets meaner.

My face burns.

"How could you understand how parents are supposed to act? What kind of mother walks out on her kid? And your dad sticking around was hardly better. I read your file." He digs a finger in his ear. "Parental neglect. That's what the state social worker called it. It says she found you eating on the floor like a dog. It says you didn't know what soap was."

I'm not going to cry. That's all I can think. *I'm not going to cry in front of Mary Anne.* I pay attention to my mouth. As long as you keep your mouth straight, nobody can tell you're sad.

"Is your old man still forgetting to come get you on weekends?"

"His dad comes." Sparrow sticks up for me.

From the corner of my eye I see Mean Jack yank Sparrow back. "Let it go," Mean Jack says in a low voice.

"That was a real pain for the dean, you know? All the other parents remember to get their kids on the weekends. Except your dad. How can a father *abandon* his son? That's what the dean would say."

It's funny. Words are air and spit. But they can hit you harder than any fist or belt or slap. They leave bruises in your belly and on your heart and in your mind that will never turn yellow and purple and fade. That will ache every time you remember them.

And he's lying about the dean. I know he is.

"What kind of kid can parents like that make? You tell me, Raul. What kind of kid did your mom make?"

He's not going to stop until I talk or cry. My mouth slips.

"We understand," Mary Anne says. She steps in front of Tuffman so that me and Sparrow end up behind her. She looks him straight in the eye. "I know you'll agree that we ought to finish our task here. If we were all to miss breakfast, I'm sure Dean Swift would expect a faithful account of every deed and every *word*."

Tuffman's eye twitches. Mary Anne's playing hard-ball. Dean Swift wouldn't like it if he knew some-one was telling stories about my parents like that. Especially since they're true.

Tuffman opens the door to leave and then turns back.

"Sparrow," he says, "do you know what a loser is? A loser is someone who loses things. Things like games, or races, or mice. Try harder. Try harder not to be such a loser."

The door slams. The room moves again. Mr. Baggins's wheel squeaks. Gandalf stretches.

Mean Jack looks from me to Sparrow. "Forget about it, you two. The guy's a schmuck, don't know his head from his—"

The door opens again and slams shut. Before any of us can stop him, Sparrow has flown out of the room, sobbing.

Tuffman made Sparrow cry.

All my sad turns to mad. I must look like I'm about to charge after Tuffman and drop him. Mary Anne grabs my arm and pulls it down, like it's a leash on a lunging dog.

"Whatever you do will just make it worse," she says.

She keeps her hand on my arm, and I know she's trying to say she feels bad about what Tuffman said to me. The tears jump from my throat to my eyes.

"Yo. Forget about the jockstrap. He's just trying to get under your skin," Mean Jack says. "We got bigger fish to fry here. Has anyone seen the snake?"

Mary Anne's face goes white.

Mean Jack takes charge. "Me and Mary'll finish up spring cleaning here. Raul, you go collar Sparrow. Last thing we need is this story getting back to the authorities."

Last thing *you* need, you mean. But it's hard to hate a kid who just saved you from bawling in front of your crush. And he's right. Forget about Tuffman. It's my fault anyway. I let him get under my skin. I let him see what I was thinking. I have to be careful. Words aren't the only thing that can give my secrets away.

"Come on, Bobo," I say.

She stands up and stretches. I hear her joints crack. As we head out the door, she puts her nose in my hand. *Thank you,* she's saying. You always know what a dog really means. Did you ever think of that? A dog *can't* lie.

There's a drawer in my mind where I put things I don't like. I shove everything Tuffman just said in it.

I know where Sparrow is, and I'm not gonna let him sit there and cry all alone in the dark.

When Sparrow feels bad he runs to Fort Casey. He's stealthy. Nobody but me ever sees him go. He dashes across the big field in the middle of the fort and heads for a bunker built into the hillside. The Blackout Tunnel is the darkest, blackest, scariest place you can imagine. If by some freak occurrence a pre-historic man-eating, bone-gnawing dinosaur survived the asteroid, then *that's* where it'd be living. Put your hand in front of your face. Now bring it so close that it's almost touching your nose but isn't. If you were in the Blackout Tunnel, you wouldn't be able to see that hand.

I head out the front door. I take the path the new kid took, but nobody is going to call security on me because

1) I'm not what they call a "flight risk"—meaning I've never tried to run away—and 2) Dean Swift believes in what he calls "personal liberty"—which as far as I can tell is a fancy way of saying that kids should play outside a lot and grown-ups shouldn't bug them much. Over the front door he had me carve a sign that says *Silva Curat!* which is Latin for *The forest heals!*

I'm warning you. Do *not* ask him about the forest and its wondrous ability to Heal children. His eyes will pop up round as boiled egg yolks, and he'll talk until your ears bleed.

I agree with him, though. Only, I would've carved something different. I would've carved *The forest has secrets.* I should write Mary Anne a note and ask how to say that in Latin. But then she'd want to know the secrets.

I look around, remembering the feeling I had earlier this morning when the crows gathered. It's gone but I know it's near. Today's Thursday. Woods magic happens Friday at sunset. Everyone likes the weekend. But I like it most of all.

Bobo lopes up ahead. The path drops off and she jumps down onto the driftwood pile. Her hind legs give way and I wince for her. She forgets how old she is. But a second later she's at the water's edge, barking at the waves.

A gleam down near Bobo catches my eye. It's black and shiny. As I get closer I see it's a helmet. It must have gotten knocked off the kid's head when he got tackled.

I pick it up. Bobo sniffs it. Her eyes ask, *Good to eat?* I scratch her ears. *You'll break every one of your last five teeth on it, dog.*

I set the helmet on a driftwood log so I remember to grab it on the way back.

Sparrow doesn't want to come out of the Blackout Tunnel.

"Come on!" I yell. Even if I didn't have Bobo, I wouldn't go in there. It reeks. My nose sniffs. I don't want to but I do, because that's how my nose works. I smell wet cat, reptile cage, park toilet, and something else—something familiar. After a few more sniffs I smile.

"Get out already, Sparrow," I yell. "It smells like Tuffman's breath in there!"

Sparrow's sputter of a laugh echoes off the walls and pings toward me like a bouncy ball. That's all it takes with Sparrow. Make him laugh and his worries are over.

He races out, drops to his knees. and throws his arms around Bobo. She licks his face like it's the most important thing she'll do all day long.

"What took you so long?" he asks.

All the way back to the school he won't stop talking. It turns out it wasn't just my joke that got him to come out. He'd also found an awesome bone.

"Is it human?" he asks me for the fiftieth time as we head down from the fort to the beach. "I fink it's someone's pinkie finger bone. Maybe the monster ate all of someone but was too full for the pinkie. This is all that's left. Poor guy. In heaven with no pinkie." He looks at me and grins. "It's a monster that only eats PE teachers."

We could use a monster like that around here.

I think it's the jawbone of a raccoon that a coyote must have dragged in there, but I let him ramble on and on about the very exclusive diet of his monster.

Why burst his bubble? I've seen some things in White Deer Woods that nobody would believe.

In fact, *I* am something that nobody would believe.

I shake that thought away. It's best to keep my worlds separate, even in my head. Look what happened with Tuffman. Just thinking about woods magic can get me in trouble.

On the way up the zigzag path Sparrow wears the new kid's helmet. He's so small, it covers his head and rests on his shoulders.

"I'm Darth Vader," he says. He holds the bone like a lightsaber and waves it in front of me. "Raul," he says in a gravelly voice. "I am your father."

I smile but I must look sad, because he takes the helmet off.

"You wanna hold the bone?" he asks after a second.

I nod. Of course I wanna hold the bone.

Chapter 3

WHERE YOU DISCOVER PART OF THE FIRST
SECRET AND LEARN ABOUT LOVE

After I drop Sparrow off at the dean's office to find out about the bone, I look at my watch. Twenty minutes left before the dining hall stops serving hot food.

But to get to the dining hall you have to walk by the wood shop. Every day I do the same thing. I take one step into the wood shop, just to breathe in the smell of sawdust, and I'm hooked. I get busy carving or sanding, and before I know it an hour has slipped by.

Dean Swift told me once about the scientific method.

"Everything you need to know is in front of you, Raul," he said. "You have to figure out the design. When a scientist wants to come up with a theory and prove it, he reads and wonders and observes. The truth is there all along, sitting hidden in the facts."

It's the same with a carving. The carving is in the wood, waiting for my knife to free it.

The fishing pole I'm making for Sparrow is almost done. This is my favorite part, where I take the fine-grain sandpaper and rub the birch wood until it's soft as sugar.

My mom's hands felt that way when she would rub my back before I fell asleep. I miss her. It makes me feel bad to say that. I bet it makes you feel bad to read it. I don't want my story to make anyone sad.

So I'll tell you part of my secret: I miss her a whole lot less now than when I first got here.

Tuffman can talk all he likes. They all can. The words burn, but they're smoke, not fire—just the ashes of the truth, just what's left of it.

The truth about my mom is beyond words.

I finish sanding Sparrow's new pole. It's a beauty, way better than the last one I made for him. He broke the last one using it as a drumstick.

Do you want to know what the other drumstick was?

A lightbulb.

Did I mention I was hungry? I am ravenous, famished, voracious. *Give me food, woman,* I feel like yelling, except the cook is Patsy and she is very nice.

"Hey, Raul," she says as I grab my breakfast tray, "will you give me a smile if I give you this?" That's Cook Patsy's favorite joke.

Usually, though, it's more like "Hey, Raul, will you give me a smile if I give you a bowl Little John didn't sneeze into?" Or "Hey, Raul, will you give me a smile if I give you a spoon the chemistry teacher didn't use to mix sulfuric acid?"

Of course I always give her a smile, but today I give her a word, too. Because today she hands me a mini flashlight she found in the bottom of a box of my favorite cereal.

"Thanks!" I say, because I was not raised by wolves. That means I have good manners.

"For your nighttime, after-Lights-Out, reading emergencies," she says.

I click it on and off. It's red. Very small but powerful. And LED so the bulb will never die. I wonder how she knows about my midnight reading emergencies.

I smile at her again and slip the flashlight into my pocket. Sometimes I think Cook Patsy is looking out for me a little, the way I look out for Sparrow. It makes my throat tight, like I might cry, except it would be stupid to cry because someone is *nice* to you, wouldn't it?

Dean Swift is showing the new kid and his mom around the dining hall.

"Now," he says in the voice he uses for the parents, "boys and girls are together during mealtimes and some of our advanced classes. Our youngest residents, the Cubs, sit closest to the food service area. The older girls—the Wolverines—sit at the round tables, and the older boys—the Pack—sit at the picnic tables."

The new kid stares at the floor, driving the toe of his shoe into a crack in the linoleum. Every time I hear him sniff up his tears, I look over to make sure Mean Jack and his wake of buzzards keep their yaps shut.

Mean Jack catches my eye once and that's all it takes for him to get the message. I was grateful to Jack for a split second after Tuffman yelled at me. But now everything's back to normal. In my age group there's the boys in the Pack and then there's me.

I walk to my usual stool at the counter. The counter is at the far end of the cafeteria, set against a window that takes up the entire wall. I sit with my back to the room, looking out at Admiralty Inlet. All I can see is sky and water, and today they are the same color.

Dean Swift, Pretty Lady, and the new kid come over and stand behind me.

My stomach feels hollow. Will Dean Swift introduce me? I wish he hadn't said anything about me helping. It's not really doing the guy a favor, is it? Here, new kid, here's the boy who's been here the longest and who fits in the least. Why don't we have him show you around?

In the end the kid will join the Pack. They'll tease him. Mean Jack'll take a little of his allowance every week and all of his brownie on Mondays. But if he puts up with it and doesn't snitch, then Mean Jack'll call him a stand-up guy and that'll be that. Once you're in with the Pack, you're never out.

The stool next to me scrapes, and Mary Anne sits

down. Now my stomach feels like a trampoline with thirty kangaroos on it.

Mary Anne's a shifter, that's what I call her. Not in the way I am, though. She shifts between groups of people. *Everyone* listens to her. *Everyone* likes her.

Everyone. Including me. Most of all.

She has long hair that hangs in curls that look like the tops of small waves right before they break on the sand. If I carved a mermaid, I'd make it look like her. *Blech.* Mary Anne makes me as sappy as a pine tree. If it hasn't happened to you yet, it will. One day you'll look up and see someone who makes your heart feel like hot pudding and your mouth feel like the Sahara Desert.

Right now her face is pale. "We didn't find the snake," she says.

Prison break. Gollum at large. Mildly venomous snake on the lam. The words run through my mind, but I don't say any of them. I just nod.

"And who sits here?" I hear the new kid's mom ask.

I look back out the window. Straight ahead. *Please don't introduce me now. Please. Not in front of Mary Anne.*

"Children of all ages sit here; it's a question of temperament."

What he means is that the weirdos sit here. We're the ones who look at the water.

Most mornings it's silver and blue like the moon-light that has just said good-bye to it.

We don't mind being called weirdos. Nobody says it mean, except Tuffman. Everyone calls us that, even Dean Swift, who a second later, says, "*Freedom* from constant adult supervision, the bane of the modern child's existence! *That* is the soul balm we offer these broken winged babes: personal liberty, independence, the wonders of the forest. Because our property extends into White Deer Woods, students can fish and explore as much as they like, which makes even the weirdos here at the counter happy."

The new kid's mom gasps. "The last thing any child needs is to be labeled a *weirdo*," she says. Her voice is so sharp it hurts my ears. "This is precisely the kind of bullying we dealt with in the public schools."

From the corner of my eye I see the new kid shake his head. For a second I hate him. I'd give my teeth—all of them—to hear my mom chew someone out for me.

I hear the dean gulp. I wait for one of his lies. They are always so unbelievable that whoever he's lying to usually feels sorry for him and pretends to believe him. It's what I used to do whenever he'd try to explain to me why my dad wasn't coming to get me for the weekend.

"I didn't say 'weirdos,'" Dean Swift finally says.

I give him points for using a very hurt voice. Nice touch, Dean.

"I said 'Werewolves' because that is what the students who sit here call themselves. They are wandering wonderers and wondering wanderers with a future in the sciences."

Mary Anne covers her giggle with her hand. I don't think it's funny, though. The dean can call me pretty much anything he likes, just not that. I'm no werewolf.

Dean Swift walks toward the back of the dining hall. "I'd like to show you the kitchen, where our residents help with meal preparation."

"Come on, Mom." The new kid turns to follow the dean.

Pretty Lady steps toward the window. She looks like she's about to cry. My mom would have hated leaving me here too.

I don't want this lady to think it's true.

I'm not a werewolf. I've read about them. Werewolves are humans who got cursed. I'm not cursed. They have unibrows, and if you cut their skin you'll see fur, not blood. Two fingertips fit between my eyebrows. I bleed. Werewolves attack people in the woods and eat them. I wouldn't do that. Not even to Tuffman, and not just because he'd taste like old cheese and toe jam. Werewolves run with two feet and one hand and push their other hand back like a tail. That's just awkward.

So I turn around on my stool and shake my head at Pretty Lady. I mouth the words to her, "I am not a werewolf." I am not a monster.

She swallows and walks away fast, pretending like

she's afraid of getting left behind and not afraid of me.

Mary Anne lets out the laugh she's been holding back. "You *petrified* her. She's abandoning her child here and she has the gall to take Dean Swift to task over a *word*." She makes a *humph* sound and lifts an eyebrow. "You sure can make your eyes look scary."

My cheeks feel hot. I don't understand 95 percent of what Mary Anne says on any given day, but I think that was a compliment. *You have scary eyes*—the nicest thing a girl has ever said to me. Pathetic. But I'll take it. Beggars can't be choosers, right? Another one from my dad.

I shift around on my stool so Mary Anne doesn't see me blush.

My spine tingles. Gollum's in here. Don't ask me how I know it, but I know it. Mary Anne would like me even better if I put that snake back in its cage. Word would get to the new kid too. *Yeah,* they'd say, *the kid over there with the shaggy hair. He caught a loose snake and saved the day.* I scan the dining room.

Sparrow is at the Cubs' table. When he catches my eye, he lifts something up in the air.

"Raul!" he shouts across the room. "Dean Swift says I can keep the bone!"

I give him a thumbs-up.

Mary Anne smiles. I feel proud. I'm glad she can see that the little kids like me, at least.

"Tell them," Sparrow hollers. He waggles his hand at the boys sitting with him. "They don't believe me. Tell them it's a monster that eats PE teachers. Tell them how all I found was some tennis shoes and a whistle," he says. "And a bone."

"A *human* bone?" Little John tilts his head and looks from me to Sparrow.

Sparrows nods solemnly but says, "No. Dean Swift says it was a dog bone."

Sparrow doesn't lie. He embellishes. "And, it is very stinky in that tunnel. Like the cat box at my granma's house." He crinkles his nose. "Ask Raul. He was there. He said it smells like Mr. Tuffman's breath."

The Cubs love it. They laugh and laugh.

Little John points at me. "You should talk more. You're funny."

Mary Anne has been following the whole crazy conversation. "Yeah," she says. "You *should* talk more."

I'm so happy, I can't even smile. Mary Anne wants more words from me. *Mary Anne.*

But then I freeze. I feel someone looking at me. And I know who it is before I even see him. When I check, he's staring at me. Mr. Tuffman.

Maybe he didn't hear?

His jaw moves. His eyes are small. He didn't miss a word. And Mr. Tuffman doesn't want any more of them.

He starts walking toward me. Silence ripples across the room as everyone realizes that Mr. Tuffman heard what Sparrow said I said.

I'm so scared I forget how to breathe. Coming from a kid who never talks, my ideas are getting me in trouble a lot today.

At just that moment Dean Swift pushes open the swinging doors that lead from the kitchen. New kid and Pretty Lady are close behind.

I glance over at Tuffman. His eyes get even smaller, but he stops dead in his tracks.

"Ah. Yes. This is our PE teacher," Dean Swift says.

The new kid looks left and right and everywhere but at Tuffman.

But Pretty Lady puts her hand out to shake Mr. Tuffman's. "I'm so sorry about earlier," she says. "I hope you didn't get hurt when you fell." She stares at his hair the whole time she's talking.

Tuffman's neck gets red, and then it spreads up his face in blotches.

I almost feel bad for him. Nobody wants a pretty lady to have seen his hair sitting on a huckleberry bush without his head in it.

"Mr. Tuffman was in the Olympics," Dean Swift says. "It still amazes me that an athlete of his caliber would forsake fame and fortune to join us here at the corner of nowhere and never-never land."

Dean Swift is starstruck. When he looks at Mr. Tuffman, all he sees is the Olympian.

Mr. Tuffman stands taller. His chest puffs out. He holds on to Pretty Lady's hand and smiles down at her. But she keeps squinting at his mangled toupee. Her mouth drops open and her eyes get bigger.

Is she really that rude?

My eyes follow hers. What I see is awful. I'm so surprised, I can't remember the word, so I point. Mr. Tuffman sees me. He thinks I'm pointing at his toupee. He shifts like he's about to pounce on me. He's going to kill me and he doesn't care who sees it.

"Snake!" Sparrow shouts.

That's the word I was looking for.

Everyone looks up and screams.

Gollum dangles from one of the hanging lights, stretching down toward Tuffman's head.

Tuffman screeches. The sound is so sharp my knees buckle. My skin pricks. Woods magic. It starts to happen again.

Gollum lands on his shoulder and skitters to the floor. She's a long black streak, but Tuffman's quick. He sprints after Gollum. Everyone stops screaming. Tuffman to the rescue.

Then, at the exact same moment, we all notice the hunting knife in Tuffman's hand. It's huge. Everyone starts screaming again.

"No," Dean Swift shouts. "Don't kill her! She's not that venomous."

Tuffman doesn't hear. Gollum darts under chairs and tables, racing for the door.

"Don't kill her!" Sparrow shouts. "She's our *baby*, remember?"

The door to the dining hall bangs open. The reading teacher, Ms. Tern, walks in with her head down and an open book in her hand. Gale-force winds couldn't make that lady pull her head out of a book. Gollum heads in her direction. Tuffman is in pursuit.

"Watch out, Nicolette!" Dean Swift yells.

Ms. Tern looks up just as Gollum slides past her foot into the hallway and freedom, just as Mr. Tuffman lunges and raises the knife.

We all shout. I like Ms. Tern and her mouse-colored hair and her soap-bubble yells and her reading and walking. I don't want to see her get hurt. But I can't look away.

Ms. Tern drops her book. Her left hand flies into the air and catches Mr. Tuffman's right arm by the wrist. The knife clatters onto the floor. What a grip!

With her other hand she punches him in the gut so hard that he grunts and falls to his knees.

The room is so quiet I hear Gollum slither down a vent in the hallway. Tuffman gets back on his feet. He stands there, a little bent at the waist, rubbing his wrist, staring at Ms. Tern.

Ms. Tern shoves her glasses up higher on her nose. "Crikey. Are you very hurt?" she asks. Her British accent makes each word trip to the next.

She looks out at all of us and explains sadly, "I only just finished reading a self-defense manual. I'm afraid I took rather careful notes."

She picks up her book and walks toward the kitchen, her nose down, her fingers flipping pages as she looks for her lost place.

And then, as she walks by me, it happens. Ms. Tern smiles.

I don't think it's the book. I can see the title. *Fifty Unsolved Crimes Against Endangered Species.* Not exactly the kind of reading that's gonna crack you up.

Ms. Tern is smiling because she knocked Tuffman to his knees.

The bell rings for class. I bend down to grab my backpack. I glance to see if anyone's looking at me.

Then I smile too.

Chapter 4

WHERE RAUL LEARNS THE WRONG WAY TO WRESTLE

Nobody can stop talking about Ms. Tern and Mr. Tuffman. Has he been packing a six-inch blade all along? Can you really get a death grip and a right hook out of a how-to book? Who knew her first name was Nicolette?

Then, as we're all heading to class, Little John finds some gross stuff on the bathroom floor under the ceiling fan. He comes running out in the hall saying that Gollum got herself killed.

Sparrow starts to sob. "It's all your fault!" he screams at Mean Jack. "Your! Fault!"

"I didn't want that snake to get whacked," Mean Jack says, and he looks sad, like he means it.

"Look," Mary Anne whispers in my ear. "Even mobsters experience remorse."

I smile like a fool.

Mary Anne and the girls gather in the hall while the boys pile into the bathroom. We make a circle around the mess on the floor. It doesn't look like dead snake to me. I'm not going to write what I think it is because I don't want this book to be banned.

I touch Sparrow's arm and shake my head.

It's not enough. The tears stream down. I hug him.

"It's not her," I whisper. "I promise."

Here's the thing. When you don't talk much, sometimes your words really matter. Sparrow wipes the backs of his hands over his eyes.

"Little John," he says in a scolding voice, "that does *not* smell like snake guts."

Everyone backs away slowly.

Whack. Another one down. It's Whack-A-Mole at school today. One creepy smiling critter of a problem after another.

But my feet have little puffs of air under them. Mary Anne noticed me. She likes my scary eyes. She laughed at my joke. She wants me to talk.

I'm a fool for Mary Anne. I grin like one until I get to my first class.

My first class is PE, so I stop grinning pretty quick. This could be bad. Mr. Tuffman and I have already spent a lot of time together this morning. And he did not enjoy my company.

The new kid is sitting on the bottom bench of the bleachers. He has a brochure about the school in his hand. The dean must have dumped him here while his mom fills out paperwork.

I gotta question the Dean's judgment here. First row seats to the Tuffman Torture Hour are *not* going to make this kid any happier about living here. Just further proof that when it comes to Tuffman, the dean only sees the word "Olympian." Not "soulless psychopath," like the rest of us.

First Tuffman makes us run lines until half the class throws up. There's actually a trough under the bleachers for that.

His bad mood seems worse when he's near me. He runs next to me, calling me a wuss and a wimp. Those are his usual insults, and I don't like it, but it's not personal.

"Sneak," he hisses at me when I touch the half court line.

Sneak? Now *that's* personal. I don't understand it, but I know it's personal.

I look back at the bleachers. I catch the new kid looking away. He must have been watching me and Tuffman.

"You takin' heat from some crumb, Coach?" Mean Jack asks all of a sudden in his big voice.

Tuffman cocks his head. We all stop running and stand there, gasping for breath, grateful for Mean Jack's special skill at distracting teachers.

"You got some serious injuries there on your neck, sir. Want me to settle the score?" Mean Jack punches his fist into his palm.

Tuffman rubs his neck. When he pulls his hand away, I see what Mean Jack saw. Huge puncture wounds barely scabbed over. They look like what would happen if a wolf decided to see how good you'd taste for lunch.

My neck juts forward. I can't look away from those bite marks. I feel weird—like those injuries have something to do with me. I can't explain it. But I feel like I'm involved. Woods magic. I try to push the feeling down. It just gets me in trouble.

I am staring too hard. Tuffman senses it.

"Get a good enough look, weirdo?" he asks.

I stare back at him longer than I should. I don't know why. Maybe it's because of what he said about my mom in front of Mary Anne and Mean Jack. Maybe it's because he made Sparrow cry. Maybe it's because he ran at Gollum with a knife.

Whatever it is, I'm in that kind of mood. The kind of mood where I don't look away.

He turns away first and I get a little surge of energy, like I won some secret game.

Then he pulls down the wrestling mats.

He calls me over. That good feeling goes away.

"Let's see if you can take down an Olympian, Raul." He's circling me, his arms wide and curved like he's holding a huge beach ball. "After my injury they told me I could stay on and coach the Olympic team. Did you know that? Big money, kids, that's what I walked away from. I came here. And you know why? Because it's my mission to teach you how to find your place in this big bad world—how to claim it and how to defend it."

My nose twitches the way it does when I smell a lie. Why would he leave everything for nowhere?

"Crouch, Raul, crouch and circle. I know you've got it in you. Every boy has a predator in him. How fierce is yours?"

Then he lunges at me. All six feet, three inches, two hundred fifty pounds of him. A big gulp of air comes out of my mouth. I think it's my courage escaping.

It's about the time when Tuffman is holding me up in the air to show everyone a wrestling hold called "the fireman's carry" that I begin to wonder if this is how the kids at his old school disappeared.

"I've got my eye on you, Raul," Tuffman breathes into my face as he puts me in a half nelson. "No sneaking around. Got it? You stay out of my territory. It stinks anyway, right?"

"What territory?" Apparently terror makes me talkative. "What sneaking?" I ask.

He twists my arm back. I hear the watching kids gasp. From the corner of my eye I see the new kid stand up and take a step toward me.

Behind me, Jason says in a very thoughtful voice, "I didn't know your elbow could go that direction."

The new kid cringes and sits down.

The pain is terrible. Like someone holding a hot iron to my bone.

"See?" Tuffman calls over his shoulder to the rest of the class. His voice is really upbeat. "Now he can't move, not an inch, or he'll break his own arm. Consequences, kiddos." He tweaks my arm a tiny bit more, and I swear my bone *bends*.

He leans down over me so that only I can hear. "One wrong move, Raul, that's all. Just remember your place. Be the boy you are. You're not powerful enough to challenge me. So don't go trying to change things," he says. "Least of all yourself."

He pushes my face into the mat as he gets up off of me.

"See?" he says to the boys.

I'm splayed out like roadkill. My body feels jumbled, like a box full of puzzle pieces. So does my brain. Everything he says has two meanings. The one he wants everyone to hear and the one just for me. There's a picture here, but right now it's just a pile of pieces.

"All I had to do was stake out my space, my *territory*," he says to the class. "That's all there is to wrestling, kids. That's all there is to life. Mark what's yours. Defend it to the death."

Death? See, now *that* I get. That only means one thing.

I decide to lie on the mat until everyone has left. Especially the new kid. I can't look him in the eye. I wanted to make an impression on him, but this wasn't the one I had in mind.

Finally I hear them open the ball cage. Everyone heads out to the field. I look at the bleachers. I'm alone. I might have a cold. My head is stuffy and my nose feels runny and my eyes are all watery.

Am I about to cry?

I head to my room to change. Why did Tuffman have to do that in front of the new kid? Why didn't he demonstrate that hold on Mean Jack? Mean Jack would find it useful for his future career as a crime boss.

It makes me feel sick. I shouldn't have let Dean Swift and his dumb idea get me all excited. Some of us are born loners.

Tuffman's voice rings in my head. What did he mean when he called me a sneak? That joke I made about his breath smelling like the Blackout Tunnel was disrespectful, not sneaky.

And what does he mean when he says not to change? Does he mean puberty? Do I have facial hair? I rub my chin, but it's smooth.

I'm the same as I was when Tuffman got here. He showed up a year and a half ago, in the fall. It was just about the time my dad stopped coming to get me on the weekends and the woods magic started happening and I decided to stop talking. I was as much a weirdo then as I am now.

Then a scary idea pops up. For a second the puzzle pieces start to make a picture.

I blink at myself in the mirror above my dresser. Does he mean the other way I change?

There is a window next to my mirror. I look out of it. On the far side of the ravine a deer and her fawn nibble on the short grass at the edge of the cliff. The cliff is red and brown and black, and tree roots stick out of it here and there. Every time it rains, chunks of it fall to the beach below, and the colors of the cliff change. The cliff changes every day and nobody notices.

How could Tuffman know my secret? I'm like the cliff. Nobody notices me.

I take a big breath. This calls for the scientific method. I organize the facts in my scientific journal. I use my most scientific handwriting.

Phenomenon (that means unusual event): Tuffman is picking on me and it's personal.

Duration (that means for how long): Targeting began during animal care and increased during PE.

Observations: How was today different than yesterday?

Item 1: Tuffman chased new kid, toupee mashed

Item 2: Tuffman made Sparrow hide in the Blackout Tunnel

Item 3: Tuffman overheard my joke during breakfast

It would make sense if he was trying to get back at me for the crack about his breath. But he didn't mention that. All he talked about was territory and changing and sneaking. I stare at the page for a long time. Then I write down the most rational explanation.

Theory: Tuffman is a jerk.

It doesn't make my arm throb any less or the embarrassed feeling go away, but it does make me smile. Maybe he's just a jerk. Jerks don't have to have good reasons for being jerks, that's what my dad used to say.

Chapter 5

WHERE RAUL MAKES FRIENDS

I decide to wait until the free period after lunch to go up to the new kid's room. After the Trauma With Tuffman I need a little sustenance.

"Pizza cut in triangles," Cook Patsy says when I walk up with my tray.

My favorite. How did she know?

I take two slices.

Then she pulls my tray toward her and puts a little book on it. *Crack Any Code!* it says on the front.

"What are the odds?" she asks. "Two prizes in one day."

"Thank you," I say. I pick it up and flip through it. On every page it tells you how to decipher a different kind of code. This is very useful. I can already see myself showing it to the new kid. An icebreaker, that's what you'd call it.

Cook Patsy holds on to the tray and looks at me for a second.

"I heard Tuffman was pretty harsh on you in gym

this morning. I know you're no snitch, Raul, but can I tell the dean about it? It seems like something he ought to know."

I shake my head. It's strange, but the whole "don't be a rat" rule applies to teachers, too. If a teacher is too mean, then the kids find a way to settle the score without getting the authorities involved. "Poetic justice" is a term we just learned about from Ms. Tern, but we've been doing it here forever. It means the punishment fits the crime. Take the last reading teacher—the one Ms. Tern replaced. He made Mark, the kid who wears the weighted vest, bend over and stand on his fingers in the corner for a whole class period. Yeah. Think about that. Now try it. Really, try it. How do your fingers feel?

Next morning that teacher picked up his coffee mug and couldn't let go of it again. Superglue. It was hard for him to pack up his desk with only one hand, but Mary Anne helped. She gave him lots of suggestions for ways he could make the most of a mug hand. *It'll be great when you stand on the street corner and ask for spare change.* And, *If anyone tries to break into your car while you're sleeping in it, you can just whack him in the side of the head.*

But I'm not the kind of kid who needs a grown-up or anyone else to fix my problems. Grown-ups are the ones who cause all the problems anyway, so I don't know why they think they're so great at teaching kids how to solve them.

Cook Patsy is watching me. She's still holding one side of my tray so I can't leave. "Well," she says, "if he bugs you again, you come to me. I can take care of Tuffman pretty quick for you." She lets go of my tray and flexes her arms down low, like a wrestler on TV before a match.

I gulp. Cook Patsy is what Mean Jack calls "ripped." She winks and picks up her spatula.

"I got your back," she says as I head to the counter.

The last of the bad feeling starts to go away, but for some reason my eyes sting like I'm going to cry.

The view from the stool is gray. A seagull the color of rain and cloud flies by and looks in at me, its beak wide open like it thinks I'm gonna toss in my last piece of pepperoni. Dream on, bird.

I wonder if the new kid ate lunch alone in his room.

Birds of a feather flock together. That means when you have something in common with someone, it's easier to make friends. We've got one thing in common, at least. We both got pummeled by Tuffman today.

And another thing—we've both got problems.

My problem is that my mom disappeared one day when I was five. My dad couldn't take care of me. I think he was too sad. He forgot to take me to school sometimes. Some days he would get me in the car and get me buckled in and then he'd rest his head on the steering wheel. Someone came over to the apartment one day to see how we were getting by, a "social worker," she was called. She saw that for breakfast he put my bowl of Cheerios on the kitchen floor. She said that was bad and that a kid should eat at a table. She said I needed a haircut and a bath and that my pants were two sizes too small. She gave him the name of this school and said it was the best solution until he started to feel better. She said I would be happy and he would visit me on the weekends.

So that's my problem. What about the new kid?

Only runaways live on the top floor, so that's one clue.

But running away is never the problem, is it? The problem is the thing that makes the boy run.

There are just a few rooms in the north wing of the fourth floor, and it's easy to tell which is his because the door is half open.

"Help! Help!" I hear a voice inside the room. It's kind of a whisper and kind of a scream.

I open the door, and the new boy is huddled on top of his desk, shaking. A long black line darts into the hall. I turn and see Gollum slip under another door.

"Should we call the dean?" the new kid asks, peeking around his door. "You know, to tell him which room it's in now?"

I shake my head. Snakes like to be with their own kind, right? And that's Mean Jack's room, so I'm sure they'll get along just fine.

"Man, it's stuffy up here," the new kid says. He walks to the window and yanks at it. He's still trembling from Gollum's welcome party.

The window sticks shut.

I tap him on the shoulder and tip my chin up so he knows I want to give it a try. He steps back and looks at me funny, and I see myself as he must see me: skinny, with my hair hanging in my eyes.

How is this kid gonna do it, when I can't? That's what he's thinking.

The window makes a popping sound and slides up. Freaky strong, that's what Mean Jack calls me.

The new kid nods like he just figured something out.

"So *that's* why Tuffman was messing with you," he says. "You must be the strongest kid here."

All my embarrassment about Tuffman tossing me around like a ragdoll disappears.

"Yeah," he says. "Jerk jocks always pick on the kids like us 'cause we're the ones who threaten them the most." He says it with a sneer, like he knows all about it and it's happened to him a million times.

Did he say "like us"?

"You got the craziest teachers here I've ever seen," he

says. His eyes are shiny. I can tell he laughs a lot. "Do they wave knives around and punch each other every morning?"

I smile so big I cover my mouth with my hand. The older kids here used to call me Dog Boy, because my teeth are so pointed. Most of them have gone back to live with their moms and dads by now, but I still hide my teeth.

With a quick twitch of his shoulders, the new boy sticks his head and as much of his body as he can out the window.

He's tall and thin, with glossy black hair and a sharp, long nose. At first he keeps his hands on the windowsill, but when a gust of wind comes up off the water, I see him lift his hands and flutter them gently, the way a bird ruffles its feather before it takes flight.

My stomach feels empty and my palms are damp. It would be good to have a friend my own age. I'm pretty popular with the Cubs, since I take them fishing every Friday. And maybe—my heart flops like a trout hooked on a line—maybe Mary Anne likes me. A little.

But I see the other Pack boys. They talk about video games and sports. They chase each other and laugh and play games and sometimes they even fight. Not me. As soon as I walk up—and I don't, not anymore—but as soon as I'd walk up, they'd look away like they hadn't seen me. Then they'd stop talking and slowly move away.

Nobody is mean to me. But nobody is nice, either.

"Do you like the woods?" I make the words come out.

The boy pulls himself back in the window.

"Are there trails back in there?" he asks. "I race dirt bikes. I'm a champion in my class. Did the dean tell you that already? My mom says she'll bring me my bike if I'm good."

His window is on the same side of the building as the dining hall and faces the water. He points to the ravine. "Is that where the school property ends?" he asks.

He must already be thinking about how to get away once that dirt bike comes. "Yeah," I say, "that ravine cuts all the way back to the road that leads to the school. You can't climb down it—it's way too steep." I decide to keep talking. I can tell he's really listening. He's worth the words. "There's a way around it, though. I'll show you one day, if you want. And you can pretty much walk out of this place any time. There's no fence keeping you here. Just the Terror of Getting Lost in the Dark Woods." I say the last sentence in a spooky voice.

He smiles at my little joke. "My name is Vincent. You're Raul, right? That boy across the hall said you're a weirdo. But you don't look like one to me."

I forget about my weird teeth. I smile again, really big.

"You have wicked cool teeth, man!"

～～～～

55

My elbow hurts when I bend it, but I feel good inside as I head into science.

First off, because I think I might have a friend. And second, because Advanced Science is the one class I have with Mary Anne. So it's safe to say that I'd feel happy right now even if I knew Tuffman would be waiting after class, ready to yank me into a Bavarian pretzel and sprinkle me with rock salt.

Some kids think science is boring, but that's because they don't have Dean Swift for a teacher. And they don't have Dean Swift for a teacher because he won't let any kid who thinks science is boring into his class.

This year he only let four of us into the class. He teaches it in his office. There aren't any desks. We can sit on the soft carpet or lie on our stomachs or, if we get there early, flop in one of the big leather armchairs.

Lately Dean Swift's been talking about the human body. We're studying cells and how every part of your body is made of them. There are skin cells and heart cells and eyeball cells. Mean Jack must have gotten extra fist cells. Tuffman got extra rude cells. Mary Anne must have gotten extra pretty cells. I must have gotten some extra weirdo cells.

But then Dean Swift says something so interesting that I forget about Mary Anne and Tuffman. I don't forget about the extra weirdo cells, though, because from what the dean says, I might be on to something.

"The center of each cell is called the nucleus. Now, in the nucleus of every cell, you will find your DNA. DNA is a code telling your body how you should look, and even how you should act. Have you ever seen a recipe in a cookbook? That is like your DNA," he says. "And it is different for each human. Half of it comes from your mother and half of it comes from your father. It is the recipe for *you*."

I like how he always gives us a picture idea. I think of the cards in my mom's old recipe box. I haven't opened the box since we all lived together. But I imagine a million copies of one of those recipes, written out in her handwriting, floating around everywhere in me. *Kid-Kebab. Raul Stew.*

"Scientists have begun to map the human genome. It will take many generations to fully understand. It's a bit like cracking a secret code."

Then he stops talking. He sits there with his mouth open and no words coming out.

When Dean Swift stops talking, it means that in a minute or two he is going to tell us something he didn't mean to tell us. It's something he doesn't know yet but is trying to understand. It has nothing to do with the learning target. And it's always the most interesting thing anyone will say to me all day long.

"I wonder. Do you know there is another kind of DNA?" he says slowly. "It's a DNA we get only from our mothers. It's in each cell but outside the nucleus. It's a shorter code than the DNA inside the nucleus. It's a special recipe that tells your cells how to turn the food you eat into energy." He writes *mtDNA* on the board. "It's called mitochondrial DNA, but we write it like that. And you only get it from your mother."

He stands and walks to the window that looks out over the ravine. I get a shiver, the kind I usually get when I'm deep in White Deer Woods and I'm me but not myself. My spine sparks like it does when I change.

"This kind of DNA you get from your mother has to do with your body's growth and development," he says. "Sometimes there are mutations. That means changes." He turns around and looks right at me—or right through me. "They only happen very rarely. That mutation will be handed down from mother to child. We know about the problems such mutations might cause. They affect vision and hearing, muscles, and the heart in particular." He pauses and shakes his head. "But we don't know if there are mutations that cause *improvements* in hearing and vision, greater muscle strength, or a heart that beats harder and stronger and longer. We don't know about that because there are no documented studies on that. Not yet, anyhow."

He sits down and looks at me. This time I'm sure he sees me. "Scientists don't really know what gifts our mothers have given us. Only we do."

Dean Swift really has a way with words sometimes.

I look down, because my eyes are saying too much. Maybe Dean Swift guessed how much the new kid coming today reminds me of the first day I came here and how sad and lost I felt. He wants me to know my mom is everywhere inside me all of the time. That it's not just words; it's science.

The bell rings and we pick up our stuff to leave.

Mary Anne holds out her hand for the dean to shake. "Dean Swift," she says in her most grown-up voice, "you soar high above the knowledgeable but pedestrian scientist when you weld wisdom to feeling."

I get the gist of what she's saying. But for me there's a lot more to it than feeling.

Vision, hearing, heart—these all have to do with my secret.

Maybe *that's* why the secret came to me. The secret was my mom's first. Or her grandma's grandma's grandma's. Each mom gave it to her child until it got to my mom. Then she gave it to me.

You can call it magic or you can call it science. I think it's a little of both.

Chapter 6

WHERE YOU HEAR ABOUT WHITE DEER FOR THE FIRST TIME

When I wake up, the first thing I think is, *What's Vincent's class schedule?* And the second is, *It's Friday.*

I hurry to get ready. Maybe Vincent will sit next to me at the counter.

But as I'm going in to breakfast, Vincent is coming out. He's telling a story to Mean Jack and Jason, and the two dimwits are laughing so hard they can't breathe.

So that's that. I know it's dumb, but it feels like someone has taken a rake and dragged it back and forth over my lungs. Vincent is already part of the Pack— the pack I'm not part of.

But Vincent stops when he sees me.

"Raul, my man," he says. He grabs my hand and shakes it. With a flick of his chin he tells the other two to go on without him. "I was waiting for you. Save me a seat at lunch, okay?"

It's crazy how relieved I feel. But I wonder. How long will it last? How long will he be able to be friends with me and with them? A week, I bet.

"I can hardly understand what those two are saying," he says. "It's like they speak their own language. Don't throw me to the wolves like that again, okay?"

He doesn't even know how funny that last comment was.

Fishing Friday. It's my job here. Every Friday after lunch and before parent pick-up I take the Cubs fishing at the lake at the edge of White Deer Woods.

Today Dean Swift joins me at the counter for a quick meeting.

"No sign of Gollum?" he asks.

I shake my head.

Dean Swift exhales. His shoulders drop. "Very unfortunate. But we have another small crisis that is slightly more pressing. Remember the bone Sparrow found in the Blackout Tunnel?" he asks.

I nod.

"The bone undoubtedly belonged to a dog. Last night I explored the Blackout Tunnel myself. It appears that over the winter an animal used it as a den." Dean Swift stares out the window like he's thinking. "That new housing development they put near the ferry terminal has been a catastrophe for so many of our animal friends. I believe we are dealing with a predator—most probably a coyote—that has been displaced from its territory." He shakes his head sadly. A second later, his spine straightens, his elbows jut out a little, and he begins a Lecture.

"In packs, coyotes have been known to attack humans. However, the animal that has claimed the Blackout Tunnel appears to be a loner. And if his territory is centered around the Blackout Tunnel, I doubt you would encounter him so far north as the lake. Especially in the middle of the day. I believe that suspending our normal activities would teach a lesson of fear to our young Cubs. Fishing Friday is their sacred hour free from adult supervision and in the tutelage of that divine preceptor, Mother Nature. But I'm counting on you to keep your eyes open today. Bobo must go with you, as usual. She will function as an early warning system."

Coyotes don't scare me. But I know what he means when he talks about the new housing development. It borders the far side of White Deer Woods, and coyotes aren't the only predators the new human families are making nervous.

After breakfast the Cubs all follow me out of the dining hall and line up in front of the equipment room so I can hand out their poles.

If the dean only knew how Fishing Friday normally goes down, he wouldn't waste his breath warning me about a coyote.

Six times Jane has hooked me, not a fish. Four times Tim has eaten deer poop. Now, the little turds *do* look like berries, but after the first three times you'd think he'd make a mental note of it. Three times I lost one of them for more than an hour, and we all had to fan out in a long line and form a search party. Twice Little John was sure he saw a witch and got so scared he wet his pants. I keep telling him that yes, there is magic in those woods, but no witches.

Before we leave, I line them up and hand out the equipment—poles, hooks, and bait.

Sixty times someone's pole has floated away to the middle of the lake.

When it's Sparrow's turn, I hold his brand-new pole out to him and then jerk it back a little as he grabs for it.

He laughs. "I won't bust it up, I promise," he says.

I hand it to him and squeeze the back of his neck lightly. His hair is soft and wispy.

He flips the pole over in his hand and then looks up at me with his face really still. I can tell he's too happy for words when he gets that look. He traces a finger along the design I carved. It's of two wolves, and they're running around the bottom, tail to mouth. It's the best carving I've ever done. And he gets what it means, he knows what I'm saying to him. I'm saying, *Hey, Sparrow, you're no cub, you're no weak runt, you're a wolf. You're in my pack.*

Five times Sparrow has slipped his hand in mine while we walk back to school from the lake.

You know what Sparrow's problem is? It's so bad it's hard for me to tell it. When he first came here he always had a couple of bruises on his cheek or his arm. Over the week they would fade and turn into yellow smears. Then Friday night he'd go home with his mom.

When he came back on Sundays he'd run to his room, open the door, and chuck in his duffel bag. Then, quick like a bunny, he'd head down to Fort Casey all by himself. But every single time, Sparrow would come back with more bruises. He'd tell the dean that he'd fallen on the stairs at the fort, or that he'd stood up under the cannon and gotten a lump on his head.

I had a bad feeling about it. How can one kid get hurt so much and so bad?

So one Sunday afternoon after his mom dropped him off, I decided to find out. First, he ran to his room and put his bag away. He came back out wearing a too-big baseball cap, and I followed him over to Fort Casey. You know where he went. To the Blackout Tunnel.

Before he stepped into the tunnel he looked back, like he wanted to make sure nobody was watching. He lifted his head up, and for the first time I saw what the baseball hat hid. A huge bruise under his eye.

He stayed in the tunnel for a while and then came out. When he got back to the school he ran up to the dean and said, "Dean Swift, a little boy playing on the field at the fort hit a baseball right into my eye."

Dean Swift clucked a few times, put an arm around him, and took him to the nurse.

I was confused. *Nothing* had hit him at the fort.

My gut told me that Sparrow shouldn't go home on the weekends. But I kept my mouth shut, because I didn't know who to tell or even really what to say. It was just a feeling, that's all.

It turned out Sparrow's mom was hitting him—not because he was bad but because *she* was. I heard the dean telling Cook Patsy one day when they forgot I was in the kitchen. I couldn't see his face, since I was chopping up onions and had to keep wiping my eyes, but I've never heard his voice so furious. Those were the worst onions I've ever chopped.

The dean had found out that Sparrow was lying about getting hurt at the fort because he didn't want his mom to get in trouble. I think he was just sitting in the Blackout Tunnel feeling sad and trying to imagine accidents that would match the bruises his mom gave him.

Now his grandma picks him up for the weekend, and he *never* has bruises anymore.

So I take special care of Sparrow. I should have told the dean what I saw that day at the fort—even though I didn't understand it. It took another month before the dean figured it out. How many more times did Sparrow's mom hit him in that month?

Dean Swift says we have to forgive ourselves when we make mistakes. He has a funny reason for it too. He says if you don't forgive yourself for making a mistake, then you get so that you never want to admit that you made one.

I'm still chewing on that one.

Today Vincent is coming fishing with us, even though he's not one of the little kids. It was the dean's idea—to give the new kid a chance to have some fun.

"If he has a great day today, it will make it easier for him to return on Sunday night," he said.

Here's the thing about Dean Swift. He lies, sure, but only because sometimes it's easier than explaining everything. He's disorganized, but that's because he's always thinking. Studying the natural light phenomena of the island is a big job.

But the main thing is, he's kind. And that's all that matters, isn't it? To us, anyway, to the ones who got left on the edge of an island with nothing but a suitcase full of clothes and a head full of trouble.

No kid here is lucky, but we're all lucky to be here.

When it's Vincent's turn for equipment, I hold up a fishing pole in one hand and a slingshot in the other. Then I shrug a little so he knows he can choose one or the other. Some kids think fishing's boring. But every-one loves a slingshot.

Twenty times I've been hit so hard with a rock in the back of the shin or the private parts that I almost fainted.

Vincent looks from one to the other. "Can I just hang out and watch?" he asks.

I nod. Vincent's not a little kid, but I've seen lots of little kids act like this. As far as I can tell it's just that they're afraid of messing up. So when Vincent says he wants to sit and watch us all have fun, I make sure he sees that I'm packing the slingshot. In case once we're out there in the woods, he changes his mind and decides to try something new.

The dean opens the door for us and hands me the walkie-talkie to use in case of emergency. To him a scraped knee is an emergency.

That man has *no idea* what happens in those woods.

We walk single file in the weeds along the roadside. Bobo leads the way. No traffic on this road, since it only leads from Highway 20 to the school. The lake is ten minutes away, halfway between the highway and the school.

While we walk, I think about my problem. The counselor says I have "trust issues." He says it's because the people I relied on most—my mom and dad—have not been able to take care of me. He says that's why I don't like to talk very much.

Wrong, is what I want to say to him—but not enough to say it. The reason I don't talk is because I can tell nobody is really listening. What I have to say doesn't really matter.

The things that matter happen in the woods. The things that matter don't need words.

Today is Friday. So tonight matters.

Once we step off the road and into the woods, we all breathe in deep to smell the trees and dirt.

Bobo runs off on a scent. There's nothing I'd like more than to drop to all fours and follow her.

I point up into the fork of an old oak tree.

Vincent follows my finger. "A bike! How did that get there?"

It's a rusted red ten-speed. In five places, where the branches of the oak have grown around it, the bike has become part of the tree. It'll be there until that oak falls, and by that time, a boy walking by the trunk won't even know the bike is in there—the oak will have swallowed it up like a snake does a mouse.

Sparrow answers, "Raul put it there."

Vincent laughs like it's the coolest thing ever.

My dad gave me that bike. It was way too big for me. He pushed me around on it a lot the Friday afternoon he brought it up here. Put on a good show for the other parents. When he stopped coming, I decided to give the bike to the tree. It's just as likely to learn to ride it as I am.

We keep walking; we're at the end of the path. The lake is in front of us. On the other side of the lake the trees are so close together and the blackberries scrape and the nettles sting so sharp that nobody has ever gone beyond them. Nobody but me, anyway.

"What's that?" Vincent asks in a whisper.

Pin pricks in my fingers and on my head. For a second I wonder if I'm going to look where he's pointing and see the secret that changed my life.

I follow his finger with my eyes. He's pointing to the straw man that I nailed to a huge cedar last year after Tuffman tackled Sparrow during touch football.

We use it for target practice. It's wearing Tuffman's favorite sweatshirt that says *3X Olympian*. I stole it from the laundry room. He turned the whole school upside down looking for that shirt. Not one of the Cubs ratted me out though, not even when Tuffman leaned in and hit them with his foul breath and a deadly speech about honesty and thieving and the awful punishment you get for stealing a man's clothes.

On the head of the straw man I nailed an old crow's nest that looks like Tuffman's toupee. Cracks me up every time I see it.

I pull my sling out of my back pocket. It's a little harder to use than a slingshot, but it's my weapon of choice.

I walk over to the straw man and point to the feet, the chest, and the shoulders.

"Five points," Sparrow yells out.

Then I point to the knees, and Little John shouts, "Twenty points." A runner's knees are valuable. I can see by Vincent's nod that he gets that.

I point to you-know-where on the shorts.

"Fifty points." I have to say it myself because all the kids are laughing to bust a gut.

I walk back to Vincent. I reach down and scoop up a smooth stone, the perfect shape.

A sling has two cords attached to a leather pouch in the middle. I set the stone in the center of the pouch. I hold the ends of the cords with the fingers and thumb of my right hand. I look at Vincent to make sure he's watching.

I start to spin it above my head. Vincent's eyes follow it. The Cubs whoop as the sling arcs faster and faster. For a minute I just swing and stare at the straw man, finding my rhythm.

I can't help but show off. I close my eyes.

I let the end of one cord go. The stone flies out of the pouch and makes a straight line toward the old cedar.

Thwack. I hear the kids shout and I open my eyes. I look at Sparrow.

"Fifty points," he informs me, and reaches out to shake my hand like a gentleman.

Vincent shakes his head. The look in his eyes means more than any compliment.

I'm about to hand him the sling, but then I think better of it. I want him to do something he can be good at right away. I pull the slingshot out of the knapsack.

It's a lot easier to learn how to use than the sling. And it's a lot safer while you learn. You let go of that sling a little too soon and some kid has a rock between the eyes.

I hand him the slingshot. I show him how to hold the Y-shaped piece of wood and where to put the rock, but I can tell he already kind of knows. I leave him alone to practice and go help the little kids bait their hooks. *Whiz.* I hear Vincent's rock sail by the cedar tree. *Thump.* It falls on something soft, like a big mushroom. *Whiz.* Another one. *Fwip.* A leaf on a branch. Progress.

Whiz. Thwack.

Now *that* hit straw.

I turn back and give him a thumbs up. He stands taller, throwing back his shoulders like a major league pitcher on the mound.

Thwack, thwack, thwack, the sound follows me all the way to where the little kids are squatting over their hooks.

One problem down, another pops up.

Little John is bawling. Tears are streaking through the dirt on his face and snot is running from each nostril like two yellow slugs. He looks at me and sobs, "Wahoul, I don't wanna kill Mr. Wormie."

"It's just a worm," Sparrow says to him. He stabs three of those suckers onto his hook.

I lead Little John by the hand to the edge of the lake.

"Look," I say. I point to the pollywogs swimming around the shiny smooth rocks. I scoop up a bunch and let them wriggle in the palm of my hand.

Little John bends down to look. He stops crying. He starts petting the pollywogs. Nothing like the life cycle of amphibians to get a boy's mind off his troubles.

Before I can stop him, he pops four of them into his mouth. He swallows. A huge gulp. "They're good," he says, rubbing his tummy.

"Oh man," I say. I'm gonna zuke.

Then my scalp tingles.

Something in me says to look up. Woods magic.

I look up.

I look up and see a glowing ball of blue-green fire floating across the lake. Will-o'-the-wisp. I mouth the words but no sound comes out. I've seen it once before—when I first noticed the woods-world. And it takes the breath from my lungs this time too.

Will-o'-the-wisps are one of the light phenomena that Dean Swift studies. *Ignes fatui* it's called in Latin, and that means "foolish fire." People have been seeing it for centuries, but it's still a mystery. Dean Swift says most scientists think it's some kind of chemical reaction caused by a bunch of dead stuff breaking down. He says it with bigger words, but you get it.

When I researched it on my own, I found out that a long time ago people thought will-o'-the-wisps would lead you to treasure or to a secret doorway where you could get in and out of heaven and see people you loved that you had lost.

They were on to something.

I watch the ball of light skip above the water. Tonight I'll go again to the place the will-o'-the-wisp led me a year ago, and I will feel like I am home, and I will find what I have lost.

My breath comes calm and slow like it does when I'm deep in the woods with her.

Little John looks up, his cheeks bulging and a little trickle of slime in the corner of his mouth. He doesn't see what I see.

Then I hear Vincent shouting behind us. "You guys won't believe what I just saw!"

The coyote! I jump up. I can see Sparrow by the lake, but where's Bobo?

Everyone runs toward Vincent. As I hurry to catch up, I notice that they've all dropped their poles. Six poles are floating in the water, heading slowly toward the middle of the lake. I change the count—sixty-six poles have gone adrift. I'm about to say one of those bad words Jack is always saying, when I see a shadow by the big hemlock. It's Sparrow. He's got his new pole in his hand and he's setting it on a thick bed of pine needles far from the water's edge. He looks up and sees me. "I told you I'd take care of it," he calls to me. Then he lopes over, and we head toward the old cedar and the straw man.

Six times he's put his hand in mine.

The kids are all gathered around Vincent. I let out a little puff of air when I see Bobo behind him, her ears flat. Her tail is tucked as far up under her body as it can get.

"It was over there," Vincent says, pointing to the other side of the lake, where White Deer Woods begins. On that side, the water comes right up to blackberry brambles and trees. It takes four legs to find the rabbit and deer paths in that tangle of branches, needles, and thorns.

"What?" I ask. "What did you see?" My heart pounds, *keblam, keblam, keblam.*

My fingertips tingle. I can feel my ears stretching the way they do when the woods magic happens.

Something tells me Vincent's not going to say "coyote."

"I saw a white deer with huge black antlers," Vincent whispers.

"Did it talk to you?" I put my hand over my mouth too late. That was not a question I should have asked. Obviously.

"Did it *talk* to me? No, it didn't talk to me." Vincent's voice sounds strange.

I clear my throat. "I said did it *walk* to you." And that, kids, is called taking a play from Dean Swift's book.

"It looked like it was going to walk across the lake toward me."

"And nobody else saw it?" I ask.

"No. I heard a noise like a jet engine. They ran over when I shouted." Vincent points to Beth, Maggie, Peter, and Paul. "We were all looking at the same spot there, but I was the only one who saw it. It was huge." He hops from foot to foot.

The truth hits me.

Two times now White Deer has come to the far edge of the lake.

Three times and it'll be science, right?

Vincent is staring at me. Bobo is staring at me. The Cubs are staring at me. Am I changing? I lick my teeth, but they feel the same. I realize that they're probably all just surprised at my talking so much.

"My grandma's eyes play tricks on her when she's tired," Sparrow says all of a sudden.

Everyone looks at him instead.

We pack up to leave pretty quick after that. As we step from the path onto the paved road, Vincent grabs my arm.

"I was lying," he blurts. "When I said it didn't talk."

I had a feeling. But why?

He answers my question before I ask it. "I didn't want everyone thinking I'm crazy. But it did. It *talked* to me. It kept saying the word 'raven.' *Am* I crazy?" he asks.

We hear a blaring honk.

It's Sparrow's grandma tearing up the road in her huge blue pickup, coming to get him for the weekend. All we can see of her as she rips by us is her curly white hair and the top rims of her enormous glasses. I'm not sure that lady should be driving.

"Trickster," I say after the dust settles. "The raven is a sweet-talkin' trickster."

Vincent looks at me like I'm speaking gibberish. Maybe I am. But all of a sudden my mind fills with black feathers. Remember the murder of crows swarming over Vincent when he made his wild run for freedom? Woods magic. The crows flew to him the way the wolves once ran with me.

I step closer to him. I want to ask him if he saw the will-o'-the-wisp too. If its light pulled at him so he had to follow. I want to tell him that it will take him to the lighthouse so deep in the woods only the light knows the way in and out. I'm about to tell him everything about my mom and my dad and the wolves in the woods. Then I stop myself. Because I see him shaking his head. A little at first and then a lot.

"Nah," he says, licking his lips. "That's just crazy. Crazy like talking to your cereal crazy. Crazy like riding your bike on the freeway crazy. I'm just tired, like Sparrow's granny says."

He looks confused. "But I didn't want to lie to you. My mom says I have to stop lying before I can come back home."

We walk the last few yards to the circle driveway, scuffing our shoes in the dirt.

I like him for telling me the truth, even if he did lie at first. I like him even more for keeping his promise to Pretty Lady. But I don't think I'll try to explain to him about the magic in the woods and the way it works for me. Because if White Deer couldn't get through to him, how could I?

Chapter 7

HOW RAUL FIRST FOUND THE LIGHTHOUSE

After fishing, we all wash up and eat lunch. Two hours of class. Snack. Doors slam, dresser drawers creak open and shut, the zippers and Velcro on overnight bags zip and rip, tennis shoes squeak up and down the stairs as kids remember stuff they almost forgot. Then motors chug up the driveway, with Pretty Lady's Harley roaring above them all. Hugs and kisses and moms asking in worried chirpy voices, *How are you? Did you have a good week?* and dads crabby from the long drive, grumbling, *It's time to get on the road, Let's try to beat some of that ferry traffic,* and *We're going to hit Seattle at exactly the wrong time.*

Vincent jumps from the bottom step into his mother's arms. She's crying. That's how happy she is to see him, and they've only been apart one day.

It only makes me a little sad before I remember to be happy for him.

"Look!" Mary Anne is next to me, pointing at the sky. The crows are wheeling and tumbling, blackening the sky with their wings, swooping over the Harley. The hair on my arms stands straight up.

"His name is Vincent, isn't it?" she asks.

I nod.

"What an amazing coincidence!" she says. "St. Vincent of Saragossa, renowned for his eloquence, is the patron saint of ravens. After he was martyred by Roman soldiers, ravens guarded his body from marauding animals. To this day the site of his tomb is famous for the multitude of ravens that flock there. And here we have these crows, such close relatives of the raven, offering a fitting farewell to our own Vincent."

Vincent and his mom roar away.

My mouth is dry. The coincidence isn't amazing— it's magical. Mary Anne's story happened a really long time ago. But White Deer called Vincent "raven" just a few hours ago. Is the woods magic everywhere and in all times?

She pats my arm to get my attention. "Your name means 'wolf' in Old Norse. Did you know that?"

I shake my head. My stomach wobbles like a rock rolling down a hill. No, I didn't know names were part of the woods magic. Do our names call the animal? Or are we named for the animal we call?

"I guess we don't really want a pack of wolves escorting you off school grounds, though, do we?" she says.

I grin. She's funnier than she thinks. Running off

with a pack of wolves for the weekend isn't as bad as it sounds.

Mary Anne's parents pull up in the circle driveway and honk their horn. She gives me a little wave and runs down the steps. I watch her leave. The trunk pops open. She sets her bag in and slams the trunk.

Her parents drive away.

I'm serious. They go almost all the way around the circle before they jam on their brakes so hard the back of the car rocks up. Mary Anne walks very, very slowly to the car. Even from the window I can see that her face is bright pink. *You shouldn't be embarrassed,* I want to shout. *They should be.*

Mean Jack brushes by me. "See you later, weirdo," he says.

I just grin. Because as he walks away I see something black and shiny, long and reptilian, wiggling out of the half-closed zipper of his bulging overnight bag.

That's gonna be a real fun car ride, isn't it?

One by one all the kids get picked up. And then it's me and Dean Swift standing in the room we call the parlor, looking at the empty driveway.

"Can I drop you off at the bottom of the hill?" The dean asks me the same question he asks me every Friday afternoon.

I shake my head. I don't want Dean Swift anywhere around when my dad picks me up, because my dad stopped coming to pick me up a year ago and nobody knows it but me and him.

Here's how it happened, or like they say in the cop shows, here's how it went down.

At first my dad came every weekend for a long time. We took the Mukilteo ferry and drove to his apartment in Seattle. Saturday mornings we had breakfast at the Sound View Café in the Pike Place Market. He had an omelet and I had a bagel with cream cheese and lox. Lunch was a meat bun from the hum bao stand. Dinner was a can of soup in front of the TV. Sundays we ate at the French bakery. He had coffee and a little loaf of bread. I had three cream puffs, an éclair, and orange juice. That gave me a stomachache that lasted until we got in the car and drove to the ferry to go back to school.

Usually at the ferry we'd run into one of my classmates.

"Would you mind driving Raul in?" my dad would ask. He'd shove his hands in his pockets and look at the ground like he was doing something wrong but couldn't help it.

I don't know if I had fun with my dad or not on those weekends. But I was glad to be with him. And I hated leaving him. I knew that when I was with him he thought about my mom more, but when I wasn't with him, he missed her more.

Then one weekend about a year ago he didn't show up. We waited. It got dark. The dean went to his office and made a call.

"Your dad's car broke down on the way to the ferry, so I'm afraid he won't be able to make it," he said when he came back into the parlor.

I cried, right there sitting on the blue sofa.

The dean sat next to me.

When I could get the words out, I asked, "If my dad can't come, then will my mom?" I don't know why I asked that. I hadn't seen her in years.

Dean Swift swallowed and shook his head.

"Is she dead?" I asked. It was the first time I asked that question out loud. Nobody ever talked to me about her.

Dean Swift's mouth made a long line. "No," he said. "She's not dead. There is no evidence to indicate that. But she's not here. I'm sure that she would be if she could."

He looked right into my eyes. "I don't know where she is. Nobody does."

I don't know why, exactly, but that made me feel better. Sad still, but better. I was glad I had asked that question. And I was glad that he didn't lie to me. Another point for the dean.

The next weekend my dad showed up. He had presents for me and a bottle of wine for the dean.

Then it happened again. All the kids were gone. The sun went down. The night came. The dean called. That time I waited to cry until I got to my bedroom. I cried until the muscles in my throat hurt and my nose was stuffed up and I felt like I had a really bad cold.

The third time it happened, I was mad.

And what was the dean supposed to do with me? See, normally he shuts the place up for the weekend and sends the staff home. He lives in Coupeville, a tiny town a few miles from the school. But if I was stuck at school, then so was he. "I can't leave you here all alone, now, can I?" he said to me with a big laugh the first time, like it was no big deal. We ate beans straight from the can and made sardine and peanut butter sandwiches. I think he had as much fun as I did. But the second and the third weekends? He was missing his family too.

So then Dean Swift took me home with him. He lives in a house painted pink. Victorian style is what he calls it. His wife called me poor little runt the whole time. I did not like her, and, strange thing is, I don't think the dean does either. But he has three teenage daughters. I'm going to marry one of them one day—unless, of course, things work out with Mary Anne. But Mary Anne is a real long shot.

Dean Swift's youngest daughter, June, is a cheerleader, and that weekend she walked around everywhere in her cheerleading uniform even though there wasn't a game. The skirt was very short and so was the top. The Dean kept walking up to her and tugging the skirt down. This made more of her tummy show, so then he'd put his head in his hands and walk away very sadly. I thought she looked like a movie star. She let me curl her hair with the curling iron. I only got a little burned.

May, the middle daughter, took me for a ride on her moped. "You don't need a helmet," she said. "Like, that's totally for sissies." That made the dean upset too, when he saw us come riding back with my hair all wild from the wind, but it was the best hour of my life.

Then April, the oldest, took me to the movies with her. The dean about exploded on Sunday morning when he found out which one we saw. I guess that movie was not for children. There were a lot of parts I didn't understand, but I really thought the party scene was funny. Maybe the actors and actresses should have had on more clothes.

One thing I know is that when I get my license, I'll drive like May taught me—speed up into the corners and turn your headlights off when you're going down hills on country roads at night. The goal, she told me, is to leave part of your tires on the road. Burning out, she called it. *Totally* an adrenaline rush, she said.

Anyway. The dean apologized to me all the way

back to the school Sunday afternoon. It was the greatest weekend of my life, so I don't know what he was so
sorry about, but I could tell I wouldn't be going home
with him again. Which was too bad, since April told
me she'd teach me how to use her rifle next time, and
May said there was a beach party with a bonfire and
she'd let me use her lighter and some gasoline to get
the fire going.

The next Friday, when the dean took me into his
office and said my dad couldn't make it because the car
was at the garage, I had some hard thoughts. *They don't
want to talk about the one thing that matters the most to me?*
I thought. *Fine, then. I'm not talking about it anymore
either.* I was done waiting for the grown-ups to decide
what to do with me.

Later that afternoon I called the dean from the phone
in the hallway of the top floor. I pretended to be my
dad.

"Oliver," I said, because that's the name the parents
call him, "the car is running good. It can't make it
up that big hill to the front door, though. Please have
Raul wait for me at the bottom of the hill, by the turn-
off from Highway Twenty." Then I hung up.

I knew the dean would be easy to fool. I knew he'd
be too tired to walk the two miles down the hill to the
highway. Plus, people are happy to be tricked if they're
getting what they really want from it. And the dean

really wanted to spend the weekend with his family.

So when the other kids were jumping into their cars to go home, I went to the dean and shook his hand and thanked him for watching out for me the last few weekends. "I think my dad has figured some things out," I said, then swung my backpack over my shoulder and headed down that hill.

Really, I was the one who had figured it out. I decided right then and there, as my feet hit the asphalt and I looked up at the thin strip of blue sky above the tops of the cedars and pines that lined the road, I was on my own. One day I'd find my mom, and maybe one day my dad would come back with an excuse better than one the dean could think of. But until then, I'd take care of myself.

I had a plan. First, walk to the highway. From there, take the footpath Tuffman makes us run through the woods. Then wait near the lake, and when everyone was gone, climb up the madrona and into my room through my unlocked window.

As I walked down the hill, cars zoomed by me in both directions. Parents coming and going with their kids. The road twists and turns pretty good, and at some point I got worried the drivers might not see me. Becoming roadkill was not part of my plan.

So I cut into the woods sooner. There was no path. The dirt was squishy and dark and covered with pine needles and cones. The woods smelled alive. I was happy to be me, to be there, to have a weekend to do whatever I wanted, whenever I wanted.

Then my skin prickled. My ears stretched like they do when you're in bed alone in a pitch-black room and you hear a sound that only something alive could make. Something alive that's *not you*. I looked behind me and saw a flash of white fur. Maybe it was just a ray of sunlight streaming down through the cedars. I stuck my chin out. I squinted. Eyes stared back at me through the low, bending branches of the cedar.

Animal eyes. I was so scared, my stomach tumbled and my mind lost every thought.

I stood very still. When I looked again, the eyes were gone but the branches were swaying. I started to step away. I sensed it watching me. I walked more quickly. I didn't know which direction to go to get out of the woods. I couldn't think.

I heard a snuffle and a hard crack.

I ran. I ran so hard my lungs burned. I ran so hard I didn't see where I was going.

Branches slapped my face, and blackberry brambles scraped my arms. Whatever it was, it was running on the other side of the trees beside me. I couldn't tell if there was one or more than one. I couldn't tell if it was chasing me or running with me. Was I part of a hunting pack or was I being hunted?

I ran until I ran out of island. One minute I was in the middle of cedars as tall as a mountain, and the next I wasn't. I was in a narrow meadow twenty feet from the cliff's edge.

I looked back a hundred times. Nothing followed me out from the cedars. My breath was so ragged and jagged, it scraped my throat and I tasted blood.

At the end of the little meadow the cliff dropped straight down to a pile of driftwood and then a strip of sand and then the blue, blue water of Puget Sound.

I started to shiver. It was almost dark. Sometimes all your choices seem bad. Was I going to spend the night on the edge of a cliff with a pack of animals watching from the trees, or run back into the forest and try to get home before whatever chased me here caught me?

If I went left, I was pretty sure I'd end up in sight of the school, but not within reach, because of the ravine.

I looked right. Farther down, the trees circled the meadow and came up to the cliff. I stared into the trees. There was a building nestled among them. I walked closer.

It was a lighthouse.

Nobody had been near it for years. Animals maybe, but no humans. The tower was as tall as the tallest trees around it, and its white paint was dappled with a pale green lichen on the landward side that helped hide it in the cedar fronds. At its base was a small cabin with a red roof. Blackberry and huckleberry and ferns and waist-high fir trees surrounded it. I pushed back the ivy covering the door.

I heard the click of little paws scamper across the stone floor as I stepped inside. It was cold and dark and musty. The first thing I thought was how I'd show it to my dad next time he came. The next thing I thought was how stupid can a kid be.

I shut the door behind me and shoved an old wooden chest in front of it.

Something out there was watching me. I could feel its eyes.

As soon as I saw the stairs, I ran up them. The light-house light was gone. The windows were cracked and broken and missing, and the edge of the ceiling was packed with the mud nests of swallows. The wind smelled like cedar and salt and wet wood. It was the most magical place I had ever seen.

I spent the night up there, with the moon coming in through the paneless windows. Before I fell asleep, I made a sling from an old leather belt I found in a chest, and gathered up as many rocks as I could.

In the morning I walked back through the woods, my sling in one hand and a rock in the other. No eyes watched me from behind the shaggy trunks of cedar.

There was a big surprise when I got back to the school: Bobo. I wasn't the only one who had been forgotten. Whichever kid was supposed to take her home for the weekend hadn't.

Boy, was she glad to see me. She charged out the door to pee and then charged right back to knock me down and lick me. She was very thorough. I never knew how happy it'd make me to have slimy sandpaper rubbed over my face.

The rest of that weekend went more or less as planned. During the day I wandered through the woods, but I made sure Bobo was trotting along at my heels. I stayed in sight of the road to the school, and before dark I was in the parlor, parked in front of the TV with Bobo for a pillow.

I found out canned pumpkin tastes really good straight from the can. In one of the chem lab closets, I found out what happened to all the crickets from that science experiment we never finished. I found out dead bugs really stink if you get enough of them piled up in an aquarium.

Turns out a German shepherd will eat those dead bugs if you forget to cover the garbage can.

Turns out cleaning up dead cricket barf will make a boy barf.

Best weekend ever.

Later the next week I called my dad one night when I was sure everybody in the whole school was sleeping.

I told my dad not to worry about me for the next few weekends because I'd be going home with different friends. He told me to take the time I needed, whatever that means.

When the next Friday rolled around, I felt a lot better knowing exactly what was going to happen. It felt good to be in charge. I told the dean my dad would pick me up at the bottom of the hill again. He asked if I would like a ride down. I said no.

I only had to call my dad that one time. He never came again. That's the bad part of the phone call. Finding out how happy and relieved he was not to have to be with me.

The good part is that's how the whole adventure, and all the magic that made it, got started. Because my dad stopped coming to get me. Because the dean didn't know what to do with me. Because a pack found me and ran alongside me. Because I got tired of being pushed around.

Don't be like dandelion fluff, shining bright but getting tossed around by the wind.

If people won't take care of you, then guess what? You gotta take care of yourself.

And in the end, I *made* the magic happen.

Chapter 8

WHERE YOU LEARN THE REST OF THE SECRET

Since then, I've found out there's a lot more at the lighthouse than swallows' nests and broken windows.

And so tonight, like every Friday night, I leave Dean Swift at the door with a smile and a wave.

I start down the road. At first I think about the other kids and what their weekends will be like. It's Mary Anne's turn to take Bobo home and I wonder if her mom will be mad about the dog hair on her car upholstery. I wonder if Sparrow's grandma lets him crack the eggs this time when they make brownies. I should write her a letter and tell her not to worry so much about salmonella. That's what soap and water are for, lady! I think about the Venn diagram Vincent made showing me how he was going to prank his stepdad. A flow chart would have been more effective.

I wonder what will happen when Mean Jack sticks a hand in his bag for a clean pair of socks and comes up with Gollum. Man, I'd like to hear that mobster yelp.

Then I notice how the brown branches of the cherry trees have green buds.

The winter months are the hardest. It's cold and the snow hurts my hands and feet when I walk. The woods get dark too early, and there is a lonesome sound in the wind.

In the spring, though, the wind talks to the new leaves. And the birds answer back, each with its own song. I'm always part of the conversation there. The sound of my breath when I run hard tells the woods I'm alive too, and so does the thump of my feet as I skim across the forest floor and the howl of my voice as I seek and find the moon and my mother.

But wait. This afternoon there's a big problem. As I'm walking down the road, I feel someone watching me. I stop. I turn around. The road behind me is empty. I keep walking. But the feeling won't go away. I stop again. I look into the trees. And up into the branches.

Tuffman.

He's sitting in the forked branches of an ash tree, and he's watching me. I catch most of my scream but not all of it. He drops to the ground. It must be twenty feet or more. He lands on both feet, his knees slightly bent. Like it's *nothing* to jump out of a tree and land on your feet and not break every bone in your legs.

"Hiya, Raul," he says.

All the hairs stand up on the back of my neck. His

voice sounds like the voice of a bad guy in a movie. Friendly, but like he wants to hurt you.

"You headin' down to meet your dad?" he asks.

My chest feels empty and my head is too full to think.

"It's funny how he never comes to the door like the other parents," he says.

I shrug.

"You ever hear of natural law? It's the way of the woods. Big things chase little things chase littler things," he says. "You're not safe alone. Not in these woods."

You know how sometimes you get a tiny voice whispering to you to get out of a bad situation? Right about now my tiny voice gets a megaphone. *Get away from this guy.*

I start walking again. Quickly. But something in me thinks that if I run, he'll chase.

He follows along, a step behind me.

We pass the point where I usually duck into the woods and head toward the lighthouse. Every step I take, my stomach feels emptier, my hands wetter, my pulse quicker.

Why won't he go away? I don't want to miss sunset. The secret only happens at sunset. Will it work if I get there after? If I miss a weekend, will it work the next one?

Here's the problem with magic. What if it's like baking bread? Cook Patsy told me that flour, water, sugar, salt, and yeast will only make bread if you use the exact right amounts and the exact right temperatures. What if the magic of White Deer Woods only works when every step is exactly right?

We can see the highway. I don't know what to do. Will he wait for my dad with me? When my dad doesn't come, will he make me go back to school? Will he make me climb the rope and run lines in the gym all weekend and drink protein shakes that taste like barf and chalk?

The wind comes down the hill from the water behind us. My nose twitches. There's a bad smell somewhere in it. On top of the smell of pine needles there's a kitty litter reptile smell I know from somewhere.

When I look back, Tuffman is staring at me.

"You worried about that coyote living in the Blackout Tunnel?" he asks.

Bingo. It's the Blackout Tunnel smell. For a second I feel relieved, like you do when you figure something out. Then it terrifies me. Because it means his nose is as sharp as mine.

"The area has too many predators already, doesn't it?" he asks. "I'm curious, Raul." He takes a long stride and then swings around and stops in front of me. "I'm curious," he repeats. "Dean Swift tells all the teachers that you're the expert on White Deer Woods."

Dean Swift talks about me to the teachers?

"Tell me, Raul."

The proud feeling shrivels up. I don't like how he keeps saying my name.

"Tell me about the woods. What kinds of predators have you come across out there, Raul?"

Tuffman's eyes are so intense, they paralyze me. For a second I don't see anything but the yellow rings around his pupils.

I feel like I have to answer his question.

He stares at me. "Anything bigger than a coyote out there, Raul?"

I open my mouth. The secret is about to fall out.

We both hear the engine coming down the hill at the same time. My mouth shuts. Tuffman glances back over his shoulder.

When he looks away from me, I blink. I've been keeping this secret for a year. Did I almost tell it to Tuffman just now? I cross my arms over my chest. I'm cold.

He turns back to me. "You should stay out of the Blackout Tunnel, Raul."

I nod. I'm trying not to look at him, but when he says my name I can't help it.

"Coyote'd make a meal of a loner like you. I guarantee it. You go back to that tunnel and you'll be sorry."

A car passes us slowly. It stops and backs up. Dean Swift rolls down the window. I'm so happy to see him that if he reached over and unlocked the door, I'd jump in.

"Is everything okay?" he asks.

"Raul and I were having a chat about the natural order, about the way there can only be one predator in a territory," Tuffman says.

Is *that* what we were talking about?

Dean Swift tilts his head and looks at me. His eyes pop a little. I must look as freaked out as I feel.

"I thought you left hours ago, Mr. Tuffman," the dean says.

Now it's Tuffman's turn to blink and look a little nervous. "I forgot something," he says. "So I came back for it. I forgot the key to my house, can you believe it?"

Dean Swift looks like he can tell Tuffman is lying. Then he looks at me like he's trying to figure out what the heck is going on here, exactly. He gives me a quick smile. I take another breath. I can tell it'll be all right. Somehow I'll get to the lighthouse by sunset.

"So," Dean Swift says finally. "Did you get it?"

"What?" Tuffman asks.

"Your key? Did you get it?"

"No."

"So where are you going now, Tuffman," Dean Swift says really slowly. It's a question, but he doesn't make it sound like one.

Tuffman's face is bright red. "To get the key," he says with a big gulp.

Dean Swift nods. "Hop in. I'll give you a ride back.

Unless you think you left your house key in the middle of this road."

Tuffman ducks his head. He lopes over and gets in.

Dean Swift starts to put the car in reverse and then looks out the window again. "You need anything, Raul?" he asks.

I give him a huge smile. "No, Dean Swift, I think I'm okay. My dad'll be here any minute."

Dean Swift nods at me. *Okay,* his face says to me. *You go meet your dad.*

I keep walking. I feel Tuffman watching me in the side-view mirror as the car turns around and heads back up the hill. I turn slightly and then stop myself. It's a woods instinct alive in me. Don't look back at an animal who is stalking you.

My mind focuses. My muscles tense.

The truth is sitting hidden in the facts, like Dean Swift says.

I'm not the only one of my kind. I'm not the only one with the secret.

Didn't White Deer call Vincent this morning? And the swarming crows? And his *name*! Isn't that proof? Woods magic happens to other people too.

Maybe it happened to Tuffman.

Okay, now you *need* to know what happens in the woods.

Remember how I found the lighthouse? There's more.

Two weekends later I was fishing in the lake. It was a Friday right before dusk.

First the woods went silent. Every warm body covered in fur or feather went still. Every bird twitter, every frog croak, every cricket thrum, every bee buzz, every leaf flutter, every rabbit nose twitch, every pebble click, every water lap—every living noise stopped.

Then in the middle of that silence there was a *BOOM* so loud that I thought someone had fired one of the old cannons hidden in the cliffs.

I looked across the lake in the direction of the sound.

From behind the low, swinging branches of a red cedar appeared a big white deer with antlers as black as a newly paved road.

It walked toward me and it spoke to me. It told me what to do so that someone I had lost could return to me. I listened so hard I forgot to breathe.

What would you do to see your mom if you had lost her? Would you go hungry? Would you run for miles and miles? Would you walk in the snow barefoot or under a boiling sun in a fur coat? Yes. Yes. Yes, you would.

I can't tell you the exact words White Deer said. That will always be a secret that I must keep. All I can say is that White Deer told me the light of the woods had spoken to my mother and told her where to find me. That she had been lost to me but that I could never be lost to her.

I put my pole down. Dandelion fluff floated everywhere. I walked out into the water, the twirling seeds catching the last of the day's light and dancing all around me. I dunked my head three times and said the things White Deer told me to say.

Then the woods were illuminated, but not from the sky above. It was from under and inside every dark, damp place. I saw light everywhere. Glowing hunks of green gold in the crevices where logs rotted to the forest floor. Foxfire. Then I saw the will-o'-the-wisp. Over the lake it bounced and shimmered, reaching back to me and hurrying ahead of me, drawing me forward.

As the sun slipped back and away behind the sea, I followed a path of light to the old lighthouse. I felt something watching me and running beside me again, and this time, because of White Deer, I knew who it was and my face was dripping with tears. I wasn't bawling. It was just like water flowing down a river. It was my whole heart in that river of tears, and I was happy.

When I came to the clearing on the cliff, the lighthouse was lit up. The light wasn't coming from inside it, though. The lichen on the tower glowed pale green like water breaking on sand in the morning.

On the threshold, the flowers called bleeding hearts bloomed. I pushed aside the red-green-gold ivy that covered the door. The soft leaves bent toward me and then away. They whispered to me in the language of leaves.

I walked into the lighthouse.

I took off my damp clothes, folded them, and tucked them into the iron stove like White Deer said.

Wings beat in the lantern room above, and I remembered the swallows and wondered if they had come home too.

Then the change came. I can't tell you how it happens. It doesn't hurt. My spine sparks. My skin prickles; it feels warm like it does when you stretch out in the cool grass under a summer sun. My ears pull up, my nose twitches, and my teeth sharpen. The pads of my fingers and toes press against the broken-up linoleum floor of the lighthouse. Do you know how good it feels to have a tail? Humans were meant to have tails. You don't know until you have one just how much you've missed it. You can't imagine what I smell—clover, dirt, bee pollen, frog spit, moss, bunny-rabbit breath, blackberry leaves, water. You can't imagine what I hear—worms sliming, bats hanging, leaves fluttering to the ground, tree trunks heating in the sun.

It's true. Every Friday night at dusk, I become a wolf.

Not a werewolf, don't say a werewolf.

A werewolf is a story someone made up to scare little kids. It's a monster that's half man and half wolf *at the same time.*

Me, when I'm a wolf, I'm a wolf. When I'm a boy, I'm a boy. Do you get it? It's not all mixed up. I'm one and then I'm the other. I change and I change back. I'm not some knuckle-dragging, hairy-faced monster who eats people.

A werewolf changes when he sees the full moon. He can't help it; he has no control over how he acts—it's why he's always gonna be alone. You never know if he's gonna feed you or eat you.

But for me it's a choice. White Deer told me the recipe, but I choose to follow it.

And when I'm a wolf, I'm never alone.

A white wolf meets me as I come out of the lighthouse door. She licks my face and my fur. In her throat she makes happy sounds, and in my throat the same sounds purr and rumble. Together we go to the woods on the side of the lake that nobody knows. We howl at the moon and we chase rabbits. When we walk through the woods together, the other animals fall back into the shrubs and leap under the fallen trees. Our shoulders touch as we sway along, our tails flick the wind.

We don't speak, of course not, don't be silly. We have calls that mean only true things. Not like words.

I have one that means *Where are you?*

She has one that means *I'm waiting right here.*

We have ones that mean *Watch out* and *There's a rabbit nearby, don't look but he's there in the blackberry leaves* and *I'm hungry* and *I'm tired* and *The sun feels good* and *This water is cold and fresh* and the one I hate that means *It's time for us to say good-bye.*

On Sunday mornings I become a boy again. I forget a lot of what happens when I'm in my wolf skin. But I remember enough.

When I'm tired I sleep, curled into her flank, and she watches over me, making soft music in her throat.

She's my wolf mother. She's my mother.

She followed me here all those years ago. She's been waiting for me to find a way to be with her. The lights in the woods told her. White Deer helped her. Those things I know because those are the things she doesn't need words to tell me. The important things, right? The things that matter.

I don't know why the change happened to her in the first place, or why she can't change back and be a human during the week like me. Maybe she forgot the recipe. It's why I'm always so careful to do everything the same way every single time. It's like with bread. If you forget the yeast, then the dough won't rise. Only with magic, when the recipe is wrong, what you get is a lot worse than crackers instead of bread.

And now that Dean Swift has helped me get rid of Tuffman, I'm going to go meet her tonight.

Chapter 9

WHERE RAUL LEARNS THAT SOMETHING HAPPENED IN THE WOODS

On Sunday my wolf mother and I return to the lighthouse. I'm always sad on Sundays. But this Sunday I'm worried, too. Something bad happened to her last week. When she met me Friday she had a deep scrape about eight inches long slicing down her left side. It was red and puffy. I could tell it had bled a lot.

There's nothing big enough in White Deer Woods to hurt her like that.

It has to be the new housing development. Because of it, she won't go as far north as she used to. White Wolf must be moving into another predator's territory. Maybe she's going south toward the fort to find food. But it can't be the coyote. A coyote would take one look at White Wolf and run off with flat ears and its tail squished up against its belly.

Something else is out there. I hope she stays out of its way this week.

A rabbit sits in the tall grass. We smell it before we see it. Twice its nose flutters open and shut.

White Wolf swings her head to look at me. *Go on. Get it.*

There's a reason people say "quick like a bunny." I charge into the underbrush. The smell of the rabbit is to my wolf nose what a paved road is to a boy's eyes. A path.

Rabbit scrambles under a fallen log and I leap over it. The air lifts me and for a minute I fly. I can't see anything but the chase. Boulder, ditch, log, thorn bush—my wolf body leaps and scampers and stretches and tumbles.

Rabbit turns. He's heading toward his burrow.

Bad idea, bunny.

The scent path opens up in front of us now. It's like he turned on headlights. He's been back and forth, in and out of that burrow so many times I can smell where he is going.

I corner him against a rock. *Snap.* I'm quick. Rabbit felt nothing. I promise.

I carry it back to her by the nape of its neck.

She makes a low growl. *Eat, Raul, eat.* She used to say that to me in a funny accent. It must be a line from an old movie she liked. I bet by now we would have watched it together.

I push the rabbit toward her. I'm returning to the world of refrigerators. She's recovering from an injury.

She growls, but I nose the meat toward her again. I

look at her, my neck straight, and my eyes speak to her. *You eat. You get strong.*

She puts her nose against mine.

Wolf kiss.

The bunny chase has brought us to the meadow where the wind has shoved back the trees. Every Sunday White Wolf leads me back to the lighthouse. There's a small growl that comes with a little nip that she only makes at the edge of the woods, and it means *Go now and be the boy you are.*

Her tail drops. She's sad to see me leave.

But there's more to it. White Wolf has regrets. I think she's sorry that we have to meet the way we do.

I lope toward the lighthouse.

White Wolf settles down under a big cedar and rests her head on her paws. The bunny is next to her. She better eat it.

My clothes are in the stove where I left them. As I put them on, I lose my wolf face and my wolf ways. When I walk out of the lighthouse, I'm no longer my second self, I'm no longer wolf me. I'm Raul, and the White Wolf who loves me is gone.

I head back toward the school. The sky is gray. A mist creeps up over the cliff, spreading a wet and glaring light into the woods.

The dean will be back by now, turning on the heat and the lights, making coffee and setting out cookies for the parents who take the time to come in. Some of the kids, like Mary Anne, just jump out of the car. Her parents don't even turn the engine off. They hit a button that makes the trunk pop open so that she can pull out her bags.

Dean Swift always runs down to help kids whose parents do this. He puts his arm around the boy or girl and takes the bag.

Sometimes I see Dean Swift look after the parents' car as it drives away, and his face looks like my insides feel—angry and sort of like he can't believe it. What kind of grown-up is too busy to carry his kid's suitcase up the stairs?

Thinking of the dean makes me feel better about going back. It'll be good to see Sparrow and hear about this weekend's disgusting casserole. His grandma throws everything she didn't eat that week into a pot for Sunday lunch—cottage cheese, refried beans, creamed spinach, spaghetti, fish sticks—if it's in her fridge Sunday morning, it's on Sparrow's plate at noon. She calls it Dutch soup, but me and Sparrow and some of the other kids like to make up different names for it. I draw pictures until someone guesses the name. So far we have barf bowl (Sparrow's), rat bath soup (mine), fungus 'n' feces (mine), poo punch (Sparrow's), dog drool dumplings (Dean Swift's), calamity casserole (Mary Anne's), and the newest one, stomach acid stew (Vincent's).

Maybe Mean Jack got to know Gollum. Do they pump your stomach for a mildly venomous snake bite? I'll ask the dean.

Maybe Vincent pranked his stepfather so good that he moved back out.

And maybe at dinner tonight Mary Anne will sit next to me at the counter.

I have a great idea. If I get there in time for drop-off, I can be the one to help her with her bag when her parents drive up. Dean Swift should be pretty easy to outrun.

Then I do what I do every Sunday when I'm halfway to the lake. I sniff until I find the stinkiest stick on the forest floor. It'll keep Bobo busy all week long.

I can tell by where the sun is in the sky that I'm earlier than usual, so I head toward the lake. I'm laughing over two new ones I thought up—scab surprise and maggot meatloaf.

But when the path opens out to the lake, I stop laughing pretty quick.

Tuffman is standing in front of the straw man.

"Was this your idea?"

I look at him. I remember the crazy idea I had about him on Friday afternoon—that he was one of my kind. I must be losing my marbles, as my dad would say. I think White Deer calls to people who need a second self because their first self has lost something so big it's not whole anymore.

Tuffman isn't the type who loses anything.

"You better talk to me, weirdo. I'm not playing games." He yanks the straw man off the tree. The heavy-duty ropes I used to tie it to the trunk snap like old rubber bands.

I can't believe it. The kids call me freaky strong, but the only word for Tuffman-strong is superhuman.

"You think it's funny to steal a man's clothes?" He strips the straw man.

The blood pumps in my neck. I want to run.

"This shirt means something," he says. "It means I'm a champion." He's ripping the straw man up as he talks. "Kids think they're the only ones with dreams. Grown-ups have dreams too. Dreams that die just like yours will unless you listen up and listen good."

He unzips his running jacket. He's not wearing a shirt underneath. The skin of his chest is smooth and tan and muscles bump and bulge. He turns around and points to a scar on his back. It's white and raised. It looks like he has two spines, almost.

"That's what happened to my dream. I was running in the woods one day, just like you." He steps toward me. "One wrong move, that's all it took." He tilts his head and I see his eyes glow. "They told me I'd never walk again. One wrong move in the woods, Raul, and everything changed. And now I'm a joke to you, huh?"

I shake my head. Nothing about Tuffman makes me

want to laugh. The scar is awful, like a thick seam of doubled-over skin.

"Bet you think that story has nothing to do with you. It has *everything* to do with you. You think you get to choose what happens next." He steps toward me again. "Well, you don't. Life happens to you."

He's about three feet away. I can sense he's about to grab me. The hairs on the back of my neck stand straight out.

"Listen, Raul," he says. His eyes fix on me. I can't move.

"Here's the moral to the story. Not just *my* story. *Your* story too. I was like you. I wasn't alone in the woods that day either. I was with a friend, Raul. More than a friend. She was family. I loved her like a little sister. She did that to me." He twists around again to show me the scar.

My mouth pops open. The scar has changed color. The muscles in his back twitch, and for a second I think it's a bloodred snake slithering along his spine.

"She broke my back. Maybe I had it coming. I'm the one that taught her to fight, that woke up the predator in her. I never thought she'd turn on me. I hate her sometimes, but I shouldn't. It's natural law. The strongest one wins. That day, she won."

He zips up his jacket.

"What are you doing out here, anyway? Is this your

territory?" He smiles a little, like he's teasing. But his eyes glow like he's not. He shifts.

I imagine the snake of a scar, twisting red with his every move. I remember the wounds in his neck that Mean Jack pointed out. My skin crawls. Everything about him is awful.

"Raul?" He says my name again.

I know better than to look in his eyes.

I run.

My second self is still awake. After the first step I go down on all fours and race wolf-style off the path and through the underbrush.

I hear Tuffman shout and curse, crashing down the path behind me. I barely have a head start, but I know these woods better than he does, and he only has two legs. I have four. I just have to make it to the road. It's drop-off day. Parents will be coming soon, right? Tuffman wouldn't want them to see him force-feeding me that bird's-nest toupee.

When I get to the road, I stand upright like a boy. The woods behind me are quiet, but I know he's in there, breathing hard and watching.

I brush my hands off on my jeans. I'm shaking. It's not just fear and adrenaline. It's shame. Tuffman saw me run on all fours like a wolf wearing the skin of a boy. It's like he saw me naked.

But that was a choice. I *chose* to run like a wolf.

I book it up the hill.

Please let Dean Swift be there. Please let the doors be unlocked.

I try the handle of the front door. I sigh with relief as it turns.

Bobo comes up and puts her nose in my pocket. *Give me the stinky stick.* Here's a conversation I understand. I give her the stick. She shoves her smooth head into my leg for a second. *Thank you.*

Welcome back to the world of doggy doors, kibble, and leashes. Where dogs are dogs and humans are humans.

I lie down on the blue sofa in the parlor. I feel like the straw man—like everything that holds me up snapped, and the stuffing got ripped out of me.

"What are you, sick?" a voice asks.

I scream a roller-coaster scream. "Eeeeek!"

Mary Anne is standing over me. She jumps when I scream and drops her notebook. I sit up and put my head in my hands. She sits down next to me.

"Sorry, Raul, I didn't mean to startle you," she says in a very kind voice. Then she starts to giggle. "That was funny, though."

It makes me laugh too. I can't remember the last time I laughed so hard. Maybe when Little John filled Mean Jack's shoes with crabs that had washed up dead on the beach. Or when Tuffman was showing us the proper form for sit-ups (*NO LIFTING YOUR BUTTS*

OFF THE FLOOR, YOU WEENIES), and he farted.

This is better, because there's no ghastly odor. Mary Anne smells like honey and daffodils. Trust me. If you had a wolf nose you'd know what a daffodil smells like, and it smells like it looks—yellow and frilly. Did you notice daffodils are always, always nodding yes at you? Remember that. Whenever you have a day where everyone is saying no to you, just find a daffodil. It will say yes.

Man. This is what Mary Anne does to me. Flowers and giggles. I make myself sick.

I stop laughing and look at her. Why is she here so early?

She reads my face. "My mom has to fly to Chicago tonight, so she dropped me off early. I got here before Dean Swift did." She frowns and then smiles quick to hide it.

I know how that feels. I wonder how long she sat on the front steps with her suitcase, waiting in the fog. No wolf coat to keep her warm. I pat her on the shoulder.

"No big deal. I'm working on a novel," she says. "I have the setting—Norway. And the villain—a sorcerer named Rodrigo who has a secret formula that will turn the world into a huge ocean. I have a heroine, a mermaid whose parents work for Rodrigo. But I need a hero."

She looks at me for a long time. Her eyes get very small like she's thinking hard.

"You could be a hero," she says slowly.

I look down at my hands. I got a few cuts during that tussle with the rabbit. Do not, I repeat, do *not* get the wrong end of a rabbit that doesn't want to be eaten.

Mary Anne's words make me feel so good it's embarrassing. I want to float away and bury my head under a pile of blankets at the same time.

Then I hear Mary Anne sigh. "No," she says in her serious voice, "no, the hero needs to be more . . . hmm." She pauses, scratching her chin. "More what, exactly? What is the word I am looking for?"

I feel a little irritated. I watch her from the corner of my eye. Just because I don't talk much doesn't mean I can't hear.

"More heroic," she says finally. "You'll make a fine helper for the mermaid. But the hero needs to be more . . . There's only the one word for it, isn't there?"

I get up from the couch and head up to the bathroom to take a shower.

What a day. Five minutes of conversation with Tuffman and I felt like I'd been doing sudoku for three hours straight. Five minutes of conversation with Mary Anne and I went from king of the world to feeling like a worm a bird pecked in half and then left because it didn't taste good enough.

There's been too much talking already today, and I haven't even said a word.

Chapter 10

A JOKE WITH NO PUNCH LINE: ONE DAY THIS PREDATOR WALKED INTO A FOREST . . .

Bad news at dinner Sunday night.

"Children." Dean Swift comes into the dining hall to make an announcement. "Listen! There is no call for panic, but it appears that a cougar has taken up residence near Fort Casey. Two guards and three tourists have described hearing the cry of a cougar while walking in the park at dusk." The dean clears his throat. He throws his head back and opens his mouth and makes a screech like a cat screaming and a dog snarling and a ghost sobbing.

The sound makes cold sharp fingernails walk up my spine.

But Mean Jack has to make a joke. "Was that a wildebeest burp, sir?"

Dean Swift doesn't even notice the Cubs laughing. "No, it's a cougar, Mean Jack, uh, I mean *Jack*," he answers, and then his face gets red and his eyes bulge because he said "mean Jack" twice now instead of once. "Scratch marks have been found about nine feet up on the trunks of several trees near the road to our school. This tells us it is a large cougar, and that it is actively roaming our grounds. Chances are good that it will move on shortly. But until it does, we must take precautions when we leave the building."

A cougar? The word gives me a strange feeling. It's like an itch in my brain I can't scratch. After a minute I realize it has to do with what happened in the woods this weekend. Sometimes what happens when I wear my wolf skin is hard to remember when I'm a boy.

My mind scratches around, and then Vincent sits down next to me.

"Don't look at me," he warns. "I'll die laughing if you look at me."

I stare straight out the window at the water.

"So I hid behind the bathroom door," Vincent says. "I put on the zombie mask I told you about. My stepfather was watching the game, and he drinks a lot of beer when he watches a game, right? So I knew he'd have to go to the bathroom, right?"

I look at him with a face that says, *Yeah, yeah, you told me all this on Friday*. There's a little piece of wolf worry left dangling in my head, and I'm not gonna feel like joking around until I rip it off.

"Okay, right. I told you that." He starts to giggle. "So look out the window, okay? I can't tell it without laughing if you look at me."

By now all the weirdos are leaning across to listen, and a couple of the kids from nearby tables have come over.

"So he comes into the bathroom, and he's unzipping his pants, and boom! I jump out at him and he *screams.*" Vincent can hardly talk, he's laughing so much. "He screamed like a wee little girl, and then he peed his pants."

I can't help it. I laugh so hard I forget my wolf worries.

Nobody's eating anymore, everyone's laughing, and the story starts flying around the room. By the time it gets to the little kids' table, it's turned into *Vincent's dad went pee in his pants.* That's enough of a story for the Cubs, and half of them laugh so hard they fall out of their chairs and roll around on the floor. Little John ends up with nacho cheese mashed into his hair. Three peas get jammed up Peter's nose.

After dinner I realize it's no joke. Vincent has changed everything in less than a week.

Normally during TV time I sit in a ratty old armchair off to one side. All the other kids sit on the floor or the sofa. Nobody makes me sit where I sit. But nobody ever sits in my chair either.

Tonight, when Vincent walks into the TV room, everyone shifts around a little. Mary Anne scoots closer to Jenny to make a space for him next to her on the carpet. Mean Jack punches Little John in the shoulder to get him to slide down from the sofa to the floor.

Vincent doesn't notice them. He scans the room. When he sees me, he walks over and perches on the arm of my chair.

"Hey," he says. "I almost forgot. I told my mom about you this weekend. She wants you to spend spring break with us."

I can feel everyone's ears stretch toward us.

"Will your dad be cool with that?"

I nod. I can see the other kids look at me like they've never seen me before. Vincent has cool. It's contagious. Now I have it too.

All the chairs are turned toward the TV as usual, but the kids sitting in them are turned toward Vincent. He has a million and one jokes and stories. My armchair is the center of the room. Once or twice I start to open my mouth. I don't say anything. But I could have. I think they would have listened.

Later in bed I turn on my LED flashlight from the cereal box.

I hate the dark. It was hardest when I first got here. The sound of the madrona's branches scraping the window made me think of monsters. Even now I wake up sometimes in the middle of the night, and at first I'm half asleep and I forget that White Wolf found me. It's a feeling like night is inside of me.

Let's not talk about it.

Tonight I think I have a friend. It's a light inside me. But it scares me a little. I wonder how I can make him keep liking me. I wonder if he'll get tired of me.

There's no answer to that. I take out the code-cracking book Cook Patsy gave me. Last week I thought I'd need it to start up a conversation with Vincent. Like making friends was an uncrackable code.

I must fall asleep, because I wake up in the dark. The flashlight is on the floor. I hear footsteps in the hall outside my room. My heart bumps. A voice mumbles. My mind wants me to run, but my legs aren't listening.

A monster or a murderer jiggles the doorknob to the utility closet next to my room.

The next doorknob in the hall is mine.

Did I lock my door?

In my mind I see Tuffman's glowing eyes. I hear him saying my name. I can't move.

I wonder if they will find my last will and testament in my sock drawer. A cold sweat covers my body. I go over the distribution of my earthly possessions.

Sparrow will get my clothes and my books.

Cook Patsy gets my mom's box full of recipes. I've never opened it, so they will be good as new.

Dean Swift will get my shark-tooth necklace for his science cabinet.

My dad—if he's not too busy to come and pick it

up—will get the shoebox where I keep things that remind me of my mom: her velvet headband that used to smell like her, her gold bracelet with her name engraved on the inside and flowers and vines on the outside, a CD she used to play when she rocked me, one of her gloves that for a long time I put my hand inside whenever I slept.

Keys jangle. The utility closet door opens. I hear feet on steps. Whoever heard of a closet with stairs?

I scrabble my hand across the floor until I find the flashlight. When I flip its beam at the clock, I see it's midnight. This is a strange time for someone to be concerned about utilities.

I lie there for a long time. It feels like five hours, but the clock says it's only been two minutes. I tiptoe to the door and stand there with my ear to it for another five hours that turns out to be one minute. Slowly I open my door.

I look to the right. The door to the closet is ajar. I peek in and see a staircase. The stairs must lead up into the north turret, overlooking White Deer Woods. From the outside of the building it's obvious my room is just beside and below it. But from the inside I never thought of it as anything but a utility closet. Maybe because the sign on the door says UTILITY CLOSET.

I creep up the stairs. Somehow I know exactly where to put my feet on each step so that it won't creak.

Except on the third to the last one when I step dead center and the stair groans like a bull.

I stand very still. I get ready to bolt back down.

When my thoughts stop crashing around, I hear a scratching sound and the rustle of papers. Someone's writing up there.

Do assassins have diaries?

My nose twitches. I don't think that's Tuffman.

"Eureka," a man's voice says. "Perhaps the cougar saw the light."

The voice belongs to Dean Swift.

I hear a click like a button being pushed.

"Midnight. March seventeenth." He must be speaking into a recorder. "After years of searching, I have found Fresnel's secret treatise. It is titled most tantalizingly *On the Generative Power of Light*. My hunch was correct. Numerous prisms on the old lighthouse lens were never correctly installed. Using Fresnel's measurements, I have exponentially increased the power of the light beam. Is it mere coincidence that there are reports of cougar activity south of White Deer Woods? My investigation of its den on the fort grounds indicates it has been in the area for approximately one month. The timing corresponds with my first lighting of the lens since I applied Fresnel's secret calculations. Questions: Is this simply a predator displaced by the new housing development? Or, as per Fresnel's theories, did the light from the lens draw him to us?" A button clicks.

My mind is scratching around. *Its den on the fort grounds?* That was no coyote den in the Blackout Tunnel. It's the cougar's.

I stretch out and peer around the low wall that keeps people in the room from tumbling down the stairs. I'm looking at Dean Swift's back as he sits at a messy desk. Every once in a while he looks up at something in front of him. It takes a second for my eyes to adjust to the low light, but when they do, I almost somersault backward down the stairs.

It's an enormous lighthouse lens. And when I say enormous, I mean it's ten feet high and five feet wide. It fills most of the room beyond Dean Swift's desk.

Even though I've never seen it before, I recognize it.

I sneak back down the stairs to my room, my blood hot and my skin alive. I need to be sure.

I lie belly down on my bed and slide the books out one at a time. There are about twenty. It's my personal library on lighthouses.

I pull out my favorite, *Lighthouses of the Pacific Coast*. There it is, on page 127. A photo of the Point Reyes' first-order Fresnel lens, manufactured in 1867. First-order means it's the biggest kind. It has 1,032 pieces of glass. Twenty-four of those pieces are bull's-eye lenses so powerful they could start a fire if they're not exposed to direct sunlight.

That's a first-order Fresnel lens upstairs. Everything tingles. My skin, my hair, inside my belly, my brain and my heart.

Is it mine? The question burns in me. I've always wondered what happened to my light. The books all say that the first lighthouse on the island, named Red Bluff, was lit in 1861. Forty years later it was destroyed, and a new one was built a few miles away with a brand-new lens. I've figured out that the books are wrong about one thing. Red Bluff never got torn down. It's where it always was, at the edge of the cliff deep in White Deer Woods, where the meadow meets the cedars and the cedars meet the sea. I don't know why I'm the only one who knows about it. And I don't know why its lantern room is empty.

Because none of the books say what happened to Red Bluff's first-order Fresnel lens. You can't lose one of them. Those suckers cast a beam for thirty miles!

I'd bet my wolf skin that's my light in the turret.

But how did it get there? No way you could fit it up the staircase, or in through one of the little square windows.

There's only one way, and it makes me dizzy to think about it.

The school must have been built *around* the lens.

You know how an earthquake happens when two plates of the earth's crust slam into each other? My school-world and my woods-world just smashed together. It's all connected, but I don't know how. White Deer told me the lighthouse is my place between places. It's the door I walk through to find my other self.

But this school where I live was built to hold its light long before I was ever born.

Chapter 11

A RECIPE FOR A HERO

Monday morning.

I wake up to the sound of the madrona branch scraping back and forth across the window. Rain spatters. The wind howls.

My first thoughts are wolf worries. I hope White Wolf is dry and warm under our ledge. I hope she ate the rabbit. I hope the wound in her side is better and that the rain has washed the rest of the dried blood out of her pretty fur. Then I remember the lens and my lighthouse and Dean Swift's *eureka*.

The wind slaps the branch against the glass. The books are still spread across the floor. The dean said the light brought the cougar. I sit up. I finally scratched that brain itch I got last night at supper when Dean Swift first mentioned the cougar.

The cougar gave White Wolf that scrape. For a minute I can't move again, like last night when I thought Tuffman was lurking outside my door. This is worse, and it's true. A cougar attacked my mother.

I can't lose White Wolf.

I can't lose her and I can't help her. I sit on the edge of my bed in my underwear. My back hunches so my elbows touch my knees, and my hands cover my face. My skin is cold and my hands feel like ice.

The feeling is called Despair.

Nobody can help us.

In the dining hall I grab three boxes of cereal. Raisin bran, granola, and Lucky Charms cover the three major food groups—fruit, fiber, and marshmallows.

I need sustenance. I need a plan. I need to think this through.

I have to push past about ten kids to get to my usual seat. Vincent is on the stool next to it, and as I set my tray down, he lifts his jacket off of my stool without even looking at me.

Nobody has ever wanted to sit by me enough to save me a seat.

I'm so surprised that it takes me a minute or two to notice that the weirdo counter is really weird today. Kids from all the groups are hanging around, holding trays filled with their dirty dishes, listening to Vincent tell a story. Their fingers are white and blue from gripping the trays, and I can tell by how they shift from one foot to the other that they're tired of standing, but they don't want to miss a word.

After Vincent finishes talking and while everyone is repeating the punch line, he turns to me. Without saying a word, he pulls a plate from his tray and puts it on mine. Then he turns back around to answer some dumb question.

It's a plate full of bacon and sausage and ham. I haven't had hot food for breakfast in forever. It's cold by now, sure, but it *was* hot once, and that's good enough.

I don't say much. Vincent doesn't seem to mind. Everyone's listening, but after a while I get the feeling he's telling his jokes for me.

"Yeah," he says when I finally crack a grin. "I *knew* you'd be the only one to get it. We got the same sense of humor."

All this time I thought it was my fault that I couldn't figure out how to fit in. But now I see. You can't ever fit in like a number or a letter, because friendship's not a puzzle or a cipher. There's no answer that you get right or wrong. You don't "get" friends. You are one.

You have one.

I stare out the window.

Vincent keeps yakking away next to me, drawing a diagram on a napkin, making the weirdos laugh until they almost puke. You can't be a dummy and be that funny. He's got street smarts is what my dad would say—the kind of smarts that keep you alive.

"Are you done?" he asked as he scoots his stool back. When I nod he grabs my tray and stacks it on top of his.

"Save my place at lunch," he says, picking up our trays and heading off.

Maybe Vincent can help me protect my mom. I don't know how. But I think he would if he could.

How much would I have to tell him?

I've got kitchen duty, so when I'm done I put my plate on top of the other dirty dishes in the bus tub, pick it up, and head back to the kitchen.

"You like the meat plate special?" Cook Patsy asks when I swing open the doors.

"Thank you," I say.

She looks at me for a second and then taps her head, like she's just got an idea. She pulls a cookbook from the shelf. "You choose what we make for lunch. Anything you want. And then if we have time, why don't you let me teach you some wrestling? I was state champ in high school."

I stare at her, totally confused. Now *Cook Patsy* wants to wrestle me? Maybe it's a virus, a terrible pandemic, a contagion spreading through the teachers.

ChokeHoldococcus. PinaStudentitis.

"I cleaned the rubber mats and everything," she says.

I look down at the black mats that cover the kitchen floor. All the little wet bits of food and slime are gone. It reeks of bleach. So that's good to know. When my face gets pushed into it, it will be very sanitary.

"I thought about it all weekend," she says. She

looks worried. There are circles under her eyes.

Then I understand. She doesn't want to squish my face into the mat. She wants to teach me to squish *Tuffman's* face into the mat.

"I can't let you get pushed around," she says. "I can't let Tuffman bully you. But I respect that you want to solve your own problems."

She lifts up the cookbook. "It's the kitchen code. Follow the recipe. And my recipe always calls for a fair fight. So I'm going to teach you to defend yourself. But let me tell you, I don't think a fight between a teacher and a student can ever really be fair. So if I hear one more whisper of him picking on you, I'm going to the dean."

She hands me the cookbook. "You choose."

I look down at it for a long time without opening it. She turns around and punches the button to start the dishwasher. Cook Patsy is trying to look out for me. I bet my mom would've talked to me like that too. A little sharp, so it sounds like she's mad, but she's not mad, she's worried. About me.

I open the cookbook. Whatever we make for lunch, I'm not chopping onions. My eyes are already watery. It's allergy season, I guess.

I get a good idea. It must be all the protein. "Wait," I say.

I race out of the kitchen and up to my room. I come back down with the recipe box.

I mean, what if I don't die? She'd never know I wanted her to have them.

"Hmm." She thumbs through the cards. "Tuna Surprise?"

I shake my head.

"Beef Stew?"

I shake my head. She holds the box back out to me. "What, then?"

I've never really read the cards before. The sight of my mom's handwriting makes me smile and feel sad at the same time. I pick one card up just so I can touch it where she probably touched it. All that's between her hand and mine is seven years.

Cook Patsy watches me for a minute. Then she pats my shoulder and lifts the door on the huge dishwasher. Steam pours out. I feel her glance over at me.

I look at each card. There's no order to the recipes. It's not alphabetical like Apple Pie to Yam Surprise, and it's not in the order that you eat them, like appetizers to desserts. Meringues is the first recipe, and the one after is Ham with Pineapple. But I keep them like she left them. I want to read them the way she wrote them.

"They were my mom's," I say.

Cook Patsy reaches up and hangs a pot on the hook above the stove. "I figured as much. Let's make lunch a feast in her honor, how about that?"

I nod. My throat is tight.

I take the next two cards without looking at them and hand them to Cook Patsy.

"Bacon and Cheddar Omelet. Now that's a good lunch for a Monday," she says. "And Island Cobbler for dessert." She sets the cards down on the counter and opens the fridge. She goes back to read the cards. She looks up at me. A long line appears between her eyes.

I can tell she's really thinking about what she wants to say.

"Raul, was your mom a good cook?" she asks. "I mean, do you remember actually eating the food she made for you?"

I shrug.

"'Cause I want you to take a look at this and tell me if it sounds right. Maybe it's her handwriting."

I look at the recipe for Island Cobbler.

3 pineapple

2 sprigs mint

4 oranges

1 egg

3 cups milk

2 tsp cinnamon

3 oz liver

7 cps blackberry

1 cp sugar

7 pats Butter?"

When I get to the three ounces of liver I make a face.

"Yeah, right? You don't often see liver show up in a dessert recipe. Or a question mark, either." Cook Patsy looks like she doesn't know what to say. "I'm sure she was really good at lots of other stuff," she says after a minute.

I close the box.

She was good at being my mom.

In honor of my mom we decide to make grilled cheese sandwiches and canned tomato soup for lunch. Then Cook Patsy teaches me a couple of really good moves.

"The main thing," she says, "is to be aggressive. Don't let him choose what's gonna happen next. *You* choose."

After kitchen duty I go to my room. My mom was a rotten cook. Maybe it's weird, but this makes me happy. I know something about her now—something only her kid would know about her, something only I could tease her about. It's like Sparrow and his grandma's Dutch soup. I've got a joke with my mom now too.

I keep thinking about it, shaking my head. Liver in dessert? No wonder she messed up the recipe to change herself back.

Have you ever taken a joke too far? That's how that thought makes me feel. Bad and sad, like you would if you were teasing someone and took it too far.

How do I get her back? The question aches like a bruise. And how do I protect her from the cougar until I figure it out?

Last night it sounded like Dean Swift thought the cougar had something to do with the lens. My books are still spread out all over the floor. It sounds crazy, but I go ahead and look for words like "measurements" and "formula" in some of the BOBs. (That's what Ms. Tern calls the Back Of the Book.)

I find a few pages listed for the word "measurements" in a book about lighthouses during the Civil War. It turns out that in wartime lighthouse lenses got taken apart so enemy ships couldn't navigate the coastline. After the war some lenses got put back together wrong. That's not a big surprise, since all one thousand prisms have to be angled in just the right way. If the measurements are off, the beam won't be very strong.

It reminds me of what Dean Swift said about making the beam more powerful. I squint to remember how he said he figured out the correct measurements. Did he really say he found them in a "secret" book by Fresnel? I'm pretty sure the title was something like *The Generative Power of Light*. I pull out my dictionary. "Generative" is the adjective for "generation," and that means "to bring into being or existence." So to make something live.

I think about it for a while. Light makes things

live. But why would that be a secret? Even Little John knows about photosynthesis. We've all put dirt, water, and a bean in a plastic cup and set it in the light or out of the light or to the side of the light. The sprout is phototropic. That means it will grow toward the light.

I sigh. It's hard to believe that Dean Swift thinks the light made the cougar come here, like a sprout turns to the sun. A cougar is not a bean.

Maybe I didn't hear him right.

I feel like a dog biting his tail, going around in circles. My mom and her wolf skin and me and mine, the cougar and a light made by a flame and 1,032 prisms.

Then I stop. My mind sits down. It's all very simple. Who knows when Dean Swift will light the lens, or why he thinks the cougar has turned toward it. I can't control that—just like I can't tell my mom where to find her human skin.

But I do have a choice. There's one thing I can choose to do that will keep my mom safe and give us more time to figure out her recipe. I can get rid of the cougar.

A funny thought comes to me.

You want a hero, Mary Anne? You're looking right at him.

Chapter 12

WHERE RAUL LEARNS VINCENT'S PROBLEM

I wait until midnight. Then I put my flashlight in my pocket and stand at my door for a minute, listening. All is quiet.

"Come with me," I whisper to Vincent five minutes later.

He pokes his head out from under his covers. He screams. I hold the flashlight up so that he can see it's me.

"What are you doing in here?" he asks. "How did you get in?"

"I opened your door. It wasn't locked," I say. "I need your help for an undertaking of great importance."

He hops out of bed and pulls on his jeans. "Do I need a jacket?" is all he asks.

That's a friend for you. The kind of kid who grabs a jacket and goes with you—even when you are waking him up in the middle of the night to sneak out a window and climb down a tree taller than a three-story building and walk out into the pitch black to *hunt a wild cougar.*

I lead him out of his room to the end of the hall. The madrona that goes past my bedroom window reaches all the way up here. The window groans as I lift it. I go out first and then point the flashlight up so Vincent can see where to step.

He drops from the lowest branch and lands even more quietly than I do.

The flashlight makes a circle of light at our feet. Outside of that circle, we can't see a thing. We walk very slowly, since we are walking toward a cliff. Very. Slowly. We step off the mowed lawn of the school grounds and onto the zigzag path.

We walk one behind the other, Vincent in front and me in back.

"Maybe we should get Bobo," Vincent says. "Just to scare off the cougar if it's out there."

"No," I say. "That's our mission. We *want* to find the cougar."

Vincent stops so suddenly that I run into him and we end up taking a shortcut down the hill to the beach. In the beginning we do something very like somersaults, but by the end we have crashed into enough stuff on our way down that we have straightened out a little and are rolling on our sides like kids do down grassy hills for fun.

Only this hill is not grassy. And we are not having fun.

Of course I drop the flashlight when we meet the raccoon.

When we finally fall onto the wet sand at the bottom of the hill, we lay there for a while, breathing. The air smells good, like fish and salt and the tar they paint on wood that sits near water. Sand fleas are jumping all over us. I pull some leaves and small branches out of my hair. I'm bleeding—just a little bit—in about twenty places.

After a minute I start to wonder, why is the sand so wet this far up the beach? I get a bad feeling.

Then I hear it.

Keep in mind, it's pitch-black.

But I know a killer wave coming when I hear it.

"Get up!" I yell to Vincent. We barely have time to jump up onto the driftwood pile behind us before it hits.

We hang on to a big log as the wave washes over us, bashing us against the wood and leaving us sputtering and coughing.

"Move!" I shout as I hear another wave gathering itself up.

Vincent and I scuttle over the rest of the driftwood logs. We find the zigzag path and sit down. Our teeth are chattering. Sand crunches between my molars. My nose and throat have that scratchy feeling you get after you throw up.

"At least it washed all the twigs out of my hair," Vincent says.

"And the salt in the salt water is antiseptic," I say, trying to look on the bright side too. "That's why all of our cuts and welts and scrapes and abrasions hurt so especially bad."

"Yes," says Vincent. "It's good to think that we won't have to worry about any minor infections."

We find the flashlight at the top of the path, right near where we bumped into each other. I pick it up and we set out across the lawn to the school.

"Try again tomorrow night?" I ask.

Vincent takes a long time to answer.

"Listen," I say, "I'll get us headlamps. And I'll check the tide tables in Dean Swift's office to make sure no waves sneak up on us."

"Yeah, yeah," says Vincent. He sounds a little grumpy. "I'm in."

I sigh. I'm sticky, soaked, bruised, and battered. But I'm glad to have a friend like Vincent.

We start up the tree. When he gets to the window and I'm in the fork of the two biggest branches, we hear it.

The cougar's screech fills the night. I can see the sound like a funnel cloud, almost, narrow where it begins and then opening out into the sky. The sound is coming from the edge of the fort closest to the beach.

The cougar screams again, and a shudder jerks my head hard to the side. That animal is close.

It's on the beach.

Near the driftwood pile.

Where we were standing ten minutes ago.

We climb through the window. Vincent is shaking now, and I don't think it's just the wind and his wet clothes. I think he can see the cougar in his mind the way I can see it in mine, the huge cat pacing, sniffing the wet wood, leaping onto the pile and pausing, one paw up, its nose in the air, tracking a scent.

Our scent.

"Tomorrow night, same time," I say when we get to his room.

"But why are we doing this?" Vincent asks.

"We need to get that cougar," I whisper. "I think it's trying to hurt someone I love."

Vincent turns his back to me. He opens his door without saying a word.

I can't blame him for bailing out. The mission tonight was a ridiculous disaster, a miserable failure, a complete catastrophe. And that's only if you look at it in a really, really positive light.

He steps into his room and then turns around to face me.

"Then we'll take care of it. You and me together. We'll get it." His eyes are scared, but he bobs his head up and down like he really means it.

"You know why?" he says. He pulls me into his room. "It's a secret. Nobody at the school but Dean Swift knows. And he only knows part of it."

I sit down on the desk chair next to his bed. He sits facing me.

"This summer there was a fire in my house. Me and my baby brother were sleeping upstairs. I tried to run out the door, but there was too much smoke. I ran to the window. My mom was down there. She was crying. She said to get the baby and climb out the window. I couldn't move. I started shaking and shaking and I fell down. I was so scared. Then a fireman broke through the door. Another one came through the window. They picked us both up and got us out of there." He stops talking, and I let him. I'm soaked and frozen to the bone, but I know better than to rush a kid through his secret.

"The firemen gave me a sticker and said I was really brave. But that was a lie. I didn't think about my brother once. I didn't try to save him or anything." His mouth pulls out into a straight line, and I can tell he's trying really hard not to cry.

"I think it's why my mom sent me here," he says. "She wants me to get tough."

After a minute he looks up at me sideways, so I can only see half his face.

"You know how that fire started?"

I shake my head.

"It was me. I found some matches in my stepdad's jacket. I wanted to see what it felt like to light one. Right before bed, while they were giving my brother a bath, I hid in the coat closet and lit them all up. I thought I stomped them out. But I missed one." He covers his mouth with his hand. "You're the only person who knows. My mom would leave me here forever if she knew."

"I won't ever tell," I say.

Then all of a sudden he grins. "My mom blamed my stepdad for the fire. She almost kicked him out for it. Wouldn't that have been great? She made him give up smoking. He'd *kill* me if he knew it was me. Whenever they argue, she brings it up and says how his smoking almost fried us all."

I try to smile, but I don't think that's funny. I know Vincent hates his stepdad. But that's a whale of a lie.

"This time I'm not gonna let anyone down." Vincent keeps talking. "You're gonna put a rock in that sling of yours and you're gonna hit that cat between the eyes. You're gonna knock him out, and we're gonna hog-tie him. When we get back to school, I'll tell everyone the whole story and you'll be a big hero."

I imagine the look on Mary Anne's face when she hears about it.

"Yeah, then that Mary Anne will notice you for sure," he says with a grin.

My cheeks get hot.

"What, you think I didn't know you're crushing on her?" He rolls his eyes. "She likes you already, but this will show her what you're made of."

As I walk back to my room, I leave squishy footprints in the carpet and on the stairs. I'm cold. I'm wet. But I'm warm inside as I think about Vincent.

A hero and a storyteller. They go together. You can't have one without the other.

Chapter 13

WHERE RAUL LEARNS ABOUT COUGARS AND HUNTERS AND DRAWS A DANGEROUS DOCUMENT

I wake up thinking how last night I missed the cougar by ten minutes. Did it find White Wolf? The worry hooks into my heart like a claw.

And there's a new problem. I'm scared now. I can hear that shriek in my head. It put a bone-deep, teeth-chattering, knee-knocking kind of fear in me. What makes me think I can catch a cougar with a sling and a little help from a friend?

I need information. How much do they weigh? How fast are they? How well do they see in the dark?

I stop by Dean Swift's office on my way to breakfast. He's busy writing, but for once the words won't wait.

"Do cougars hunt wolves?" is the first question I ask. *Say no,* I think. *Please say no.* If the answer's no, then I'm barking up the wrong tree.

Dean Swift looks at me for a long time.

Maybe he knows I was spying on him in the turret, and he's so furious he doesn't even know what to say. What if he calls my dad about it? There's a can of worms I'd like to keep sealed.

Then I see that even though he's staring right at me, his hand is writing. The man isn't listening.

"Do cougars kill wolves?" I ask again.

The question finally sinks in. His eyes bulge.

"Well," he says. He stands up and puts his hands in his coat pockets so his elbows stick out a little. He looks like a penguin.

Bobo is at his feet. She sighs.

I sit down. I sigh too.

When Dean Swift looks like a penguin, we all know he is about to give a lecture.

Sometimes, when Dean Swift is very interested in and very informed about a subject—like cougars and wolves it turns out—he takes a very long time to get to the point.

I am very hungry. But I listen long and hard.

Here's the point: Cougars attack wolves, but only rarely. It has to do with territory. Sometimes a cougar gets "displaced," which means it doesn't have a territory of its own. Then it might try to move into a wolf's territory. Or a wolf might feel its territory shrinking due to human population growth. It may begin to hunt in a cougar's territory. Either way, there's bound to be a fight. If there's more than one wolf, then the cougar doesn't stand much of a chance. The wolves will follow the cougar around, and then when it makes a kill, the wolves will leap in and chase the cougar off and eat his dinner. Cool, huh? Well, not for the cougar. It spends so much energy making kills it can't eat, it eventually starves to death. Or it gets so hungry it does something risky—like pounce from too high—and ends up snapping its spine.

So much for the good news.

Here's the bad news: In a fair fight between predators—when there's only one wolf and one cougar—the cougar will most likely win.

First period is PE. It might as well be. It's not like the day is going to get better.

Tuffman calls my name for roll like usual. Maybe he's not holding a grudge about our voodoo doll in the woods. I don't see the bird's-nest toupee anywhere handy. He doesn't say much of anything to me. Instead he throws a ball out at us and barks, "Dodgeball!"

His feelings toward me become pretty clear though, when the first round ends.

"Raul, stand at the wall!" he yells. "And the rest of you little blue-haired ladies, don't tell me you can't hit him."

Oh yeah, he's still mad. Guess he decided that since I used the straw man of him for target practice, he'd turn me into a bull's-eye.

"I'll give a quarter to whoever leaves a mark," he hollers. He jingles the change in his pockets. They look very, very full.

I gulp. And dodge and duck and dart for my life.

Tuffman's pockets are empty in fifteen minutes. When the quarters run out, kids get dimes. Then nickels. The darnedest thing is that those kids throw just as hard for the pennies, in the end.

The good part is that every time Vincent gets the ball, he heaves it, granny-shot style, at the hoop at the other end of court. The bad part is that even though everyone laughs every time he does it, nobody copies him.

Of course Tuffman's gonna put a stop to that. The next time Vincent gets the ball, Tuffman booms, "What are you two, besties?"

He stalks over. "Vincent. You hit him fair and square, or you drop and give me fifty."

Vincent glances at me.

All the boys start to chant, "Hit him, hit him."

Fifty push-ups? Vincent doesn't have five in him.

Vincent lifts the ball. He stares at the ground. Then he looks up and takes aim.

My stomach jumps.

Right as he's about to throw it, Tuffman smacks the ball down.

"See?" Tuffman says. "Some things never change. It's always your best friend who betrays you in the end."

They don't even know what Tuffman's talking about, but all the boys hoot.

"Burn!" says Mean Jack.

Vincent looks off to the side.

All I can do is remember Tuffman's story about how his best friend broke Tuffman's back in the woods. Why is everything he says to me lately so personal? It's creepy.

Game over, people. I'm done.

"Where you going?" Tuffman asks when he sees me heading toward the locker room. "Don't be a quitter. We're only going after you because you're so good at running away. Heck, you can get down on all fours if you want."

My cheeks burn. I look around to see if any of the other boys heard. But Mean Jack is picking his nose, and Little John is scraping off the scab on his elbow and eating it, and Jason is walking around the room doing a chicken dance.

Tuffman sends the ball at Jason, so hard his last "squawk" comes out like a scream.

Vincent walks over to me. "I was going to take that ball and slam him with it," he says. "He wouldn't have known what hit him."

You promised your mom not to lie, I almost say to him, but instead I nod like I believe him. It's not easy to change. And it's hard not to do what Tuffman wants. It's the way he says your name.

I don't blame him. But I would've done all fifty push-ups with him.

Tuffman looks over at us, the ball raised high. I pick up the bathroom pass that's on a hook by the locker room door and hold it up to him.

"Wimp!" he hollers at me. Then he says, "Okeydoke, Mean Jack, you're up. You take Raul's place."

The last thing I hear before the ball starts slamming is Tuffman shouting, "I'm out of money, kids, so you're hitting Jackie-Girl here for the glory of it, all right?"

It almost makes me smile.

The nurse makes me ice my shins so long, I'm late to reading.

This is Ms. Tern's first teaching gig. I don't think she knows yet that the teacher is supposed to be mad at kids who come in late. She smiles when I open the door.

Ms. Tern always makes me feel better. I feel safe in her room. Is that weird?

Especially since she makes us read stories where dogs die and spiders die and moms die and sometimes a nuclear bomb falls on people and then they die later after being sick for a long time. If anyone complains, she says, "It's the curriculum." Her voice is so sad when she says it that even Mean Jack gets a wrinkle between his eyes and looks sympathetic.

She gets up from her desk and hands me a copy of the sheet she's reading from.

"Brilliant. I thought you might fancy learning something about the history of the island."

When she says "you" I realize she means me. Just me. I look down at my desk.

I wish I could tell her everything. I think she would believe me. I don't think she'd be afraid. Not with a right hook like she's got. She'd be a great cougar hunter, I bet.

Then she reads us the worst story I've ever heard.

Forty years ago some hunters got in little planes and boats and came to the Salish Sea and chased an orca family that scientists call the L pod. The male orcas and the grandma orcas tried to trick the hunters. They broke off from the mothers and babies and swam farther north to draw the hunters away from their families. But the hunters in the planes figured out what they were doing. They used loud noises and nets and got the whole pod trapped in Penn Cove. It's not far from Fort Casey. Then the hunters loaded the baby orcas onto trucks. They wanted to sell them to water parks where they would be trained to perform. The hunters let the rest go. But the orcas wouldn't leave. They waited in Penn Cove to see what would happen to their babies. They waited until the trucks drove off. Finally they swam away. Since that day the L pod has never returned to Penn Cove.

I'd rather spend the day bombed with dodgeballs than ever hear that story again.

Ms. Tern is a teacher, so she keeps reading. "Some of the mother orcas died that day trying to save their babies. They fought so hard they got tangled in the nets and suffocated. The hunters filled the bodies of the dead mother whales with rocks so they would sink to the bottom of the ocean floor. The hunters feared that animal rights groups would protest if they found out how many orcas had died. Eventually all these dark deeds came to light. Evil always does. And that particularly evil day has gone down in history as the Penn Cove Massacre."

Ms. Tern sets the book down. "Right." She wipes a tear away. Her voice is a little high up in her throat like she's got more tears bunched up in there. "I know a bit more."

Please don't tell me any more, I want to say. *Please.* I have the ache I get when I remember my mom tucking me into bed.

"As it turns out, two of the mother orcas were spirit whales," Ms. Tern says. She smiles softly. "That means they were pure white. They disappeared entirely. Nobody ever found their bodies."

My throat squeezes tight, but something in my belly jumps like it has little wings. Spirit animals. The story is sad, but now I have a name for something so important to me that I didn't think there could be a word for it. Animals that are white that shouldn't be white are spirit animals.

"Many cultures throughout the world prize spirit animals for their quote unquote 'magical' properties." Ms. Tern raises a skeptical eyebrow at me.

I stare back at her. Would she raise her eyebrow like that if I told her my secret?

She keeps talking. "Often times these animals are used in traditional medicines or sold illegally to wealthy individuals for private collections. International wildlife organizations believe a man named Luke Ferrier is the criminal mastermind responsible for the Penn Cove massacre as well as the disappearance of countless other spirit animals," she says. "He is a ruthless killer."

A chill of fear runs from my ears down my neck. I imagine a hunter in a red cap raising a rifle, white fur flashing through a screen of blackberry bushes.

"It is imperative that I find him before he further decimates endangered populations," she adds.

Have you ever looked in someone's eyes and seen the words they don't say? Like *I'm sorry.* Or *I love you.* Or *I just lied.* The words in Ms. Tern's eyes go like this: *I said too much.*

But I'm the only one listening. So I'm the only one who knows that when Ms. Tern should have said "they" she said "I." And that she meant it, or else why would her eyes look worried? Does Ms. Tern think she's part of an international organization looking for an infamous spirit-animal poacher?

I shake my head. Vincent's right. We do have the craziest teachers here.

"Right," Ms. Tern says. Her voice is very tidy and neat, like she's trying to sweep a little mess under the rug. "Now, let's have a look, shall we, at another document related to this issue." She begins to read aloud from a book. "The orcas of Puget Sound are called Southern Residents. The J, K, and L pods frequent these salmon-rich waters. Many facts about these animals would surprise you. Did you know that in local native lore the orca is related to the wolf?"

Orcas and wolves? Is that what she said?

But then my spine lights up. Gollum has returned. I turn, and she stops with the tip of her tail under the door. The gold ring around her body gleams under the fluorescent lights.

Mean Jack hollers, "I got a beef with you, snake!"

I remember Gollum's tail flicking out of Mean Jack's duffel bag last week. What did that snake do to that mobster over the weekend?

Mean Jack lunges at Gollum and lands flat on his belly. Half the kids are shouting, and the other half are standing on their chairs.

"Do *not* harm her!" Ms. Tern says in her popped-soap-bubble voice.

Cook Patsy and Mary Anne are right. Choices. You gotta make 'em. Ms. Tern needs a hand here. I pick up a big bin, dump out the crayons, and toss it to Mean Jack. He slams it onto the floor right on top of Gollum and shouts in a Cuban accent, "Say hello to my little friend!"

His aim is perfect. Almost. All I see is a flash of black and a glint of gold streak across the floor, over Ms. Tern's shoe, along the long wall, and back out under the door.

Mean Jack shakes his head at himself. "Man's gotta know his limitations."

Ms. Tern starts reading out loud again, but nobody's listening.

The classroom sounds like an F5 tornado. Paul, who gets to sit on an exercise ball instead of a chair, is bouncing across the classroom on it, smacking it and yelling "Yippee-kie-ay" and a bad word. Mark takes off the weighted vest they make him wear to keep him calm and starts swinging it above his head like a shot-put. Jason is making animal calls. He's good, and my pulse runs wild when he howls.

I put my hands over my ears, but then I can't draw.

Only the back corner of the room is quiet. A group of boys have pulled their desks around Mean Jack. They sit and watch carefully as he teaches them how to make a weapon out of a paper clip and a ruler.

"It's called a shiv," he says.

When the bell rings, Ms. Tern puts the book down.

The floor is covered with paper and broken pencil tips and Kleenex and paper clips, and each of Mean Jack's students has fashioned a perfect shiv.

"Beastly boys," I hear Ms. Tern whisper.

I'm halfway to lunch when I notice I forgot my drawing. Let's just say it's a dangerous document. I don't want it to end up in the wrong hands. It's a picture of a man getting chased by a hungry lion. The man's toupee is hanging from the lion's fangs. I kept the blood to the absolute minimum, considering the mortal injuries the victim has sustained.

Did I mention that the man looks a lot like Mr. Tuffman?

I run back to the classroom, but I'm too late.

Ms. Tern has taped my drawing to the blackboard.

My hands start to sweat. I'm going to be in big trouble. I don't get in trouble very often. I don't like it. Plus, Ms. Tern is my favorite teacher. I don't want her to be mad at me. I know she'd probably just give me sad eyes and whisper, "Raul. You know better than that." But is there anything worse than a teacher who never gets mad at anyone getting mad at *you*?

I step back into the hallway.

I peek in to watch as Ms. Tern picks up one of the shivs Mean Jack's crew was making. She walks to the back of the room. She glances at the door.

I don't move.

And then she sends that shiv flying. It slices the air. I hear a little pop and then another as the blade drives into the blackboard.

I push the door open a little wider and put my head in farther. I can't help it. It's what my dad would call professional curiosity. I'm a pretty good shot myself, but her form is phenomenal.

"Did you forget something?" she calls. She's standing at the blackboard, untaping my drawing.

I stare at the back of her head, frozen. My thoughts are frozen, my mouth is frozen. Should I ask her for the drawing? Does she hate Tuffman or just enjoy target practice? Will she rat me out, or does she believe in solidarity?

When she turns and looks at me, her eyes are sharp and intense like I've never seen them before. I'm used to Ms. Tern looking Defeated and In Despair. Right now she looks Tough as Nails.

"Would you like your drawing?" she asks.

My eyeballs feel dry. I've forgotten how to blink.

"It's a very good likeness," she says. "You're quite a gifted artist."

She walks over and hands it to me.

I don't look at the drawing until I'm out in the hall. It's not just her form that's phenomenal. It's her aim. There are two slits—one where the shiv hit Tuffman's heart and another where it tagged him in the head.

How did she make the blade *bounce* with such accuracy?

I turn back and stand in her open doorway for a second. It flashes through my mind that maybe Ms. Tern isn't delusional. Maybe she really is some kind of secret agent.

She's sitting at her desk. She looks up at me.

"Have we both got a little secret, then?" she asks. "Right. It looks to me like we'll just have to trust each other, eh?"

Can you be in love with two women at the same time? That's a question I'd like to ask my dad. Could I love Ms. Tern and Mary Anne both? Is it legal? Is it wrong?

I stop in the middle of the hall.

Could she do that to a cougar?

Chapter 14

WHERE RAUL FINDS OUT HE HAS FAMILY

After classes are over I head back toward my room. I have a lot on my mind. I want Vincent to like me enough to do fifty push-ups for me. I want Mary Anne to call me heroic. I want Ms. Tern to grab her shiv and help me get the cougar.

"Raul!"

The dean's voice makes me jump. I step into his office. Maybe he found out more about the cougar.

Dean Swift is at his desk. My nose twitches. Then I notice Tuffman sitting behind him, in the corner by the window. On the table next to Mr. Tuffman there's a lamp with a stained glass shade. It throws a blotchy pattern of light onto his face. Like he's wearing a coat of many colors.

"Mr. Tuffman and I were just having a little chat," Dean Swift says.

The drawing. Ms. Tern ratted on me. How could she?

"Someone gave the dean here the impression that

I've been picking on you," says Tuffman. "You got any idea who that might be?"

I almost smile, I'm so relieved. Cook Patsy must have got wind of the dodgeball disaster.

"You think that's funny?" Tuffman asks.

"No, no, Mr. Tuffman," says Dean Swift. "We're not here to accuse anyone, not Raul or you or *any* member of our staff. We are here to open the lines of communication."

The dean beckons to me. Ready to listen. Tuffman half stands. Ready to pounce.

I don't know what comes over me.

I bolt like a bunny in the woods.

Tuffman's on me before I hit the stairs. He grabs me by the back of my shirt. With his fist he gathers the material in tight like a straitjacket and steers me to the office.

"Keep your clothes on," he says in my ear. "Today you're gonna talk."

I shudder. Like that bunny in the woods when my wolf breath hit its neck.

Tuffman lets go of me before we get to the office. As we walk in, he rests his hand on my shoulder. He goes back to his chair in the corner.

I squeegee his spit out of my ear with the cuff of my sleeve.

"Have a seat, my boy," Dean Swift says. "I'm sure

we'll find that this is nothing more than a little misunderstanding."

"I've been coming on too strong," Tuffman says to me. "Let me tell you why." He leans forward. The shadows from the lampshade flicker across his face. I see that they are shapes—a red butterfly on his forehead, a playful kitten on his mouth. "We got history, kid, you and me."

Dean Swift looks back and forth between us, big-eyed.

"I didn't even know it until I got here and read your file. Then I thought it was best to keep quiet. I could see Raul was traumatized," he says to the dean. "And I was recovering from my last surgery. I didn't have the strength to tackle the problem. You get that, right?"

"Indeed, serious injuries like yours can take a grave emotional toll," Dean Swift says.

Tuffman clears his throat. "I knew your mother, Raul. I coached her at the university. When she went to Nationals she broke all the records. I bet she never told you, did she?"

His lies are getting personal again. I don't like it.

"I was the only one who could outrun her. Your dad couldn't come close to keeping up with her."

My *dad*? Now he knows my dad? Liar.

"Your mom had a real shot at the Olympics. It was your dad who put an end to all that. He got a job studying whales or something. She had to choose between him and the team. She chose him. Last I heard they were living in a one-man tent on Orcas Island."

I sit up. That part's true. I was born on that island.

The lampshade shadows shift. Now a running dog rests on Tuffman's cheek. His voice is soft. "Your mom was an amazing woman. *Kind*. No ego. Always putting everyone else first."

I stop hating Tuffman. I stop hating him because in his voice I can hear that he loved my mom too.

"Raul," he says softly. He comes across the room. He reaches out like he's going to touch me. I flinch. But I want to hear what else he has to say.

"When I got here and found out who you were and what all had happened to you, I thought that maybe fate had sent me for a reason. Your mom gave up her dream for your dad. She had disappeared a long time before she disappeared, if you know what I mean. You're a lot like her, the way you hide yourself. I started thinking that maybe if I toughened you up, you'd learn to put yourself first. My heart's in the right place, Raul. I didn't mean to scare you."

It makes sense, in a strange way. Maybe his heart *is* in the right place. "Thank you for telling me," I say. "I never knew my mom could've been in the Olympics."

It fills me up with pride. Since she left, my mom has become a shadow to me. A warm shape in a dark room in my mind. The more time passes, the darker the room gets, the harder it is to see her. Tuffman just walked into that dark room and turned on a nightlight. I can see her better now.

I see my dad better now too. I don't think he means to be selfish. And I guess it's good to know that I'm not the only one he was selfish with. Forgetting about me has more to do with him than me. It's not because I'm so easy to forget. It's just who he is.

"Your mom and I were so close. I miss her." Tuffman's voice breaks. "See, I'm no good at all this." He puts a hand over his eyes. His Adam's apple bobs up and down. When he takes his hand away again his eyes are damp.

I put my head down in my hands. I knew he'd make me cry.

"So you gotta tell me how I can help you," Tuffman says. He kneels down in front of me. "You can't trust everybody you meet. Even best friends will betray you. But you can trust me, Raul."

I think of White Wolf and the scrape in her side and the broken-necked bunny I left for her in the grass. The relief runs over me like rain on your face when you look up into the sky. He will help me help my mom.

"Tell me about the woods, Raul." He opens his arms.

I slip from the chair.

"I know everything about your mom, Raul."

I can't say the wrong thing to him. He knows everything already. The words rush up. The whole story of how she found me and I found her.

"It started last year," I say. "I was so sad about my dad forgetting me." My voice is very small. It's because the words are so true. The truer the word, the closer to silence.

"Oh, we all were," Dean Swift says quickly and kindly. "We *all* were."

"Just tell us what happened, Raul," Tuffman says.

I lift my arms. I put them around him. He squeezes me to him. Warmth. Nobody has hugged me in a long time.

I don't mean to. But through his polo I feel a long raised river of skin. His scar. The second I touch it his fingernails plunge into my back. They bite into my skin through my thin shirt. My shoulders jump up, and, just as quick, he pulls away from me and pats me gently.

He looks down so I can't see his eyes.

I get a deep, bad, black feeling. The eight half-moons left by his fingernails on my back burn. This is the kind of guy who can hurt you when he hugs you. This is *Tuffman*.

I sit back in my chair. Far back. I almost told him everything! I watch him as he hangs his head. I forget to blink.

Finally he looks up. He's still sitting on his heels in front of me still. His eyes search the air above my head. He's looking for the words to make me forget those half-moons.

"Raul, I can't keep this secret anymore. Your grandma was my sister."

"Oh!" Dean Swift gasps. "Oh goodness. You're his family!"

I look at Tuffman. I don't see the resemblance.

"Your grandma was a lot older than me. Before she died I promised her I'd take care of your mom. I was barely twenty. She was around your age. I did the best I could by her, Raul."

Tuffman taps my knee to get me to look at him. He says my name again. *Raul.* He wants me to talk, but I can feel the sting of his nails in my back.

"I'm your great-uncle. What else can I say to convince you, Raul?" he asks. His voice has a hard edge to it.

I can feel how desperate he is. The more he wants my words, the less I want to give them to him.

He gets to his feet. His left hand reaches back. I think he's touching his scar.

"I loved her like a little sister," he whispers.

The words send a jolt through me. I've heard them before. Didn't he tell me that it was family who injured him? Someone he had loved *like a little sister*?

I shiver. My *mom* gave him that scar.

I smell it. Something wrong. Something bad. Story time's over, Tuffman.

But I can't look away from him. My neck won't let me. It's tight and stretched and forces my face in his direction.

He lowers himself into the chair by the lamp. His back must hurt from crouching in front of me for so long. Shadow leaves from the lamp flutter across his face. He looks tired out. He looks how I feel when I'm deep in the woods and I've spent an hour chasing a bunny and at the last second the bunny darts into a hole just big enough for my nose but too small for me to get my mouth open.

Dean Swift honks into his pocket handkerchief. "For the love of St. Jude, I never foresaw such a turn of events," he says damply. "Never in all my years. To witness such a reunion. Happy day. Happy day."

The bell rings.

I back out of the room.

Tuffman watches me through half-closed eyes. "We'll talk later," he says. He smiles softly at me. "There's more to the story, Raul."

I race upstairs. I'm out of breath, but I can finally breathe.

Tuffman was suffocating me. It's that feeling you get when someone stands too close or looks over your shoulder while you're reading or tries to get you to give them things you want to keep for yourself—like your dessert or your mom's soul. It's not just that he was in my space. It's like he was trying to climb inside of me.

I almost told him everything.

Vincent is standing at my bedroom door. He looks worried. "What happened, man? Did you get in trouble? I saw you running down the hall, and then Tuffman grabbed you and marched you into the dean's office."

"Later," I say. I'm done talking for the day. I push past him to open the door. I'm about to shut it, but Vincent has already stepped in behind me.

"Friends tell each other stuff," he says.

For a split-second I want to push him out of my room. But there's a look on his face that stops me. He wants to listen to me because I listened to him last night. He thinks he owes me. It's like sharing stuff, only it's not your baseball mitt or a book. It's words.

"Tuffman says he's my great-uncle," I say it quick, like ripping off a Band-Aid.

Vincent blinks. "No way. Tuffman?"

"Tuffman," I say. Then I say more. It just pops out. "It's so embarrassing. I'd rather have Mean Jack for a twin. Or Gollum for an aunt."

Vincent cracks up like the whole thing is just some crazy, random joke. It makes me smile too.

"My mom says you can't pick family, you just take what you get and lump it," Vincent says after he stops laughing. "But if I could, I'd pick you to be my brother."

He stretches out his hand. "Brother," he says.

"Brother," I say back.

We shake.

People always tell you talking will make you feel better. But it's not the talking that makes you feel better. It's the person listening.

Vincent picks up my code book and flips through it for a while. Then all of a sudden he sets it down. "So why's he being such a jerk to you, then?" he asks.

I shrug. "Maybe it's because he's a jerk."

"You know what? He's just like my stepfather. All he wants is to boss me around. It's like he's trying to get his claws into me, so I do what he says the second he says it."

I grin. I pull up my shirt. I can see the reflection of my back in the mirror when I turn to show him. Just above each shoulder blade are four red half-moons.

"He did that to you?" Vincent asks.

"Yeah, this is the side effect of a hug from Tuffman."

Vincent's eyes glint. "I'm gonna get him for you, just like I got my stepdad."

"Don't bother," I say. I'm happy he cares enough to want to. But I've got bigger fish to fry, if you know what I mean. I've got a cougar to hunt and a girl to win.

Vincent shrugs like it doesn't matter anyway. He holds up the code book and heads to the door. "Can I borrow this?"

"What's mine is yours," I say as he leaves. That's what my dad always said to anyone who wanted anything. And he meant it too. He's the kind of guy who would give you the shirt off his back. You ask for it, it's yours.

Tuffman's the kind of guy who will *take* the shirt off your back. Then he'll put it on and take a nap in your bed.

It makes me think.

Tuffman didn't lie about everything. But he twisted the truth like a wolf twists a bunny's neck.

My dad's not selfish. He'd give you everything even if it meant he'd end up with nothing. Maybe that's what happened when my dad lost my mom. He had nothing left.

Chapter 15

WHERE TUFFMAN GETS A GUN AND MARY ANNE MEETS A BULLET

I can't sleep. I wake up early. My plate is full of bacon and eggs and sausage and they're so hot the steam is coming off them. It cheers me up a little. Protein will do that for you.

Today I'm gonna ask Ms. Tern to help me hunt the cougar. She has skills, there's no denying it. And she's got a little more crazy in her than your average teacher. That's a plus in my book.

Mary Anne sits down next to me. "Vincent said to give this to you."

It's a plastic Easter egg. I crack it open. A paper clip and a strip of paper fall out.

I smooth the paper. Mary Anne leans over. Her eyebrows are pinched together.

"Paper clip code," she says after a second.

She takes the paper clip out of my hand. My hand buzzes when her fingers brush my palm.

I glance up and catch her staring at me. Right away she looks down. Her cheeks are a little pink. I get a fluttery feeling. Does Mary Anne like me, too?

"Now," she says in her teacher voice, "you lay the paper clip flat over the line of letters, with the double loop end to the right and the other end around the first letter. Whatever letter is in that double loop is the one you want. Then you slide the paper clip right, like this, so that the end loop goes around the letter the double loop was around. See?"

Together we spell it out. *LAKE. NOW. ALONE.*

We look at each other. I get off my stool and grab my tray.

"I'm coming," Mary Anne says. She sets her tray on top of mine, puts everything back in the Easter egg, and shoves it into her pocket.

Vincent said *alone*. But am I ever gonna tell Mary Anne she can't do something she wants?

As we run out the front door and down the steps, Bobo joins us.

The sun has just risen. It's very cold. The sky is filled with crows. I run hard.

We hear it before we get off the main road. *Crack.* The crows caw and croak. They swoop and tumble. Someone's shooting a gun in the woods.

I'm ahead of Mary Anne. I stop running and wave my hand at her to stop. We're not going into the woods if there's a hunter in there. But she races by me. Bobo is at her heels, and she looks back at me too, her tongue flopping out of her mouth.

"Come on," Mary Anne shouts as she turns off the road and onto the path to the lake. "That gunshot came from miles away."

For once Mary Anne is dead wrong. But they get to the oak tree with my bike stuck in it before I catch up. I sprint in front of her and block her way on the narrow path. Bobo sits and pants. Mary Anne puts her hands on her hips and looks at me, breathing hard.

"Stop," I say. Then the hairs on the back of my neck stand up. We're not alone in the woods. Is it the hunter?

My blood freezes.

The *cougar*? I reach toward my back pocket, but I already know there's no sling there. How could I be so stupid? Dean Swift said to stay close to the school.

When I turn to look behind me, toward the lake, Mary Anne darts ahead. "You worry too much. Last one there is a rotten egg."

Bobo streaks after her.

The early light is loose and filtered, falling through the fog and cedars. The lake is straight ahead. I look into the distance, just to the left of the path. I feel it. Something alive is in there. It's hard to see. The morning sunlight glares down from above, while the night still sits in the cold shade below.

I squint. Whatever it is, it's not moving. It's a man. The man's lifting something. It's a rifle. It's Tuffman. He's aiming at something on the other side of the path.

I'm trying to see what he's shooting at when I realize that Mary Anne is running straight toward the lake. My feet pound on the path before my brain screams *Run!* In a second Tuffman will be on her left. His target will be on her right. She's heading straight into the line of fire.

I hear the gun click.

"Don't shoot!" I yell. At the same time, I leap. The gun goes off. I grab Mary Anne and pull her down. She screams. We hit the path. The bullet whizzes over us. There's a sound like a bunch of little explosions, and we look to the right, where Tuffman was aiming.

Fireworks. Mary Anne and I sit up slowly and stare. Fireworks are popping and blazing out of something that looks like a busted-up piñata.

When I look the other way, I see Tuffman walking out of the trees toward us. He starts shouting. "I almost shot your head off!"

Mary Anne and I are sitting on the path side by side. She looks like she might cry. I put my arm around her shoulders. Bobo comes sniffing to see if we're alive.

"Who gave you permission to be out here at this time of day?"

We stare up at Tuffman. He's got two little spit balls, one in each corner of his mouth. He's frothing mad, but I can tell it's because he's scared pantsless about what he almost did.

A shadow falls across us. Tuffman wipes his mouth.

"What the dickens were you thinking, Mr. Tuffman?" comes Ms. Tern's clipped voice from behind us. We turn and see her standing over us in a jogging suit.

"I saw a cougar out on the road this morning," Tuffman says. I hear the nervous shake in his voice. "I got my gun and followed it. It was right there." He points to the thing with the fireworks popping out of it every so often. "I didn't see the kids until it was too late."

Ms. Tern looks over at the fireworks. "Your cougar appears to be a piñata in the shape of a lion. Either you have a very strange idea of a good time, or someone has played a rather complicated trick on you."

Mary Anne and I glance at each other. Vincent went a little too far this time.

Before we can blink, Ms. Tern snatches the rifle from Tuffman. He jerks his hand back and then holds it out and looks at it. There are four long scratches across Tuffman's skin where Ms. Tern's nails cut him as she took it.

Ms. Tern does something quick and clicky with the rifle to make sure it's not loaded. Then she puts her hand out and stares at Mr. Tuffman. "Don't make me go after them," she says.

Tuffman gulps. He rubs his hand, reaches into his front jeans pocket, and gives her some bullets.

Ms. Tern is now armed. Something tells me that if Ms. Tern aimed that rifle at the cougar, she wouldn't miss.

"Have you been injured?" she asks us. She helps Mary Anne to her feet. She makes a *tsk* sound at Mary Anne's ripped jeans and bleeding knees.

She glares at Tuffman. "I've got my eye on you."

"What about my gun?"

"That's the second time I've stopped you from trying to kill an animal. That cougar has as much right to be walking in these woods as you."

Here's a problem. Ms. Tern has the right skills and the firepower but the wrong attitude. She's never going to hunt the cougar with me.

She herds us down the path in front of her. "I'm taking you two directly to the nurse," she says.

I glance back at Tuffman. He looks angry and confused. He's made me feel that way often enough that it makes me a little happy. But he looks scared and sorry, too. He's a jerk, but even a jerk has his good side, I guess.

"You, young man," Ms. Tern keeps saying over and over.

I'm afraid she knows about Vincent's prank and thinks I was in on it.

Finally she says more. "I am speechless. I've known courageous men in my time. Men who would sacrifice

173

their lives to make this world a better, safer place. But only rarely have I witnessed such bravery, such speed, such agility."

I'm proud and embarrassed. I didn't know she saw what happened. I'm glad she thinks I'm so great, but I just did what my gut told me to do.

Mary Anne nods. Her mouth moves, but for once she doesn't have anything to say.

At the oak, Bobo stops to sniff. My eyes follow her nose up into the branches of the tree. My mouth pops open. Vincent is sitting up there on my bike. He puts a finger over his lips.

I stare at him. I don't know what to think. That was one heck of a prank.

When we reach the driveway, Mary Anne takes my hand. "Thank you," she says. She gives me a hug. "I was wrong. There *is* a synonym for 'heroic.' It's *Raul*."

Her hug pins my arms to my sides. I lean my head down toward hers. My cheek touches her hair. It's soft, like cherry blossoms.

Solidarity. Mary Anne and I don't say anything to anybody about what Vincent did. Ms. Tern would say that I am *conflicted*. Part of me gets all pumped up whenever I think about it. Cook Patsy taught me to wrestle Tuffman, Dean Swift made me talk to him, but Vincent scared the daylights out of him.

The other part of me knows it was the worst, dumb-est, stupidest idea in the world. Obviously Vincent didn't expect Mary Anne to come running through that scene. But Tuffman, a gun, and a piñata full of fireworks? Nothing good's gonna come of that.

Vincent doesn't mention it either. He looks a little worried around Mary Anne at first, but she just tells us her usual stories about Samish princesses married to sea gods and children kidnapped by shape-shifting otters. In the dining hall Vincent sits to my left and Mary Anne to my right. Sometimes Mary Anne's shoulder brushes mine and neither of us pulls away.

Tuffman doesn't know what hit him or who got him. For a day or two he's a shadow of himself. He pulls out a parachute and lets us play popcorn in PE. Every once in a while he calls me "son." It makes me want to shove him away. *There's only one man who calls me that,* I want to say. *And it's not you.*

Ms. Tern has us read informational texts on gun safety. She's not going to help me get the cougar, I've figured that much out about her. But she gives me a little wink every now and then that makes me glow inside.

Nobody hears or sees the cougar. I bet it's gone away.

On Friday morning when it's my turn to help out in the kitchen, Cook Patsy gives me a hug.

"It's nice to see you looking so happy," she says. "You and your friends."

I knew she liked me. But I didn't know how much.

"Thank you," I say. I always mean it when I say that. I hope she knows how much.

Chapter 16

WHERE EVERYTHING STARTS TO GO RIGHT BUT IS REALLY GOING WRONG

On Friday at lunch Dean Swift comes into the dining room to make an announcement.

"I'm sorry, children," he says. "Due to the high volume of phone calls from concerned parents regarding the cougar, there will be no fishing today. Instead, we will all enjoy an extra hour of free voluntary reading in our rooms."

All the Cubs moan and stomp their feet on the sticky floor.

I look out the window. The sky is the blue that makes the cedars so green. The air is cold and the sun is hot. There's enough wind to make your blood skip in your veins.

Nobody's heard that cougar all week. It's either long gone or sound asleep.

Vincent leans forward so he can see both me and Mary Anne. "I'm going fishing," he says. "Are you two in?"

Don't get me wrong. I love to read.

But I'm with Vincent. Mary Anne takes a second longer.

There's hot wet breath on my elbow. I look down. Sparrow. "Me too," he says.

I smile and mess up his hair.

"But keep your trap shut about it, okay?" Vincent says.

I shoot him a look. Nobody talks rude to Sparrow. Not even Vincent.

We sneak into the equipment room with the key Dean Swift gave me a few years ago. While I'm looking for a pole for Mary Anne, Sparrow shows Vincent the carving I made on his. Vincent traces his finger over the head of one of the wolves.

He looks up at me and whistles. "Wicked cool. This is some quality work."

"It's not done yet," I say. "I'm going to paint it, but I have to read a little bit more to make sure I do the colors right."

"It looks good to me," Vincent says.

"Dean Swift says there are rules about where you put which colors in Native American art," I explain. "It has to be authentic." I'm talking a lot. They all look at me with big eyes.

Sparrow pulls on the pole to take it back, but Vincent holds on to it a minute more.

"Will you make one exactly like it for me?" he asks when he finally lets Sparrow take it.

"No," I say.

Vincent opens his mouth like he can't believe it.

I try to explain. "I only make a pole once. It takes a long time to figure out the right carving for the right boy. The wood tells me what it wants to become."

Vincent raises an eyebrow. He's about to call me a weirdo. But instead he just nods.

I glance at Mary Anne. I can tell she likes something I said.

Now if I could just figure out which words, I'd say them again.

It's easy to sneak out the window in Sparrow's room, since it's on the ground floor. After the first bend in the road, nobody can see us from the school, so we slow down and relax.

Vincent has a big surprise for us when we get to the picnic table. "Look," he says, and opens up his backpack. "Candy feast."

Sour watermelons, candy necklaces, bouncy balls, tattoos—it's all my favorite stuff. There's enough loot for twenty kids. Mary Anne and I look at each other. We're thinking the same thing. We're thinking this is what you get when you gut a lion piñata to make room for fireworks and other incendiary devices.

"And I saved us some sparklers," he says.

Sparrow is jumping up and down. Mary Anne and I say thank you. Vincent shrugs.

Something tells me Vincent is trying to say he's sorry for almost getting us killed, but without actually saying it.

Mary Anne does a sparkler dance. Sparrow shows us some survival tricks you can do with bubble gum, pee, and some string. Vincent sticks a tattoo on his forehead.

Sparrow polishes off four packets of Pop Rocks and ten candy rings before we even notice him lying under the table singing a weird little song.

It's the best time I've ever had at the lake, even though the fish won't bite. In the end, Sparrow is the only one who catches something big enough to keep.

"It's my lucky pole," Sparrow says as I unhook the beautiful trout.

I get a glimpse of Vincent's face when Sparrow says that. He looks the way you look when the lunch lady gives the piece of pie you've been eyeing the whole time you're in line to the kid in front of you. Jealous.

It makes me feel bad and happy at the same time. I don't want Vincent upset. But I know all about jealousy. You only get it for the good stuff.

All of a sudden it starts to rain so hard, the ground turns to mud in seconds. With every gust of wind, the trees shake water down at us along with the sky, and so we all take off running back to the school.

This time I even outrun Vincent. Must be all the gummy peaches. Halfway up the main road I look back and see him standing where the path meets the road. He's hunched over like he's winded, but when he sees me staring he hollers for me to go on ahead.

"I dropped something," he yells. "I'm gonna go back and get it!"

His voice sounds funny—like it did when he lied and said White Deer hadn't spoken to him.

But why would Vincent lie to me?

After I change into dry clothes, I notice the recipe box sitting on my bedside table. I can't believe the whole week has gone by.

All my wolf worries hit me like a punch. Is White Wolf all right? What if the cougar *isn't* gone? What if it's out there and I did nothing all week but laugh at Vincent's jokes and think about holding Mary Anne's hand?

I can't watch the other kids leave today. I grab my duffel bag, run downstairs, and tell the dean that my dad got here early. Then I slip back into my room, lock the door, and keep the light off. Nobody will know I never left. After I see Dean Swift drive away, I'll sneak out my window and run to the lighthouse.

I lie on my bed and wait. The curtains are open and the light coming through is gray and wet. I'm mad at myself. Maybe this is what happened to my dad. Maybe he meant to do the things he was supposed to do but would forget right up until it was too late. I wonder if he has this same heavy dragging feeling when he thinks of me.

Ms. Tern said I was the bravest kid she'd ever seen. But I'm not. I'm a little chicken, afraid of a big cat. Why didn't I go after that cougar again?

I open my mom's recipe box. I flip through the cards. She feels more real to me now. I don't like Tuffman. He's a snoop and a jerk. But he did something nobody else did. He introduced me to my mom before she was my mom. I can't explain it very well. But I know her better now.

It's like what Dean Swift said about the mtDNA. Our family is a secret code, inside of us. I wonder if I'll ever crack the code of why my mom and dad did the things they did.

Most of the cards she wrote in blue ink. But right in the middle of the box there's one written in faded pencil. Tuna Surprise. I squint to make out the words. There's no tuna in it. But there are muffins. And coconut.

Nobody puts coconut and muffins in tuna casserole. *Everybody* puts tuna in it, though. My mom had to know when she wrote it that it wasn't right. You can't make that big of a mistake.

I get a tingly feeling.

My thought is typed out and italicized in my mind, just like the chapter title in the code book Cook Patsy gave me. *It's a List Code.*

What if my mom wasn't a terrible cook? What if her recipes are codes?

I grab my clipboard. I clip Tuna Surprise at the top. Then I take the inside of a candy bar wrapper and make a chart. For a list code you use the number in the front to tell you which letter of the ingredient to use. You ignore the measurements.

2 tsp ginger	I
3 muffins	F
4 tsp cumin	I
2 oz meat	E
3 oz liver	V
5 pats butter	E
2 tsp cream	R

If I ever. I suck my breath in. It *is* a code.

I pull out the recipe after Tuna Surprise. It's Frog Eye Salad.

3 oz cod	D
2 tsp ginger	I
1 steak	S
3 oranges	A

1 tsp pepper
1 cup pearl pasta
5 frog eyes
1 apple
2 grapes

By the time I get halfway through Frog Eye Salad my hand is shaking.

I was wrong when I thought the cards weren't in order. They are. They're in the order of my mom's story. I keep going. It's five o' clock. I hear Dean Swift walking the halls, turning off lights. He jiggles the handle of the utility closet to make sure it's locked.

I stop taking the time to write out the ingredients and just copy over the letters. My mouth is dry like dust. After Crock Pot Spaghetti and Jim's Lasagna I put the pencil down.

If I ever disappear: I know his secret. T wants to kill me.

I look at my clock. It'll be sunset soon. I put the cards back in the box. My head feels full, like an overpacked suitcase. There's such a big mystery raining down all around me, and I can't see my way through it. I push the recipe card box far back under the bed. I throw the window open and scramble down the madrona tree.

I don't mind the rain or the cedars whipping in my face as I run.

I think about the questions Tuffman asked me. I

think about how he kept trying to find out where I go when I go into the woods. He's looking for her.

Maybe she didn't lose the recipe to turn back. Maybe she stopped using it. Maybe she turned into a wolf to escape him.

The rain stops. I slow down. Is he following me? Am I leading him straight to her?

What will he do if he finds her? Does he want to help her? Or does he want to kill her?

I stand real quiet and listen. I don't hear anything. I lift my face and sniff. The woods are wet and silent, and the little wind that rises tells me that they are all mine.

Of course. I exhale slowly. I tricked him today, without even trying. Usually I take the road down to the highway. He's waiting for me there. I get a sick feeling in my stomach when I remember how just last week he was hiding in the ash tree, waiting to pounce on me.

Chapter 17

IF YOU GIVE A BOY A ROCK . . .

As I get closer to the lighthouse I move more slowly. The rain stops, but the cedar fronds bob and drip. In the clearing at the edge of the cliff the sun has dropped right out of the clouds.

Worry tugs at me. I turn around and look at the path darkening behind me.

Through the trees I see something spark in the distance, back near the school. I freeze.

Is it Tuffman with a flashlight? Is it a cougar with glowing eyes? I take a breath and stare hard. The flashes are coming from the north-wing turret. Of course. Dean Swift has lit the Fresnel lens again. I squint, one hand shading my eyes, and the light swings at me, pouring through the tiny windows in the turret. Even the bricks of the building are glowing, like the light is coming through them, too, somehow.

The beam drenches me.

The light flickers in me like flames. It flows through me like waves. Fear and wonder quiver up my spine. That light makes me feel as if I'm wolf and boy at the same time. I'm wearing my two skins at once. The blood in my veins is thick and hot. Strength radiates from inside me.

The trunk of an alder tree is on the ground in front of me, fifteen feet long and maybe six feet around. The storm must have brought it down. I tap it with the tip of my toe. It flies thirty feet away into the horizon, off the edge of the cliff.

My strength is superhuman. It is superwolf. It's the light. Its power pulses in me.

It's magic, I whisper to the shuddering leaves.

The sun has wedged itself between the water and the clouds. Between the dark ocean and the dark sky is a thick slice of white and yellow. And I'm like that lemon-meringue pie of a sky. In my heart, hope jams itself between my fear of Tuffman and my worry about my mother. Because if I'm that strong, then how can Tuffman hurt anyone, or any wolf, that I love?

I run across the grass to the lighthouse.

I wait in my wolf skin on the doorstep of the lighthouse. The darkness of the woods deepens and spreads its shadows over the edge of the cliff and down into the blue-black water below. My hope disappears with the coming of the night.

White Wolf is late. And then she is later. And then she is very, very, very late.

What if the cougar found her?

I whimper. It's a sound that crumbles out of me.

At last I hear a whimper in return. Low and soft, the sound creeps toward me under the cover of dark and above the bed of quiet grass and bleeding hearts.

The moon comes up suddenly from below the line of treetops. I see a flash of white from the edge of the woods. In my wolf shape I lope from the lighthouse doorway to where she waits for me. *Thank you,* I say. *Thank you.*

She's weak and gets slowly to her feet. Her nose is dry.

Has she been waiting as long as I have? Waiting, but too sick to come to me?

I sniff her side. The wound has almost healed. But my nose tells me she is hungry and thirsty and tired. Was the rabbit I left for her on Sunday her last meal? It makes me ache inside to think of White Wolf alone and suffering without me.

Why isn't she eating? The woods are full of deer.

As I lead her to the lake, I catch the smell of the cougar here and there, coming at me on different currents of air. The cougar hasn't come into our territory, but he's roaming its edges. The scent of cougar gets stronger the closer we get to the lake.

I stand guard as she drinks. We're at the edge of the fishing area and White Deer Woods. We've never come this close to the school, but I need to find food for her and I know there are plenty of deer here. I sniff the ground. I smell Sparrow and Vincent. I smell human me. We've come so often to the lake that it would take more than a little rain to wash us away. I follow the whiffs and puffs of cougar scent that I pick up in the air. A pair of footprints in the mud near the picnic table makes my nose twitch. The prints are fresh and from not long ago. Expensive running shoes. Tuffman's the only one with feet that big wearing Pumas around here. The prints are his, but the smell is cougar.

My nose and mind work together.

Tuffman is the cougar. Tuffman, my uncle. Tuffman, the one my mom calls "T," the one who gave White Wolf that vicious scrape, the one my mom hurt in the woods long ago.

When wolves get scared, they get mad. My blood pops hot and slow, like boiling tar. That cougar's asking for trouble. He's gonna get it.

Once she's had enough to drink, I lead White Wolf back to the ledge. The cougar scent disappears inside White Deer Woods. He hasn't come into our territory. She's safe in here, for now.

All Saturday I hunt. I make sure White Wolf eats her fill. I kill everything I can and cache what she can't eat now so that she will have something during the week. The beam of light keeps pulsing in me. Nothing I chase outruns me. Nothing I lunge for slips past my teeth.

By Sunday morning White Wolf looks strong. Her eyes sparkle and her nose is damp and her fur glows white in the sunlight. I follow as she roams to the edge of our territory.

And then it happens.

One minute I'm looking off into the underbrush for a bunny snack and the next White Wolf is backing up. For a second I'm filled with her fear. Then I get a whiff of cougar.

When I'm in my boy skin, the cougar scares me. In my wolf skin it infuriates me. No litter-scratching cat is going to tell my mom where she can go, when she can eat, or what skin she can wear.

I push past her. She whimpers and stands still, her head tilted. She wants to go back and she wants me to come with her. But I'm not leaving her like this. Not for a whole week. If that cougar is up ahead, then I'm going to find him and finish him. I'll run him off the edge of the cliff.

I messed up during the week. Boy me spent his time eating candy and looking sideways at Mary Anne. But wolf me is going to take care of the problem.

I run harder as the cougar scent gets stronger. I head directly toward it, and a second later I feel her behind me. My wolf mouth smiles. Our feet beat in time against the hard dry dirt under the cedars.

Two against one. This is how wolves chase off a cougar.

We're so close to the lake I can smell the pollywogs Little John hasn't eaten yet. The cougar scent is so strong I almost choke on it.

Then I hear a whistle, and a split second later I'm lying on the path, a searing pain in my right shoulder. I can hardly breathe, it hurts so bad. White Wolf sniffs me. She whimpers. A second later she growls like a wild animal and dashes past me.

I struggle to my feet and follow her.

White Wolf's growl rumbles in the quiet woods ahead.

"I didn't know there were two of them!" a boy's voice screams out.

Humans.

I race through the pine trees. The lake is just ahead. I want White Wolf to turn around and come back. We hunt cougar, not humans.

What if they have a gun?

"Get up here on the table," a man's voice says.

I hear a boy sobbing.

"No!" the man shouts. "Get off the ground!"

As I come into the clearing, I skid to a stop, stunned.

White Wolf has brought Tuffman and Vincent to bay on the picnic table. They're wearing running shoes and shorts. There's a little stack of pink flags on the ground.

They are staking out the 5K practice run for PE. When did those two get to be such good buddies?

I look at her. My mother is a magnificent beast. Her teeth are sharp and gleaming. Her fur is standing on end so that she looks twice her usual size. And her usual size is about twice the size of any wolf you've ever seen.

"Stand up," Tuffman yells.

Vincent is on his hands and knees on top of the table, shaking with fear. Tuffman grabs him by the back of the neck and yanks him upright. He shakes Vincent hard.

"Pull it together," he says angrily. "I'm not about to lose her after all these years just because you're chicken."

Vincent has the slingshot I gave him. That must be how the rock hit me so hard. He's bawling his eyes out and shaking and trying to put another rock into the strap.

Rock or no rock, White Wolf is going to kill Vincent.

No, I want to shout. *Stop. He didn't know what he was doing.* My mother is going to kill my best friend. She's going to jump on him, pin him down, and do to him what we do to weasels and rabbits and deer.

I rush between them, barking and dancing around in front of White Wolf, trying to get her to calm down.

You can't reason with a wolf. Nose nudges and nips aren't going to stop her. Never—and I mean *never*— mess with a wolf mother's baby.

Whiz. Whack. Another rock hits me, this time in the back of the head.

White Wolf lunges to protect me, positioning her body between me and the table. She's barking so hard now she's like a machine gun.

I whimper but stay on my feet. I've got to get between her and them again. I'm the only one who knows everything. And one thing I know is that a wolf that attacks a human will be hunted down by the park rangers and killed within the week.

But when I look up at the table again, I see it's Tuffman who has the slingshot now. That last shot came from him. The smell and sight of him remind me of what he is. He's the cougar. He wants to hurt White Wolf. He asked me questions so that I would lead him to her.

Listen up, feline. Did you ever hear the saying: Curiosity killed the cat?

My fur goes electric. Every muscle in my body tightens. I turn to stand side by side with my wolf mother. Together we advance, growling fiercely. White Wolf shifts her weight, and I see she's about to jump. I gather up my strength.

Sorry, Vincent. This can't be helped. You're too close to my territory. I'm going to do whatever a wolf has to do to get you out.

Tuffman makes a little scream. Apparently, we are two really scary wolves. He drops the slingshot. He leaps off the table and is running before his feet hit the ground. Vincent follows.

White Wolf and I give chase. Vincent is still bawling, but he runs so hard he catches up with Tuffman. If I had a stopwatch and opposable thumbs, I bet I'd clock them at forty mph.

Before they even reach the road, White Wolf and I stop. We flop, panting, in the shade of the oak tree that is growing around my bike. As the thrill of the chase fades, I realize how bad my head hurts where Tuffman hit me with the rock.

I meant to take the cougar down with my sling last week. Looks like Tuffman found a rock with my name on it first. That is what Mary Anne would call ironic. I rest my nose in my paws. Why did Vincent hit me in the first place? I didn't give him that slingshot so that he could use it to hurt animals.

Before the sun reaches the middle of the sky, I get up and follow White Wolf back to the lighthouse. We're not the usual dynamic duo. I feel dizzy. There's blood in White Wolf's fur. I sniff it. It's the old wound. Running so hard must have reopened it a little. If the bunnies and deer have come up with any revenge fantasies, this would definitely be the time for them to act on them. They could pelt us with pinecones and green berries and we'd go belly up.

I'm worried when I walk into the lighthouse. But if

White Wolf stays near the ledge, she'll have plenty of food. And just because I'm not with her doesn't mean I won't be hunting cougar.

This week I won't get distracted. This week I'll remember what matters.

It takes me a long time to shift. I keep losing track of what I'm doing. I manage to walk out of the lighthouse fully dressed. I find out later my underwear's on inside out and my T-shirt is on backward, but at least I zipped my jeans. By the time I get to the school, I'm out of breath and dizzy. My head aches. My right shoulder burns.

Bobo meets me on the front steps. She jumps up and rests her paws on my chest.

Oh no. How could I forget her stinky stick? I gently help her down to all fours. She gets herself into a pickle like that sometimes where she has just enough strength to get up but not enough to get back down. Old hips, young heart.

I'm sorry, I whisper as I scratch just under her left ear. She licks my hand and then my cheek. *Forgiven.* It's simple between animals.

I see Mary Anne's suitcase in the foyer when I come in. She beat me again.

I walk into the TV room. I need to sit a second before I can make it up to my room.

Mary Anne takes one look at me and sets her book down.

"Dean Swift," she calls, running up the stairs before I can stop her.

I stand there and stare at her book for a long time. My brain can't turn the letters of the title into words. Finally I get it. *The History of Paris.*

The two of them come down half a minute later. I'm still staring at the book. It makes me feel less dizzy. Dean Swift's face is bright red from the dash down the stairs, and I can see that whatever Mary Anne told him has got him worried.

"See?" she says, pointing.

I look around. But she's pointing at me.

Dean Swift comes up and puts his face very close to mine.

"What have we got here?" he says softly. He touches my chin gently with his fingers and lightly turns my head one way and then the other. The pain in my head makes my knees buckle. Dean Swift catches me around the waist and settles me into a chair.

He kneels in front of me. "Mary Anne, bring me the flashlight from my top desk drawer."

She races back upstairs.

Before I can stop myself, I lean over the arm of the chair and throw up into a wastebasket.

Dean Swift pats my back. He hands me a tissue.

"Nice aim," he says, like it's nothing to be embarrassed about.

"Turn out the lights," he calls as Mary Anne comes back down the stairs.

"Now look into the flashlight when I hold it up to your eyes."

I do what he says, even though the bright light aches.

The dean whistles low. "Concussed, my boy. You have been concussed. How did this happen?"

"I was climbing a tree," I begin. "To get my kite. And I fell." I have to stop a lot because I'm making it up as I go. "Right on my back," I add. "And there was a big rock. I fell backward onto a big sharp rock." I pause. It throbs where Vincent tagged me with that rock. I better cover all my bases. "Two rocks. My shoulder landed on one."

I see Dean Swift glance at the phone by the front door.

"My dad knows," I say quickly. "He was there when it happened. We were having a picnic lunch at Fort Casey before he dropped me off. I told him I was fine. He said to tell you if I felt worse."

Dean Swift's jaw tightens. He can't believe my dad could be so heartless.

But I'm not done. "And you can't call him because he's flying to Paris tonight," I say quickly. Why did I say *Paris*, of all places?

"It must be that international conference for wildlife biologists," Dean Swift says, stroking his chin. "He's published some interesting work lately, your father."

I blink. Bingo. That was the lie to tell.

"I'll have to watch you carefully," he says. "If you're not better by this time tomorrow then I'll have to get ahold of him."

I sink back in the chair. I am now an official specimen in Dean Swift's curiosity cabinet. I will be observed. Conclusions will be drawn. I'm too sick to care.

Bring on the science. The magic's killing me.

"Stay with him while I call the doctor," he says to Mary Anne. "Don't let him fall asleep."

They only call the doctor when a kid is really sick. Is he going to give me a shot? Will they have to operate?

I touch the soft, sad, painful spot on the back of my head. When I pull my fingers away they are wet and red.

Mary Anne makes a little noise. Her eyebrows crinkle. She sees it too.

"Don't worry," she says. I can tell she is forcing herself to sound calm. "You'll be fine. Head injuries tend to bleed a lot. It's to be expected."

She takes some tissues from a box on the end table. "You should apply a little pressure. The doc will be here soon." As she stretches the tissues toward me, I can see her hand shaking.

I sit back in the chair. I close my eyes so that Mary Anne doesn't have to work so hard to pretend like she's not worried about me.

After a second she grabs my hand and squeezes it. "You have to stay awake. Okay?" She doesn't let go. "I'd read you my novel, but my dad says it puts him to sleep. *Best cure for insomnia ever.* Those were his exact words."

She frowns and then smiles real quick, like her dad's dumb, mean joke is actually funny.

Anger surges up in me. My skin burns. Wolf rage. *Hey, Mary Anne's dad, I've got an even better cure for insomnia. A nocturnal visit from a wolf. You'll never wake up again.*

I exhale slowly. I better calm down. I'm in boy world again.

I listen to her voice. I feel her press gently on my hand whenever I close my eyes. If all it takes to get Mary Anne to hold my hand is a rock smashing into my head, then bring on the meteor showers.

Because this is love.

The doctor is very jolly for a guy who spends his day jabbing people with needles. He explains what a concussion is.

"Your brain has been bruised," he says with a big smile. "Exactly like a melon that has been dropped on the ground. If your brain really were a melon, I'd suggest that you eat it up quick before it spoils, but since you're a boy, I suggest that you stay in bed for a few days and don't go doing those boy things that bruised your melon in the first place."

He's very pleased with his explanation, but I'm not. Eating my bruised melon brains? Where's that wastebasket again? And he prescribes bed rest. That's it. Not so twenty-first century. I wonder what he'd recommend for a sore throat. Leeches?

Chapter 18

WHERE THE HEARTACHE BEGINS

In the middle of the night I sit straight up in bed. I'm wide awake.

I remember the feel of the scar on Tuffman's back, the way he clawed me when I touched it. My mother did that to him, a long time ago. I remember the marks on the back of his neck that Mean Jack pointed out. White Wolf gave him those, I bet, when the cougar scraped her.

What else did she write on those cards?

I can't find my flashlight, so I flip on the bedroom light. I dig under my bed until I find the recipe box. As I'm pulling it out, my lighthouse books topple over and spill onto the floor.

Someone taps on the door. I stop scrabbling.

The tap turns into a rap. I am so quiet I stop breathing. My face feels like it's on fire. *I'm not about to lose her after all these years just because you're chicken.* That's what Tuffman said to Vincent.

Tuffman knows my mom is White Wolf. He's been hunting for her.

The door handle turns.

And he knows what I am too. He's come to finish what he started on the table by the lake.

"Raul?" Dean Swift peeks in.

I'm so relieved, I almost start to cry. I'm on my bed, the open box in one hand, the recipe for meringues in the other, my secret stash of books scattered out onto the floor.

"Oh, my child," Dean Swift says when he gets a look at me and my sad, scared eyes. "You must sleep. Give me that."

I shake my head.

"You can*not* read when you have a concussion." He takes the box from me gently. "I'll keep it safe," he says. But when he looks at it, his whole face sinks with sadness. He hands it back. "How can I take this from you? Please promise not to read them tonight."

I sniffle. I wipe my nose with the back of my hand. "Dean Swift," I whisper. "Tell me about the Fresnel lens."

Because I can't just ask him how to get rid of the cougar, can I?

The dean's spine straightens. I can feel him move away from me the tiniest bit. He looks at the wall that separates my room from the stairs to the turret. Then he looks at me. He looks at my books on the floor.

"Something tells me you know as much as I," he says.

"Please," I say.

I must look pretty pathetic with my face all wet and my head all banged up and my mom's recipe box on the pillow next to me like some kind of metallic, sharp-edged teddy bear.

He perches on the bed. "If you close your eyes," he says, "I'll tell you everything I know."

I tuck the box under my pillow and keep my hand on it. I close my eyes. I listen.

"My family has been the keeper of the Fresnel lens for three generations. This is how it began. Long ago there lived a French engineer named Augustin Fresnel, who believed that light traveled in waves. Most scientists mocked him. But Fresnel used mathematical equations to prove his theory. And then he applied everything he knew about light to design brighter lighthouse lenses. His innovations have saved countless lives from shipwrecks. After Fresnel died, his brother found that he had been working on a formula for a lens so powerful it could transform the energy of light and focus its life-giving properties. Fresnel's theories about what the lens could do were so unbelievable that his brother kept it secret. He didn't want to destroy the reputation Fresnel had fought so hard to earn. But my great-great-grandfather, Admiral Swift, got ahold of that formula." Dean Swift chuckles. "I'll tell you *that* story when you're older."

I hate it when they say that. *Tell me the whole story, you old baboon,* I want to shout. But I don't. Obviously.

"When Admiral Swift settled on the island, he had a lighthouse built in White Deer Woods, and he used Fresnel's secret formula to make the lens. For years he secretly studied the lens, and his first experiments apparently proved Fresnel's wildest theories. Admiral Swift began to tell people he had discovered something that would change human life forever. He invited famous scientists to come to a conference to study his claims. In those days it took years to organize such an event. In the meantime, a treaty was signed by the settlers that granted the return of White Deer Woods to the care of the local tribes, for whom the land was sacred. All the buildings that had been constructed in White Deer Woods, including Red Bluff Lighthouse, were torn down. Admiral Swift had helped to write the treaty. His wife, my great-great-grandmother, belonged to the Kwakiutl tribe. With the last of his seafaring fortune, he built this school to house the lens and provide a place for scientists to live and study it."

Dean Swift stops talking. The bed creaks as he stands.

"More," I say. The word is thick on my tongue.

The dean sighs and sits back down. "What happened next, nobody could have predicted. When the lens was moved to the school, it never worked properly again. Every experiment failed. It looked as though my great-great-grandfather had been losing his mind for quite some time. He became a joke—literally. Whenever a scientist formulated a particularly unlikely theory, others would tease, *Go measure your lens again, Admiral Swift*. He died a broken man. I never knew him. I wish I had. I don't think he was crazy. In fact, I know he was *not*. Because one day when I was a young man, I was in the woods and something happened. It made me wonder if Admiral Swift's first experiments had as much to do with White Deer Woods and its light phenomena as they did with Fresnel's special lens. I devoted my life to the study of bioluminescence, never quite knowing exactly what I was looking for. And then, not long ago, I was in the kitchen with Cook Patsy, selecting items to donate to charity. And do you know what I found folded up among the cookbooks?"

Sleep smothers me. I answer, but the words don't make sense. "A cougar?"

He stands up softly, his knees popping. He whispers, "Fresnel's secret formula."

The last thing I see before sleep crushes me is Dean Swift stretching his spine, his elbows pushed back. In profile he looks like a hawk launching himself from a branch.

I spend the night trying to wake up. I need to read the cards. My hand won't listen. It won't turn on the light, it won't open the box. My body is weighed down, stuck in the bed, but my mind wanders everywhere. Dean Swift has fixed the lens. Remember? He found Fresnel's measurements. The lens has a secret power. It has to do with the cougar. The cougar has to do with White Wolf.

The light behind my window shade is gray. Morning. My mouth is dry. My skin burns. The first thing I see when my eyes finally agree to open is the recipe box sticking out from under my pillow. I reach for it, but push it off the bed instead.

Dean Swift must hear the clang of the box as it hits the floor. He comes in and touches my forehead. His hand is ice cold.

"The cards," I whisper to him. "The whole story of my mom is written on them. She knows a secret, and I do too."

A drop of water falls on my cheek.

I look up. The dean's face is wet with tears.

"I'm going to put this in a safe place," he says, picking up the box. "I'm sorry. But we have to keep you calm."

"Please, please turn off the light," I beg. "For my mom."

He flips the switch as he leaves. But that's not the light I meant.

I fall asleep again. When I wake up the doctor is back. The doctor never comes twice. He says I have a fever. He says the wound in my head is infected and gives me pills. I have to take two of them three times a day. Each pill is the size of the rock that Vincent hit me with.

At the door I hear the doctor whisper to Dean Swift, "Don't be surprised by his fever talk. Children often say very strange things with a temperature running that high."

"He misses his mother," says Dean Swift, and the words sound full of tears.

"Don't we all?" the doctor says kindly. "Keep him hydrated."

The door closes.

Where are my cards?

All day people come in and check on me. Ms. Tern reads to me. Her voice is so sweet and she smells so nice that I can't tell her that her stories are like big boots stomping on my heart. She puts her hand on my forehead and smiles at me softly. "We'll have you sorted out in no time," she says. Dean Swift comes in and checks my pulse a lot. Really he's just holding my hand, but we both pretend he's checking my pulse.

The next morning I feel better, but they won't let me get up.

Cook Patsy brings me a diary. When she sees me look

worried because a diary is such a girl thing, she says, "You can live by those boy-girl rules everyone makes up for you, or you can make up your own. Your choice."

I put the diary under my pillow.

Mary Anne is in charge of bringing me soup and hot chocolate. I drink so much, I have to pee every half hour. But it keeps her coming back all day long.

Once I think I hear Sparrow breathing outside my door.

Later that night Mary Anne brings Vincent.

I'm afraid to look at him at first. Has he figured out that I'm the wolf he hit with a rock in the woods? Remembering what he did makes me want to lunge at him and take him to the floor. My chin juts forward. My muscles clench.

But Vincent just perches on the edge of my bed and shakes my hand.

"Are you better?" he asks. "Are you going crazy in here all by yourself?" He looks so worried for me.

I nod, *Yes* to both questions. I'm better and I'm crazier.

A shiver runs over me. It scares me, how angry I just got. A door in my mind opens. The thought behind it terrifies me. What would have happened if Vincent had tripped when wolf me was chasing him?

I shut that door quick.

I realize Mary Anne is talking to Vincent about me.

"No, he's not like *us*, Vincent. He's happiest alone. He's an artist. A scientist. An observer."

I can tell by the expression on her face that she thinks she's complimenting me. But the way she says "us" makes me feel like something scientists found in the deepest trench of the Atlantic ocean—pale, squishy, and one of a kind.

I'm a loner, but that doesn't mean I like being alone.

I'd tell her that, but I'm not sure she notices I'm alive right now. The way he's sitting on the bed and she's standing just inside the door makes it so that they're facing each other. I'm lying here behind Vincent like some unrolled sleeping bag.

I thought they were here to visit me?

Jealousy, like a wet little worm, squiggles in me.

"I didn't tell Raul what happened this weekend yet," Vincent says to her. "Should I?"

My jaw clenches. There's no way I can lie here like a lumpsucker and listen if he's found a way to turn those horrible fifteen minutes in the woods into a funny story.

The doctor said I should expect to have some trouble controlling my emotions for the next few weeks. It's part of bruising your brain. "You'll wear your heart on your sleeve. You'll be grumpy and sad," he said.

So I make my face as blank as I can. But neither of them notices me anyway.

Mary Anne looks like she's about to clap her hands.

"Yes! It's the best story." Then she does clap her hands. "You should write it down! It'd be a great first chapter."

Doc's right about one thing. I'm grumpy.

Vincent smiles. His teeth are white and straight. His skin is tan and his black hair gleams under the lamp.

Charming. That's the word for Vincent. I swallow it down like a piece of meat you can't quite chew and don't know how else to get rid of.

"Okay," he begins. "It's not really a story. It's more like a . . ." he pauses and looks at Mary Anne.

She mouths the word back to him.

"Right, it's more like a *development*."

She nods.

"I spent the whole weekend fishing on the pier with my stepdad," Vincent begins.

Mary Anne looks at him like it's a real cliffhanger of an opening line.

"All day long we sat there, shooting the breeze and hangin'. He let me bait the hooks. He showed me how to gut the fish *with his knife*. I mean it. He let me use his fishing knife. It's *that* big." He measures out about two feet with his hands in front of my face. I notice a big white bandage on his thumb. "Look!" He shoves it at me. "Ten stitches."

I try to smile, but my mouth feels stiff. I'm happy for him and his injury. I really am. So now he gets along with his stepdad. And Mary Anne loves him. And when his mom comes next weekend she'll tell him to pack his bag, because he's going home. And Mary Anne loves him.

Vincent looks worried. He can tell I'm upset. He should know why.

"Don't sweat it," he says. "I promise, next time we go to the lake I'll sneak into the kitchen and steal one of Patsy's knives. I'll show you how much quicker you can gut fish. You'll never want to use that Swiss Army knife again."

He's being so nice, how can I hold a grudge? He's willing to resort to thievery for me.

He takes the bandage off his thumb and shows me the stitches.

"It hurt like you-know-what," he says. "The doctor gave me a shot with a *huge* needle. I mean *huge*. Right in my thumb."

Mary Anne nods. "A local anesthetic."

"I'm telling you, it did *not* work. They started to stitch me up, and I could feel the needle going in and out. Do you know what it's like to have thread pulled *through* your skin?"

"Not good," Mary Anne says.

He's charming. She's pretty. He's witty. She's smart. Why wouldn't they get along?

He knew how much I liked her. Everyone else likes him better than me. I don't mind that. It makes me proud to be the best friend of the most popular kid in school. But couldn't he have let Mary Anne like me better?

My belly burns with the bad feeling. "Grumpy" is not the word for it.

"Won't Vincent make the best hero for my novel? He looks like a Nordic god, doesn't he?" she asks.

No, Mary Anne, I think. He doesn't. He looks like a kid so dumb he split his own thumb open with a knife.

After they leave I pull the diary out from under my pillow.

Cook Patsy was telling the truth. I'm gonna need this.

I pick up my favorite pencil, a number-two Staedtler, and practice my cursive on the first page. *Tuffman was right. Your best friend is always the one who betrays you.* I stare at it for a while.

I erase it.

My brain must really be bruised to think Tuffman could be right about anything.

Have you ever been sick with a fever and stayed in bed all day? At night you never really fall asleep. You toss around a lot and wait for morning. You might think about your crush liking your best friend better than you, and how that's nobody's fault, really, not hers and not yours and not his, either. You might think about the cougar invading your wolf territory. You might wonder if your mom is safe without you. You might wonder if her uncle is out hunting for her, and which skin he's in.

But then I hear the cougar screech.

My ears stretch upward, my mouth feels wet, my legs tighten, and I can actually smell the thing. It's the smell you smell when you go to the zoo and you watch the lions or other big cats pace. A little like old meat, a little like wet fur, a little stale.

White Wolf is out there alone.

I need the recipe cards.

I swing my legs out of the bed. I stand up. My head aches and feels empty at the same time. I fall down. The door opens. Ms. Tern helps me back into bed.

"My mom is a wolf," I say to her.

She pulls the covers up to my chin. Her hand is cool on my forehead.

"Mine was an orca," she whispers.

In the morning when I wake up, my pajamas and hair are soaking wet. Something happened in the middle of the night, but I don't know what.

As I look out the window, the memory of the cougar screech echoes in my head. Right after it comes the feeling of Ms. Tern's words brushing my ear. It makes my skin tingle to remember. I try to shake it away. The doctor said the fever would give me weird dreams. The weirdest thing about that dream is how it seems so real.

I don't have long to think about it.

When Mary Anne comes in with my breakfast, her eyes are red and puffy and I can tell she's been crying.

I bet Vincent has already broken her heart. I know it's wrong, but I'm crossing my fingers so hard my knuckle cracks. Please. Please. I would never break your heart.

"He doesn't want me to tell you," she says. "But I think you should know."

It's all right, Mary Anne, I know. He's charming. But I'm loyal.

"Dean Swift wants to tell you later. But I *hate* secrets." She starts to sob. "The cougar," she says.

My head pounds. Has the cougar hurt White Wolf?

"The cougar attacked Bobo," she says.

Bobo? I can't believe it.

"Bobo has been grievously wounded. The vet says her hind leg will have to be amputated." Mary Anne takes a breath. "I thought you should know that her chances of survival are slim. The truth, even when it is sad, is something we must all learn to live with."

I turn my face away from her. The ache fills my head and my chest so that I can't think or feel anything but it. A little later I hear the door shut.

What did Bobo ever do to him? Nothing. Bobo did nothing.

My skin is still hot from the fever, but inside I'm cold. What will he do to White Wolf? My mom knows his secret. And she's the one who cracked his back.

I need the recipe cards. I need to know how to get rid of my uncle.

Chapter 19

WHERE THE ENEMY MIGHT BE THE FRIEND

Thursday morning I get up and go downstairs before anyone can come and tell me that I can't. I need to see Bobo. I need the cards. My head hurts and I'm clammy. But the sooner Dean Swift thinks I'm healthy, the sooner he'll give me what I want.

I stop by his office to ask for the recipe box. The door is open, but he's not there.

I step in. Then I turn and look down the hallway, both directions. Nobody's coming. I close the door behind me. I open every one of his desk drawers. I know I shouldn't. But I need to learn the rest of my mom's story.

Why did she hurt Tuffman that day in the woods? What is Tuffman's secret?

I can't find the box. It must be in the turret. I'm going to have to get my hands on a key.

Next stop: kitchen. I left Bacon and Cheddar Omelet and Island Cobbler in there.

I sneak in the side entrance instead of going through

the cafeteria. There's nobody in the kitchen, either. The search takes a while. There are lots of drawers and cupboards to look through. Finally I think to look at the corkboard near the phone. An envelope with my name on it is tacked there. I pull it down and open it. Cook Patsy has slipped the recipe cards into plastic protectors so that they won't get stained by splatters when she's cooking. She's always looking out for me.

"Thank you," I say, even though she's nowhere around to hear it.

I look at the recipe for Bacon and Cheddar Omelet.

4 cubes Che"ddar	D
1 onion	O
5 tsp honey	Y
2 tsp yogurt	O
2 oz rum	U
1 walnut	W
1 apple	A
5 oz bacon	N
1 tsp thyme	T

I hold my breath until I figure out what's written on the next card.

Island Cobbler.

3 pineapple	N
2 sprigs mint	P
4 oranges	N
1 egg	E
3 cups milk	L
2 tsp cinnamon	I
3 oz liver	V
7 cps blackberry	E
1 cp sugar	S
7 pats Butter ?"	?

I must have done something wrong. Ignore the measurement. I change the *P* to *I*. *Do you want nine lives?* That's better. Or is it? What does that mean?

I shake my head and then stop because that hurts. I look again. Why are there quote marks in front of the *D* and after the question mark? I add them in. "Do you want nine lives?"

Is this part of a conversation?

I step out of the kitchen, tucking the cards into my pocket.

In the hallway I run into Ms. Tern. I scream like you do when you get caught doing something or being somewhere you shouldn't.

"Are you looking for Bobo?" she asks.

I stare at her. Maybe it wasn't a dream last night after

all. The memory of it feels so real. Finally I remember to nod.

"She's in here," Ms. Tern says. She walks to the storeroom next to the kitchen.

I don't follow. I don't want to see Bobo suffering.

"Don't be afraid." Ms. Tern comes back to lead me in. Her hand is cool like it was in my dream. "She's a bit groggy from the anesthesia," she says as she opens the door. "I put her in here since it's quiet during most of the day and warm because of the kitchen."

I step in. There's a pile of blankets on the floor. Bobo lifts her nose.

I don't think about it. I just do it. I lie down beside my friend.

"Oh!" Ms. Tern says. "Please get up. That floor is filthy."

I rest my hand under Bobo's muzzle and bring my face in close to hers.

I don't think I'll tell you any more of this part.

Ms. Tern leaves me alone with Bobo for a while. When she comes back, I let her convince me to get off the floor and go get breakfast. It's good to let grownups feel like they're helping you even when nothing can help. Everybody needs to feel useful.

What I see in the dining hall doesn't cheer me up. Vincent is on my stool. Mary Anne is next to him. When I come over with my tray, they're looking at something together.

"I like that scene," he says. "But what if you made the bad guy handsome?"

They look up when I sit down a few stools away.

"Sit with us," Vincent says like I'm crazy.

My new place is next to Vincent and not between the two of them. I try to look like I don't notice. But I feel like one of those reversible puppets. On the outside I'm a cheerful Little Red Riding Hood. But if you flip the puppet over you'll find a really angry wolf inside.

Dean Swift comes into the dining room.

Tuffman is behind him. A growl starts in my throat. Vincent looks at me sideways. I tap my chest and pretend it's a burp.

This weekend, Tuffman. You and me. In the woods. I get it now. It's the only way it can go down—when we're both what we are in the woods. Natural law, right?

"Children," the dean says, "the vet tells me that we must prepare for the worst. Bobo is an old dog. But a heroic one. The vet says that her injuries prove that she fought valiantly against her attacker. She lost three teeth in the fight." He gives a shaky smile. "And it is not unreasonable to assume that she left them deep in the beast's hide. The cougar will feel the bitter sting of Bobo's bite for many days to come."

I'm so proud of Bobo, I almost stand up and make a toast with my orange juice. *Here's to infected dog bites! Let there be pus and inflammation!*

But the dean keeps talking. "Nevertheless, we must be realistic. In preparation for a memorial service, please write down your memories of our dear old friend—" His voice cracks. He covers his eyes.

Tuffman finishes the dean's sentence. "And give them to a teacher. We're gonna make a memory book so we can always honor the good times we had with our four-legged buddy." His voice is high up in his throat, like he's got a lump of tears in there as big as mine. His mouth is turned down at the corners. His eyes are red and wet.

He's as sad as I am. I can feel it.

There's a word Ms. Tern uses: "gobsmacked." It means the look on someone's face after they get smacked in the gob. That's your mouth. My gob looks smacked.

Nobody can lie like that. Not even Tuffman. You would have to have two hearts and two brains and two tongues, not just two skins.

After a minute Dean Swift looks up again. "Well said, Coach. Because of this attack, nobody will leave the building without my permission."

The room erupts with chatter. Then above it all, Tuffman shouts, "We'll have that cougar in a cage by midnight tonight!" The anger in his voice sends an electric charge through the room. "Midnight tonight!" he shouts again, and we all stand up like soldiers, ready to fight.

Dean Swift nods and walks out of the room. Tuffman stomps out after him. Everyone is quiet for a long minute. Then there's a murmur, and the voices get shrill and loud and they're all talking about the cougar.

My throat clamps up. I'm about to start bawling. The doctor said the concussion would make me emotional. He said to try not to think about anything worrisome until I'm better. But *everything's* worrisome right now.

If Tuffman's the cougar and the cougar attacked Bobo, why would Tuffman look so broken up? And Bobo took a bite out of the cougar. Wouldn't Tuffman look a little worse for wear if he had three canine teeth stuck in him somewhere? Look at me. I'm living proof that a wound on one skin leaves a wound on the other.

My head hammers. I focus on my evidence. It's like I see it written out on a page in my scientific journal. First, set aside the science and the magic. The Fresnel lens, the spirit animals, and the mtDNA are all theories. Set aside the coincidences. Look at the evidence.

Item 1: Sneaker prints in the mud smelled like cougar.

Scents can get mixed-up. Especially after a rainstorm.

Item 2: Tuffman says a lot of weird things and stands too close to me and follows me around.

Little John practically stands on my feet half the time he's near me. And last week he walked up to me in the bathroom and said, "The thunder's moving east." What does that mean? But only a pollywog would accuse him of homicidal tendencies.

Item 3: My mom's recipe card said he wanted to kill her.

It said T wanted to kill her. T doesn't have to be Tuffman. It could be Ted or Tina or T. rex or Tinker Bell. Why would she call her uncle by his last name, anyway? Who does that?

But what really doesn't make any sense is this: Why would Tuffman have fallen for Vincent's prank if he was the cougar? When he was shooting the piñata, Tuffman *thought* he was shooting the cougar. My head whirls.

Conclusion: I can't make one until I have my mom's whole story.

I look around the cafeteria to calm myself down.

Little John is tapping the kid next to him on the head with a spoon. The kid is just shoveling cereal into his mouth like this is a normal part of breakfast. Mean Jack is twisting a wrapped-up string cheese around and around. Mark is wiping his face off with the dishrag that's for cleaning up spills.

At the little kids' table, Sparrow won't look at me. It hits me: He didn't come visit me. He didn't slide one of his drawings under my door, either, like he normally does when some nasty contagious stomach bug has half of us quarantined. And now, every time I try to make eye contact with him, he turns his back to me.

I try to pay attention to the funny story Vincent is telling Mary Anne. She laughs a lot and then asks, "Can I use this in my novel?"

I stop listening and start thinking about what's wrong with Sparrow. He's hiding something from me. It feels like an explosion in my chest when I realize what it must be. He must be hiding a bruise. His grandma must have let his mom come see him. She must have hit him again. He doesn't want her to get in trouble anymore because even though she's a terrible mom, she's *his* mom and he loves her. That's how love works. You can't always stop it, even when you probably should.

It makes me so angry. I can't take another bite. I put my tray in the dirty dishes bin and walk over to Sparrow's table.

I kneel down and put my hand under his chin and make him look up at me. There's no bruise on his face, but his eyes fill up with tears pretty quick.

I tilt my head so he can see I'm ready to listen.

"I lost it," he says, and makes a huge gulping sound. "I lost your fishing pole."

"What?" I ask. I spent so much time on that pole. It's the best carving I've ever made.

"I left it at the lake on Friday. When I went to look for it after Grammy dropped me off on Sunday, it was gone." He starts to cry really hard now.

All morning it's been cooking in me. Rage. And now it's like when frozen fries get thrown into a deep fat fryer and the oil spatters and jumps. Someone is gonna get burned.

"You promised. How could you?" First I whisper it. Then I say it louder because it makes me feel good to shout. "How could you?"

Sparrow's face crumples.

I don't stop. "Tuffman's right," I say. "You *are* a loser."

Everyone in the dining hall stops talking and eating. First they look at me, but my face must be even more scary than normal, because right away they turn and look at Sparrow. He can't stop crying, and now everyone is staring at him crying.

Good, I think. Now they'll think he's a baby, and he *is* a baby because a baby can't be trusted with important things.

Sparrow says something, but I can't understand it since he's sobbing so hard. I only hear the word "rain."

I stomp out of the dining hall and up to my room.

But before I even get to the second floor, I feel terrible. What is wrong with me?

He's only five. A five-year-old is going to lose things from time to time. When I was five, I lost plenty of things. Like the time I lost my mom's favorite bracelet. I remember how she almost started to cry, she was so sad, how she said she got it from her mother and her mother had gotten it from her mother and so on and so on. But did she yell at me? No. She hugged me and said she knew I felt even worse than she did and that even though the bracelet was a gift that reminded her of all the mothers who had made her, I was the gift who had made her a mother herself.

She found it a week later in the trunk of my Flintstones car, along with the remote for the garage door, an old slice of cheddar cheese, and twenty-five paper clips. How many times did I hear her tell that story to someone on the phone, saying it like it was the funniest, smartest thing a kid could do?

I turn around and head back to the dining hall. I'll tell him not to worry about it. We'll find the pole. And if we don't, then we'll go out to the woods and look for another straight branch so I can make him a new one. It won't be as great as the last one, that'll be the lesson for him, but it will still be pretty darn good.

Halfway down the hall I slap my hand to my forehead. *Rain.* That's what he was saying. It's why he forgot the pole on Friday. He wasn't being careless. It was raining so hard and so fast we all scrambled out of the woods like the cougar was after us.

I feel bad all right, but not as bad as I'm going to feel, because when I turn the corner, guess who is standing in front of me with a look in her eyes so mean it could shatter a window or make a building fall down or bend a telephone pole? You got it. Mary Anne.

"Was I wrong about you!" she says in a very quiet voice. "I thought you were different from all these other primates." She stares at me like I'm more disgusting than mushroom casserole. "Jack is a real Prince Charming next to you, you know that?"

I look down.

"You're out of the book," she hisses, knocking into me as she walks past. "You get that? You're *out* of my novel."

I hadn't known I was in it, but there's nothing she could say that would make me feel worse.

"I guess I shouldn't be surprised. There's a saying for it. The apple doesn't fall far from the tree. You didn't get Tuffman's looks, but you sure got all of his cruelty," she calls back.

I was dead wrong. She *could* say something that makes me feel worse. And that was it.

I can't believe Vincent told her I was related to Tuffman.

Chapter 20

WHERE RAUL LOSES SPARROW AND FINDS BOBO'S TEETH

I couldn't find Sparrow. After about ten minutes I had to stop looking and go to class.

Have you ever done something as bad as what I did? Lose your temper like that, make a little guy who looks up to you cry, make the girl you love hate you? But it gets worse. At lunch I don't see Sparrow at his table, so I go pound on his bedroom door. He doesn't answer, and when I hit it one last time the door opens a little. I peek around the corner. Maybe he's hiding behind the door. But he's not. He's not under the bed or in the closet, and when I've looked inside and under everywhere a five-year-old could hide, I notice how cold the room is. The window is open. It's a short jump to the ground even for Sparrow's little legs.

I run to Dean Swift's office and stand in the open doorway. Four teachers are hunched over his desk.

The math teacher is talking. "I think we're looking at a boy with anger management issues."

The social studies teacher clucks. "I'm not sure he

should be supervising the little ones on Fridays."

Ms. Tern shakes her head. "You're both mad. The doctor told us that the concussion could make him prone to irrational behavior. If anyone's at fault here, I am. I saw him acting strangely before breakfast. He was deeply affected by Bobo's injury. I should have taken him back to his room."

"Hey, Nicky, we all dropped the ball on this one," Tuffman says. "I should've checked on him first thing this morning. I can tell you from personal experience, a concussion brings out the worst in a man. Add that to the family temper and kaboom, whaddya expect?"

Have you ever walked into a room where everyone's talking about you? You know how part of you wants to run away and part of you wants to act normal so nobody can tell how much it hurts?

They all turn to stare at me, long wrinkles between their eyes. Ms. Tern looks worried. Tuffman looks sympathetic. Dean Swift looks disappointed.

In me. He's disappointed in me.

I hang back a little as we head into the dining hall. It's the middle of lunch and the noise makes me feel like someone stuffed a pillow in my brain. But the minute the kids notice the dean, four teachers, and me, all standing in the doorway, it gets as quiet as the library on a Saturday.

"Children," the dean says, "Sparrow has not come to

any of his classes. Please finish your lunches quickly. We will start a search. Students will work with a supervising adult."

Dean Swift doesn't look at me as he chooses his group, and Mary Anne flounces over to him before he even calls her name. Me, Mean Jack, Vincent, and Little John get assigned to Tuffman. The cafeteria bustles and booms as everyone starts talking and Cook Patsy distributes flashlights for the tunnels and walkie-talkies.

But when Dean Swift raises a hand, the room goes silent in a split-second. "Children," he says in a voice so serious it makes my skin tingle and my ears burn, "you must stay within sight of an adult at all times. *Do You Understand?*"

Why doesn't he just say the word we're all thinking? *Cougar.*

I made a mistake. Everyone knows it. Me most of all. And now I'm going to fix it.

"Come on," I say, pushing my way out the door. "I know where he is."

No one else knows it all. I know where Sparrow hides when someone he loves hurts him. I know his hideout is also the cougar's den. I guess we all know the cougar has three German shepherd teeth sunk in him and is getting meaner by the minute.

But I'm the only one who knows—who *really* knows— how dangerous a wounded predator is. Because I'm the only one who's ever worn that skin. I keep thinking how I charged Tuffman and Vincent down by the lake. What would I have done if one of them had tripped as he ran out of my territory? Would the boy in me have been able to reason with the wounded wolf?

I sprint down the zigzag path to the beach. I don't care how many spiderwebs break up on my face and arms. I don't care how many blackberry thorns rip my shirt and scrape my bare legs. I run. Tuffman and Vincent are right behind me as I jump from the path to the driftwood pile and then onto the sand. We are racing three across now, our feet pounding in the hard-packed sand. Behind us, Mean Jack stumbles over the driftwood. I glance back and see Little John at the top of the zigzag path. He's throwing rocks as hard as he can down at Mean Jack and whooping every time he hears the big kid curse and moan, "You're breakin' my heart Johnny, you're breakin' my heart."

We don't need them anyway.

I turn up the path that leads from the beach to the fort, and Vincent and Tuffman stay beside me. We're a team and we're running like one, our feet hitting the ground all at the same time.

Tuffman reaches out and punches me lightly on the shoulder. "We'll find him, Raul," he says. "You lead the way. It's your show, Raul."

I swallow hard. Tuffman drops back, like he knows

I'm about to cry and he doesn't want to embarrass me. Man, was I wrong about this guy. It's just been a misunderstanding, like the dean said. He's on my side. Look how he's treating me now, like he has respect for me. Like I made a mistake and he respects me enough to let me be the one to fix it.

Maybe he does know my mom is White Wolf. Maybe he's looking for her because he wants to help her.

Didn't he tell me *twice* that he loved her like a little sister?

The thought gives me a burst of energy. We pound across the field. A group of police officers is getting out of a squad car in the parking lot as we run by. They nod at us, and I feel another surge of energy as I see that our team is part of a bigger team. We're gonna find Sparrow. He'll be all right.

The Blackout Tunnel is on the far side of the fort, separate from the main building. It's a U shape, with two ways in or out. As we get nearer I put my finger to my lips. I signal to Tuffman to guard the first entrance to the tunnel in case Sparrow runs out that end. I try not to think about the cougar.

"Wait here," I whisper, and Tuffman gives me a sharp salute.

"You bet, Captain Raul," he says.

I've been thinking like a lunatic. This is what happens when you've got a bruised melon for a brain.

Thank goodness I kept my yap shut. One good thing about being the quiet type—even your fever talk is all in your head.

Vincent and I creep toward the other entrance. Then we hear it.

The cougar scream. It rings on and on with a cold, echoing sound, like it's coming to us from the bottom of a well.

When you were little, what scared you? Toilets flushing? Spiders? Or dogs? For me it was being alone in the dark. When I saw my mom's hand reach up to turn off the lights, my whole body felt like it was screaming NO!

That's how I feel when I hear the cougar screech.

I'm a big No. My legs are a jelly of No. My head has no thoughts but the word "No." My stomach jumps like a trampoline that squeaks the word "No."

I look at Vincent, and my eyes are so wide open, I wonder if I'll ever be able to shut them again. Vincent stares back.

"We gotta get Sparrow out of that tunnel," I manage to say.

Vincent starts to shake all over. He falls to the ground.

Looks like I'm on my own.

"Sparrow!" I shout. Halfway into the tunnel I trip over something. I scream. The thing on the ground screams. It jumps on me and starts scratching and clawing me.

It's not the cougar. It smells like maple syrup, for starters.

"Sparrow," I say after a second. My voice is very calm. The scratching stops.

"Raul?" his little voice asks.

"Yeah, it's me," I say. I try to pull him up, but I can't tell which end of him I've got.

We shuffle around for a second.

"Sorry," he says with a little sob once we're sitting shoulder to shoulder with our backs to the wall.

"No, Sparrow, I'm sorry. I acted like a total jerk. I know you only forgot it because of the rain," I say.

I stand up, because all of a sudden my legs want to run really fast. I sense the cougar. I try to keep my voice calm. "Okay, which way did I come in?" I ask, reaching down and patting around to find Sparrow again. I pull him up next to me.

"It doesn't matter," Sparrow says. "Either way leads out."

If either way leads out, then either way leads in. And I only know one thing for sure—the way I came in there was no cougar.

"Stay with me," I say. I walk with one hand on the wall to my left and the other hand holding tight to Sparrow's. It's so dark, I realize I've closed my eyes.

There's no point in keeping them open. I could not see my finger even if I stuck it into my eyeball.

The screech of the cougar echoes toward us. The back of my neck prickles. The tingly, chicken-flesh feeling spreads all the way from my neck up over the top of my head and then down into my ears.

I hear a sound like claws clicking on the cement. I look back. Two yellow eyes glow. Then I *feel* the cougar's low growl and the hot breath that carries it. I sense the cougar tensing its back, leaning into its hind legs, gathering all of its muscle into a force strong enough to knock the two of us down with one pounce. I can't explain what happens next. It's the wolf in me. It's the light in me. Without having any idea of what I'm doing, I scoop Sparrow up with one hand and then I leap blindly into the air, grabbing at a ladder that I somehow know is bolted to the wall in front of us. My hand grasps the middle rung and I pull us both up to safety in one insanely accurate jump into total blackness.

Below, the cougar pounces and lands on cement. I can hear him scrabble around, like he can't believe it, and then I can feel the air sweep beneath us as he stretches up against the wall and paws at the emptiness.

With Sparrow holding tight to my neck, his legs squeezing around my waist, I scramble up to the top of the ladder until my head hits the ceiling. We are out of rungs.

I push Sparrow up so that he is sitting on the top rung. I'm pretty sure the big field in the middle of the fort is above us. Some kid's up there flying a kite, I bet. In a minute, when I've caught my breath, I'll feel around on the ceiling for the hatch this ladder must lead to, but I doubt it'll open—it's probably been locked tight for half a century.

I hear claws scrape against something metallic. That cougar is trying to climb the ladder! I cling to the bar and curl my feet in. I'd sure like to keep them attached to my ankles.

Scrape, scrape. My ears flinch. I don't want to die in the dark.

Then I hear shouts.

It's Vincent's voice hollering at us, but I can't tell where he is.

"We're at the top of a ladder, but the cougar is trying to climb it," I shout back.

"Hang on, boys!" Dean Swift calls. "The police are going to fire a flare to scare him off. Stay where you are and plug your ears."

I put Sparrow's hands over my ears and mine over his and then I press down as hard as I can.

There's a flash of light and a loud bang.

A second later I hear the sound of a gunshot and then the screech of the cougar.

They've killed it.

We scramble down and head out of the tunnel as fast as we can in the dark.

As we come out into the daylight, Sparrow looks up at me. I can tell by the shape of his mouth that he's about to cry. I stop walking and kneel down so that I'm his height. It feels good to get low—my legs are wobbly. I hug Sparrow.

"I'm sorry," I tell him.

I look around as I pat him. We're all alone. This is where I left Tuffman. So much for calling me captain and promising to obey my orders.

Dean Swift runs over to us from the other entrance. A few of the teachers and some of the policemen follow. Vincent comes too, but he hangs back. He must feel embarrassed about how he acted when we heard the cougar.

"Thanks for going to get help," I say as I walk up to him. "You saved us." I say it loudly so that the grown-ups will remember to give him credit for doing the right thing.

His face gets red.

People start crowding around us.

Vincent leans in and whispers, "Promise you won't tell anyone."

Like I'd do that.

"Promise," he says again.

"I promise." I don't have much time to think about

it, but it bugs me a little that he doesn't trust me—
that he needs me to swear to it.

Then the grown-ups are all over me and Sparrow,
asking if we're okay and did we get hurt and are we
frightened and do we need to talk and the counselor is
waiting for us back at the school and here's some juice
and brownies that the Fort Casey guards brought over
for you.

When they quiet down for a second, Sparrow asks,
"Did you get the cougar?"

Dean Swift and the policemen all sigh at the same
time.

For the first time I notice Ms. Tern is standing there,
holding a rifle.

One of the Fort Casey guards speaks up. "The durn
thing got clean away!"

Dean Swift frowns. "Not clean away, you can't say
that. The bullet nicked him. I saw it as he darted by.
She managed to graze his cheek."

Ms. Tern bites her lower lip. "I hoped I could stop it
without killing it."

Dean Swift shrugs. I can tell he wishes Ms. Tern had
done a little more damage. But he just puts an arm
around me and Sparrow and says, "I have been assured
by the guards that it will be easier to track, thanks to
the trail of blood. The suspense will soon end."

"Hey, there you are!" A voice cries out.

We turn around to see Tuffman walking out of the tunnel from the same side Sparrow and I had just run out of. The side where Tuffman saluted and promised to stand guard.

Tuffman is ready with an excuse before he can even see the look on my face. "I got worried. I went in to look for you. It's dark in there!"

My blood feels cold. My thoughts click together like puzzle pieces. How could he have gone in that side and not passed me and Sparrow as we were coming out?

Oh man. Maybe a wolf's nose is never wrong.

"I cut myself pretty good, huh?" Tuffman says. He's holding his bandana to his cheek. "There are some hooks stuck into the wall—right at face level. Wonder what the soldiers used them for."

How can it be a coincidence that Tuffman is bleeding in the same place where the cougar got hit?

The whole solidarity thing as we ran across the fort grounds—that was all just a big show, wasn't it? He was trying to distract me and make it easier to hide shifting into his second skin. His *cougar* skin.

"Missed it, Nicky? Well, it takes skill to use a gun that big," Tuffman says to Ms. Tern.

"Just because I didn't slaughter the animal doesn't mean I missed my shot," Ms. Tern says. She grips the stock of the rifle.

I watch them argue. I crack my jaw. It makes me

calm, to know the truth and to be certain of it. I'll take care of Tuffman in the woods.

But then I think of Bobo. Fury pulses in me. Because what would the cougar have done to me and Sparrow if I hadn't leaped onto that ladder?

It's not human—the anger in me is all wolf. I see and hear like I do when I'm deep in the woods. My nose is full of scents, each one resting above or below another, like layers on a tall cake.

Everyone is moving away from the Blackout Tunnel, crossing the field and heading to the beach and the school. Tuffman's at the back of the pack. He's wiping his cheek with his bandana.

I sense how he feels—frustrated but safe. He's tired and off his guard.

I move behind him slowly, tracking him. I stare at his back. The closer I get, the harder I sniff. I can smell his blood. I sniff deeper. I smell Bobo.

I found her teeth.

"Hey," I call to him. "Thanks for helping."

"And they say the kid never talks," he says in his jokey way as he turns to face me.

If he knew me better, he'd know that I always say *thank you*.

"Put it there, pardner," I say. I put my hand out.

He thinks I'm dumb as bricks. He reaches for my hand.

I don't think we've been properly introduced. Meet your nephew, the wolf.

I grip his hand tight in mine. With my left hand I pat him on the shoulder. I reach around a little to the back, where I can feel the shape of a bandage under his shirt. I sink my fingers into the wound. *Bobo wants her teeth back.*

He winces. His shoulder twists and drops down. I keep digging. He tries to yank his right hand out of mine. But I squeeze harder. I have my wolf strength in me.

"There's more than one way to skin a cat," I say to him.

I let go. I don't want him to start screeching. Not yet.

I turn to walk away, but he reaches out and swipes at me.

When I look back, his face is pale with pain but he's smiling. "Hey, pardner," he manages to say. "I had that coming. No hard feelings, yeah?"

My ears bend back. I want to snarl, but my mouth only works that way when I'm a wolf.

"What?" I bark.

"You two were in my territory, like the dog was last night. Remember the other day at the lake?" he asks. "Me and Vincent were in your territory, right?"

It's so strange to hear him say my secret out loud. He's talking about it like it's normal.

"Don't tell me you wouldn't have destroyed us if we'd given you half the chance," he says. "It's in our nature, that's all." His voice is calm and matter-of-fact, like this is just some weird family trait like a knack for math or bad teeth.

But it's true. I don't know what I would have done to them. I look away.

"You're strong, Raul," he says.

I shrug, but I can't help it—I feel proud. It's funny. Tuffman's the only one who could notice that about me. Nobody else sees what we can see.

"We need to work together, Raul," he says. "We can help each other—keep normal people out of our territory so they don't get hurt."

It all starts to sink in. What I've been hiding, why I've been hiding it, and now here it is out in the open. Someone knows my secret. And he's not afraid of me and he doesn't hate me for it.

He smiles. "I mean, it's not like we're monsters."

Mary Anne says I'm a loner because I want to be. But all this time, I've been a loner because I have to be.

He steps closer to me. "And, Raul, I can show you how to live forever."

His eyes wrap around me. I can't move.

Under the sharp March wind or above it is a puff of warmth. Spring. I sniff and smell the yellow stubs of sprouts and the white-green of rising bulbs and the cracking shells and cocoons of every insect and bird waking to life.

And I can't look away from his gold eyes and the promise that I know somehow is not a lie.

"Both of you," he says. "I can help her, too, Raul."

I blink. Of course he can.

He reaches back and rubs his shoulder where I dug my fingers into him. His hand comes away covered in blood. He stretches it out to me. "Shake on it?"

I begin to raise my hand. With a swipe so quick I don't even see it, his fingernail slices across my palm. I stare at the rising red line.

Blood brothers with Tuffman?

I drop my hand.

He steps closer. "Don't chicken out on me, kid. Here's the deal. A cat's got nine lives. A wolf can too," he says.

The words in my head are all in capital letters: DO YOU WANT NINE LIVES?

He made my mom the same promise.

I almost drop to all fours. I race to join Sparrow and the others.

The wind comes up off the water. The sky is whipped cream and blue. The grass along the cliffs is tall and golden. I smell salt and seaweed and driftwood.

Yeah, I want to live forever. But not with him.

I wipe my hand on my jeans. The cut isn't very deep.

On the walk back to the school everyone surrounds me.

I tell myself to look calm. Dean Swift will give me

the recipe box as soon as we get back. Until then, I'd best act like my brain isn't bruised and my uncle isn't a man-eating cougar who thinks he can live forever.

I say "Thank you" when Mean Jack says I make one heck of a capo. He wants to talk to me privately later about whether I'd consider taking the vow of *omertà*.

"Code of Silence, you wanna take that? Everyone knows you can keep your trap shut. But now you proved you got what it takes to be a made man," he whispers.

Mark, swinging his weighted vest over his head, hollers to me, "I woulda *Peed. My. Pants.* I mean it."

Little John grabs my hand. "Did you hear that joke? Is it wet on Uranus? Only it means the planet and it also means your butt. Right? You get it?"

When Sparrow takes my other hand, the pressure on the cut takes the sting away. He holds it like he'll never let go.

All the grown-ups tell me I must be the bravest kid in the world. But I know what I did. What I did was lose my temper, scare a little kid who looks up to me, and put him in danger. That's what I did. I acted as vicious as a wounded animal.

And I've still got to save my mom. Inside, the wolf rage dies down. The boy in me thinks. I might have messed up there, too. Maybe I shouldn't have let Tuffman know I know. Maybe I shouldn't have let him see how strong I am.

Who is he, really?

Cook Patsy comes over and calls me heroic. I look around to see if Mary Anne heard. It takes a while for me to spot her.

She's at the back of the crowd. With Vincent. A little drop of jealousy rains in my heart. Then it sprinkles when she whispers something in Vincent's ear. He smiles and nods like she said something reassuring.

Then it's a downpour. Because when she loses her balance and moves away from him a little, I see that they are holding hands. He pulls her back so that she doesn't fall.

It's a hurricane in my heart.

Chapter 21

WHERE RAUL FINDS THE KEY TO HIS QUESTIONS, BUT THE ANSWERS ARE WRONG

On the steps of the school, Dean Swift and Ms. Tern stop me. Their eyes drill into me.

"Straight to bed for you," the dean says.

I'm hot and sweaty. There's an 88 percent chance I'm going to barf. I sit down hard on the bottom step.

"He's knackered!" Ms. Tern says.

Dean Swift bends over me. Something small and metallic falls out of his pocket and lands on the step. A key. I point to it, but he has already stood up. His head is swiveling around, searching for help.

"We need a pair of strong arms to get you up to your bed," Dean Swift says.

I barely hear him. My eyes focus on the little key. The top of it is in the shape of a lighthouse. The key to the turret. I set my hand over it. I need the recipe cards more than ever.

"Mr. Tuffman," the dean shouts. "Mr. Tuffman, come here!"

While he's shouting, I slip the key into my pocket.

I hear Ms. Tern scolding the dean. "You're going to *humiliate* him. Really, Oliver, you haven't got a clue, have you?"

I look up and see Tuffman heading toward us. That's when I realize the dean wants Tuffman to carry me up to my bedroom.

Are you kidding me?

I jump up and take the steps two at a time. Dean Swift and Ms. Tern can hardly keep up with me. The sooner I get into bed, the sooner they'll leave me alone. I have the key to the turret, and the answers to all of my questions are in that recipe box.

Dean Swift flips on the light in my room. "You will stay in bed until tomorrow morning. We can't risk a relapse."

He turns to leave, then stops in the doorway. The air feels heavy all of a sudden. He's going to say something that maybe I don't want to hear.

"We all make mistakes, Raul," he says.

I nod. The scratch Tuffman gave me throbs. I'm glad it hurts, because I deserve it.

"It is through our failures—not in spite of them—that we triumph," the dean says softly. "You disappointed me this morning. You made me very, very proud this afternoon."

I swallow hard and look down.

"Pajamas!" he says as he turns out the light.

I put on my pajamas and listen to him and Ms. Tern bickering as they walk away. It's funny, they act like old friends even though she's new. I can't make out what they're saying, but I have a feeling it's about her shooting the cougar. I think she calls him a twit. Did he just tell her to put a lid on it?

I listen until the hallway is quiet. I open my door and peek out.

A second later and I've unlocked the utility closet. I glide up the steps. The recipe box is on top of Dean Swift's tape recorder. I grab it.

On the second step down the stairs I see the door-knob turn. For a split-second I'm so scared, I can't move.

"You forgot to lock it?" It's Ms. Tern.

"Never!" I hear the dean say as the door opens.

I turn around. I put the box back and dart under a small table pushed against the wall.

"You're an absentminded old duffer," Ms. Tern says as the steps creak and Dean Swift starts to puff-puff his way up them.

I pull a desk chair in under the table to hide myself better. I barely stop my scream. Coiled on the seat is Gollum. She lifts her head and looks at me. The back of my neck tingles. Then she drops to the floor and glides away.

"So you think this is why the cougar is here?" Ms. Tern asks.

They're so far from the truth they can't even see its tail end. The cougar is here for the wolf. I almost crawl out from under the table to tell them. But then I'd have a lot to explain. The key feels hot in my pajama pocket.

"It's a theory," says the dean.

"But it supports mine," she says.

"I don't see how." Dean Swift sounds tired.

"Luke Ferrier has spent a lifetime hunting rare predators. What if you're right? What if the Fresnel lens attracts them?"

There's a long silence. *Luke Ferrier*. My brain scratches around. Where have I heard that name before?

"It doesn't *call* them, exactly," Dean Swift finally says. "It's more complicated."

My ears stretch, I'm listening so hard.

"It's not a theory. It's a hunch. Perhaps the light of this lens has the power to open a kind of doorway in the natural world between different states of being. I think White Deer Woods is one of those doorways. And maybe certain types of predators are attracted to that power threshold."

I shiver. I'm hot and cold at the same time. The dean only has half the story. He's wrong about why the cougar's here, but he's right about the door. White Deer told me my lighthouse in the woods was a place between places. That's a good definition of a doorway, isn't it?

But here's what Dean Swift doesn't know. The door the light opens isn't White Deer Woods. When the light hit me last Friday on the edge of the cliff, it opened the door inside *me*—the door that separates wolf me from Raul me.

"What if you're right?" Ms. Tern asks. "Let's say that the light draws *certain types of predators*. What if Ferrier got wind of your experiments somehow, and decided to hunker down on this island and wait to see what your light would bring him?"

"If that were true, then the Fresnel lens would be like a baited trap!" Dean Swift sounds horrified.

"Precisely," says Ms. Tern. "Forty years ago, the Penn Cove Massacre brought Ferrier two spirit animals in one felonious swoop. Why wouldn't he return to the scene of his most successful crime? Especially if he thought that your light would lure his prey to him."

It clicks. Luke Ferrier is the criminal mastermind she told us about in class.

"I've been fiddling with the light for years," Dean Swift says. "Why would he show up now? It doesn't add up."

"It does, in fact, add up. This fall when you sent me the fundraiser flyer for your school and I saw the photo of your new coach, I knew it was him. The bio matches perfectly. I've been following Ferrier for years, always one step behind. Seven years ago the trail went cold. Interpol determined Ferrier must have died. I moved on to elephant poachers. But seven years ago—that's just about the time Tuffman broke his back, isn't it? It's been one surgery after another for him since then. No wonder he hasn't been in shape to hunt."

Ms. Tern should stick to tossing shivs and reading novels. Tuffman isn't Luke Ferrier and he isn't here to hunt the cougar. He *is* the cougar.

Dean Swift isn't buying it either. "How could *our* coach be *your* Luke Ferrier?"

"Look," she says. "It's a photo of Ferrier taken in August, 1970, just after the massacre."

"That photo is over forty years old!"

"Stay on topic, Oliver. The resemblance is uncanny."

"I am on topic. He looks thirty in that picture. Does Mr. Tuffman look like a seventy-five-year-old man? Or is he ageless? It's not rocket science. It's arithmetic."

I hear Ms. Tern's heels click angrily on the wood floor. "Didn't you see him try to kill that snake? Tell me how many coaches at primary schools carry hunting knives about in the pockets of their tracksuits. And do you care to know how I came by that rifle? Tuffman—*Ferrier*—was out hunting cougar with it. The man is a predator. And take our little prodigy, our little Raul, with his big eyes and sharp teeth."

What does she think I have to do with it?

And I don't know if I like that description.

"Raul *hates* him. That boy has instinct. Today, in fact, I saw him shake Tuffman's hand," her voice slows.

I hold my breath. I didn't know she was watching us. What did she see?

"I saw Tuffman's knees buckle. As if Raul—the skinny thing—gripped his hand too hard. And when I walked by just after, your coach's face was white with pain. Blood was seeping into his shirt where Raul had touched him."

Dean Swift doesn't say anything.

"Oliver?" she asks.

"Yes."

"You do realize that Raul is one of our kind?"

My eyes get watery. So it wasn't a dream the other night. She really did tell me her mother was an orca.

Her mother must have been one of the ones Ferrier filled with rocks or one of the white ones that disappeared. No wonder she hates him. My face is wet, and I turn my head to wipe it on my shirt. I think of White Wolf and how alone I would be if I lost her.

In the silence I can feel Gollum staring at me from some dark corner. I try not to sniffle. What kind *are* we?

You'd think it would make me happy to find out that it's not just me, my mom, and Tuffman. Instead, I feel a little angry. I don't know why. But shouldn't they be trying to help me?

The dean just stands there with his hand resting on

my mom's recipe box. I can't see his face. What is his second self?

"It's too early to know. It'll be years before he's called," Dean Swift says. "And you must be mistaken. Our kind or not, a child his size could hardly have injured Mr. Tuffman."

That was a low blow, dean. He's a mole, I bet. Don't they have eyes that can't see?

"I'm telling you what I witnessed. And, if Ferrier is Tuffman, and Tuffman is Raul's uncle, mightn't the boy be in danger? Shouldn't we warn him in some way?"

During the long silence that follows, I get nervous. My hands get damp and I can feel the blood beat in my throat. What are they going to do about me?

"We shouldn't be talking about this," the dean finally says. He smacks his desk with his hand. "Keep the woods in the woods, Nicolette. It's the way we survive. We know each other there, and that's enough. He's far too young to be shifting anyway. And even if he were, I can only help him if he asks. I'm not allowed to intervene. And you can't either. It's the way."

His words sink in. Finally something one of these two says makes sense. We know each other in the woods. We don't talk about it. We keep our selves separate. That's what my gut has been telling me to do all along. It's how our kind has managed to survive, the dean is saying, and hearing him explain it gives me a feeling of peace. I understand the rules—the way—of my own kind instinctively. It's why nobody can help me. I will figure it all out on my own.

"It's time we organize ourselves, Oliver," Ms. Tern says so softly I almost can't hear her. "It's time we make new ways. We must defend the wild."

"Silence is our only defense. The old way is the only way," Dean Swift says.

They're both quiet for so long my feet fall asleep.

"Turn off the light," Ms. Tern finally says. "Until we know what it does."

"How can I know, if I turn it off? Show me more than an old photo and a cold trail. Until then, I'll believe the most rational version of events. Ferrier is a very old man or a dead one. His days of destruction have ended. And Coach Tuffman is an Olympian who has boxed up his medals in order to forge a relationship with his long-lost nephew."

"There's no talking sense to you." Ms. Tern stomps down the stairs.

Dean Swift tinkers around at his desk for a while.

"Gollum," he whispers. The snake slithers across the floor, and he lifts her onto his desk. "Guard the light," he says with a little smile in his voice.

Then he takes the stairs slowly, his knees creaking as loudly as the steps. At the door I hear him mutter, "Now I must find that key."

Chapter 22

WHERE VINCENT WORRIES AND RAUL SAYS TOO MUCH

I take the stairs quick, two at a time. I want out of there before the dean decides to come back and look for the key. The second after I slip under my covers, I hear a tap at the door.

Vincent walks in with my dinner. I smile like I'm happy to see him, but I'm not.

I want to be alone, so I can think about every crazy thing I just overheard. I want the story and all its pieces out in front of me.

And I kind of want to cry, because I just realized that I left the recipe card box in the turret.

Vincent sets the tray on my desk under the window. It smells good. Fried chicken and mashed potatoes. Gravy—the good kind, homemade. And green beans with salt and basil. My stomach grumbles and moans and shouts and screams.

It's funny how good food can make you feel better.

Vincent sits down. He seems to have forgotten my dinner.

"Please promise you won't tell anyone what a loser I was."

"I won't tell," I say. Didn't we go over this already? I look at the food.

"Promise? I don't want them to call me chicken like they did at my last school."

Would it be rude to get my tray? Since Vincent is sitting between me and it, I'd have to climb all the way down the length of my bed. Or leap over Vincent.

I eyeball it. I could probably almost clear his head.

He blurts out, "*Everyone* likes me here. At my old school nobody would even sit next to me at lunch."

"I promise." I understand now. Vincent got type-cast. That's when you get a reputation for being bad, or stupid, or a crybaby. You get stuck with that word and you can't get anyone to drop it. And when you come to a new school, you think you'll finally change that word.

There's nothing worse than finding out the word for you is always the same.

After a minute he walks over to my window. It's dark out, so all he can see is his own reflection.

I watch the steam coming off my plate next to his hand. I swallow my spit.

"So I know it and you know it. I don't want anyone else here to know it. Especially not Mary Anne." He whispers her name.

I get a mean little feeling. Because it's true—Mary Anne is looking for a hero.

But I say it nicely. "I won't tell."

"But you might."

"I won't."

"How can I be sure?"

"I won't tell." From here the gravy is looking less like gravy and more like jelly.

"It's hard to keep a secret," he says. "Are you sure you won't tell Sparrow?"

Starvation makes me desperate. He's not going to let me eat until I make him believe me. And I want to tell him anyway, don't I? I want him to help me make all the pieces of the puzzle into a picture.

"I have a secret too," I say. "What if I tell you my secret? Then you'll know something about me that nobody knows."

Vincent looks relieved. "Yeah, okay. But it better be bad."

What can I say, it seems like a good idea to a kid with a bruised brain and an empty stomach.

I tell him my secret. You know it already.

While I'm talking, I get up, go over to my plate, and devour my dinner standing up.

I tell him about the lighthouse and leaving the clothes in the old oven on Friday night and getting them on Sunday morning. I tell him that on the weekends in the woods I live in the skin of an animal. I don't tell him about White Wolf or Tuffman. Those aren't my secrets to tell.

I leave something else out. My melon isn't *that* cracked. I don't say "wolf."

Because he already met wolf me, and I don't think he liked me much.

When I'm done, he looks at me. "Do you think that's what the talking deer wanted?" he asks. "Do you think it was telling me I have a second skin too?"

I nod.

"A raven? Isn't that just a crow? I don't want to be a garbage-eating bird." He shakes his head. *No no no no,* like his body has to say the words even when his mouth doesn't.

He tucks his hands into his sweatshirt pocket to hide the trembling.

"I don't wanna change. And I don't want *you* to change either."

His eyes get big, like he just thought of something. "What animal are you?"

I look away. I don't want to lie to him.

Luckily, the more upset he is, the more he talks. "The woods are scary. Some cougar would snap me up in one bite. Look what it did to dumb old Bobo."

Bobo's not dumb.

"I'm not supposed to tell anyone, but something

happened to me in the woods this weekend. That scene with the cougar in the tunnel was *nothing* compared to it," he says.

This little talk is taking a turn for the worse.

"On Sunday I was helping Tuffman mark out the 5K race." He pauses. "You're *nothing* like him, I don't care what Mary Anne says. When I told her you were his nephew, she acted like it made sense because you're both antisocial or something. But you're nothing like Tuffman."

I think he thinks he's giving me a compliment, but it feels like a kick to the gut. Why'd he tell her in the first place? Didn't he know that was a secret?

I get a heavy, scared feeling. I think the word for it is doom. Because that secret really didn't matter much. But the one I just told him does.

I bet he knows the difference, right?

Vincent keeps talking.

"When we were down at the lake, a pack of wolves came out of nowhere. Twenty of them circled us, barking and snarling. I pulled out my slingshot. Pow. I hit one. Killed him cold." Vincent's moving around, acting the scene out. He doesn't look nervous anymore.

"Tuffman was useless. They chased us clean out of the woods and all the way up to the school. I've got bite marks on my calves." He lifts his pant leg up half an inch like he's gonna show me and then drops it again before I can see so much as a pimple.

"I barely managed to slam the door shut on them. They would've killed us if they caught us. *They're* the ones that got Bobo, bet you ten to one."

"Why didn't you tell Dean Swift?" I ask.

Vincent shrugs. "Tuffman. He said it was my fault for teasing them, but they just attacked me when I was totally minding my own business. He said the dean will always take nature's side in any argument—whatever that means—and that I'd get in big trouble with him. Plus he said they'd make him cancel the 5K run, and *that* would get me in trouble with Tuffman."

"So what kind of animal are you?" he asks again. "A chickadee? A squirrel?" he teases. Then he laughs. "Are you a werewolf?"

Man, I hate that question. "No, I'm not a *were*wolf."

I didn't mean to say the word the way I did.

Understanding ripples across his face like a wave at the tide line. He backs toward the door.

"Wait," I say. I try to make my eyes not so scary. "Listen. I think it's something genetic—you know, like coded in my DNA. My *mitochondrial* DNA. And it's White Deer Woods, too. It's a special place. It has something to do with bioluminescent fungi and the power of the light in the woods. I'm not sure how it all works, but it probably has to do with the wave theory of light and the measurements of the lens."

I'm mixing it all up and sticking it all together, everything I've heard and thought over the last few weeks.

He's staring at me like I'm a mad scientist who's been sniffing his test tubes.

"I don't hurt anyone," I say. "I don't care about humans at all when I'm in the woods."

He gets a look like he just figured something out. "What about dogs?" he asks.

I keep talking. I talk for a long time. I never admit to being a wolf. He doesn't ask again. But deep down, he knows I'm a wolf, and I know he's a liar.

After a while he starts to nod like he's convinced, but I can tell he just wants to get away from me. He's inching toward the door. He's careful not to turn his back on me as he steps into the hallway.

"The dean told us at dinner that Bobo won't make it through the night," he says as he shuts the door. There's a mean look on his face.

That's when I realize that he thinks maybe *I'm* the animal that attacked Bobo.

And Bobo won't make it through the night.

I get into bed. I should never have gotten out of it this morning.

My parents have come and gone. Teachers have come and gone. Kids have come and gone. But Bobo's been here with me the whole time. She's run through the woods with me and slept on the floor of my room. She's a tear licker, a heel nipper, a pillow, and a friend.

I never got to say good-bye to my mom. There are lots of things I would've said and done if I'd known the last time was the last time. I can't let Bobo leave without saying good-bye.

I get out of bed.

I can't let my best friend die alone in the middle of the night.

Maybe there's some leftover bacon in the kitchen. Dogs know love when you feed it to them.

I pick up my tray to take down with me. It bumps into my pajama pocket, and I feel the key. I take it out and stare at it for a second. I remember how the light made me feel when it pulsed through me. I remember how it made me so strong I could tap a tree trunk with the tip of my toe and send it flying across the meadow and over the cliff.

I grab the key and the tray and run out the door.

I run all the way down to the kitchen. I forgot to light the light. I smack my head, which hurts more than it would if I didn't have a smushed melon for a brain.

I run all the way back upstairs. Turn the light on first. Right? Doesn't that make sense? Turn the light on, get the dog, put the dog in the light.

Everyone's in the bathroom getting ready for bed.

Vincent opens the door and sees me run by. I see

myself in the big mirror. I look crazy. I've got a tray full of dirty dishes in one hand. I'm clenching the key in the other. My eyes are lit up and intense like Dean Swift's when he starts talking about fungi. There's a bandage wrapped around my head, and my hair is standing straight up around it. How many days since I washed it? Yikes. I'm one dirty dog.

Vincent just stands there and stares. Man, I could use his help. I don't know why, but I shove the tray at him. He takes it with a surprised look. The words are on the tip of my tongue, but he ducks back into the bathroom like he's afraid of getting stuck alone with me again. I hear the dishes clatter on the tray, and then the door slams shut.

I blink. I take a breath. My right eye twitches. This job I've got to do on my own. I wouldn't know where to begin explaining it to him, since I don't understand it all and I'm pretty sure the dean—the one who's in charge—doesn't either.

Ha! If the dean doesn't know, then nobody knows. If nobody knows, then anything's possible.

I race to my room. I stop and stand in front of it. I wait, quiet as a mouse. The hall is silent. I step one big step over and put my ear to the utility closet door. Silence.

It only takes me a minute. The matches are on the desk. The wick is ready.

Slash goes the match. Flicker goes the flame.

I don't even watch as the light fills the room.

"Guard the light, Gollum!" I whisper like a maniac as I fly down the stairs.

Everyone's awake, but I know where they are. The dean is in the basement, locking the gym doors. Cook Patsy is in the dining hall, wiping down tables and setting up for breakfast. Ms. Tern is monitoring the girls. Tuffman is monitoring the boys.

And I'm alone in the kitchen.

By the delivery door there's a low cart for moving big boxes. It's like a huge metal tray on wheels. I pile all the kitchen towels I can find onto it. Quick as I can, I wheel it over to the storage room.

The room is so quiet that it's only my wolf sense that tells me Bobo's alive, because she doesn't move.

I lift her. It's not easy. I know I hurt her. She whimpers, and I put my hand just above her eyes. *I'm sorry,* I say, but I don't have to say it out loud because she knows it already.

I push her back into the kitchen and out the delivery door.

I walk slowly along the edges of the driveway so that the noise of the cart wheels is muffled by the grass. The back left wheel creaks. I head toward the trees. I look up. Wings rustle in the oak. The crows are huddled there, each with one eye open.

Suddenly the driveway is flooded with light. I stop dead in my tracks. Someone must have seen me. Someone has turned on the lights. If I run with Bobo, she'll get tossed around. If I stay, I'll get caught. I shrink back as much as I can into the shadow of the great oak tree.

A second later and the crows have swooped down, silent.

At first it feels like I'm in the middle of a black feather storm, like there's no order or meaning to what they're doing. Then they settle. They surround Bobo and the cart, like a great dark shadow. They hover next to me, one above the other, sheltering me from the lights and the eyes that might be watching from the school.

Did Vincent call them garbage eaters? They're guardians, that's what they are.

Slowly I move on behind my shield of black feathers. I know that the woods love me.

As I push Bobo away from the school, I realize that must be why nobody ever sees White Wolf. It's why the cougar can't find her unless she leaves the woods. As long as she stays in White Deer Woods, the woods magic shelters her.

The crows wheel off, one by one, as we reach the lake. Bobo is so quiet. The path is rough. I wince every time the cart bounces. I can feel how it must hurt her.

As I get closer to the lighthouse, I catch flashes of

the light off to my left. I'm taking her to the meadow between the edge of the woods and the edge of the cliff, where the light struck me last week.

But it begins before we get there. Every time the beam catches my eye I feel it. It's so powerful that I flinch a little when I see it coming, the way you do before you touch something that you know will give you a little shock.

In the meadow I pull the kitchen towels off Bobo. I get down beside her and try to make her open her eyes. I don't know if the power happens when it hits your skin or your eyes.

The light swings at us. It drowns me. My skin hums. I look down at Bobo. Her fur is standing on end. Her eyes are half open. A tremor runs across her nose.

We stay there until the light goes out.

I imagine Dean Swift standing up there, scratching his head. "I do not recall lighting the lens," he must be saying to himself.

I cover Bobo back up. She looks awful. The light has made me even stronger. Pushing the cart is like pushing one of those toy lawnmowers with the popping balls.

When we reach the lake, I hear it. She whimpers. It's a sound of pain, but it brings tingles all over my skin. I stop pushing and run up to her. Bobo lifts her nose and sets it in my hand. Her eyes are open. I see the sketch of a tail wag.

Chapter 23

WHERE BEST FRIENDS FIGHT AND DON'T MAKE UP

Friday. I sleep late. At breakfast there are only weirdos at the counter. Mary Anne is with the Wolverines, whispering sadly about Bobo. Vincent perches on Mean Jack's table, telling them how he saw the cougar coming out of the tunnel and tagged it in the face with a rock. He says it so convincingly, I'd believe him too, except that I was there.

Vincent and Mary Anne don't look at me when I sit down at the counter, but I can tell they notice me. I have a heavy feeling inside. Are we still friends?

The dean walks into the dining hall. We can tell by the look on his face that he's here to tell us about Bobo. Even Vincent stops talking.

Dean Swift stands there for a minute. "Bobo," he says finally. His mouth is crooked and his voice is full of tears. He shakes his head and raises a finger.

The girl next to me starts to cry. I stare at the counter. I really thought the light would save her. Sometimes a bad situation is just a bad situation, no matter how hard you try to fix it.

Dean Swift clears his throat. "I'm sorry. I am over-come with emotion. The vet said Bobo will live. He said it is a miracle."

The room goes wild. Everyone starts to chant, *Bobo, Bobo.* The boys in the Pack and the Wolverines stand up, grab their chairs, and slam them up and down to the beat. The weirdos smack the counter with their open palms. The Cubs stamp their feet.

Cook Patsy walks over to me with a plate full of bacon. "I saw you," she says.

I freeze. Maybe she was the one who turned on the driveway lights.

"I saw you sleeping next to Bobo in the storage room," she says. "You're the reason why." She nods. "Love heals all, that's what they say." She pulls something out of her apron pocket and hands it to me. It's a friendship bracelet.

"Do you know why rings and bracelets always stand for friendship and love?" she asks.

I think about it. I want to give her a good answer. "Because they're like chains that lock us together?" I ask.

She laughs. "Well, that's one way of looking at it. But I always think it's because a circle never ends. It goes on and on, around and around, no matter what. *Nothing* can stop it, because it never ends once it begins."

I look down. She's a sneaky one. She's talking about my mom.

"Thank you," I say.

Right after breakfast a motorcycle roars up. A lot of us are in the upstairs bathroom, and we rush over to look out the window.

I lift Sparrow up to see. He weighs as little as a feather to me this morning. Bobo's not the only one the light fixed up last night. I'm wearing my bandages, but there aren't any bumps or bruises under them anymore.

We see Vincent tearing down the front steps, yelling, "Mom!"

I squeeze Sparrow a little tighter. Sometimes that's a hard word to hear.

Pretty Lady hops off and unstraps something tied to the side of the bike. She lifts it up and waves it at Vincent. "You forgot something, kiddo!" she says with a huge smile.

Even from up here, we can tell it's not just any fishing pole.

It's the one I made for Sparrow.

Vincent stops and glances up at us. Then he hurries toward her, his hands spread out in front of him like he's afraid of falling or like he's telling her to put that pole away.

On the last step Vincent trips and stumbles into his mom. She drops the pole to catch him and it falls in a long line going up the steps. We can all see it's about to happen before it does. He steps back to get his balance. The wood splinters as his foot comes down on it.

We all let out a big breath.

His mom bends down and starts picking up the pieces.

Vincent stands over her. "Why did you come so early today? Why would you bring that?" He chews her out. Like it's all her fault.

"I was vacuuming and found it under your bed," she says. Her voice is thin and confused. "I thought you go fishing on Fridays. I didn't want you to get left out. Vinnie, I took the whole day off work to bring it to you."

"You never get *anything* right," Vincent shouts. He kicks the Harley's tire and runs to the zigzag path, just like he did on the first day.

Only this time, no one is cheering about it.

No wonder his mom dumped him here.

I set Sparrow down. I rest my hand on the back of his thin little neck.

Vincent let me yell at *Sparrow*. My jaw crunches my teeth together. How low is that?

"That rat stole the pole and made the bambino take the fall for it?" Mean Jack can't believe it either. "What a *cafone*."

Mean Jack's got a way with words sometimes.

My chest hurts like I got punched. And I did—I got punched with the truth.

The truth is, Vincent's worse than Mean Jack. His dumb prank almost got Mary Anne blown to smithereens. He's the kind of kid who throws rocks at animals. And he's a liar. He lies even when it doesn't really matter. He lies until he thinks his lie is the truth. I never knew someone so low down.

And he broke my pole.

The other boys leave for class. I hear them calling Vincent a sneak and a cheater.

From the window I watch Vincent run.

Chicken. That's what they called him at his old school. That's what he is. Always doing the wrong thing and too chicken to admit it.

Since Dean Swift had to cancel fishing and outdoor time again, he decided to make it up to us by giving us an extra hour of PE. I like Dean Swift, but I don't think we have the same idea of a good time.

When I get into the gym, Mean Jack is on the bleachers with the Pack. "Me and Tuffman just had a little sit-down. I was telling him how Vinnie told us about clipping the cougar. Coach said forget about it. Coach says the second our boy heard that cougar, he hit the turf bawling. Coach says there's no way our friend so much as looked that cat in the eye, let alone whacked it."

Jason comes up, and Mean Jack tells him, too.

Jason makes little wings with his arms. "What a chicken, yeah?"

For some reason, I don't like it. I don't want them ganging up on Vincent. He's a jerk, but he was a jerk to Sparrow, not to any of them.

The gym gets quiet. I look up and see Vincent walking in through the side door that leads down to the beach. I don't think he was expecting us to all be in here. His eyes are red like he's been crying. His face is all scraped up like he got tackled again down on the beach. When is he gonna learn that when you run, they chase? It's called Consequences, Vincent.

He sits down on a pile of gym mats by the side door. He looks so sad that a weird thing happens. I start to feel sorry for him.

The Pack stares at him from the bleachers. Mean Jack cracks his knuckles. Little John puts his fists to his eyes and pretends to be a bawling baby. *Wah-wah.*

Anger flashes in me. I want to run over and shut them up. Vincent's *my* problem, not theirs. Fresnel fury, that's what I should call it. The light makes me strong for a while after I get hit with it, but it makes me angry, too.

I've got to control myself.

I start to walk over to Vincent. I'm still mad at him, but I understand about jealousy. He was jealous of that pole. Sparrow left it in the rain, Vincent went back to grab it. I bet Vincent meant to give it back. He just got in over his head. The lie went too far—like a bad joke. It's not his fault if I lost my temper and scared Sparrow. *I* did that. Not Vincent.

Friendship goes on and on like a circle, right? And Vincent's the only person I've ever known who would save me a seat or hunt cougar with me or try to make me laugh when I was worried. He invited me to his house for spring break. He may have stolen Mary Anne, but he made her notice me too—he made her my friend.

I'm halfway across the court when I hear it.

"Bok, bok, bok bok BAWK!" I turn around, and Jason's on the bleachers, doing his chicken dance. Everyone is pointing at Vincent, laughing.

Vincent glances at them and then stares at me.

"You said you wouldn't tell," he says.

He jumps up and runs at me. He wraps his arms around me and tries to take me to the ground, but I won't let him. He starts punching and kicking.

Strength pulses in me. One punch and he'd be on his back on the mats again. But I'm not gonna do it. No matter what Tuffman says, I'm not like him.

The Pack surrounds us, yelling, "Fight, fight, fight!"

I bob and duck quick enough that his fists go flying most of the time. When I grab his wrists he head butts me, and a second later hooks his foot around the back of my knee.

We fall to the floor. Twice he tags me on the head,

right on my bandage like it's a bull's-eye. Like he's trying to kill me.

I roll and get up on my feet. "Listen," I say. "It wasn't me. I didn't tell anyone."

Something feels loose in my mouth. I spit out blood and a tooth.

The sight makes the Pack hoot and howl.

He comes at me again, and this time I can't stop myself.

I pull my arm back. The shouting stops. Everyone stares as my fist connects with his chin. All anyone hears is the crack of my knuckles hitting his bone.

Vincent staggers back, back, back three steps and then lands on his butt.

Mean Jack starts counting.

"One, two, three!" Everyone counts along. Little John is jumping up and down, holding his crotch like he's trying not to pee. Jason's eyes look red, and Mark starts to unzip the weighted vest.

What if I broke his jaw? Will the police arrest me?

"That's enough," Tuffman says, shoving everyone aside. He winks at me. "I knew you had it in you."

How long has he been watching? I hate myself. I am what he says I am.

Tuffman drags Vincent up by the armpits. He inspects his chin. "You're fine. Don't start bawling. You had it coming."

Vincent stares at me like I'm less than dirt. "I know all about you," he says.

"I'm not the one who told," I say, but Tuffman is carrying him out of the room. "I didn't tell!" I shout after him.

I can taste blood. My tongue finds the hole where my tooth was.

"Where'd you learn to fight like that?" Mean Jack asks in a whisper. He pulls back like he's scared of me when I look at him.

Everyone is looking at me like I'm a monster.

I didn't want to hit Vincent. But I did. I'm turning into what I don't want to be—a creature that's half wolf and half boy.

There's a name for that.

I spend the rest of the day sitting on the floor of the storeroom with Bobo.

Ms. Tern tries to make me come out. "Do join us, Raul," she begs.

"Will you tell the dean I need my mom's recipes?" I finally say to her.

My eyes must look weird. Did I growl at her?

She backs out of the room, nodding. "Certainly," she says.

Chapter 24

WHERE RAUL FINDS THE TRUTH AND LOSES THE WORDS TO TELL IT

Finally there's nothing left to do but pack my bag to spend the weekend with my dad who never comes. I head up to the boys' wing. I sense Tuffman as soon as I step in the hallway. The door to my room's open. I smell burnt matches.

"Hey, kid," he says before I step inside.

He's stretched out on my bed, wearing my stocking cap. In one hand he's holding a silver lighter and in the other a recipe card. Tuna Surprise.

"Dean Swift said to bring these back to you. After all the hullabaloo, he thought you could use some time with family. And I'm all you got."

He grins and the lighter clicks. The card curls black, a little line of orange flame eats it all down to a corner. When the flame hits his thumb, he blows it out.

There's a pile of charred corners at the bottom of the garbage can. He drops in what's left of Tuna Surprise.

He takes five or six more from the box and makes them into a fan. "I appreciate her effort, you know, with the code. But it's a little obvious, isn't it? She put sawdust in her biscuits, just because she needed that *W*."

I reach over and bat the lighter out of his hand. It skids across the floor.

"Fine," he says. "Let's read them together." He squints at the cards. "'He killed a deer. Above the deer I saw the shadow of the head of a woman. I refused to eat. He was angry.'"

He tosses the cards onto the floor.

"I like her style. Good grammar. She gets right to the point, but there's attention to detail. And I *was* angry."

I pick up the box. It's empty.

"Go ahead. I'm done with it now. You want to know why I was so angry when she wouldn't eat?"

I stare at him.

"Have you ever tried to reason with someone who's going crazy? You try to be patient. But it's hard. Especially when you love that person the way I love your mom. I *raised* her, Raul. We were all we had."

He sighs and looks down. "So when she started to lose it, and I mean really lose it, it was hard for me. She always had a big imagination. When she was a little girl she thought she saw faces in trees."

I'm listening. He's telling me about her again. Things only someone who loves her could know. I saw faces in the trees too, when I was little. I still do sometimes.

He keeps talking. "You, me, and your mom—we change. Once the change happened to her, she went berserk. She didn't know where her second skin ended and her imagination began. She thought she could see human faces in the animals we hunted. She wouldn't eat. She'd get weak. Yeah, it made me angry. I couldn't stand watching her starve."

He stares at me. "Has she ever done that to you, Raul?"

It's been hard to get White Wolf to eat this spring. Is he telling some part of the truth?

"You don't trust me because of what happened with Bobo and Sparrow. I won't lie to you—when I'm an animal, I'm an animal. You go into my den, then that's what's gonna happen. I warned you, didn't I? I tried to put some fear in you so you'd stay away." His eyes hold me. "Raul, you and me are a lot alike. I had to run like the devil when you chased me and Vincent at the lake. And I saw you turn on Sparrow, I saw you knock Vincent across the room. Thing is, sometimes you act like a wolf when you're a boy. That's gonna get you in trouble."

I look down. He's not lying.

"Listen up. I've been tough. I've been nice. Now I'll be honest. You're younger than you should be. I've never known the change to happen so early. It wasn't until you went to my den that day Sparrow found the bone. I smelled the wolf in you. And you're stronger than you should be. Look what you did when you shook my hand." He stretches it out. On the back of it are four fingertip-shaped bruises.

He grins—like it's funny, like he's proud of me. "That's not normal. You can reach all your wolf strength in your boy skin."

That's true too.

"It's gonna take the two of us to talk some sense into her. You gotta lead me to her, Raul," he says.

My ears stretch at the sound of my name. I feel like I'm being called. "I need to think about it," I say.

"Raul," he says.

I look into his eyes. They're gold. I see a raised red scar in each of his pupils. But it doesn't scare me.

"Raul, I'm the only one that can help her. I know what she lost and I know where she lost it. I can take her back to the place where she can change."

He can help me. He has her recipe.

I feel light for a second. Like I've been carrying a backpack full of bricks and someone just reached down and lifted it off of me.

"She won't come with me. She attacked me a few weeks ago—chewed up the back of my neck and forced me to take a swipe at her. You saw her that day at the picnic table. But she'll trust you, Raul. See, I can't track her. For some reason, I lose her scent in the woods. I need you to tell me how to find her."

It's true, everything he says makes sense. The words gather in my throat.

"Raul," he says, "I got a question."

I nod.

His face is strange. Not nice. Not mean. I can't think of the word, exactly. "Your mom wasn't white when I knew her. She was a gray wolf, like you. Are there any other white animals in the woods around here, Raul?"

Hungry. That's the word. His face is *hungry*.

I take a step back. Stop saying my name.

I know his secret. That's what my mom wrote. I look at the ashes in the garbage can. He burned her words. What is he hiding?

"Bobo's going to live," I say. I want him to go away. I don't trust myself with him.

He looks me up and down. He sighs. "Well, I guess some dogs never do learn," he says. He stands up and brushes the ashes off his pants.

"We'll talk again later, Raul," he says as he opens the door to leave. "I'll give you a chance to pack for the weekend and change your clothes."

The last thing I see as he shuts the door are his eyes, laughing like it's a joke. It sends shivers up my spine.

I snarl at myself. What's wrong with me? Did he almost get me to take him to White Wolf?

I sit on the edge of the bed with my elbows on my

knees and my head in my hands. I keep talking to the wrong people.

At pick-up time I grab my duffel bag and join the rest of the kids on the front porch. The clouds are high and the sky is pale blue. Nobody comes near me. I don't blame them. I'm scaring myself lately too. Mary Anne looks at me sideways.

Did Vincent tell her? I swallow hard. Now that would be a rotten thing to do.

Sparrow's grandma is the first to show up. He jumps into her truck. At the bottom of the circle the truck lurches to a stop. Sparrow hops out and tears back to the porch.

"Wait, Grandma," he hollers.

"Look, Raul," he says when he gets to me. "I saved it." He stretches his hands out to me.

I smile at him even though I don't feel like it. I look at his little treasure.

It's part of the busted-up fishing pole I made him. The best part. It's the carving I did, of the wolves chasing each other around, tail to mouth. I trace the grooves with my finger. I was wrong. Vincent wasn't my only friend. He wasn't my best one either.

"I'll make you another one, but even better," I promise.

"No." He shakes his head and runs to his grandma's truck. "Not better. The same. The same is the best," he calls as he climbs in.

The bitter bad feeling goes away. Sparrow's forgiven me.

His grandma reaches over and hugs him like seeing him is the best thing that's happened to her all week. Then she hits the gas and the brake at the same time. The truck jerks and peels away. Blue smoke pours from the tailpipe.

I remember how Sparrow used to lie about the bruises his mom gave him. Back then I had a bad feeling about it all, but I never said anything to anyone. Sparrow's mean mom hit him a lot more times before the dean figured it all out.

I gotta use my brain here. Bobo almost died this week. Things could get even worse if I wait much longer to get help. I don't know what Tuffman wants or who he really is, but I do know one thing—I've got a bad feeling about it all.

I've got to tell Dean Swift.

I don't know why I've waited so long.

The words won't stay down anymore. I can tell they're important, because I feel them in my throat like the sounds I make when I wear my wolf skin.

Once all the other kids have gone, I'll walk up to him. I'll say, *Dean Swift, I have a secret I've been keeping. Can you help me?*

While I'm waiting for everyone to leave, I keep Bobo company. The tip of her tail moves gently while I stroke her side. Forty-five minutes to sunset. I press my forehead against Bobo's and tell her I'll see her soon.

I feel jumpy and nervous. I don't know where I'm going to begin the story. Does it start with White Deer? Or Tuffman?

But when I go into the living room, Mary Anne is sitting on the sofa, writing in her notebook. She doesn't look up at me. My hands are sweating and I can't sit still. Come on, Mary Anne's dad, come get your kid.

Out of the blue, Mary Anne starts talking.

"Some individuals are uncivilized. They do not understand the most basic elements of the *social contract*," she says to her notebook.

I'm pretty sure Mary Anne is just thinking out loud until she says, "I can't believe you told everyone his secret."

It's like she ripped the last of a hangnail off. It stings. *I didn't,* I almost say, but I can tell she's not in a listening mood.

"He's broken," she says. "He looks up to you."

I shake my head, because I don't know what she's talking about.

"Vincent doesn't know who he is or where he fits in. That's why he lies so much. He's hoping if he tells enough stories about himself, he'll finally tell one that's true."

She wants me to feel *sorry* for Vincent?

"You're not like everyone else. You *know* who you are. You're the strong one," she says.

My throat hurts. How can she be disappointed in me when she doesn't even know what happened? *I didn't tell.*

"And then you go and hit him? There's an expression. *Noblesse oblige.* It means that the stronger you are, the greater your obligation to take care of the weak."

She's wrong about most of it, but she's right about that. I *hate* her.

I hear a car honk. *Just leave, Mary Anne.* I need to talk with the dean.

The car horn honks again, louder and longer this time.

Mary Anne shoves her notebook into her bag and zips it up so quick that she catches the corner of her skirt in the zipper. She looks at the door and tries to undo the zipper. I hear the fabric rip.

A week ago I would have felt sorry for Mary Anne for having parents who can make their car horn sound like they're irritated with her when they haven't even seen her in a week. I would have felt sad to see her rush around and act nervous for making them wait for her for two minutes when she's been waiting for them for an hour.

You're just a kid like the rest of us, Mary Anne.

You've got to love them too, no matter what they do to you.

I don't feel sorry for her today.

I hear a car pull into the driveway. The front door slams. Mary Anne must have forgotten something. But it's Sparrow.

"I forgot!" he yells, even though he's standing in front of me. "I forgot and then I remembered. Here. Dean Swift couldn't find you. He says this is yours. He says it fell out of your box."

He hands me a card. Then he hugs me and runs out the door.

I look at it. I smile.

Skagit Oatmeal.

She must have been running out of cards. It's the longest recipe of them all and the craziest. Is *haggis* part of a healthy breakfast? And the seventh ingredient isn't food at all, it's just a number. 1750 what? Oat flakes?

But this is what it says: *Born in 1750. Preys on white ones. Their flesh makes him immortal. His power is your name.*

It's the last piece. And the picture the puzzle makes is a nightmare so bad, nobody's ever had it yet.

Ms. Tern was right. Tuffman is the spirit-animal hunter. Tuffman's the guy in her photo.

And the dean was right too, even if he meant to be sarcastic. Tuffman is ageless.

But neither of them could ever guess the secret my mom knew: that the hunter is one of our kind, and that he's ageless because he eats us.

Only one thing makes me feel better. It's awful, but it makes me feel better. He gets power over you by repeating your name. That's why I kept telling him stuff— whenever he'd say my name, I'd turn into his slave.

I jump up. My thoughts are zinging around in my head like a BB shot in a metal room.

What was it Tuffman said at the end?

Your mom wasn't white when I knew her. My ears bend back. He tracked her here to kill her so she wouldn't tell his secret. And now that he knows she's a spirit animal, he wants to eat her too. And I thought *Vincent* was a bad egg.

My skin creeps when I think of how he smiled at me when he shut my door. Like he had something up his sleeve.

I look at the clock. Sunset in ten minutes. It's time to go. I can't mess up the recipe this week of all weeks.

Dean Swift is standing at the door when I get to it. He's looking at me funny.

"How's the old noggin, Raul?" the dean asks. "Could I drive you down to meet your dad this week and tell him how sick you've been?"

I stand there with my hand on the doorknob, shaking my head. The clock is ticking, the sun is setting, the magic is happening. I don't have time to talk about it.

I'm not a dandelion. Tuffman can't puff me away.

Mary Anne got one thing right. I am the strong one.

Dean Swift puts a hand on my forehead. He's been doing it all week, checking if I have a fever. His skin smells like fire.

"Don't you need your bag?" he asks. We both look back to the parlor where my duffel bag is still on the floor.

"Did you light the lens?" I ask instead.

He looks startled. He nods slowly.

"Good," I say. "I'm gonna need it."

As I walk out the door, I turn around. The dean is standing in the foyer watching me. His face is gray and old and he looks so worried. I know if he could help me, he would.

"Thank you," I say. "I'll see you soon."

"I can only help you if you ask me," he says. "It's the way."

He says it sadly, like he'd give anything to save me. I'm tempted. But I don't have the time. I need to get to the lighthouse as quick as I can, and we've been over this, haven't we? When it comes to running, Dean Swift does *not* live up to his name.

"Just keep the light on," I say. "I've got it all taken care of."

Then I'm out the door and I'm running as hard as I can. My ears are stretching and my teeth are pulling and I can feel my body changing as I race. Every part of me is alive and alert and listening and sniffing for the cougar.

There's no time to talk.

Chapter 25

SOMETIMES THE GLASS IS HALF FULL BUT THE OVEN IS EMPTY

In the meadow the light blasts through me.

I stand in it so long my skin pulses. Then I walk into the lighthouse.

I step over the threshold with four legs. I'm a wolf with a purpose. I'm a wolf that means business.

I'm ready for whatever Tuffman has cooked up.

All weekend I watch and listen. I lead White Wolf to the lake, just outside the protection of White Deer Woods. But I never catch a whiff of the cougar or the man who wears its skin. We hunt and eat and sleep, but all I want is my chance to fight the cougar.

White Wolf makes me leave on Sunday morning. She nips and nudges me. I want to stay. How will I protect her if I'm not here? Two wolves together can defeat a cougar, right? But one alone cannot. My tail drags as I cross the meadow.

I wish we could speak to each other with words. *Stay in White Deer Woods,* I want to say. *The woods magic will protect you.*

There's a scent on the doorstep of the lighthouse. It makes me cold. I see them in my mind before their names come to me. A boy with hair the color of a raven's feathers and a man with a scrape on his cheek that could have been made by a hook stuck in a wall or by a bullet grazing his skin.

At first all I feel is fear. I race back to the edge of the woods to warn her. But White Wolf is gone. Will she be safe? Is this a trap? I stare into the woods. I listen. I sniff. Nothing moves. The cedar fronds sift the sharp gray light that falls across the green grass. The woods are still.

From a distance I watch the lighthouse. I am gray like the light, and I stay in the shadows of the trees as I walk the woods around the building. There's no sign of a boy or a man or the gun he might carry.

I nudge the lighthouse door open. I stop. I listen. But all I hear are wings above in the broken lantern room.

They've come and gone.

Vincent told Tuffman about my lighthouse. What will this do to the magic?

I put my nose to the ground and sniff. The scent trail leads from the door to the oven. The oven door is open. My clothes are gone.

In my wolf's mind's eye I see Tuffman's laughing eyes and the last words he said to me. *Change your clothes.*

Vincent didn't just tell him about the lighthouse. He told him everything he knew, and that was all Tuffman needed.

At first I'm stunned, like when someone hits you in the back of a head with a rock. It's that solid kind of ache like when a bone breaks—sharp and hurting the same amount of bad everywhere.

Then I wonder. Was Vincent laughing when he reached into the oven? Did he wear his zombie mask? If I open one of the kitchen cupboards, will golf balls come dropping out?

Does Vincent know this isn't a prank? This isn't stealing or lying. This is a kind of killing. He's stolen the boy in me, and forced me to stay a wolf forever.

It takes the air out of my lungs.

Has someone ever punched you or kicked you? It hurts, right? But what's worse is the way you feel ashamed, like you let it happen, like you had it coming, and now everyone can see how you are stupid and worthless and weak.

What will Dean Swift think? What will Sparrow think?

I know what it's like to lose someone. I don't want them to feel that way.

Bam goes my heart. Will they call my dad? He doesn't need to feel any sadder than he already does.

Tuffman will think he's won. He must be the one who

trapped my mom, too. This way we can't tell his secret. This way he can keep trying to kill us and nobody will know or care. Nobody goes to jail for shooting a wolf.

And Vincent? If there's one thing I know about Vincent, it's that when he does something wrong, he'll never admit it.

Remember the fire? He started it.

Remember the fishing pole? He broke it.

Remember my clothes? He stole them.

I stumble out of the lighthouse. I need White Wolf. I don't want to be alone.

But I am.

Maybe she only comes on Fridays at sunset. Maybe the magic only works at the moment I change.

I sit down in front of the lighthouse and put my nose on my paws. I feel the lump in my throat and I wait for the tears to come. But wolves don't cry. After a minute I swing my head up high and stretch my neck. I howl my sadness to the great gray sky.

When I stop howling, the woods fall silent. I think every bird feels my loneliness beneath its red or brown or blue feathers. The rabbits and the foxes, the voles and the moles, the frogs and the snakes, they all burrow down deep into the earth at the sound of my sorrow.

And then I hear a crack at the edge of the cedars.

When I look, I see White Wolf loping toward me. I

stand, my tail wagging with a joy so great only a tail can truly tell it.

Together we return to the woods.

We don't do much that day. We listen. I hear cars on the road below. The parents are bringing everyone back.

It may sound strange to be grateful for anything when you've just found out your best friend has stolen your life and that you'll never again eat with a fork or play pinball or baseball or wear shoes or read a book or watch a cartoon or fly a kite or use a straw to drink a soda.

But I'm grateful White Wolf returned when she heard my call. I'm grateful to find out that the magic doesn't happen just when I change. It's always there.

Chapter 26

HUNTED

Most of the time, I try not to think. I feel the sun in my fur. I chase a rabbit.

When I do think, I worry about what they told my dad.

The sun rises, and we stay under our ledge because we can hear the men and women and children searching. Most days I try to sleep through it.

The cougar is always a shiver of anger running along my spine. When the sun sets, sometimes we hear the cougar yowling. White Wolf keeps moving us deeper into White Deer Woods, sidling between shaggy cedars and widespread oaks and flowering chestnuts.

Trees have their own magic, I learn. The faces I once saw in their trunks—a wolf sees them too. But a wolf hears them sigh and sing, remember and regret, whisper and worry as well. It's all alive out here. Once you know what to look for, you see everything.

One morning I'm padding along so softly on a thick layer of pine needles that I startle a snake coiled on a rock, where the sun streaming down through the branches strikes it and heats it. I stop and raise one paw. Gollum. Her tongue flickers out toward me. When she looks at me, I think for a second that I can see the shadow of a girl's head floating just above her. Whoever said a wolf has no imagination? Quick as can be, she uncoils and slips into a crevice in the rock.

A warm feeling spreads through me. I'm happy to see this old friend.

The days grow long and the nights grow short. It must be almost summer.

After a while there are no more searches.

The 5K race comes. I hear the gun shot that starts it.

Did Tuffman get his rifle back? I hope when he comes, he comes as a cougar. There's no fair fight between wolves and guns.

The wind carries the scent of the runners to us as they follow the road that leads down to Highway 20 all the way around White Deer Woods to the ranger station. This is the first year I don't run it, and the only year that I could win it. If I raced in my wolf shape, that is. Ha-ha. A little dark wolf humor there.

Is Vincent sorry?

At first that's all I want. I want for him to be sorry. I want him to be terrified at what he's done. He's killed half of me. Doesn't he understand?

Many times, more than a wolf can count, I return to the lighthouse. Dean Swift keeps his word. The light of the lens is flooding a corner of the meadow every night I find myself there. I let it pulse through me until I feel too big to fit my skin.

White Wolf lets me come alone, to say good-bye to the part of me I have lost. I slink in slow, cautious. I stick my nose into the oven. It's always empty. Each time it surprises me. Each time it hurts.

After a while I just want Vincent to be terrified. He'd better not ride his bike too deep into the woods. A flick of my paw and he'd be over the cliff, swimming with the seals.

One evening the cougar attacks as I leave the lighthouse. He springs at me from a screen of fern and crushed bleeding hearts.

All I see from the corner of my eye is a flash of teeth and a red mouth coming at my throat. But I've stood in the light so many times. I'm quick. I dart away and he gets nothing but a mouthful of air.

I turn back and growl. The cougar jumps up onto a rotting stump of cedar.

Go ahead. Take the higher ground. It won't save you.

I've been waiting for this moment. All my anger—at Vincent, at Tuffman the man and Tuffman the cougar—surges through me.

As I gather my strength to charge, White Wolf streaks from the cedars, barking short and vicious barks. She's trying to protect me. Even she doesn't know what the light has done to me.

The cougar pounces. His claws dig into her back, his mouth gapes, and his teeth plunge toward her neck.

I leap at him, knocking him off balance. He twists and tumbles and just barely finds his feet. He hisses and turns to face us. White Wolf and I crouch. We advance, he retreats. We back him across the meadow and into the woods. White Wolf and I keep moving forward, our heads low. When the path narrows, White Wolf tries to push ahead of me, but I won't let her. Side by side, that's how it's gonna be this time.

You see, cougar, alone you can hurt us. Together we are strong.

Along the right cheek of the cougar is a hairless pink scar. The sight of it infuriates me, and I lunge at him.

I hear White Wolf warn me. My teeth pierce his skin, and I taste blood.

That's for the scrape in White Wolf's side, I rumble.

I shake my head as I bite down harder, ripping his hide. *That's for Bobo's leg.*

His huge paw comes up, claws stretched, and he bats me away.

The blow knocks me off balance. I stagger and fall against White Wolf. Before I can get back up, he's racing off ahead of us through the woods. We give chase, but everyone knows you can't catch a cougar. When we stop running, we are miles from the moon-dappled forest floor. Small lights illuminate the cement walls and rusty ladders of Fort Casey. The cougar has fled to his den.

A burning pain hits my haunch. Did I get shot? I didn't hear the rifle. But maybe the cougar led us here so Tuffman could shoot us.

I look at White Wolf. *Help,* I want to say.

She's dragging herself toward me, making sounds that mean *I'm coming. I'll help you.* Then her eyes cloud over and close.

Oh no, she got hit too. Oh no. Maybe we're dying. My head is dizzy and my haunch stings like something—a bullet? a thin sharp stick?—is stuck into me.

Then I see a ranger. I recognize the uniform. I stumble and fall to the ground beside White Wolf, trying to cover her with my body.

The man leans over me. His face is so kind and familiar. I feel safe.

"We got you, boy," the ranger says.

I can feel sleep pushing my eyes shut, but I struggle to stay awake. Who is he? What has he done to me?

"That's only a little tranquilizer shot," he says, stroking my side. "You two will be all right in the morning. We've been looking for you for a long time."

It's the most peaceful thought I've ever had. I was lost and now I've been found.

More voices join in. "Did you get the cougar?" one asks.

"No, but we got the wolves," says my man. "We can tag these two and release them up north." I'm glad he keeps talking. His voice is so familiar. I've been wanting to hear it for so long.

I can feel him looking me over; his fingers are deep in my coat. "I wonder what brought them all the way over here tonight. You think they got in a tangle with that cougar?"

Whoever he is, the clearest thought-in-words I've had in a long time comes to me as the strength in my wolf body fades. *I need to show him who I am.* It's the Raul me saying this. I fight the numbness that makes every muscle in my body feel like hot chocolate.

"My goodness!" the ranger says. He's surprised by what I do, but he doesn't move his hand away. "Can you believe it?" he calls to the others. "Look at this gray one here. He's licking my hand. Tame as a puppy."

I keep licking. He tastes like roast beef and cheddar cheese.

Feet surround me. Black shoes, polished. Hiking boots, expensive. Tennis shoes, very well used.

"Well, I'll be," someone says.

I lick the ranger's hand some more and then slowly

place my front paw on his hand. His face is familiar, his voice is familiar, and so is the feel of his hand in mine. What is happening? The hair on the back of my neck stands up, but not from fear. From wonder. The magic must be working again.

"Now, that's a new one. I never seen that before," says a woman. "That wolf is trying to tell you something, I think."

I do my best to nod my head and wag my tail.

I must have done a pretty good job, because they all stop talking.

"Did you see that?" the woman in the hiking boots finally asks. Good style *and* good brains. I reach over with my front paw and pat the toe of her boot very gently.

"I've got goose bumps," someone says. "That animal is trying to say something to us."

"I've never seen the likes of it." The woman sounds amazed. "Not in thirty years working these woods. He's thanking me for noticing. You realize that, don't you? That wolf's not just tame. He's downright civilized."

The ranger gets down low to study me; he must be crouching on all fours. He looks into my eyes. I bark a happy bark. I *do* know him. That's my dad.

In the distance a shot rings out.

"Got him!" a voice cries. "We got the cougar!"

Chapter 27

WHERE A WOLF IS NEVER WRONG

Budget. That's the word I keep hearing my dad say on his phone as he paces between a trailer and the kennel where White Wolf and I wake up.

To my dad, it's a bad word. He says a lot of real bad words when he's talking about the budget—worse even than the ones Mean Jack used to use. Sometimes he slams the trailer's screen door shut when he gets off the phone.

To me, "budget" is a good word. It's the reason why White Wolf and I are still here with him. The "budget" doesn't have the money to transport two wild wolves from an island in Puget Sound all the way to Montana and "integrate" them into a new environment. There's a red wolf exhibit at the Point Defiance Zoo, but they don't want us. Thank goodness.

The cougar went straight to Woodland Park Zoo in Seattle, where he has a cage all to himself. Since he tried to attack me and Sparrow, they consider him too dangerous to release back into the wild. *Ha.* Tuffman's too wild for the wilderness. They got that right, even if they don't know the half of it. Lock him up, boys, lock him up and throw away the key.

The trailer where we're staying is located at the ranger station on the far end of White Deer Woods. At first my dad keeps us out back in a big cage. It's a huge square of chain-link fence with a cement floor and a wooden roof.

Whenever my dad's not at work or yelling at someone on the phone about the importance of saving the wild wolf population of this country, I do what I can to show him that I'm not a wolf like any other.

When I see him, I sit on my hind legs with my front paws stretched out in front of me. Sort of like I'm bowing to him.

When he greets me with a "Hey, gray wolf," I yip in return.

One day, instead of stretching out in a bow, I sit up and offer him my paw. He blinks at me for a long time. Then he says, "Well, I'll be," and takes my hand and shakes it.

It doesn't take long to train him. He's a smart man. By the end of the week he opens the cage door and leads us into the trailer.

"Don't tell anyone," he says to us. "I'll lose my job if they catch me with wild animals for roommates."

I don't know who exactly he thinks I'm going to

tell. The blue jay who hangs out near the kennel? Yeah, he's a real chatterbox.

My dad lives in the trailer. It's his home.

In the last year he must have moved away from Seattle. He must have gotten a job as a ranger in the White Deer Woods.

But if he was living so close to the school, then why didn't he ever come see me?

Once we're inside, I realize he's been seeing me all the time.

There are pictures of us everywhere. Pictures of the three of us at the Woodland Park Zoo with the penguins. Me in a little kiddie car on the sidewalk in front of our apartment. Me and mom standing by the sound sculpture at Magnuson Park. Me trying to eat a pinecone at Green Lake. Man, I was a dumb baby!

I sit down in the middle of the room and look at the pictures.

The ranger kneels next to me. He puts a hand on my back. "My family," he says, and his voice sounds squeezed—like there's a lump in it that won't let the words past. "See," he says as White Wolf walks up and sits on the other side of him, "you two are lucky. You still have each other. I'm gonna make sure it stays that way too."

I learn things when he talks on the phone. I learn he took the ranger job so that he can live here next to my school. Sometimes he talks to the photos of us on the wall. He asks the picture of me why I didn't want to see him anymore, why I wrote him all those letters and told him to stay away. He says that if he hadn't listened to me, then none of this would have happened and he and I would still be together. He says he moved out here to be as near to me as he could be, until I was ready to see him again.

I never wrote him a letter. I don't know what he is talking about. Did someone play a trick on us? Was it Tuffman?

I sit close to him then. His sadness is the same as mine. We can't say what we want to say to each other. I guess I was wrong. I guess sometimes words matter.

One afternoon he has to go to town to get some supplies. He opens the trailer door and White Wolf and I walk straight into the cage.

"You two must really like it here," my dad says.

When he comes back, I hear voices.

"The wolves are out here," I hear my dad saying.

The back door opens. I smell him before I see him. Mean Jack.

Do you know what is strange? I'm happy to see him. I push my nose through the wire, and before my dad can tell him not to, Mean Jack has his hand right in front of my mouth. I lick him all over. Beef jerky and lemonade. This is my kind of kid.

"Never," my dad says sternly as he comes out the door, "*never* do that with a wild animal. Promise me you'll never do that again."

Mean Jack freezes and then yanks his hand back. "I'm sorry, Mr. Ranger. Please don't tell Dean Swift."

My dad puffs his cheeks up and blows the air out. "I won't tell him if you won't! I promised him I'd let you guys take a look, not get your hands bitten off."

Mean Jack nods. It's crazy how respectful he is with my dad. Maybe it's the ranger uniform. Or maybe Mean Jack is a nicer kid than I thought.

"Anyway, there's no real danger with this gray wolf, but he's somewhat of an anomaly," my dad says. "You know what that is? An anomaly is something unusual. And this gray wolf loves people."

"Anomaly comes from the Greek," I hear another voice say. "'An' is a prefix meaning 'not,' and the middle part, 'oma,' is a shortened form of *homos,* meaning 'the same' or 'equal.' So anomaly means 'not the same.'"

Mary Anne. The prettiest dictionary walking God's green earth.

I'm even happier to see her. I don't mind how mad she was at me the last time I saw her. Vincent had us both fooled.

"If this wolf is not the same as any other, then why *shouldn't* I do this?" she asks, and sticks her hand into the cage. Dean Swift always says she is too impertinent.

But I rush over and lick her hand like crazy. Wolf me is not shy, not one little bit. Sigh. Honey and blackberries.

My dad stares at her, but he doesn't chew her out. That's the power of Mary Anne. She can get away with anything. Words and beauty—a killing combination.

"I'm conducting research," she explains, even though nobody asked. "I'm penning a novel about a wolf family. I need to experience the precise texture of a wolf's tongue." She reaches through the fence and strokes my fur. "And its coat. Coarse." She pulls out a notebook and takes the cap off her pen with her teeth. "And a little . . . sebaceous." She lifts her hand and sniffs it, then makes a face. "*Sacre bleu!* For such a civilized specimen of *canis lupus*, he would do well to consider a bath."

After a minute my dad glances up to the trailer. "Where's the other one?" he asks.

Mary Anne shouts, "Come on, I thought you wanted to see them in the flesh."

"Is it safe?" I hear a worried voice ask.

The smell of him makes my nose twitch and my lip curl up. Vincent.

Then I see him in the doorway, chicken as usual, only this time he's got a really good reason to be.

"Of course," my dad says. "Dean Swift says you've been asking about these wolves since the day we caught them."

"If you nourish even the slightest hope of illustrating my story, then you had better come feast your eyes," Mary Anne says. "These animals are *magnificent*."

Yeah, Vincent, come on. Let me illustrate something for you with my teeth.

The growl starts low in my throat. Mean Jack hears it first. He steps away from the kennel. But Mary Anne stands her ground, watching me with her lips moving slightly.

Take a mental note, Mary Anne, because this is what a wolf looks like right before he attacks.

My hair stands on end. My muscles tense, but I stay perfectly still. Then the growl in my chest explodes into a round of barks so loud every other noise disappears. Even the trees stop talking to the wind.

I leap up against the fence. I'm taller than Vincent now, stretched long against the wire links, 155 pounds of rage. The cage rattles with the weight of me. I push my paws and chest against the metal and shake it so that it clangs and bangs.

Vincent screams and falls to the ground like a bird that has flown into a closed window. As he falls, his arm scrapes against the cage and my outstretched claws. A strip of his shirt rips away, and a thin line of red appears on his skin.

My dad looks at Mean Jack. Mean Jack looks at my dad. They both look down at Vincent. The whole time, Mary Anne stares at me.

So that's all it takes to get her undivided attention.

"No!" my dad shouts.

I jump down. I tuck my tail under and creep to the back of the cage. I curl up against White Wolf, who has watched it all so calmly. I sink my nose onto my paws. In one second I have ruined everything. My father will think I'm as wild as any other wolf. He'll forget all that I've done to show him who I really am.

"I've *never* seen that wolf do that," my dad says as he helps Vincent sit up. "Are you all right?" He pulls Vincent's arm out to look at the cut.

Vincent looks like he's seen a ghost. He should. I'm the ghost he made.

"It's a superficial flesh wound," Mary Anne announces after she glances at Vincent's arm. "It may or may not leave a scar."

"That wolf is dangerous," Vincent says, moving away on his knees. "You're gonna have to put it down," he says to my dad. "That's what happens, isn't it? When a wild animal attacks a human? It gets put down."

I feel a snarl start in my throat. I glance at White Wolf. Her body is tense. She moves forward slightly.

"Now, see here—" my dad starts to say.

But Mary Anne interrupts. "*Nobody* knows what you are saying, Vincent. *Nobody* saw that wolf attack you. I, for one, will testify that it was the fence and not the wolf that caused your injury. *Everyone* here will say the same thing."

My dad and Mean Jack nod. "I think the lady has made a fine point," says my dad.

There's a long silence, and then Mean Jack says in a voice like he can't believe it, "It was like the wolf had a score to settle."

I sit up. My humans are smarter than I thought.

"That wolf despises Vincent." Mary Anne nods.

Interesting. Whatever Vincent did to Mary Anne since I saw them last must have been pretty rotten, because she sure doesn't like him anymore.

"All I know," my dad repeats, "is that I have *never* seen that wolf act that way."

"Mr. Ranger here and me can vouch for this wolf. So, Vinnie, you gonna tell me why it thinks you're a problem?" Mean Jack asks.

Vincent starts walking really fast up the little steps to the back door.

"You wouldn't sink so low as to tease an animal, wouldja?"

I'll never call Jack "Mean" again, and that's a promise.

I slink over, really low to the ground. Then I push my nose out toward my dad. He scratches the top of it gently, the way I like.

All of them—even Vincent at the back door—stare at me. The blue jay comes to sit on the lowest branch of the cedar that shades the kennel. I could swear she winks at me.

Then Jack, Mary Anne, and my dad turn. Now all of us stare at Vincent.

My dad asks, "Dean Swift said you take your dirt bike out on the trails in the woods. Did you come across these wolves once and harm them somehow?" He glances back at White Wolf. He noticed the scar in her flank when we first got here.

Vincent looks at his feet. He digs his toe into the plank of the step and shakes his head.

"You can tell me the truth. It would be the right thing to do." My dad walks toward him.

Vincent runs back into the trailer. We hear the front door slam.

"There's a mystery here," Mary Anne says. She caps her pen and sits down on the bottom step.

Jack sits down on the step below. "Well, I, for one, ain't got nothin' better to do this summer than solve it," he says.

I sit down and look at them. I'm grateful. Even though I know Jack has the attention span of a fruit fly and Mary Anne will probably spend days looking up synonyms for the word "mystery." Even though I know the chances of the two of them working together well enough and long enough to figure this out are slim, to say the least. But it's funny to think that of all the kids I've ever known, these two are turning out to be my best friends.

The mobster and the novelist.

Chapter 28

WHERE TUFFMAN'S NEFARIOUS DEEDS ARE REVEALED

A few evenings later there's a knock at the door. Dad gets up to answer it. He must be tired because he forgets to send us outside.

"Hello, hello," a cheery voice says.

I sniff. My tongue rolls out of my mouth, I'm so happy. Dean Swift.

He comes in and sets a shoe box down on the table.

"It's been a few weeks since . . ." Dean Swift stops like he doesn't want to say the rest.

My dad finishes for him. "Since the search for Raul was called off."

"This has been a hard couple of months for all of us, and you especially," says Dean Swift. "But I have discovered something that might answer at least one question."

I stretch and crawl out from under the table. I come at Dean Swift very low, on my belly almost, with my tail droopy and my ears back. Dad is looking at me, waving his hand to tell me to get back under the table, but I know better than he does. If anyone can help, it's Dean Swift.

"Is that one of the wolves?" asks the dean. He doesn't sound as surprised as you'd expect.

"Yeah." Dad nods. He scratches his head. "The white one's over there, in front of the TV. She really likes prime-time dramas. This one stays close to the food. The darnedest thing—he loves cereal."

Dean Swift looks down at me. I scoot up closer and try to put words into my eyes so that he can see the Raul me inside them.

Instead, what I see stuns me. Above Dean Swift's head I see the shadow of an eagle's head. And behind him, I see wings. Well, not *really* wings. More like a hologram of wings—like I could push my hand through them. Like the ghost of a skin.

In his eyes there's a flash that tells me that above my wolf head he sees the shadow of my Raul skin. He smiles and touches me above my eyes.

We know each other in the woods. That's what he said to Ms. Tern. This is what he meant. This is the shadow my mother saw when she hunted with Tuffman. This is why she wouldn't eat his kills. This is how she figured out his evil secret.

Dean Swift takes a big breath. He smiles at me and then pushes the shoe box he brought toward my dad. "I found this among the belongings of our former PE teacher. He left us suddenly." The dean glances down at me. "In fact, he disappeared the night the cougar got shot."

There's a long silence. Then he says, "Jimmy, there is no question that I made a serious mistake. Not once have you blamed me, and yet you should. I should have kept track of where Raul went on the weekends. I thought he was with you. You thought he was with me. I've been trying to figure out how I could have been so negligent."

My dad looks sad, like he does whenever anyone talks about me.

"Well, here's part of the answer." The dean opens the box. "It was Mr. Tuffman." He pulls out a couple of yellow notepads.

"Do you see the traces here?" He points to the top sheet on one of the pads. "He pressed down so hard with his pen when he wrote that it left the imprint of the word on the next page. I took a pencil and gently shaded over the blank page."

He reads aloud, "'Dear Dad, We have been very busy. I go fishing with Sparrow and the Cubs. I have a lot of friends. I don't want to see you yet. You remind me too much of Mother. Please send more money because my shoes are too small. All my love, your son, Raul.'"

My dad swallows and his lower lip moves a little. *Don't cry, Dad. Please don't cry.*

"How much money did you send him?" Dean Swift asks.

My dad puts his head in his hands and shakes it. "I don't know. Couple hundred—a thousand. It doesn't matter. The money doesn't matter."

"If we could only figure out where Raul went during all those weekends, we might have a chance of finding him." Dean Swift pauses and then looks at me. "Of bringing him back," he corrects himself. "In the meantime, it's now clear that Tuffman took advantage of Raul's loneliness and your desire to do whatever Raul needed to cope with the loss of his mother. We'll notify the police. But I wanted to know how many letters he sent, and if you kept them?"

My dad nods. He gets up and walks with hunched-up old-man shoulders to the bedroom.

Dean Swift bends down and whispers, "I suspected you were one of my kind. But I thought it would be many years before your second self would call you. We can recognize each other now only because we are both wearing our second skins. It's the way of the woods. It prevents us from hunting one another."

I nod. He smiles. Then he stares at me, a long thinking line between his eyebrows.

"Are you hiding from someone in your wolf skin?" he asks.

I shake my head.

"Are you trapped?"

I nod.

"Have you lost your threshold?"

I tilt my head at him.

"The place where you shift."

No.

"Have you lost your light?"

No.

"Have you lost your clothes?"

Yes.

"Was it Tuffman?"

Yes.

Dean Swift runs his hands over his face. "I'm a fool. Ms. Tern warned me about him, but I refused to see the truth."

He jumps as a crash comes from the back of the trailer.

"I'm all right," my dad calls out. "It's a mess in here, that's all."

Dean Swift exhales and then leans back down to me. "So few of our kind harm one another that it seemed impossible. I went down to the fort the night they captured the cougar. When I saw the shadow of Tuffman's face above the skin of that cougar, I began to wonder if he had something to do with your disappearance. I searched his room but found nothing. This morning Mary Anne came to my office and told me about her visit here. She wanted to know about white wolves. It reminded me of Ms. Tern's strange theory that Tuffman is a notorious hunter of spirit animals. I decided to search his room again. What I found has led me to believe that he was trying to separate you from your father, and worm his way into your trust. But why? Was it simply to get to the white wolf through you?"

Yes.

My dad comes back with a stack of papers.

Dean Swift sits up straight and clears his throat.

"Here are all the letters," my dad says. He drops the stack on the table and slumps back in his chair. "And you're telling me Raul didn't write them."

I put my paws up on the chair and rest my head in his lap.

"No," Dean Swift says. "He didn't write even one of them."

"He must have wondered why I stopped coming," my dad says sadly. "He must have thought *I* abandoned him too. Now he'll never know how much I love him. That I think of him every second."

Dean Swift looks at me and talks to my dad. "I imagine he knows the truth. Children always do."

He stays until the sun starts to fall behind the cedars, cruising down toward the water, lighting it up so that the blue sea glows like my wolf mother's eyes. They don't talk much, my dad and the dean. But Dean

Swift's silence is a kind of hug, warm and filling the room with his understanding.

When he leaves, he bends down and scratches my ears. "I'll get you out," he whispers. "I will make inquiries. Have no fear."

Chapter 29

SOMEONE'S BEEN CLEANING MY LIGHTHOUSE

In the morning the phone rings.

"No," my dad says. "We can't separate her from the gray."

He listens. "They have to stay together."

He listens. "No. You can't put her in a zoo."

He slams the phone down.

I learn more when he calls a friend. "They're coming for the white one later today," he says. "It's all about money."

When he hangs up, he sits on the floor next to me. White Wolf settles down on the other side of him. I don't know how much she understands. Sometimes I think she's been a wolf so long she doesn't understand words.

I look at her for a long time. Ever since Dean Swift left, I've been looking at her. But no matter how hard I look, I never see the shadow of my mother's face above White Wolf's head. What does that mean?

Soon we will all be separated again. It will be like

when my dad stopped coming to get me and I hadn't found White Wolf. Only now I don't have Bobo or Sparrow. I don't have the other half of myself anymore either.

Cook Patsy is right. Love is a circle. It goes on forever. But I'm right too. It's also a chain that means you belong to someone. My family's chain keeps getting broken. When they take White Wolf from us, and me from the ranger, then I won't belong to anyone anymore. And nobody will belong to me.

I will have lost so much that there won't be much of me left.

I look again for the shadow of my mother's face. Maybe that's what happened to White Wolf.

I put my nose in my paws. It's despair. I can't change what's happening. Turn the light on me as much as you like, I'm just a dandelion seed floating in the wind— shining bright and alive but helpless.

That afternoon is so hot the trailer feels like the inside of a volcano.

"Come on," my dad says as he opens the back door. "You two will be more comfortable outside in the shade."

He trusts us. He knows we'll walk from the door of the trailer straight into the cage.

I nip White Wolf as she trots out the door. She

swings her head back at me. I make a low noise in my throat.

Right then we hear a truck coming up the dirt forest road that leads to the trailer. My dad turns at the sound. The blue jay darts up from her branch and flaps her wide indigo wings to the sky.

We bolt.

My dad hollers.

White Wolf is already at the edge of White Deer Woods. I'm close behind her. I slow down and stop, right in the shade of an enormous cedar. I swing my head back toward my dad. I give him one long last look. I make the sound that means *Good-bye.*

Then I hear him say it. "Go!" It's a whisper of a shout. "Go!" I can see him take his hat off and wave it at me. "Go!"

We run and run.

The woods are deep and dark and cool. The rabbits haven't missed us.

We return to our ledge deep in White Deer Woods. I know the ranger won't try to track us. We'll keep quiet and he'll keep quiet and soon the others will forget us.

We're free from our cage, but White Wolf and I are trapped. Nobody can help us. We'll be wolves until the day we die.

I'm melancholy. Do you know the word? If you were a melancholy wolf, your tail would droop. If you were a melancholy boy, you would shut the door to your room and listen to sad songs. If you were a melancholy kite, your streamers would straggle. A melancholy ball would go flat on one side.

At the lake I can smell the fish and frogs. I look to where the Tuffman straw man once hung. Now it's just a pine like any other. I look at the bicycle up in the oak. I look at it for a long time because something is different. I sniff. Fresh sawdust. I trot slowly toward the tree. I see the marks of a saw's teeth in the branches. Someone is trying to cut the bike from the tree. Soon every trace of me in these woods will be gone.

Late that first night, very, very late, I lope out to the lighthouse. By the orange light of an enormous moon I see that the shrubs and brush around it have been cleared. A small garden has been planted. I sniff. Broccoli, carrots, kale, basil. It makes me so mad I could growl. I'll never be able to eat those things again; to crunch and chew and taste something other than meat and bone and fur.

Who has uprooted the bleeding hearts and fern?

I nose the door open carefully. The room has been swept and cleaned.

I sniff. The smell is familiar—like the dining hall after Cook Patsy has sprayed the tables down with her special cleaner.

I look in the oven, even though I know it will be

empty. The ashes and bits of wood and charcoal have been swept out.

It has to be Vincent.

The wolf rage simmers in me. He took my skin and now he wants my lighthouse.

I'm going to play a little prank on him. I'm going to scare his pants off.

I come back often, staying in the shade of the cedars at the edge of the clearing, waiting. My gray fur makes me look more like a shadow than an animal. It's how I feel, too. I'm between skins, between shadows, between shapes.

One day I hear them.

They are coming out of the woods from the path I used to take.

"Are you *sure* Raul wasn't the one?" Vincent asks.

"*He* didn't tell me," Jack almost shouts, like he's been giving the same answer to the same question for an hour. "Give it up, already. Raul never told nobody nothin'. *Tuffman* told me you freaked when you heard the cougar. Then *I* told everyone else—'cause it was funny, that's why. Nobody ever told me not to tell."

As he gets closer, I can see Vincent's eyes darting all around. Is he looking for me? Good. 'Cause I'm looking for him.

I push the growl down. I'm not in a hurry. I've got him right where I want him, finally.

"How'd you know this was out here?" Jack asks as Vincent leads him toward the lighthouse.

Vincent stops on the threshold. "I'm fixing it up. In case Raul comes back."

"Why do you look so scared, Vinnie?" Jack asks. "You do something off the record?"

If he's scared now, just wait until I come charging out of these woods and run him right up to the edge of the cliff.

"You remember that gray wolf at the ranger's place?" Vincent asks.

I hold my breath. Is Vincent actually going to do the right thing?

The two of them step into the lighthouse.

A few minutes later they come out.

"We better get the ranger," Jack says. He's shaking his head.

"No grown-ups," says Vincent.

"Face it, it's too big for the two of us," Jack says.

"He's Raul's dad. He'll hate me," Vincent says.

"Well, you ain't gonna come out of this smellin' like roses." Jack shrugs. "But we don't have to tell the whole story, get it? Let Tuffman take the rap."

They're walking away from me now. My heart is beating so hard the blades of grass on the ground in front of me are trembling.

I can't stop myself.

I run out from under the cedar. I sprint across the meadow. They turn and see me. Vincent screams and falls down. Jack stays on his feet, but he looks scared. I trot the rest of the way to them slowly, tail wagging, tongue out of my mouth, lips drawn back in one wicked smile.

"Get up, Vincent," Jack says in a tired voice. "It's just Raul."

I jump and put my front paws on Jack's chest.

Jack scratches my ears. "Don't worry, we're gonna get your dad."

"Tuffman made me do it," Vincent says, his face pressed into the grass.

I walk over to him and sniff at his back. He's shaking like a leaf on a tree.

"I'm sorry, Raul," he says. "I'm really, really sorry."

What can I say? Nothing. Those are the words I've been howling to hear.

I wait at the edge of the forest. White Wolf waits with me.

The sun is high in the sky. It gets lower. Then lower still. The light of the setting sun streams down through a small opening between leafy branches, making a tunnel of speckled, spackled, dappled light from sky to earth. Through this tunnel of filmy light two boys walk. Behind them are two men. I take a big breath. Thank goodness. They brought Dean Swift.

White Wolf sits up. I nudge her with my nose. *Stay,* I'm saying to her. Because my only fear is that White Wolf will leave.

"I'm still not clear as to how you knew Raul's clothes were on the top rung of the ladder in the Blackout Tunnel?" Dean Swift asks.

"Tuffman told me," Vincent says. "But I didn't remember until just now."

Dean Swift makes a face like he can't believe what he's hearing. "You didn't *remember*?" he says.

Then he sees the lighthouse. He whistles softly between his teeth. "So they never destroyed it. Red Bluff has been here all along. I should have guessed." His face lights up like it does when he learns something new.

I get up and walk across the meadow. We meet in the middle. Tears stream down my dad's face, and he kneels to stroke my fur.

My dad looks up at Vincent. "This better not be some game."

Then he stands up. "Give him the clothes." He yanks Vincent by the arm so that he's standing in front of me. Vincent stares at the ground.

"Wait," says Dean Swift. "Let's put the clothes in the oven. Isn't that where Tuffman found them? And then the rest of us should step back into the forest."

Vincent doesn't look at my dad, but I hear him whisper, "I'm sorry, Mr. Ranger."

My dad nods, but there's an unforgiving look around his mouth.

Vincent takes a big breath and walks over the threshold.

Dean Swift tilts his head curiously. "So this is where Vincent has been coming all summer. He told me he had made a memorial garden for Raul." He scratches his head. "But how did he find the lighthouse?"

Jack pipes up, "Raul told him it was a place you could only find if you knew it was there."

Dean Swift looks at my dad. I can see them put it all together. My dad cracks his jaw. He looks after Vincent with pure hate on his face.

"Vincent knew about this all along, didn't he?" the dean asks Jack.

Jack lifts his left hand in a lopsided shrug.

Dean Swift's face turns purple. "Here I've spent endless hours reviewing every account of these kinds of occurrences, trying to find some way of bringing a boy back, and that little traitor had the answer the whole time!"

Now Jack and my dad look at the dean with surprise.

"You knew Raul was stuck in the gray wolf?" Jack asks the question before my dad can figure out how to say it.

"Thirty years of research has given me one irrefutable and entirely *natural* fact: These woods are magic.

Native cultures the world over and throughout time believe that there are places scattered over the earth where thresholds, or doorways, exist that allow us to move between the physical world and the world of the spirits. And in these special places, white spirit animals, like the wolf that accompanies Raul, are messengers between those worlds. The local tribes have always considered White Deer Woods to be one such sacred *locus*."

See how he does it? He only tells as much as he thinks you need to know. He's not going to mention that Fresnel lens. Even he doesn't know how the lens fits into the woods magic, just like he doesn't know that the white wolf is my mother. He knows more than anyone else, but he doesn't know it all, and he'll never tell all that he knows.

"So you're sayin' Raul's a wolf because of these woods?" asks Jack. "Can they turn me into a bear, then?"

"Well, yes, and I don't know. I believe the ability to shift between human and animal states and gain access to these thresholds is passed down genetically from mother to child." The dean speaks slowly. "The unusual forms of light in these woods are most certainly involved. Either these lights actually give special powers to certain people or they activate those powers in individuals who carry the code.

"I can only make observations," he says. "The light

phenomena in these woods spoke to me long ago—first as a scientist and then, well, then in the way that only Raul can understand."

He looks down at me. And I see the shadow of eagle wings on his back. The feathers ruffle in the breeze.

My dad looks skeptical, but he keeps his mouth shut. I mean, here he is in the middle of a clearing at the edge of a cliff on an island in the far west of the country, waiting for a lighthouse to turn a gray timber wolf back into his son.

So what's he really gonna say? That he doesn't believe in magic?

When Vincent returns, they all enter the woods.

I hug my old clothes when I pull them out of the oven. Joy, relief—I can't tell you how happy I am.

I found myself. I am right where I was.

Socks. My feet are warm. My jeans won't button and my shirt and shoes are snug, but I feel light, like I'm walking on two inches of air. My skin is smooth and my head is full of thoughts and words and things I have to say.

I run out of the lighthouse, and before I know it my dad picks me up and holds me tight.

"White Wolf," I say. The words come out like a creak and a growl.

We both look over to where we last saw her.

She's gone.

"It's Mom," I tell my dad. "I'm sure of it."

Dean Swift's eyes bulge. "That never occurred to me."

Dean Swift is flabbergasted, but my dad acts like I just told him mom got stuck in a traffic jam somewhere. Like it's no big deal. "Don't worry," he says. "We'll bring her back. We just have to figure out the right steps."

Do you see how quick a man of science can become a man of magic?

Seeing is believing.

"We'll fix it," he says.

He's my dad. So I believe him.

Chapter 30

ONCE UPON A TIME THERE WAS A HAPPY ENDING

Let me break it down for you. Even happy endings feel sad, so let's make it quick, right?

First we go back to the school.

Mary Anne skips down the steps, throws her arms around me, and squeezes me so tight I burp. How's that for a hero's homecoming? My belch cracks everyone up, but Mary Anne doesn't seem to mind. She keeps saying I'm the most heroic boy in school. I'm not sure what kind of lie Dean Swift has come up with to explain it all, so I just smile. Now, if I can figure out how to make the things I want to say to her sound like words instead of gastric distress, maybe she'll do a slow dance with me at the Christmas party this year. My armpits get sweaty just thinking about it. Ha! *There's* something I didn't miss when I was a wolf. Nervous perspiration.

Jack is my new best friend. He's rough on the outside but smooth on the inside. Like the birch branch we found last week in the woods. I'm showing him how to carve. For a mobster he has excellent fine-motor skills. Right now we're making Sparrow that rod.

Sparrow is still Sparrow. When he heard that I had come home, he ran and hid under his bed. He wouldn't come out until I had crawled under there with him. No easy feat, since I gained a lot of weight in the woods. Berries and raw meat apparently meet all of a wolf-boy's nutritional needs, and then some.

The police are looking for Tuffman. If they ever find him, he'll be charged with fraud for pretending to be me and writing letters to my dad and asking for money. I'd tell the police to go check out the new cougar at the Woodland Park Zoo, but then they'd send me off to the loony bin, and that has to be worse than being stuck in a cage or a wolf skin.

Vincent never says he's sorry again.

"Look," he says instead one day. "I sawed this from the tree and cleaned it up for you."

It's the red bike from the old oak. "A little grease, a lot of paint, and she's as good as new," he says. He spins the back wheel. He opens his hands, and I see the blisters and calluses he got from using the saw. On the inside of one arm he has a long thin scar, like what you'd get if you fell down against a sharp wolf claw.

"Thank you," I say. I know he really feels sorry for what he did. I just wish he had felt more sorry, sooner. A lot sooner. Like so soon that he had never done it.

I wish I could say I forgive him, but it's hard. I still

wake up some nights in a cold sweat, my head filled with the cougar's screech and the sight of him pouncing on White Wolf.

Vincent tries to explain it. One night he tells me how White Deer calls him Raven whenever he goes into the woods.

"I don't want to be a bird, Raul," he says. "I don't ever want to change. I want to stay the same."

I just look at him when he says that. Everyone changes. We can't help it. And maybe if he tries to be a raven, he won't be such a chicken anymore.

One day when I'm not so mad at him, I'll try to help him figure out that when you change, part of you stays the same. There's more than one of you inside you. Don't be afraid of that. We were made for this world and we belong everywhere in it, wearing all the skins that fit us.

And what about White Wolf? She came back, the very next Friday at sunset. She's not going anywhere. Love goes on and on. *That's* the magic.

The big problem is how to help her find whatever she lost. When the dean talked to me that night when I was a wolf with the shadow of a boy's head and he was a man with the shadow of an eagle's head, he asked me if I had lost my threshold, my light, or my clothes. My mom must have lost one of those things, or all three.

The day after I get back, I open the dean's office door.

"I have a question," I say. "And I'm afraid of the answer."

Dean Swift nods.

"I never see the shadow of my mom's face the way I saw the shadow of your eagle wings," I say. "Does that mean she's been trapped in her wolf skin so long that her first self is gone?" My mouth turns down. I've said most of it, but some of it I keep inside. I don't want to say it out loud because the words might make it true.

Is my mom dead? Is White Wolf all that's left of her?

Dean Swift's eyes are very soft when he finally speaks. "Think about your question," he says.

I think. He watches.

"Remember," he says, "shifters can only see each other's first-self shadow when they're *both* wearing their second skin."

My skin tingles when I realize what he means. "I understand," I say.

"Do you?" he asks.

I nod. I see him with different eyes. Dean Swift and my mom have something in common. It's their *second* skins that are human. My mom's first self is White Wolf. Dean Swift's is the eagle.

It's wonderful. And a little weird, too.

"When you're ready," he says, "I wonder if you'll

tell me what you know about the Fresnel lens?"

It's nice for once to know more about something than the dean.

"I love you," my dad says when he picks me up. Sometimes he just says it when we are opening a can of soup for dinner.

I was wrong before. Words matter. Those words my dad says matter to me.

The three of us—me, my dad, and the dean—we all agree on what to do. We all agree that not every family can be the same. Not every family can have a mom and dad and a house and two cars and two kids and money for vacations. But every family can find their own kind of happy.

So we all agree. I stay at the boarding school during the week.

In the mornings I carve in the woodshop before breakfast. At lunch Mary Anne sits next to me and tells me stories about soul-stealing shape-shifting otters. In the evenings Jack and I work on what the counselor calls our "social skills"—that means I try to talk more, and Jack tries to talk less. Cook Patsy is the new PE teacher. First thing, she burned the vomit troughs. Soon we will all be ripped. Ms. Tern doesn't come back. Something tells me she's parachuting into the jungle, a knife in her teeth and a rifle strapped to her back, looking for tiger poachers. On the first day of school, the new reading teacher rips up the curriculum and eats it in front of us.

Gollum's cage is still empty.

Jason made Bobo a little wheeled seat that attaches to her hind leg. She runs way faster than before.

There's a lot I don't understand. I think I'm becoming a wonderer, like Dean Swift. The less I know, the more there is to discover.

On Fridays I still take the Cubs fishing. On Friday afternoons my dad rides his bike over from the ranger station to pick me up. He hugs me. We bike out to the lighthouse together. My legs are finally long enough for that ten-speed. On Sunday mornings he meets me at the lighthouse again. We bike over to the ranger trailer. We draw maps. We make plans. We talk a lot, and we think even more.

We sit under the cedars by the lake, and we wait for White Deer. One day it will come back. Red flowers will pour from its mouth, and in each flower a word. And in each word, a clue to freeing my mom.

AUTHOR'S NOTE

In the late twelfth century there lived a noblewoman named Marie de France. She felt that as an author, her job was to take old stories that she had heard and write them down so that others could enjoy and learn from them. She often changed the stories to make them more meaningful to her audience.

One of her stories was called "Bisclavret." Bisclavret was a noble knight who became a wolf every weekend. When his wife discovered his secret, she was terrified. Nobody can really blame her, right? But instead of trying to understand and help her husband, she spoke with another knight who was in love with her. She got him to follow Bisclavret into the woods, steal his clothes, and trap him as a wolf forever.

There's more to the story. Believe me, Marie didn't let the wife and her partner in crime off as easily as I do Tuffman and Vincent. If you want to see how Marie went medieval on the bad guys, check out Project Gutenberg online for an English translation of her

"Bisclavret," or better yet, buy an English translation of *The Lais of Marie de France.* You'll find many more great short stories by her.

I've often wished I could thank Marie for all the joy her words have given me. A few years ago, I decided that the best way to make sure that everyone remembers her would be to do what she had done: take an old story and make it new.

ACKNOWLEDGMENTS

I wrote *This is Not a Werewolf Story* with my son, who was nine when we started it. Many of the ideas and words in the book are his. This story is dedicated to him. Without him, like most of the good things in my life, it wouldn't have happened.

The keys stop clicking when I try to express my gratitude to my husband, Mike. We've grown up together. Marie de France wrote it best: "Neither you without me nor me without you." I thank him for always thinking I can do anything I try.

My parents, Bill and Diane, filled my childhood with books. They read to me and my sister and talked with us. Above all, they gave us, and continue to give us, the precious gift of their time. Thank you more than I can say.

Nobody has believed in my dreams longer than my older sister, Kaye. She has always gone through everything in life first, and has made it all easier for me. I thank my nephew Evan and brother-in-law Jim for always cheering me on. I thank my mother- and father-in-law, Jane and James, who have shared countless books and conversations with me over the years. I thank my grandparents, Jim and Peggy, for always making a big deal about my reading and whistling skills.

I was ten when I started to write. Since then I have received hundreds of rejections for my poems and stories. I decided at some point that it didn't matter how many people said "No." All it would take was one person who said "Yes."

In my case that person was Minju Chang, my agent at BookStop Literary. To her I give my most sincere thanks for her faith, and for talking to me about my story as if it were a real book she had read. The next person to say yes to me was Reka Simonsen at Atheneum. I am so grateful for her willingness to work with a first-time author. Only with her guidance and insight was I able to find the shape of this tale. I thank Reka from the bottom of my heart. I am grateful to Debra Sfetsios-Conover for designing a cover that so perfectly captures the story, Maike Plenzke for an illustration that stuns me every time I look at it, and Adam Smith for catching so many of my errors.

I thank friends who bravely asked, "What's it about?" and then listened like they meant it: Sheri H., Kim K., Denise D., Tiffany, Derek and Ric M., Hans O., Jennifer C. I thank Michelle S., my son's compassionate and inspiring teacher during the year I wrote this. I thank the late Laura Hruska, who wrote me a rejection many years ago for an early attempt at a novel. Her letter, full of encouragement, has been taped to the refrigerator of every kitchen I've cooked in since.

I thank my teachers. Mr. Carroll, Professor Delcourt, Professor Vance, and Professor Stacey all thrilled me with their wit, intellect, and passion for old stories. I thank William Kibler, whose careful feedback allowed me to see my first scholarly article published in the journal *Speculum.* That success gave me the confidence to return to writing fiction. I thank Caroline Bynum and Peggy McCracken, whose scholarship influenced my interpretation of this story. I especially thank my students, whose kindness to one another, global awareness, and love of justice give me hope for the future.

SANDRA EVANS drew inspiration for this story from cultural sources, including the "sympathetic werewolf" stories of twelfth-century France, Celtic myths, and the folklore of the Pacific Northwest. In her research, she also studied everything from *ignes fatui* to mitochondrial DNA to wild animal behavior. She wrote this story for (and with input from) her nine-year-old son. Sandra is a native of Whidbey Island and earned her doctorate in French literature from the University of Washington. This is her first book for children.